HOW TO WIN AT GAMBLING

About the Author

Avery Cardoza is the foremost authority on gambling in the world and best-selling author of 21 gaming books and advanced strategies. His company, Cardoza Publishing, founded in 1981, represents the top authors and experts in their fields. More than 200 titles and 9,000,000 books sold make Cardoza Publishing the world's largest and most respected seller of gambling books.

Cardoza's life has been unique among all gambling writers or players in that he has counted on his gambling winnings and activities as his only source of income throughout his adult life and before. In fact, has never had a 9-5 job.

He began his gambling career underage as a professional blackjack player in Las Vegas, beating the casinos at their own game. At the age of 23, when even the biggest casinos refused him play, Cardoza took his winnings and wrote and published his first book, the best-selling classic, *Winning Casino Blackjack for the Non-Counter*, a revolutionary book that gave non-counting blackjack players a winning method. Cardoza is also the author of *Lost in Las Vegas*, a dark comedy, set against the backdrop of drinking, gambling, murderers, the mob, outrageous eccentrics and a passionate but dangerous love affair.

Though originally from New York City, where he is occasionally found, Cardoza has used his winnings to pursue a lifestyle of extensive traveling which has included extended sojourns in such exotic locales as Bahia in Brazil, Jerusalem, Tokyo, Greece, Southeast Asia as well as California, New Orleans, and of course, Las Vegas, where he did extensive research into the mathematical, emotional, and psychological aspects of winning.

In this book, Cardoza has put it all together; his years of professional play, teaching, research and knowledge into the definitive work on winning at gambling, the standard work every intelligent gambler must have – a book that shows you how to play and win at gambling.

HOW TO WIN AT GAMBLING

AVERY CARDOZA

CARDOZA
PUBLISHING

To Ron Charles

5th Edition
Copyright©1991, 1994, 1997, 2002, 2006 by Avery Cardoza
- All Rights Reserved -

Library of Congress Catalog Card Number: 2006926893
ISBN: 1-58042-189-X
Author Photo by Ron Charles

Visit us at www.cardozapub.com or write to the address below for a full list of Cardoza books, advanced, and computer strategies.

CARDOZA PUBLISHING
P.O. Box 1500 Cooper Station, New York, NY 10276
Phone (800)577-WINS
email: cardozapub@aol.com
www.cardozapub.com

TABLE OF CONTENTS

Introduction

FIVE KEYS TO WINNING

1 Prepare for the games you will be wagering on by reading the appropriate section carefully and practicing in the comfort of your home.

2 Protect your wins, limit your losses, and you're on the way to winning.

3 Make the correct strategy move on every play, all the time. Hunches and feelings are for losers. There is only one correct move for every situation and it is the winner who makes that play.

4 Never gamble with money you cannot afford to lose, either financially or emotionally.

5 Think and play like a winner.

I'm going to show you how to win money at gambling. Whether you're a novice just starting out or an experienced veteran, this brand new edition will show you how to approach gambling like a pro, and how to beat any game you might face. I've updated many of the sections with the latest information. I've also added new games including a completely new chapter on poker featuring comprehensive coverage of Texas hold'em (as well as the other major poker games).

You'll learn everything you need to know to be adept at gambling; from the rules of the games, the bets involved, and the odds you face, to how the game is played not only in America, but in casinos, gambling parlors and card rooms around the world. And for every game covered here, and there are many, you'll learn the absolute best way, with the odds, to be a winner.

I've packed these pages with winning strategies. Often, I'll show you multiple approaches to beating a particular game. This new expanded edition now covers the most important casino gambling games as well as other popular gambling games. You'll learn about casino games such as blackjack, craps, slots, roulette, poker, baccarat, video poker, Let it Ride, the wheel of fortune, keno, Spanish 21, and Caribbean stud poker, as well as other popular gambles including horseracing, and sports betting—football, baseball, basketball and prizefight betting. There is also a special bonus: Cho Dai Di—an exciting Chinese card game that originated in Southeast Asia. To my knowledge, this is the only English-language description of the game in a strategy book.

Since winning doesn't just stop at knowledge of the skills to beat the gambling games, we'll also take a careful look at money management, and lots more, because like I said, my goal here is to make you a winner.

This book is about winning and gambling intelligently. That means you must always make the best bets possible, and avoid the sucker bets, and that you must gamble with your head and within your means. Being a winner entails many things, and I'll cover them all here. What you can expect from this book is a straightforward discussion so you how things really are at the tables.

For me, the name of the game is winning. I play to win money. That's my personal motivation. Throughout my adult life, and before, I have supported myself strictly through my gambling activities. My goal in these pages is to make you a player that the casinos and your fellow players respect, the one that plays to win.

Overview

FIVE KEYS TO SUCCESS WHEN GAMBLING (HAVING FUN)

1. Play games you enjoy, but give yourself a chance to win by learning how to beat them.

2. Always bet within your means. This keeps the games fun and within safe limits.

3. Take a few minutes before playing to brush up on your strategies.

4. Stop playing when you're not at your best. First, you want to maintain your maximum edge, and second, no sense playing if you start giving money away.

5. Try to have fun. Unless you're gambling professionally, that's what it's all about.

The poker section, the first games chapter in the book, has been completely revised and expanded, and includes the super-popular game everyone is playing nowadays—hold'em. We cover no-limit and limit games, cash games and tournaments, and even online poker. You'll also learn about draw poker (jacks or better, anything opens, and lowball), seven card stud (high, low, and high-low stud) and Omaha. You can make a lot of money playing poker and hopefully, the in-depth information here will get you started on the path.

In blackjack, which we cover next, you learn how to have a mathematical edge and beat the casino. This thorough section shows how to play against any set of rules and variations and any number of decks so you're ready to play like a pro in any game around the world, be it Las Vegas or the French Riviera. Master charts for a multitude of variations and locales are included for easy strategy reference.

Spanish 21 is a relatively new casino game that has grown in popularity and thus, I decided to add the game to this edition. It is really an offshoot of blackjack, or a close cousin anyway, sharing the same basic rules but with some interesting twists to make it more exciting. Blackjack traditionalists won't necessarily be thrilled, because the tens are removed from the deck—key cards for the player—however, casual players will love the new options. Beware though: if you're a blackjack player, you can't use your regular moves—you'll have to learn new strategies to play the casino tough.

Craps is for players who love action. In this chapter, you'll learn about bets which give the house no edge at all, and how to use these wagers to beat the game. I present eleven different winning strategies from a variety of approaches—single odds and double odds, conservative and aggressive, betting with the dice or against them. This section will make you as good as any craps player out there, for you will be playing against the minimal house edge possible.

If you're going to take on roulette, this chapter will show you all the basics. This includes the rules and differences for both the European and the American game and how to make every bet possible including some little known wagers. I also present three betting systems and an actual strategy for beating the wheel with the odds.

Baccarat is a glamorous and popular European game whose odds are so good for the player that casinos sometimes can lose money at it over a month's worth of play. There are several variations of the game and I'll show how they differ. And of course, we'll discuss the winning strategies you can use to beat the casino at baccarat.

Horseracing is a tremendous gaming passion for many, and this section shows you all about the races, from the bets available, the types of races run, the odds and the important winning approaches, to eleven solid winning tips to help you win money at the track.

How would you like to be $50,000 richer? A lucky catch in keno can do the trick, and in this section, I'm going to show you ways to play and bet the game to give you that shot, the odds involved and the payoffs on winning tickets. You'll learn how to play straight, combination, split, way, special, and for you royalty-minded players, how to play the king.

Video poker has grown to be a very popular game, and for good reason—astute playing can make one a winner. You'll learn the winning hands and payoffs at all the main variations—including jacks or better, deuces wild, bonus quads, and joker wild—how to use the various options, the best strategies to pursue for straight games and progressives, and the best way to improve your chances of winning the giant jackpot.

As a special bonus, I'm introducing Cho Dai Di, a very exciting Chinese card game that's sure to please and thrill those of you who love skill, luck, and backstabbing all in one easy-to-play package. I'll show you how to play and score, plus present some winning strategies to get you on the way. I hope you do me the honor and give this section a read—it's a great game and you'll soon be hooked.

Sports betting is like bread and butter for many gamblers; billions of dollars are wagered on sports events every year. In this section I'll show you how the lines are made, why they exist and how to use inside information to beat the line and make money. Betting on football, baseball, basketball, and boxing are all covered—the different types of bets you can make at each, the odds and the payoffs and the best strategies to make you a winner.

Slots has become the most popular casino game so I have expanded and rewritten this section to reflect the new changes. I'll also look at some of the new slot machines, show the different machines available, and tell you about the straights, the progressives, the various odds and how to improve on them, the basics of play as well as showing you some insider insights on how to get the best slot odds possible and beat the machines.

There is a small section on the wheel of fortune, also called the "Big Six." I'll show you the bets available and the odds you face.

There are also sections on Let it Ride and Caribbean stud poker, two poker-like casino games that have become increasingly popular staples in the casinos. Both combine table play with bonus payoffs and large "jackpot" possibilities. These are the right combinations for players, which accounts for the increased casino floor space of these games.

Most important of all, I show you how to be a winner. There's more to winning than knowing the odds and the game. You must know how to handle yourself and your bankroll. Money management is the key to all successful gamblers and thus, I've devoted a full chapter specifically addressing the psychological and emotional aspects of beating the casino. I'll tell you how to keep the game under control, how to minimize losses when you're losing, and when winning, how to turn moderate winning sessions into big winning sessions with a minimum of risk. Finally, I'll show you how to walk away a winner.

All right then. Let's turn some pages, get more educated, and get ready to put the odds on your side. I hope you enjoy my book and it makes you a winner!

— *Avery Cardoza*

Poker

FIVE KEYS TO POKER

1 Learn the particular house rules for the game you are playing in.

2 Learn the right hands to open and fold with. Strong starting hands tend to finish strong, weak ones, tend to lose.

3 It is just as important to make good folds in poker as it is to make good bets.

4 Pay close attention to opponents. Their body language and mannerisms (tells) can give you as much information about their hands as open cards!

5 Play the right size game for your wallet and skill level, that is, not over your head. Better to be the mackerel in the sardine tank than in the shark tank.

INTRODUCTION

Poker is the greatest and most exciting gambling game, an American tradition where rich and poor, and men and women of all classes gather around a table and vie for stakes ranging from mere pennies to thousands and even millions of dollars. No other game provides the challenges of skill, luck and psychology—and the drama of the bluff—in such a fascinating wave. In this chapter, we'll show you how to conquer these challenges and be a winner at poker!

We cover the major poker variations—draw poker: jacks or better and anything opens, seven card high stud, high-low stud, hold'em, lowball: draw poker and seven card low stud (razz)—and show the basics of play for each of these games. We discuss the differences between casino and private games and go into all the fundamentals of poker: the jargon, the rules of the games, the player's options, the ranks of hands for high, low, and wild card poker, how to bet and how to play, and everything else needed to make you an informed player.

We'll show you how to apply the five winning strategies to get an edge on your opponents and to turn that edge into winnings. You'll learn how to recognize lock, strong, marginal and weak hands and adjust your strategy accordingly; how to play position at the table; how to use pot odds to determine the soundness of a bet; how to read opponent's playing styles and cash in on that information; how to play against opponents who bluff a lot or rarely bluff or are loose or tight players, and much, much more, so that by adjusting your play accordingly, you'll have a big edge on your opponents.

It's all here in this section. Now let's go out there and win!

OVERVIEW

Poker is a betting game requiring two or more players. It is played with a standard pack of fifty-two cards consisting of thirteen ranks, ace through king in each of four suits (hearts, clubs, diamonds, spades). The ace is the best and highest card, followed in descending order by the king, queen, jack, 10, 9, 8, 7, 6, 5, 4, 3 and then the **deuce** or 2, which is the lowest ranked card. The king, queen, and the jack are known as **picture cards** or **face cards**.

The four suits in poker have no basic value in the determination of winning hands.

Cards are referred to in writing by the following commonly used symbols: ace (A), king (K), queen (Q), jack (J), and all others directly by their numerical value, 10, 9, 8, 7, 6, 5, 4, 3, and 2.

THE FOUR SUITS

♣ = clubs   ♦ = diamonds   ♥ = hearts   ♠ = spades

When the cards are held together in various combinations, they form hands of different strengths. These are called **hand rankings** or **poker rankings**.

There are many variations of poker, but they all have these four things in common:

1. Players receive an equal number of cards to start.

2. There will be a wager after these cards are received; players that match the wager can continue playing the hand, players that don't match the wager, will sit out. You have to pay to play!

3. More cards are usually dealt, with players having an option to wager more money following each round of cards.
4. The winner of each hand will be the player with the best hand or the last one standing because all opponents have refused to match his bets.

Each player in poker plays by himself and for himself alone against all other players. Playing partners is illegal and is considered cheating.

OBJECT OF THE GAME

Your goal in poker is to win the money in the **pot**, the accumulation of bets and antes in the center of the table. You can win in two ways. The first way is to have the highest ranking hand at the **showdown**—the final act in poker, where all active players' hands are revealed to see who has the best one. The second way is to be the last player remaining when all other players have dropped out of play. When this occurs, there is no showdown, and you automatically win the pot.

TYPES OF POKER GAMES

For new players, the choice of poker games being offered can be bewildering. Not only do you have all the different variations, such as hold'em, Omaha, seven-card stud and variations within these, but you have different forms of playing them. There is straight high poker, low poker, and high-low poker. Then there are cash games and tournaments, as well as limit, no-limit, and pot-limit betting structures.

Huh? How do you make sense of them all? Here's a down and dirty guide so you can understand all the poker games available.

BASIC GAME FORMATS

Poker can be played in two basic forms—as cash games or in a tournament format. While tournaments get all the television coverage, the more popular versions being played in cardrooms are actually the cash games. Let's take a quick look at each one.

Cash Games

In a **cash game**, the chips you play with represent real money. If you go broke, you can always dig in to your pocket for more money. If you give the poker room $100 in cash, you get $100 worth of chips in return. If you build it up to $275, you can quit and convert your chips to cash anytime you want. Your goal in a cash game is to win as much money as you can, or if things are going poorly, to minimize losses.

Tournaments

In a **tournament**, every player starts with an equal number of chips and plays until one player holds them all. Your goal in a tournament is to survive as long as you can. At the very least, you want to survive long enough to earn prizes, usually money, and in the best case scenario, to win it all, become the champion, and win the biggest prize. As players lose their chips, they are eliminated from the tournament. Unlike a cash game, where the chips are the equivalent of cash money, **tournament chips** are only valuable in the tournament itself and have no cash value.

BETTING STRUCTURES

Poker has three different types of betting structures: limit, pot-limit, and no-limit. These structures don't change the basic way the games are played, only the amount of money that can be bet. The big difference between the three structures is the strategy. The amount you can bet changes the hands that you should play, when you should play them, and how much you should risk in any given situation.

Let's take a brief look at each betting structure.

Limit Poker

In **limit** poker, the most common game played in cardrooms and casinos for cash, all bets are divided into a two-tier structure, such as $1/$2, $3/$6, $5/$10, $10/$20. and $15/$30, with the larger limit bets being exactly double the lower limit. On the preflop and flop, all bets and raises must be at the lower limit, and on the turn and river, all bets double and are made at the higher limit. In a $5/$10 limit game, for example, when the lower limit of betting is in effect, all bets and raises must be in $5 increments. When the upper range is in effect, all bets and raises must be in $10 increments.

One form of limit poker, called spread-limit, allows you to bet any amount between the minimum and maximum amounts specified for the game. Spread limit is typically played in very low stakes games. For example, in a $1-$5 game, you may bet or raise $1, $2, $3, $4, or $5 on any betting round. There is also a $1-$4-$8 spread-limit format where all bets in the early betting rounds can be anywhere from $1 to $4, and in the later betting rounds, from $1 to $8.

In the sections on the individual games, we will go over exactly when the upper level of betting comes into effect and how that works.

No-Limit Poker

No-limit hold'em is the exciting no-holds barred style of poker played in the World Series of Poker main event and seen on television by millions weekly on the World Poker Tour and stations such as the Travel Channel and ESPN. The prevailing feature of no-limit poker is that you can bet any amount up to what you have in front of you on the table *anytime* it is your turn. That exciting all-in call signals a player's intention to put all his chips on the line. No-limit is usually associated with Texas hold'em, but this style of betting can be played in any variation.

Pot-Limit Poker

Pot-limit is most often associated with hold'em and Omaha, though this betting structure, like no-limit, can be played with any poker variation. The minimum bet allowed in pot-limit is set in advance while the maximum bet allowed is defined by the size of the *pot*. For example, if $75 is currently in the pot, then $75 is the maximum bet allowed.

The pot sizes in pot-limit quickly escalate to large amounts. Like no-limit, this betting structure is not for the timid.

HAND RANKINGS & WINNING COMBINATIONS

Poker is typically played as **high poker**, that is, the player with the best and highest five card combination at the showdown wins the money in the pot. But there are also variations where the low hand wins, and some, where players compete for both ends of the spectrum—the best high hand and the best low hand.

Of course, in each variation, the pot can also be won by a player when all of his opponents fold their hands at any point before the showdown, leaving one player alone to claim the pot—even though he may not actually have held the best hand!

HIGH POKER

The best poker hand you can hold is the royal flush, followed by a straight flush, four of a kind, full house, flush, straight, three of a kind, two pair, one pair, and high card hand. The order in which cards are dealt or how they are displayed is irrelevant to the final value of the hand. For example, 7-7-K-A-5 is equivalent to A-K-7-7-5.

Poker hands are ranked the way they are because of one cold, hard fact: the more difficult it is, statistically speaking, to be dealt a particular poker hand in five cards, the higher it ranks on the scale of poker hands. Note that all poker hands eventually consist of five cards, regardless of the variation played.

High-Card Hands – A hand containing five unmatched cards, that is, lacking any of the combinations shown below, is valued by its highest ranking card. 3-9-K-7-10, is a "king-high" hand. When the highest ranking cards are identical, the next highest untied card wins. A-K-J-10-4 beats A-K-J-3-2.

One Pair – Two cards of equal rank and three unmatched cards. Example: 5-5-8-J-K. If two players are competing with one-pair hands, then the higher ranked of the pairs—aces highest, deuces lowest—wins the pot. And if two players have the same pair, then the highest side card would be used to determine the higher-ranking hand. 5-5-A-7-6 beats 5-5-K-Q-J, since the ace is a higher kicker than the king.

Two Pair – Two pairs and an unmatched card. Example: 6-6-J-J-2. The highest pair of competing two-pair hands will win, or if the top pair is tied, then the second pair. If both pairs are equivalent, then the fifth card decides the winner. K-K-3-3-6 beats J-J-8-8-Q and K-K-2-2-A, but loses to K-K-3-3-9.

Three of a Kind – Three cards of equal rank and two unmatched cards. Also called **trips** or a **set**. Example: Q-Q-Q-7-J. If two players hold a set, the higher ranked set will win, and if both players hold an equivalent set, then the highest odd card determines the winner. 7-7-7-4-2 beats 5-5-5-A-K, but loses to 7-7-7-9-5.

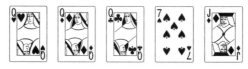

Straight – Five cards of mixed suits in sequence, but it may not wrap around the ace. For example, Q-J-10-9-8 of mixed suits is a straight, but Q-K-A-2-3 is not—it's simply an ace-high hand. If two players hold straights, the higher straight card at the top end of the sequence will win. J-10-9-8-7 beats 5-4-3-2-A but would tie another player holding J-10-9-8-7.

Flush – Five cards of the same suit. Example: K-10-9-5-3, all in diamonds. If two players hold flushes, the player with the highest untied card wins. Suits have no relevance. Thus, Q-J-7-5-4 of diamonds beats Q-J-4-3-2 of spades.

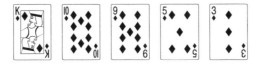

Full House – Three of a kind and a pair. Example: 5-5-5-9-9. If two players hold full houses, the player with the higher three of a kind wins. J-J-J-8-8 beats 7-7-7-A-A.

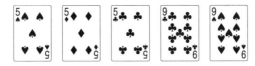

Four of a Kind – Four cards of equal rank and an odd card. Also called **quads.** Example: K-K-K-K-3. If two players hold quads, the higher ranking quad will win the hand. K-K-K-K-3 beats 7-7-7-7-A and K-K-K-K-2.

Straight Flush – Five cards in sequence, all in the same suit. Example: 7-6-5-4-3, all in spades. If two straight flushes are competing, the one with the highest card wins.

Royal Flush – The A-K-Q-J-10 of the same suit, the best hand possible. No royal flush is higher than another.

POKER PROBABILITIES

There are a total of 2,598,960 five-card combinations possible with a 52-card deck. The chart below shows the chances of receiving each type of hand in the first five cards dealt.

Probabilities of Five-Card Poker Hands

Hand	Number	Approximate Odds
Royal Flush	4	649,740 to 1
Straight Flush	36	72,192 to 1
Four of a Kind*	624	4,164 to 1
Full House	3,744	693 to 1
Flush	5,108	508 to 1
Straight	10,200	254 to 1
Three of a Kind	54,912	46 to 1
Two Pair	123,552	20 to 1
One Pair	1,098,240	1.37 to 1
No Hand	1,302,540	1 to 1

*Though there are only 13 four-of-a-kind combinations, to be accurate, this calculation must include the total number of possibilities when the fifth card is figured in to make a five-card hand.

LOW POKER

In **low poker**, the ranking of hands is the opposite to that of high poker, with the lowest hand being the most powerful and the highest hand being the least powerful. There are two varieties of low poker games: ace-to-five and deuce-to-seven.

In **ace-to-five**, the ace is considered the lowest and therefore most powerful card. The hand 5-4-3-2-A is the best low total possible with 6-4-3-2-A and 6-5-3-2-A being the next two best hands. Straights and flushes don't count against low hands.

In **deuce-to-seven** low poker, also known as **Kansas City lowball**, the 2 is the lowest and best card and the ace is the highest and worst. The hand 7-5-4-3-2 is the best possible hand, followed by 7-6-4-3-2 and 7-6-5-3-2. In this variation, unlike ace-to-five, straights and flushes count as high so you don't want to end up with 7-6-5-4-2 all in hearts, or 8-7-6-5-4.

HIGH-LOW POKER

In **high-low** poker (and its variant, **high-low 8-or-better**), players compete for either the highest-ranking or lowest-ranking hand, with the best of each claiming half the pot—with some restrictions which we'll go into in the individual game sections. With two different ways to win, these games tend to be wilder with a lot of betting. The best high hand and the best low hand split the pot, or if one player is fortunate enough to have the best high and low, he'll claim it all or **scoop**. In **declare**, which is only played in home games, players announce at the showdown whether they're going for the high, the low, or the high-low end of the pot, and they're committed to that declaration.

High-low games are sometimes played with a **qualifier**, a requirement that a player must have five unpaired cards of 8 or less to win the low end of the pot. If no player has an 8-or-better qualifier, then the best high hand will win the entire pot. For example, if the best low at the table is 9-6-5-4-2, then there is no qualified low hand and the best high hand will win the entire pot. This version of high-low is called **8-or-better**. Popular 8-or-better games are Omaha high-low 8-or-better and seven-card stud high-low 8-or-better.

WILD CARD POKER

In some home poker games, players designate certain cards as **wild cards**. These are cards which can take on any value and suit at the holder's discretion, even as a duplicate of a card already held. Any card can be considered wild with the consent of all players—possibly the jokers, deuces, or one-eyed jacks. If the deuces were used as wild cards, for example, the hand 6-5-3-2-2 would be a straight by designating one deuce as a 7 and the other as a 4.

Five-Ace Hand in Deuces Wild – The only difference in the ranking of hands in wild card poker from that of straight high poker is that a five of a kind hand—which is possible in wild card poker—is the highest ranking combination, above that of a royal flush. Otherwise, all other rankings, from the royal flush down to the high card, are equivalent.

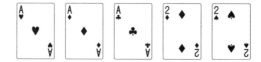

THE BASICS OF POKER

PLAYERS AND DEALERS

Poker can be played with as few as two players to as many as the 52-card deck can support, usually anywhere from eight to ten players, depending on the variation.

The **dealer** is responsible for shuffling the cards after each round of play so that they are mixed well and in random order. In a private game, the players take turns dealing, with the dealer position rotating around the table in a clockwise direction after each hand. The dealer is still an active player in a private game and enjoys no advantage other than any positional edge he may have for the particular game played.

In a casino or cardroom, the house will supply a dealer. He is not a participant in the betting or play of the game. His role is simply to shuffle the deck, deal the cards, and direct the action so that the game runs smoothly. He will point out whose turn it is to play and pull bets into the pot after each round of cards. And at the showdown, he will declare the winner, push the pot over to the winning player, then reshuffle the cards, and get ready for the next deal.

In casino variations in which the dealer enjoys a positional advantage, such as hold'em, lowball, Omaha, and draw poker, a **button** is utilized to designate the dealer's imaginary position. The button rotates around the table, one spot at a time, in clockwise fashion, so that, as in the private game, each player has a chance to enjoy the advantages of acting last.

THE CARDROOM MANAGER OR TOURNAMENT DIRECTOR

In a cardroom, the employee responsible for the supervision of poker games is the **cardroom manager**, or if there is a tournament in progress, the **tournament director**.

When a dispute arises, the dealer or one of the players may call over the supervisor for a ruling. If a player gets out of hand, the supervisors may ask the player to act more appropriately and let that serve as a warning. If the situation warrants or the abuse or infractions of the rules or decorum of the game continues, the player may be given a "time out," and will be disallowed from play for say, ten or twenty minutes, twenty-four hours, or even, permanently.

THE POKER TABLE

In a cardroom, the players and dealer sit around a table built to accommodate the game of poker. The dealer sits in the middle of the long side where there is an indentation cut into the table to facilitate access to the players. He will usually have a small rack in front of him where he can keep an extra deck of cards, chips, cash, and a few other items. In a cash game, he may also have a drop box where he will deposit money taken out of the pot as the house commission (see "Rake," later).

MONEY AND CHIPS

Poker is almost always played with **chips**, thin, circular clay or plastic units that are assigned specific values, such as $1, $5, $25, and $100. To receive chips in a cardroom, give the dealer cash, and he'll give you back the equivalent value in chips. This exchange of cash for chips is called a **buy-in** and is usually done right at the table. Dealers will accept only cash for chips, so if you have traveler's checks, credit cards, or other forms of money, you need to exchange these for cash at the area marked Casino Cashier. Then, with cash in hand, you can return to the poker table and buy chips.

In private games, players generally use chips, though sometimes the game will be cash only. When chips are used, one player acts as the bank or banker.

CUTTING THE CARDS

In a private game, the players take turns dealing, and the deck will be offered to a player, usually on the dealer's right, for the **cut**. This player initiates the cut by removing the top part of the deck and placing it to one side, face down. The dealer completes the cut by placing the former lower portion of the deck on top of the former upper section, thereby making the deck of cards whole again. In a cardroom, the dealer cuts the cards himself, using a **cut card**, a plastic card that is not part of the deck (and typically of a different and distinct color), to separate the deck into two stacks so that the top and bottom order of the packs can be reversed. This helps protect against cheating and covers the bottom card of the deck so that it is not accidentally exposed.

MANDATORY STARTING BETS

In poker, one or more players are typically required to put a bet into the pot before the cards are dealt. There are two types of mandatory bets: blinds and antes. **Blind bets,** or **blinds**, are used in hold'em, Omaha, and some draw variations. They are generally required of the first two players to the left of the dealer position. An **ante**, also known as a **sweetener**, is a uniform bet placed into the pot by all players before the cards are dealt. The sizes of the blinds and antes in home games are set by the players. In a casino, they are set by the house. Antes are used in a majority of private poker games and some casino games.

Players will frequently play aggressively in the early going, hoping to force opposing players out of the pot and pick up the antes and blinds without going further into a hand. Where there are blinds, as in hold'em and Omaha, this is called **stealing the blinds**. In ante games, it is called **stealing the ante**.

THE PLAY OF THE GAME

If the game requires antes or blinds, these should be placed into the pot before the cards are dealt. After the dealer shuffles the cards and offers the cut, the deal is ready to begin. The dealer begins by distributing cards to the player on his immediate left. He deals cards one at a time in a clockwise rotation, until each player has received the requisite number of cards for the poker variation being played. Like the dealing of the cards, play always proceeds in a clockwise direction. The first round begins with the player sitting to the immediate left of the blinds, the dealer, or, in some stud games, with either the high or low card opening play. Play will continue around the table, until each player in turn has acted.

In later rounds, the first player to act will vary depending on the poker variation being played. We'll cover the particulars of play under the sections on the games themselves.

THE PLAYER'S OPTIONS

When it is your turn to play, the following options, which apply to all forms of poker, are available to you:

1. Bet: Put chips at risk, that is, wager money, if no player has done so before you.

2. Call: Match a bet if one has been placed before your turn.

3. **Raise:** Increase the size of a current bet such that opponents, including the original bettor, must put additional money into the pot to stay active in a hand.
4. **Fold:** Give up your cards and opt out of play if a bet is due and you do not wish to match it. This forfeits your chance of competing for the pot.
5. **Check:** Stay active in a hand without making a bet and risking chips. This is only possible if no bets have been made.

The first three options—bet, call, and raise—are all a form of putting chips at risk in hopes of winning the pot. Once chips are bet and due, you must match that bet to continue playing for the pot or you must fold. Checking is not an option. If no chips are due, you can stay active without cost by checking.

If a bet has been made, each active player—one who has not folded—is faced with the same options: call, fold, or raise.

When a bet has been made, it no longer belongs to the bettor; it becomes the property of the pot, the communal collection of money that is up for grabs by all active players.

Betting continues in a round until the last bet or raise is called by all active players, at which point the betting round is over. A player may not raise his own bet when his betting turn comes around. He may raise only another player's bet or raise.

PLAYING TIP
Never fold a hand, no matter how bad, when you can check and remain active for free.

THE SHOWDOWN

If two or more players remain at the conclusion of all betting in the final betting round of a poker game, the showdown occurs. The **showdown** is the final act in a poker game where remaining players reveal their hands to determine the winner of the pot.

The player whose last bet or raise was called—if all players checked, the first to the left of the dealer position—turns over his cards first and reveals his hand. The player with the best hand at the showdown wins all the money in the pot. Players holding losing hands at the showdown may concede the pot without showing their cards.

In the event of a tie, or if there are two winners—as may be the case in high-low games—the pot is split evenly among those players.

If only one player remains after the final betting round, or at any point during the game, there is no showdown. The lone remaining player automatically wins the pot.

WHAT BETTING IS ALL ABOUT

You'll make bets for one of three reasons:

1. You feel your hand has enough strength to win and you want to induce opponents to put more money into the pot.

2. You want to force opponents out of the pot so that the field is narrowed, since fewer players increases your chances of winning.

3. You want to induce all your opponents to fold so that you can win the pot uncontested.

Limit Poker: Minimum and Maximum Bets

The minimum and maximum bets in limit games are strictly regulated according to the preset limits. For example, $3/$6 and $5/$10 are two common limits. The number of raises allowed in a round are also restricted, usually limited to three or four total according to the house rules for the cardroom. In other words, if there is a three-raise limit and the action goes bet, raise, reraise, and reraise, the raising would be **capped**. No more raises would be allowed for that round.

The exception to this rule comes into play when players are heads-up, in which case, there is no cap to the number of raises that can be made.

No-Limit Poker: Minimum and Maximum Bets

In no-limit cash games and tournaments, there is typically no cap to the number of raises allowed, though there are cardrooms that still impose the three- or four-raise rule. There is also no limit to how high a bet or raise can be. Players may raise as often as they like and for all their chips.

The minimum bet in no-limit must be at least the size of the big blind while the minimum raise must be at least equal to the size of the previous bet or raise in the round. For example, a $10 bet can be raised $30 more to make it $40 total. If a succeeding player reraises, he would have to make it at least $30 more—since that is the size of the last raise—for $70 total.

How to Bet

A bet is made by either pushing the chips in front of you—an action which speaks for itself—or by verbally calling out the play, and then pushing the chips in front of you. Simply announce, "I call," "I bet," "I raise," or whatever clearly indicates your desire, and then push your chips out on the felt. Note that if you announce a check, bet, raise, or a fold, it is binding and you're committed to the action.

Your bet should be placed at least six inches toward the middle, but not so far that your chips mingle with those already in the pot and cannot be distinguished from them. That is, your chips should be far enough away from your own stack and the pot so that they are clearly seen not only as a bet, but as your bet.

Do not throw your chips into the actual pot, which is called **splashing the pot.** This protects all players from an opponent intentionally or unintentionally miscalling a bet. This also allows the amount of the wager to easily be verified while making it clear to all players that a bet or raise has been made.

To check, tap or knock on the table with your fingertips or hand or announce "I check" or "check." To fold, push your cards or toss them *face down* towards the dealer. It is illegal to show your cards to active players who are competing for the pot.

Betting Etiquette

You should wait for your turn to play before announcing or revealing to any opponents what decision you will make. And if you fold, pass the cards to the dealer face down, so that no other player can view them. If any cards are revealed to any one player, the rules of the game require that all players see them so that everyone is kept on equal footing.

It is improper and illegal to discuss your hand or another player's hand while a game is in progress. It is also very poor form to criticize other players strategy decisions, no matter how poor they appear to be. If you think an opponent plays poorly, then that's good news for you: go win his chips.

Table Stakes, Tapped out Players, and Side Pots

You may only bet or call bets up to the amount of money you have on the table. This is called **table stakes**. You are not allowed to withdraw money from your wallet, borrow from other players, or receive credit while a hand is in progress. Getting extra cash or chips is permissible only before the cards are dealt.

For example, if the bet is $25 and you only have $10, you may only call for $10. The remaining $15 and all future monies bet during this hand—except for bets by opponents to equal the $10 called by the tapped-out player—would be separated into a **side pot.** A player who has no more table funds from which to bet is **tapped-out**.

A tapped-out player can still receive cards until the showdown and play for the **main pot**, however, he can no longer bet in this hand and has no interest in the side pot. The other active players can continue to bet against each other for the money in the side pot in addition to remaining in competition for the main pot with the tapped-out player.

At the showdown, if the tapped-out player has the best hand, he receives only the money in the main pot. The side pot will be won by the player having the best hand among the remaining players. Should one of the other players hold the overall best hand, that player wins both the original pot and the side pot. If only one opponent remains when a player taps out, then there is no more betting, and cards are played out until the showdown, where the best hand wins.

THE RAKE

One of the biggest differences between casino poker and private poker games is that in casino games the house gets a cut of the action, called a **rake**, as its fee for hosting the game. In low limit games and online, the rake can be anywhere from 5% to 10%, usually with a cap of $3 to $5 per pot. In higher limit games, the house typically charges players by time.

DRAW POKER: JACKS OR BETTER & ANYTHING OPENS

Draw poker is typically the first poker game players learn. The high version of the game is predominately played in casual home poker games among family and friends and rarely, if ever, dealt in a cardroom anymore. The low versions of draw poker games, however, still can be found in cardrooms, though with the recent popularity of hold'em and Omaha, these games are becoming rarer.

Online, however, where there is no overhead in hosting the games, you'll find draw poker games on some sites.

Though draw poker is typically played in a limit betting structure, no-limit structures are dealt as well; in fact, the 2005 WSOP lowball event was played as no-limit.

In this section, we'll cover three draw poker versions: jacks or better, anything opens, and lowball.

OVERVIEW

In draw poker, each player is dealt five face-down cards to start, and there are two betting rounds. These cards are known only by the holder of that hand. The first betting round occurs after the initial cards are received and before the **draw**, when players have an opportunity to exchange unwanted cards for new ones. In cardroom draw poker, players may exchange up to five cards. In some home games, players are restricted to drawing three cards, unless they have an ace and can draw four cards to it, but this is unusual.

After the first round of action is completed, there is a draw, which is followed by a second round of betting, and then the showdown. At the showdown, the highest hand wins the pot. If all other players have folded, the last remaining player is the winner.

Draw poker is sometimes played with an ante and sometimes with a blind, a mandatory bet placed by two players (sometimes three, sometimes only one). Rarely, both a blind bet and an ante are used as part of the structure.

JACKS OR BETTER

To open the betting in **jacks or better**, which is also known as **jackpots**, a player must have a hand with a minimum ranking of a pair of jacks, called **openers**, in order to open the betting. For example, a pair of queens, three deuces, or a straight are hands that could open betting, while a pair of sevens or an ace-high hand could not. If you hold a jacks-or-better hand, you do not have to open betting, however. You may check your turn.

Any player, even one with openers, can elect not to open. Once an opening bet is made, subsequent players can call, fold, or raise the opener. Checking is no longer permitted. If all players check on the opening round of play, the hand is said to be **passed out**. If that occurs, the cards are collected and shuffled, and the next player in turn gets the dealer's position. New antes will be required of all players and these will be added to the ones already in the pot.

The Play of the Game

The player to the immediate left of the dealer will receive the first card with the deal continuing clockwise, one card at a time, until all players have received their allotment of five cards. The first round of betting begins with the player on the dealer's left.

The first player to act must check if he cannot open betting or chooses not to open. The next player, in turn, must also check if he doesn't hold the requisite opening cards. Players continue checking until an opening bet is made. Subsequent players must call that bet to play for the pot, raise the bet, or fold. Checking is no longer permitted. Play continues around the table in a clockwise fashion until all bets and raises have been called.

The draw occurs after the first betting round is completed. Each remaining player, beginning with the first active player to the dealer's left, can exchange unwanted cards for new ones. The cards should be tossed face-down toward the dealer, who will issue an equivalent number of new cards from the unused portion of the deck. You should draw in turn, waiting for the previous player to receive his new cards before making your own discards. The dealer position draws last, if he is still in the pot.

Discards should be announced, so that all players are aware of the number of cards drawn. Players who do not draw any cards are said to be standing pat. You can indicate your choice to stand pat verbally or by knocking on the table with your hand.

The second round of betting follows the draw. It is begun either by the opener or the last raiser, if there were any raises during the round. If no raises occurred, and the opener has folded, the first active player to the dealer's left opens the betting. This player may check or bet as desired. Each succeeding player has the option of checking or betting, but once a bet is placed, active players must call, raise, or go out.

The showdown occurs after the second betting round is completed. At this time, the player who was the last to bet or raise turns over his cards first. Any opponent who claims a superior hand must show his cards while players holding inferior hands may go out without revealing what they hold. The best hand wins the pot and gets to rake in the chips.

Strategy Concepts

As with all other poker variations, the single most important strategy in jacks or better is to start out with cards which have good winning possibilities. The opening requirement of jacks or better tells you right off that any pair less than the minimum opening hand of jacks is automatically a big underdog. For example, if an opponent opens the betting, what chance would your pair of eights have, given that your opponent must have at least a pair of jacks?

Position is an extremely important consideration in jackpots. The dealer position has the biggest advantage because he not only acts last in the first betting round, but gets to exchange cards after all other players have made their drawing decisions. With marginal hands, you can come into the pot cheaply, or if the action is too stiff, you can fold. You're in a great position to bluff, and being the last to draw, you can make use of your drawing strategy to gain a powerful edge. Due to the dealer's big positional advantage, draw poker is an excellent choice in dealer's choice games.

The relative position you have at the table affects the types of hands that you should play and how they should be bet. For example, if you open betting with a pair of jacks or queens in an early position, you're in a bad situation if you get raised by several players. You have to figure the raisers for at least kings or aces, possibly better, and your lowly pair of jacks becomes a big underdog and must be folded.

Let's examine the minimum requirements for profitable play in jacks or better.

Jacks or Better • Minimum Opening Cards

First Four Positions (Early):	Kings or Better
Second Two Positions (Middle):	Queens or Better
Last Two Positions (Late):	Jacks or Better

In late position, when no openers have yet been made, the pair of jacks becomes a stronger hand. The jacks take on greater value in late position in a hand without openers, and have the advantage in that your opening bet might force opponents out of the pot and win the antes. If only one or two players call the opener, the jacks are in a decent enough position going into the draw to have a realistic chance of winning the pot.

Once someone has opened the betting, players holding jacks or queens should call only if two players or fewer are in the pot and no raises have been made. Otherwise, jacks and queens should be folded. Their winning chances diminish as the number of active players increases.

Four-card straights and flushes have good potential. They should be played to the draw, but only if the pot odds justify calling the bet. (See Pot Odds later.) Do not raise with these hands, however. At this stage they're too speculative and hold little value. Should the draw fill these cards into a straight or flush, then you've got the goods to raise and build up the pot.

If you hold kings, aces, and low three-of-a-kind hands, you should not only call the opener but raise as well. These are strong cards. If you don't force out weaker and speculative hands, a lucky draw by inferior hands could bury your favorite, making you pay the price for playing weakly. Against fewer opponents, there's less chance of this occurring. The more players that stay in for the draw, the higher the average winning hand will be, and the greater the opportunity that the kings, aces, and small trips will get beat out by an inferior hand that draws good. You've got to raise when you hold strong cards—don't make the game cheap for dreamers.

On the other hand, with a high three of a kind, such as a set of tens or higher, don't raise—call! You have a powerful hand which is favored to win without improvement. You want to keep as many players in as possible.

Do not play three-card straights or flushes, or inside straights. An **inside straight** is a four-card straight that has only one way of improving, such as 4-5-7-8. These long-shot draws are chip burners and will lead to losing session after losing session if you continually try to chase with them.

Playing a Small Two Pair

Smaller two-pair hands, such as nines over threes, are deceptive hands in draw poker and must be played carefully. At first glance, two small pairs appears to be a strong hand with good winning possibilities. In reality, however, these cards can be trouble.

While a small two pair may stand tall before the draw against three opponents, that hand becomes an underdog after the draw. If you're facing bets and raises before the draw and more bets after it, your small two pair (with 11-1 odds against improving) starts looking even smaller.

Fold two small pairs in early position if the pot is opened ahead of you. Do the same if you're in late position and three or more players are in the pot. In the latter case, raising the pot by one extra bet probably won't force your opponents to fold, but it will open you up to a reraise. This is asking for a tricky situation to get more expensive than you'd like. In last position, however, against just one or two players, you should raise, and try to get rid of them. You have good position after the draw, which works to your advantage, and fewer players to outlast.

The Draw

There is a lot of strategy involved in drawing the correct number of cards, though for the most part, the correct strategy is straightforward.

When you're drawing to a pair, your best chances of improving is to take a three-card draw. Sometimes, however, holding a kicker can be a powerful bluffing tool. Opponents have to suspect your two-card draw for three of a kind. Occasionally, using the kicker in this fashion can disguise your hand.

Drawing one card to a three of a kind is a good bluffing strategy as well. Let's say you're playing a $5/$10 game. The first two players check and the third player opens with a $5 bet. The next player folds. You're in the next seat holding three eights, and you raise the opener $5. Players fold in turn around the table. Only the opener calls your bet. He goes first and draws one card. You take one card as well.

After the draw, the opener bets $10, probably holding two pair, kings- or aces-up and figuring you for a lower two pair. You raise $10, banking on the 11 to 1 odds against his improving. He calls. Then he quickly folds his cards after you turn over your three eights.

Fold four-flushes and four-straights if they don't improve at the draw.

DRAW POKER: ANYTHING OPENS

This game is played the same as jacks or better, except that *any* hand may open the betting, regardless of strength. For example, a pair of sevens could open the betting or even a queen-high hand. Though any cards can open the betting, don't be fooled into opening or calling bets with anything less than you would play in jackpots. No matter what the opening requirement, you'll be dealt just as many good and bad hands in one game as in the other. The same minimum starting hands apply here as in jacks or better. In other words, don't enter the pot with weak hands.

Odds Against Improving Draw Poker Hands

Cards Held	Cards Drawn	Improved To	Approx. Odds Against
One Pair	3	Two Pair	5.3-1
		Three of a Kind	7.8-1
		Full House	97-1
		Four of a Kind	360-1
		Any Improvement	2.5-1
One Pair plus kicker	2	Two Pair	4.8-1
		Three of a Kind	12-1
		Full House	120-1
		Four of a Kind	1080-1
		Any Improvement	2.8-1
Three of a kind	2	Full House	15.3-1
		Four of a Kind	22.5-1
		Any Improvement	8.7-1
Four-Card Straight (Open Both Ways)	1	Straight	5-1
Inside Straight	1	Straight	10.8-1
Four-Card Flush	1	Flush	4.2-1
Four-Card	1	Straight Flush	22.5-1
Straight Flush (Open Ended)	1	Straight or Better	2-1
Four-Card Straight Flush	1	Straight Flush	46-1
		Straight or Better (Inside)	3-1

DRAW POKER: LOWBALL

This interesting draw poker variation presents a different twist to poker. The lowest hand is the strongest in **lowball**, or **loball** as it is sometimes spelled, as opposed to the standard high poker game in which the highest hand is the best.

In the ace-to-five version, the ace is still the best lowball card, but unlike in high poker, in which the ace counts as the highest card held, in ace-to-five the ace counts as the *lowest* card of a hand. The 2 is the next lowest card, and therefore the next best lowball card, and is followed in order by the 3, 4, 5, and so on, up to the king, which is the worst card.

In ace-to-five lowball, the highest card counts in determining the value of a hand; the lower the highest card, the better the hand. Hands are announced by their two highest cards. For example, the hand 7-6-4-2-A is announced as a "7-6" or "7-high," and 8-4-3-2-A is announced as an "8-4" or "8-high." Of the two above-mentioned hands, the "7-6" is the more powerful lowball hand, since its highest card, the 7, is lower than the 8, the high card of the "8-4" hand.

In instances where the highest ranks of two hands are equivalent, the next highest cards of the hands are matched up, and the lowest value of these matched cards determines the winner. Thus, the hand 8-6-4-3-2 is stronger than 8-7-3-2-A, and 9-6-5-2-A beats 9-6-5-4-A. When competing hands are equivalent, such as 8-5-4-3-A versus 8-5-4-3-A, the hand is a tie and the pot is split.

The **wheel** or **bicycle**, 5-4-3-2-A, is the perfect lowball hand. It can never be beat. At best, it can be tied by another wheel. 6-4-3-2-A is the next strongest lowball total, followed in order by 6-5-3-2-A, 6-5-4-2-A, 6-5-4-3-A, 7-4-3-2-A, 7-5-3-2-A, and so on.

Since straights and flushes do not count against the low hand, the wheel, 5-4-3-2-A, is not considered a straight. It's a perfect "5-4." An 8-4-3-2-A, all of hearts, is simply an "8-4" hand, not a flush as it would be in high poker.

Any five-card hand containing a pair is a weak hand and can be beat by any five unmatched cards. For example, K-Q-7-6-5 is a winner over 2-2-3-4-5. Two pair, three of a kind, full houses, and four of a kind are increasingly worse holdings. The odds of these hands winning a pot in lowball are steeper than a canyon wall.

The term **smooth** in lowball refers to a hand with a relatively good back four cards, such as the hand 9-5-4-3-A, a *smooth* nine. **Rough** suggests a relatively weak back four cards, such as the hand 9-7-6-5-2, a *rough* nine.

The Play of the Game

Lowball is played similarly to high draw poker, with two betting rounds, one before the draw and one after. An ante is often used as well, and that bet should be placed into the pot before the cards are dealt. When no ante is required, a blind bet is used. Sometimes both a blind bet and an ante are used.

The order of play and betting proceeds as in the other draw poker variations. At the showdown, the *lowest* hand wins the pot. The deal now moves to the left. In the case of a casino game, the former blind is now the button and can enjoy all the advantages of playing the dealer's position.

Strategy for Lowball

The knowledgeable player has a tremendous advantage over beginners at this variation, since the strategic thinking is vastly different from high poker. In lowball, players are shooting for different types of hands, and it takes the high poker player some time to become accustomed to the peculiarities of playing for low hands.

The cardinal rule in lowball is this: never play a hand which needs more than a one card draw to improve to a winner. Unlike high poker, draws of two, or even three cards are terrible draws and immediately single out a player as a weak opponent. A two-card draw is a shot in the dark. It's equivalent to trying to fill a three-card straight in high poker.

To win at lowball, you must start out with cards that can win. If the cards you're dealt are weak, throw them away unless you can get a free ride. For example, if you're the blind, and there are no raises following the forced bet, it costs nothing more to play, so you should stay in for the draw. Always play further if there is no cost, no matter the cards. However, if you're faced with a bet, fold unless you've got the goods.

Position is important in lowball and must be part of your opening strategy. Here are the minimum opening cards you should play in lowball:

Lowball • Minimum Starting Cards

First Four Positions: (Early)	8-high—pat hand 7-high—one card draw
Second Two Positions: (Middle)	9-high—pat hand 8-high—one card draw
Last Two Positions: (Late)	10-high—pat hand 9-high—one card draw

Unless you hold an 8-high pat hand or have a four-card 7-high in early position, you can't call the blind's bet or make an opener yourself. You must fold. You're too vulnerable to raises behind your position to call with these hands in the first four spots. There is a strong possibility that players will up the stakes in the middle and late positions. It is foolish to call hands in middle and early position if you will be forced to fold on a raise. Do not call bets with anything less than the minimum openers in early and middle positions. In late position, if you're facing a bet and a raise, call with a minimum holding of an 8-high pat hand or a four card 7-high draw.

A 7-high pat hand is strong enough to play aggressively. Raise the opener from any position at the table. If a raiser enters ahead of you, reraise. When you're dealt a 6-high pat hand, you have an almost sure winner. Don't raise in early position. You want to keep as many players as possible in the game. However, if a player raises behind you, and it's just the two of you and maybe one other player, reraise and build up the pot. You're sitting pretty.

SEVEN CARD STUD: HIGH, LOW (RAZZ) AND HIGH-LOW

Seven-card stud's three main variations—high, low, and high-low—pack five exciting betting rounds into play. In each variation, each player forms the best five-card combination out of the seven dealt to produce his final hand.

In **seven-card high stud**, the highest ranking hand at the showdown wins the pot. In **seven-card low stud** (also called **razz**), the lowest hand claims the gold. And in **seven-card stud high-low** (and its variant, **seven-card stud 8-or-better**), players vie for either the highest ranking or lowest ranking hand, with the best of each claiming half the pot—with some restrictions, which we'll go into.

Players will receive a total of seven cards if they play through to the end. After the first three cards are dealt (two **face-down**, or **closed**, and one **face-up**, or **open**), the first betting round commences. The following three cards—the fourth, fifth, and sixth—are dealt open, one at a time, to each active player, with a betting round accompanying each card. The last card, the seventh, comes "down and dirty," that is, face-down.

All players who have not folded now hold three hole cards and four open cards. A final round of betting follows the seventh card, and then the showdown occurs with the best hand (or hands, as may be the case in high-low) claiming the pot. In each variation of seven-card stud, a player can also win the pot before the showdown by forcing out all opponents through bets and raises that opponents won't match.

THE PLAY OF THE GAME

All antes, if required, should be placed into the pot before the cards are dealt. Once an ante bet is placed, it is like any other wager. It is the property of the pot and will belong to the eventual winner of the hand.

The dealer distributes the cards in a clockwise direction beginning with the player to his left and continuing around the table, in order, until all players have received their initial three cards. Either the lowest open card on the table, or the highest, depending on the variation, is forced to make an opening bet, called a **bring-in**, which will start the action.

Play proceeds in a clockwise direction beginning with the player to the bring-in's left and moving around the table until all bets and raises have been called. Or it will end right there if no player chooses to call the bring-in, giving that first bettor the pot. This first round of betting is called **third street**, so named for the three cards that each player holds.

The bring-in bet is usually less than the size of the smaller bet in a limit game. For example, in a $5/$10 game, the bring-in might be $2. In seven-card stud high and high-low games played in cardrooms, the player holding the lowest open card makes the bring-in. If two players have identically ranked cards, the player with the lower ranked suit plays first. For this purpose only, the suits are ranked, with spades being the highest, followed by hearts, diamonds, and clubs. For example, if the lowest ranked open cards are the 3 and the 3, the 3 will open the betting.

In low stud games, razz, played in cardrooms, it is the opposite: the player with the *highest* ranking open card starts the betting. If two or more players hold equivalent values, the high-card player closest to the dealer's left will make the bring-in.

In high and high-low seven-card stud games played in home poker, the player with the highest ranking open card usually starts the betting, with the lowest ranking hand in home poker usually being the bring-in—and remember, the ace counts as the lowest card in low poker. But, as in all home games, players may use the high hand rather than the low one to open betting.

There is no checking on third street. The first player to the bring-in's left goes next, and he must either **complete** the bet, that is, bring it up to the lower limit of the betting structure (so if it's a $5/$10 game with a $2 bring-in, then he must raise $3 to make it $5), raise the completed bring-in, or fold. All bets and raises in this first betting round are at the lower limit of the betting tier. So if you're playing a $5/$10 game, all bets would have to be for $5. If a player wants to raise the completed bring-in, it would be by $5 more, making it $10 to the next player.

When third street betting is completed, each active player receives a face-up card. Everyone now holds a total of four cards, two open and two closed. Play in this round, called **fourth street**, and all the following rounds, whether in a home game or a cardroom, begins with the best open hand and moves clockwise around the table. In high and high-low seven-card stud, the best hand is the highest ranked, and in low poker, the best hand is the lowest ranked. When two or more players hold identically ranked cards, the player closest to the dealer's left plays first.

For example, in low poker, a player showing 8-6-2-A on board, an 8-6 hand, would act before a player showing a pair of sixes, 6-6-3-2. Similarly, a 6-4-2-A board would open against a 7-3-2-A. And if players held K-K, A-Q, and 6-6 in a high or high-low game, the pair of kings would lead off the betting.

Beginning on fourth street, which is the second betting round, and continuing through the last betting round, the first bettor to act may check to open the betting since there is no bring-in bet to meet. It is only on third street that an opening bet is required for players to stay in active competition for the pot. All bets and raises on fourth street are in the lower limit of the betting structure unless an open pair shows on board, in which case players may elect to open with a bet from the upper limit of the betting. Thus, on fourth street in a $5/$10 game, bets would be $5, unless an open pair forms on board, in which case $10 could be bet.

Once fourth street betting is concluded, another open card is dealt to each active player. Players now have a total of three face up cards in addition to their two down cards. This round is called **fifth street**, and all bets and raises on this round and on the following two rounds, sixth and seventh streets, are in the upper tier of the betting limit. In a $5/$10 game, bets and raises would be $10, in a $3/$6 game, $6, and in a $15/$30 game, $30.

After this round of betting closes, active players receive their fourth open card. This next betting round is called **sixth street**, so named for the six cards each player holds. It is played like fifth street, with the highest ranking open hand acting first and concluding either when all bets and raises have been called, or when all opponents fold, ceding the pot to the last remaining player.

Seventh street is the final betting round. Each remaining player receives his seventh and final card face-down. There is a round of betting, which is followed by the showdown if two or more player remain.

THE SHOWDOWN: HIGH STUD AND RAZZ

In straight high poker and low poker, each player chooses five cards out of the seven total he holds to form his best hand. In seven-card high stud, the best high hand wins, and in the lower stud version, the five best low cards will claim the pot.

THE SHOWDOWN: HIGH-LOW STUD

The main difference between high-low stud and straight high or low versions, is that you're actually playing for two parts of the pot: half the pot goes to the player with the best high hand and the other half goes to the player with the best low hand.

High-low seven-card stud is played as either "cards speak" or "declare." In **cards speak**, which is the style universally played in cardrooms, players simply reveal their cards at the showdown—like all other poker variations. The best high hand and the best low hand split the pot, or if one player is fortunate enough to have the best high *and* low, he'll claim it all or scoop. In **declare**, which is only played in home games, players announce at the showdown whether they're going for the high, the low, or the high-low end of the pot, and they're committed to that declaration.

High-Low Declare

A player declares his intentions by hiding a colored chip in his fist and extending his closed fist over the table. At a given signal, players simultaneously open their hands and reveal their decisions. White chips are usually used for a low declaration, blue chips for high, and red chips for high-low, though using different color arrangements, coins, or writing the decision on a folded note will work just as well.

If a player declares high and loses to a higher ranking-hand, but actually has the best low hand, he gets nothing because he didn't declare low. Players are only eligible for the part of the pot they declare.

Among the players who declared "high," the best high hand wins that half of the pot, while the best low hand among players who declared "low" takes the other half. If just one player calls "high" and the rest "low," the player declaring high automatically wins half the pot and need not show his hand, while the low declarers compete for the other half—and vice versa. If all players declare high, then the best high hand wins the entire pot. If all players declare low, then the best low hand claims the entire pot.

Players that declare "high-low" risk all, and must have both the best high hand *and* the best low hand or they forfeit the entire pot. It's an all or nothing proposition. If a high-low declarer wins only one way, then he's out of the pot, and the best high hand and the best low hand split the chips. And if just one opponent remains against the high-low declarer and the one-way declarer wins his side of the pot, he gets the entire pot since the high-low hand failed to win both halves.

Sample Declaration

Let's follow a showdown in a game being played as declaration. Five players remain: Donto, Fay, Julian, Eddie-boy, and Big Phil. The first three declare "high," the fourth "low," and the fifth, Big Phil, goes all out and declares "high-low." (Flavian has already folded and both he and his cigar watch passively from the sidelines.)

Donto (Declared high)	J 10 9 8 7
Fay (Declared high)	K K K 5 4
Julian (Declared high)	A 10 8 6 3 (flush)
Eddie-boy (Declared low)	7 6 4 3 2
Big Phil (Declared high-low)	High: K 7 5 4 2 (flush) Low: 7 5 4 3 2

Big Phil's 7-5 hand is a stronger low than Eddie-boy's 7-6, but his king-high flush is weaker than Julian's ace-high flush. Therefore, Big Phil, unable to win both ways, loses his high-low declaration and wins nothing. Julian and Eddie-boy hold the best high and low hands respectively, and they split the pot. Had Big Phil declared "low" only, he would have won that half of the pot.

SEVEN-CARD STUD 8-OR-BETTER

Seven-card high-low stud is sometimes played with a **qualifier**, a requirement that a player must have five unpaired cards of 8 or less to win the low end of the pot. If no player has an 8-or-better qualifier, then the best high hand will win the entire pot. For example, if the best low at the table is 9-6-5-4-2, then there is no qualified low hand and the best high hand will win the entire pot.

This version of seven-card stud low is called **seven-card stud 8-or-better**, or simply, **8-or-better**.

Strategy for Seven-Card Stud: High Poker

The first three cards you receive in seven-card stud lay the groundwork for the future possibilities of your hand. Therefore, to build winners, you should only stay in with cards that have the right winning ingredients. Starting and staying with promising cards is especially important in seven-card stud, since the five betting rounds of this game add up to a lot of bets and raises.

With all these chips at stake, you want to give yourself every chance of winning.

These are the minimum starting cards you need to enter the betting in seven-card high stud:

Seven-Card High Stud • Minimum Starting Cards

Three of a kind
Three-card straight flush
Three-card flush
Three-card straight
Pair of tens or higher
Low or middle pair with ace or king kicker
Concealed pair with face-card kicker
Three high cards, two of them suited

Starting cards of three of a kind are powerful hands that are heavily favored to win. With these cards, you want to keep as many players as possible in the pot. Play low key on third and fourth street, calling bets but not raising. If your opponents start showing threatening signs of flushes or straights on fifth street, bet heavy. You should either force them out or make them pay for the privilege of trying to buy their hands. However, if your trips turn into a full house, you have nothing to fear from straights or flushes. You want them filling their straights and flushes—and how!

With three-card flushes and straights, call third street betting, but do not raise. In general, it is prudent to raise only if you've either got the goods or you are bluffing (and only under the right circumstances). If your three-card straight or flush doesn't improve by fourth street, it's time to say goodbye. Fold the hand. The odds against filling it are getting too steep for the cost of calling bets and chasing cards for three more betting rounds.

One interesting thing about three-card flushes that most players don't realize is that when you end up winning with these cards, your winning hand usually is *not* the flush! Along the way, you'll make two pair hands, three of kind, a straight, full house, or perhaps a high pair. So it's important to remember that you prefer your three-flush to contain high cards. Holding a 10-7-4 flush draw is not as valuable as a K-J-2 flush draw.

For example, if the highest exposed card on board is a queen—say your opponent shows Q-J-10-7-5 on his board—pairing up your king in the hand K-J-2 gives you a much more competitive hand. If the showdown ends up matching pair against pair or two pair against two pair, your big pairs will often win.

As you can see, pairing big cards is much more valuable than pairing up a 10, 7, or 4, weaker cards which form weaker pair and two-pair hands that often lose to bigger pair and two-pair hands. Of course, there are other considerations to take into account, but the high-card factor is one that must be considered from the get-go. Bigger is better.

Having a big kicker to low and medium pairs is critical, and that is why you don't want to enter the pot without an ace or a king to support your weaker pairs. If you pair up the ace or king, it gives you a good chance to outlast opponents with smaller two-pair hands than you. Of course, if there is an ace on board, your king could be playing second-best so you need to be aware of that. But if you have an ace and pair it, you have at least the top pair, and are in pretty good shape. If your small and medium pairs haven't improved by fourth street, you'll probably want to toss the hand if an opponent raises the pot before your turn or bets with a higher pair on board. It's best not to chase hands when you're probably beat.

A key factor to winning at seven-card stud, or at any poker game for that matter, is making sure you lose as little as possible in the pots you don't win. You must fold hands which have not panned out or have become underdogs. Avoid the temptation to play "just one more card." That one more card costs money and if it's not a sound call, it's a bet deducted from your overall winnings.

To be a winner, you must wager with the odds, not against them. And those odds are defined by the cards held versus those of your opponents—not on the hopes of what might happen. Again, when a promising hand's possibilities wither and it looks to be second best, bury it.

Betting intensity can indicate the strength of your opponents' hands. If betting is heavy, with raises and re-raises, expect to see strong cards at the showdown. Heavy betting usually equates to strong hands. However, if the betting is relatively light, then the opposite applies: expect the average winning hand to be weaker.

You must pay attention to all the open cards in seven-card stud. Cards in play cannot be drawn and therefore greatly impact the chances that you or your opponent will improve your hand. For example, if an opponent holds an open pair of kings and you saw two kings folded earlier, you know that, no matter what kind of luck that player has, there's no way he can buy a third king.

On the other hand, your chances of completing a four-card flush draw are greatly diminished if you see that six of the clubs you need have already been dealt to your opponents.

If you hold a marginal hand and are unsure of how to proceed, lean toward folding if cards you need are already in play, and lean toward playing if they are not.

Strategy for Seven-Card Stud: Low Poker (Razz)

In seven-card low stud, or "razz," as the game is commonly called, you use your best five cards out of the seven dealt to form the lowest possible hand. Strategic thinking is different in razz than in standard seven-card stud. Unlike high poker, where players sometimes start with strong hands, good lowball hands *always* start out as **drawing hands**, hands which need improvement to develop into winners. (See the section on lowball in the draw poker chapter for hand rankings in low poker.)

Your first four cards may be A-2-3-4, a golden start, but if the next three cards you receive are a pair of jacks and a king, then your hand melts into nothing. On the other hand, seven-card high stud presents situations where you're dealt big hands for starters, such as the starting hand Q-Q-Q, and regardless of the next four cards, these trip queens are heavily favored to win. Subsequent draws cannot diminish the inherent strength of this high hand. In contrast, lowball hands that don't improve die on the vine and become worthless.

To be competitive in seven-card lowball, you must enter the betting with strong starting cards, ones that can go all the way. Below are the minimum opening or calling hands that should be played in razz.

Seven-Card Low Stud • Minimum Starting Cards

Three-card 7-high or better (lower)
Three-card 8-high with two cards valued 5 or lower
Three-card 9-high with two of the other three cards being an ace, 2, or 3
An ace plus a 5 or a lower card, and an odd card

If you don't hold one of the above combinations, you must fold. You don't want to play underdog cards and contribute to other players' pots. If you can get a free ride into fourth street, take it, but hands weaker than those mentioned cannot call a blind or opening bet. However, if you're the blind, and no raises occur behind your position, you're already in—take the free card on fourth street.

Hands with relatively low supporting cards are called **smooth** hands. For example, the 3-2 in the starting hand of 7-3-2, a *smooth seven*, or the 4-3-2-A in the hand 8-4-3-2-A, a *smooth eight*. Hands where the supporting cards are relatively high are called **rough**, such as the 6-4 in the starting cards 7-6-4, called a *rough seven*, or the 7-5-4-3 in the hand 8-7-5-4-3, a *rough eight*. Smooth hands have greater possibilities of winning than their rough counterparts and should be played more aggressively.

If you make an 8-high hand or a smooth 9 on fifth street, you're in a strong position. You should bet and raise forcefully against players still holding drawing hands. You're the favorite, so you want to either force them out of the pot or make them pay for every card they try to catch.

Also, play aggressively against weak players when you've got the goods. They'll stay in too long with inferior hands. Why not make your winning pot that much larger?

Strategy for Seven-Card Stud: High-Low Poker

The splitting of the pot into two parts, half for the best high hand and half for the best low, makes seven-card stud an action-packed and exciting game. An astute player can win healthy sums against loose opponents, while a weak player can really get buried. Note that the advice in this section applies to both seven-card stud high-low (with no qualifier) and seven-card stud 8-or-better.

Though there are more ways to win at high-low stud, you must not let this tempt you into playing too many hands. The same winning principle applies here as in all poker games: enter the betting only with good starting cards, ones that have a good chance of winning. Staying in pots with hands that hold both high and low possibilities, but are mediocre in both directions, is a costly and weak strategy. You can work only with the cards that you're dealt.

Look for hands that give you possibilities of winning both the high *and* the low end of the pot, which is called scooping. The problem with playing one-way hands in high-low is that your bets immediately lose half their value due to the fact that you're going after only one half of the pot. If you get shut out, you lose all your chips. And if you win, you only get half of the action.

And what if you happen to get caught in a pot where one player has a lock on one part of the pot? You're going to get whipsawed for a lot of bets, making your pursuit of 50% of the action very costly if you're the player getting trapped, especially if you're the player drawing dead. The math is not favorable for you in many one-way pots.

So when you are playing for one-half of the pot, you need that hand to be *very* strong.

The best starting hand in seven-card high-low stud is three suited cards 8 or below (A, 2, 3, 4, 5, 6, 7, or 8), particularly if one of these cards is an ace or you have three consecutive cards for a three-straight flush. You have a great hand with excellent high and low potential and want to build the pot. If you're first in the pot, you should raise to build it up, but if you have raisers before you, just call.

Another big hand is a three of a kind, especially if the trips are low. This is a very deceptive hand. A pair of aces with an 8 or less to go with it, giving it two-way potential, is a strong hand as well. Other big pairs, like kings and queens, are almost worthless against an aggressive ace, as their scooping potential is limited and their high potential is vulnerable. In 8-or-better, big pairs take on more value because if low hands don't qualify, the high hand scoops the pot. However, you should never play a high hand that is not shaping up to be the *best* hand. This is an extremely important concept in high-low, with or without the qualifier.

Other strong two-way starting hands are three-straights 8 or less (A-2-3, 2-3-4, 3-4-5, 4-5-6, 5-6-7, and 6-7-8), three straights 8 or less with just one gap (such as 4-5-7 or

2-3-5), and three cards 8 or less that include an ace (such as A-4-5, A-3-8, and A-3-5). You can play these hands strong on third street, raising or handling a few bets before your position. You have a great shot at low, and if your ace pairs and there is no other ace on board, you have a good shot at the high as well.

Even if you don't pair, sometimes the ace by itself might be enough to win the high. For example, a player holding K-Q-K would have to consider folding against your ace if you bet aggressively since his one-way high hand is looking at a possible bigger pair.

If your three-straight 8 or less has two gaps and doesn't include an ace, such 4-6-8 and 2-4-6, it has some value but should be folded against heavy betting. If on fourth street, you're sitting with a four-card low topped by 8-7 or 8-6, you can't handle any action if another player looks like he's going for low as well—say by showing a 5-3 or 6-5 on board. And remember, an 8-led low hand is vulnerable against other players going low, particularly if you see no eights on their board.

You shouldn't play middle pairs without high kickers, three-flushes that don't have three cards 8 or less, three-straights with high cards (no scoop potential and only a draw to a high hand), and of course random cards that don't fit in with the starting hands discussed above. One important concept to keep in mind is that high hands can't turn into low hands, but low hands can turn into high ones if the right cards are drawn.

The nature of high-low stud calls for more aggressive play. When you have a chance to scoop the pot or you have a lock on either the high or low end of the pot, bet forcefully. You want to create big pots and make the winnings that much sweeter.

TEXAS HOLD'EM

Texas hold'em, or **hold'em**, as the game is more commonly known, is played as high poker, that is, the player with the best and highest five-card combination at the showdown wins the money in the pot. The pot can also be won by a player when all of his opponents fold their hands at any point before the showdown, leaving one player alone to claim the chips in the middle—even though he may not have held the best hand!

Your final five-card hand in hold'em will be made up of the best five-card combination of the seven total cards available to you. These include the **board**, five cards dealt face-up in the middle of the table which are shared by all players, and your **pocket cards** or **hole cards**, two cards dealt face-down that can be used by you alone. For example, your final hand could be composed of your two pocket cards and three cards from the board, one pocket card and four from the board, or simply all five board cards.

At the beginning of a hand, each player is dealt two face-down cards. Then each player gets a chance to exercise his betting options. Next, three cards are dealt simultaneously on the table for all players to share. This is called the **flop**, and it is followed by another round of betting. A fourth board card, called the **turn**, is then dealt, and it too is followed by a round of betting. One final community card is dealt in the center of the table, making five total. This is the **river**. If two or more players remain in the hand, it is followed by the fourth and final betting round.

When all betting has finished, there is the **showdown**, in which the highest ranking hand in play wins.

HOW TO READ YOUR HOLD'EM HAND

You have all seven cards available to form your final five-card hand—any combination of your two hole cards and the five cards from the board. You can even use all five board cards. Let's look at an example.

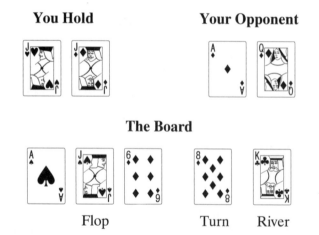

You Hold   **Your Opponent**

The Board

Flop   Turn   River

Your best hand, three jacks, is made using your two pocket cards and one jack from the board. This beats your opponent's pair of aces, formed with one card from his hand and one from the board. In both instances, the other cards are not relevant. For example, there is no need to say three jacks with an ace and a king versus two aces with a king, queen and jack—simply, three jacks versus two aces.

If the river card, the last card turned up on the board, had been a K♦ instead of a K♣, your opponent would have a diamond flush (formed with his two pocket diamonds and the three diamonds on the board), which would beat your set of jacks.

THE PLAY OF THE GAME

All play and strategy in hold'em depends upon the position of the **button**, which is a small disk, typically plastic and labeled "Dealer." The player who has the button in front of him, who is also known as the button, will have the advantage of acting last in every round of betting except for the preflop round. After each hand is completed, the disk rotates clockwise to the next player.

The two players to the left of the button are required to post bets, called **blinds**, before the cards are dealt. The player immediately to the button's left is called the **small blind** and the one to his left is called the **big blind**.

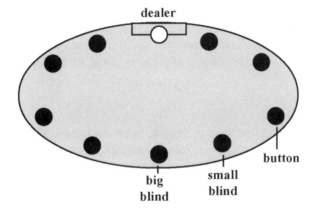

The big blind is typically the same size as the lower bet in a limit structure, so if you're in a $3/$6 game, the big blind would be $3 and in a $5/$10 game, it would be $5. The small blind will either be half the big blind in games where the big blind evenly divides to a whole dollar, or two-thirds of the big blind when it doesn't. For example, the small blind might be $2 in a $3/$6 game and $10 in a $15/$30 game.

Typical blinds for no-limit cash games might be $2/$5, $3/$5 or $5/$10 for the small blind and big blind respectively. Bigger blinds mean more action and larger games.

In cash games, the amount of the blinds are preset and remain constant throughout the game. In tournaments, however, the blinds steadily increase as the event progresses, forcing players to play boldly to keep up with the greater costs of the forced bets.

ORDER OF BETTING

Play always proceeds clockwise around the table. On the preflop, the first betting round, the first player to the left of the big blind goes first. He can call the big blind to stay in competition for the pot, raise, or fold. Every player following him has the same choices: call, raise, or fold. The last player to act on the preflop is the big blind. If no raises have preceded his turn, the big blind can either end the betting in the round by calling, or he can put in a raise.

However, if there are any raises in the round, the big blind and other remaining players must call or raise these bets to stay active, or they must fold.

On the other betting rounds—the flop, turn and river—the first active player to the button's left will go first and the player on the button will go last. If the button has folded, the player sitting closest to his right will act last. When all bets and raises have been met on the flop and turn, or if all players check, then the next card will be dealt. On the river, after all betting action is completed, players will reveal their cards to see who has the best hand.

Betting in a round stops when the last bet or raise has been called and no bets or raises are due any player. Players cannot raise their own bets or raises.

At any time before the showdown, if all opponents fold, then the last active player wins the pot.

PLAYING TIP

Never fold the big blind unless the pot has been raised. If there is no raise, there is no cost to play and you can see the flop for free.

SAMPLE GAME

Let's follow the action in a sample $3/$6 limit game with nine players so that you can see how hold'em is played.

In limit poker, the betting structure has two levels, the lower levels being the amount you must bet or raise on the preflop and flop ($3 in a $3/$6 game), and the higher levels being the amount you must bet or raise on the turn and river ($6 in a $3/$6 game).

Before the cards are dealt, the small blind and the big blind must post their bets. Once that occurs, the dealer will distribute cards one at a time, beginning with the small blind, who is the player sitting to the immediate left of the button, and proceeding clockwise until all players have received two face down cards.

The Preflop

The player to the big blind's left acts first. He has the option of calling the $3 big blind bet, raising it $3 more, or folding. Checking is not an option on the preflop as there is already a bet on the table—the $3 big blind bet.

Let's say this player folds. The next player is faced with the same decisions: call, raise, or fold. He calls for $3. Since this is a $3/$6 game, all bets and raises in this round *must* be in $3 increments. The next three players fold. The following player raises $3, making it $6 total—the $3 call plus the $3 raise.

It is the button's turn, the player sitting in the dealer position. He thinks about his cards and calls the $6. Now it is up to the small blind. The small blind has already put in $2 so he must put in $4 more to play. If there had been no raise, it would cost him just $1 more to meet the $3 big blind bet and stay active.

The small blind folds and the big blind considers reraising the raiser, but instead just calls the $3 raise. Play now moves back to the original caller. Since he has only put $3 into the pot, he must meet the $3 raise to stay in the hand. He calls and since all bets and raises have been matched, the round is over. We'll see the flop four-handed.

The big blind always has the option to raise on the preflop. The dealer will say "option," on the big blind's turn letting him know he can raise. If there had been no raises and the big blind calls, the preflop betting is finished for the round. If the big blind raises, then the other active players must meet that raise to stay active.

If all players fold on the preflop, the big blind wins the hand by default.

The Flop

At the conclusion of betting, the dealer pulls the blinds and bets into the pot. He takes the top card off the deck and **burns** it, that is, he removes it from play, and then deals the three card flop face-up in the center of the table.

Bets and raises during this round are still at the $3 level. The first active player to the button's left goes first. Since the small blind has folded, it is the big blind's turn. There are no bets that have to be met—the forced first round blind bet only occurs on the preflop—so the big blind may check or bet. (There is no reason to fold, which would be foolish, as it costs nothing to stay active.)

The big blind checks, the next player checks, the original raiser from the preflop checks, and it is now up to the button. He pushes $3 into the pot forcing the other three players to put up $3 if they want to see another card. The big blind, who checked first in this round, is the next active player. He must call or raise this bet to continue with the hand, or he must fold. He decides to call for $3 and the other two players fold. Since all bets have been called, betting is complete for the round.

We're now heads-up, the big blind versus the button.

The Turn

The dealer burns the top card and then deals a fourth community card face-up on the table. This is known as the **turn** or **fourth street**. Betting moves to the upper limit, so now all bets and raises are in $6 increments. The big blind, being the first active player on the button's left, goes first and checks. The button checks as well. Since all active players checked, the betting round is over.

The River and the Showdown

After the top card is burned, the fifth and final community card is turned over and placed next to the other four cards in the center of the table. Players now have five community cards along with their two pocket cards to form their final five-card hand.

At the **river** or **fifth street**, which this round is called, there is one final round of betting. The big blind goes first and leads out with a $6 bet. The button calls, and that concludes the betting since the big blind cannot raise his own bet. We now have the showdown. The big blind turns over K-Q, which combines with a board of K-Q-10-7-5 for two pair of kings and queens. The button's K-10 also gives him two pair led by kings, but his second pair is tens. The big blind has the superior hand and wins the money in the pot.

Had the button simply folded, the big blind would have won by default, since no other players remained to contest the pot.

On the showdown, the last player to bet or raise (or if there has been no betting in the round, then the first person to the left of the button) has to show his cards first. Losers can simply **muck** their cards, that is, fold them, without showing their cards.

The dealer pushes the chips in the pot over to the winner, collects and shuffles the cards, and prepares to deal a new hand. The button moves clockwise, so the big blind is now the small blind, and the small blind becomes the button.

HOLD'EM'S SEVEN KEY STRATEGIC CONCEPTS

The following key concepts apply to all forms of hold'em.

1. Respect Position

In hold'em, where you sit relative to the button is called **position**. In a nine-handed game, the first three spots to the left of the button are known as **early position**, the next three, **middle position**, and the last three, **late position**. In a ten-handed game, early position is the four spots to the left of the button.

The later the position, the bigger the advantage, because you get to see what your opponents do before deciding whether to commit any chips to the pot. The earlier the position, the more vulnerable your hand is to being raised and thus the more powerful your hand must be for you to enter the pot.

In late position, you have more options and leverage so you can play more hands. If the early betting action is aggressive, you can fold marginal hands without cost. And if the betting action is weak, you can be more aggressive with marginal hands and see the flop with better position.

2. Play Good Starting Cards

You must start out with good cards to give yourself the best chance to win. And while this seems obvious, you'd be surprised at the number of players who ignore this basic strategic concept and take loss after loss by chasing with inferior and losing hands. If you play too many hands in poker, you'll soon find yourself without chips. Enter the pot with good starting cards in the right position and you give yourself good chances to finish with winners.

3. Play Opponents

By watching how an opponent plays, you get all sorts of information on how to take advantage of his tendencies. For example, when a player infrequently enters a pot, he's **tight**, and you can often force him out of hands even when he may have better cards than you. You'll give him credit for big hands when he's in a pot, and get out of his way unless you have a big hand yourself.

On the other hand, an opponent who plays a lot of hands is **loose**, and you can figure him for weaker cards on average. You also need to adjust for **aggressive** players, who often raise when they get involved in a pot, and **passive** players, opponents you can play against with less fear of getting raised.

4. Be the Aggressor

Hold'em is a game where aggression brings the best returns. It's almost always better to raise than to call. Raising immediately puts pressure on opponents who will often fold right there, unwilling to commit chips to their marginal hands. Or they will see the flop but will be ready to drop out against further bets if it doesn't connect strongly enough with their cards—which happens most of the time.

5. Win Chips, Not Pots

You want to win chips and to do so, you need to win pots, particularly big ones if you can. So keep this in mind: It is not the quantity of pots you win, but the quality of them that matters.

6. Fold Losing Hands

Part of winning is minimizing losses when you have the second best hand. This means not chasing pots when you are a big underdog to win, especially longshot draws against heavy betting. You can't win them all. Save your chips for better opportunities. Cutting losses on hands you lose adds to overall profits.

7. Patience

Hold'em is a game of patience. You will often go long stretches between good hands. Winning players exercise patience and wait for situations where they can win chips. Your good hands will come, and if you haven't blown yourself out trying to force plays, you'll be able to take advantage of them and win some nice pots for yourself.

LIMIT HOLD'EM STRATEGY

In limit hold'em, where all betting is in a two-tier structure, such as $3/$6 or $5/$10, the three main factors to consider when deciding how to play a hand are the strength of your starting cards, where you are sitting relative to the button, and the action that precedes your play.

There are other considerations that enter into the mix, such as the cost of entering the pot and the aggressiveness or tightness of the table, but you should always consider these three fundamental factors first.

Starting Cards

The biggest mistake novices and habitually losing players make in hold'em is playing too many hands. Each call costs at least one bet. They compound this mistake when they catch a piece of the flop—but not enough of it—leading to more inadvisable bets and raises when they are holding a losing hand, thus making the situation even more costly. These lost chips add up quickly and set the stage for losing sessions.

So the foundation of playing winning hold'em is starting with solid cards, that is, playing the right cards in the right positions.

We'll divide the starting hands into four different categories: Premium, Playable, Marginal, and Junk.

Premium Starting Hands

A-A	K-K	Q-Q	J-J	A-K

Aces, kings, queens, jacks, and A-K are the best starting hands. They are strong enough to raise from any position at the table and should be played aggressively. You hope to accomplish two things with the raise. First, you want to get more money into the pot on a hand in which you're probably leading, and second, you want to protect that hand by narrowing the field of opponents.

The greater the number of players who stay in the pot, the greater the chances that a weaker hand will draw out and beat your premium hand.

If a player raises ahead of you or reraises behind you, reraise with aces and kings, and just call with the other premium hands and see how the flop goes. Jacks are weaker than the other big pairs because there is about a 50% chance that an over-card, a queen, king, or ace will come on the flop, making your hand vulnerable.

If an overcard flops when you have jacks, queens, or even kings, or you miss entirely with A-K, you have to think about giving up on these hands if an opponent bets into you or check-raises. For example, if the flop is Q-7-6 and you have A-K or J-J, and an opponent leads into you, you're probably donating chips. A better flop would be K-10-3 for A-K or 10-8-2 for J-J.

It's also tough to play high pairs against an ace flop since players will often play starting cards containing an ace. And in low-limit games, you'll get players seeing the flop with all sorts of hands, so if there are a bunch of players in the pot, you have to be concerned about an ace flopping when you have a big pocket pair, such as queens or kings. If you have A-K, however, that ace-led flop puts you in a strong position, especially in a game where opponents like to play ace-anything.

You're also concerned with flops of three connecting cards, such as 8-9-10 and three suited cards if you don't have the ace of the same suit for a powerful nut flush draw. These are not good flops for big pairs or an A-K.

Playable Starting Hands

A-Q	A-J	A-10	K-Q	10-10	9-9	8-8

These starting hands should be folded in early position. They should also be folded in middle or late position if the pot has been raised from early position, which suggests strength, unless you think the raiser is loose and you can see the flop for just that one bet.

If players limp into the pot before you—that is, if they just call the bet—you can limp in as well with the Playable hands. Sometimes a raise will be good if you can force out players behind you and isolate the limper. However, if you're in there against loose players who are not easily moved off a pot, which will generally be the case in low limit, you might consider calling. When you're up against opponents who cannot be chased by raises, you'd prefer to see the flop for one bet with these hands.

If you enter the pot and it gets raised after you, you have to make a decision. If the raise comes from late position and it's from a loose player, you have more reason to call then to fold. It's just one bet. However, if it's raised twice and costs you two more bets, or it looks like you might be trapped between a bettor and a raiser, get away from these hands while it's still cheap. There is too much strength against you. The problem with A-Q, A-J, A-10, and K-Q in raised pots, is when you do connect. The ace-big hands could be outkicked by ace-bigger hands, leading to a lot of trouble. Always suspect opponents for premium cards, especially when they come into the pot from early position.

If you can get your pairs in to see the flop four-handed, you have enough value to handle a raise, but only if you're confident you won't be stuck between bettors and raisers while you're holding a less-than-premium hand.

What if no one has entered the pot before you? If you're in middle or late position, you should raise coming into the pot and try to limit the field or even better, get the blinds.

Marginal Starting Hands

7-7	6-6	5-5	4-4	3-3	2-2	K-J	K-10	Q-J	Q-10	J-10
A-x (ace with any other card)						Suited connectors: 5-6, 6-7, 7-8, 8-9, 9-10				

Play marginal hands in middle and late position only if you can get in for one bet—but not at the cost of two bets. This means you'll fold these hands in raised pots or where you are vulnerable to being raised. The exception is with the small pairs (twos through sevens), where quantity equals quality. If you have reason to believe the pot will be played four-handed, you get the right odds to handle a raise, hoping to catch a set and win lots of chips.

In late position, call in an unraised pot, but if the pot has already been raised from early or middle position or you are between a bettor and a raiser, these marginal cards become unprofitable and should be folded.

If there is a raise after you enter the pot, you can call with these marginal hands—when the cost is only one bet—but fold in the face of a double raise or in situations where yet another raise can follow.

Playing Late Position

You can play many more hands from late position. You've had a chance to see the betting before it reaches your position. If the action is heavy, you fold all non-premium hands. If the action is light and the cost is cheap, you can get more creative. And if no one has entered the pot, you should often raise, as there is a good chance no one will call and you'll get the blinds.

If there are only limpers, you add **suited connectors**—hands that are consecutive in rank, such as 5-6 or 8-9 and in the same suit—to your starting hands. Suited connectors are best played in a pot with three or more players. You want multiple opponents in the pot so that you can win a bunch of chips if you hit your hand. If the pot is raised and it would cost you two bets to play, call only if it looks like there will be enough players in to see the flop.

Pairs of twos through sevens are played similarly to connectors preflop. You want to play them in late position when you can see the flop cheaply and get a multiway pot. If there are several callers, you should call, but if the pot has been raised, meaning it will now cost you two bets to play, you can quietly muck the small pair. If you've already bet and the pot gets raised, you can call that extra bet as long as you feel that you won't get trapped and raised again.

Though a pair will only improve to a three of a kind hand about one time in eight, when it does, you'll be sitting with a big hand that can trap opponents for a lot of chips. If it doesn't improve and there are overcards on the flop, you probably have the worst of it and should fold against an opponent's bet. One rule of thumb here—no set, no bet.

Junk Hands

All other hands not shown in the above categories should be folded. They are heavy underdogs with little chance of winning. If you're in the big blind and the pot is unraised, by all means take the flop for free. But if it costs you to see the flop, fold immediately. It's cheaper watching this round as a bystander.

Playing the Blinds

If you can get in the pot cheaply from the small blind for just a few chips (you already have some chips in the pot), it is often worth expanding your starting cards to see if you catch a lucky flop. And if you're on the big blind and the pot is unraised, be careful never to fold—you get to see the flop for free!

Other Considerations

If you miss the flop and think that betting will cause your opponent to fold, make the play. Otherwise, don't throw chips at longshots. Save them for better spots.

Be careful playing flush and straight draws unless they're to the **nuts**—the best hand possible given the cards on board. For example, you don't want to play a straight draw if there is a flush draw on board, or if you have, say the 6-7 on a board of 7-8-9-10-X. Any opponent with a jack will bust you here. And given that many players like to play J-10, that 7-8-9 flop is dangerous to your hand.

If you think you've got the best hand, always bet or raise. Do not give opponents a cheap or free ride. You want to narrow the field and build the pot. If you have a huge hand, however, you want players to stay in the pot, but don't give away your hand by playing different than you usually would in the situation. If opponents expect you to bet, then bet.

Most important in limit hold'em and for that matter, all forms of poker, if you don't have the winning hand or a draw to a winning hand with enough money in the pot to go for, get out. Every bet you save in a lost pot is worth the same as a bet you'd win in a won pot. Minimize your bad bets and you'll most likely win money in this game.

NO-LIMIT HOLD'EM STRATEGY

In no-limit hold'em, your entire stack of chips is at risk on every single hand—as are those of your opponents. One big mistake and they're gone. In limit hold'em, one bet is only one bet. In no-limit, that one bet could be the defining moment of your game because it could be for all your chips. And that changes the way you play hands.

No-limit hold'em appears deceptively simple at first glance, but as you get deeper into the strategies and the situations that occur, you start to see the many complexities of the game.

Starting Hands

If you're the first player coming into the pot on the preflop, you generally want to enter the pot with a **standard raise**, three times the size of the big blind. So if the big blind is at $5, make your raise $15, and if it's $10, make your raise $30. The reason you don't make the raise two times the big blind is that you make it too easy for your opponents, particularly the big blind, to enter the pot cheaply with marginal hands, subjecting your hand to lucky draws from opponents who might not otherwise see the flop.

You want your preflop raises to consistently be three times the size of the big blind so that opponents get no extra information on the strength of your hand. Players that vary their preflop raises are sometimes announcing their hands.

And if your opponents limp in to see the flop and you have a raising hand, make it four times the big blind. There is now more money in the pot and you want to make it unprofitable for them to call with marginal cards.

The hammer of the big bet or the all-in bet in no-limit hold'em puts a lot of pressure on opponents who hold marginal hands as well as strong hands in which they don't have confidence. Even when opponents think you're bluffing, it costs chips for them to find out for sure, which is often a greater cost than they're willing to risk.

Early Position

The best starting cards in no-limit hold'em are the **premium hands**—pocket aces, kings, queens, jacks, A-K, and A-Q. In an unraised pot, bring these hands in for a standard raise in early position. Your goal is to narrow the field to one or two callers and to either win the pot right there when all players fold or reduce the number of players who will see the flop.

If you have aces or kings, hopefully you'll get a caller or two, or even better, a raiser. Then you'll raise right back the size of the pot or go in for all your chips if you get reraised. With queens and A-K, you can stand a raise to see the flop, but if the raise is for all your chips and you're not short-stacked, you may need to let these hands go. If you don't want your day finished with queens, you certainly don't want to go out on jacks or A-Q! If an opponent goes all-in when you hold J-J or A-Q, or even puts in a big raise, these are grounds for folding these hands.

If a player comes in raising before you, the aces and kings are automatic reraises and the non-premium hands are automatic folds. Lean towards calling with A-K and queens. If the raiser is tight, fold with A-Q and jacks; if the raiser is loose, raising or calling are both viable options. Remember, no play is set in stone in no-limit hold'em. You need to judge hands on a situation by situation basis.

Pass on all other hands from early position, especially against an aggressive table. If the table is tight, or it's early in a tournament and there's little cost to enter the pot, you may take a flier on a hand now and then to mix it up.

Middle Position

In middle position, you can play more hands due to the simple fact that you have fewer players behind who can raise your bets. If there is a raise before your turn, consider folding all non-premium hands. You don't want to go into the flop as a big underdog, which this earlier position raise probably indicates. And if the raiser is tight, fold jacks and A-Q as well. If you have aces or kings, reraise and have no fear of getting all your chips in the middle. You can also reraise with queens and A-K, or you could just call.

If no one has raised in front of you, you will still play the premium hands for a raise and can add the second tier hands—eights, nines and tens, along with A-J, A-10, and K-Q to your list of raising hands. If you get reraised by a player behind you, consider throwing second tier hands away. These hands have value, but against heavy betting, they're chip burners.

Of course, if your opponent is low on chips and moves in on the preflop, especially in a tournament, give him credit for holding lesser quality cards and be prepared to play all premium hands—but again, use judgment. When in doubt, go with your gut feeling.

Late Position

In late position, if the pot has been raised in early position, reraise with A-A, K-K, Q-Q, and A-K. If you get reraised, you may consider just calling with Q-Q and A-K, and if the raiser is tight and goes all-in, you probably want to release these hands. And you certainly do not want to be in that reraised pot with jacks, A-Q or anything less. With aces and kings, you're always ready to play for all the marbles preflop.

If the pot is raised in middle position, reraise with the top four hands, A-A, K-K, Q-Q, and A-K. How you play jacks and A-Q is a judgment call, but it may be safer just to call and see the flop.

If there has been no raiser in the pot, you can expand your starting hands to any pair, an ace with any other card, and any two cards 10 or higher, for example, Q-10 or K-J. Generally, it's best to come in raising. Most of the time, you'll win the blinds, which is good. If you get callers, you have some value to see the flop.

If you get aces or kings in late position and you think you'll get a caller, raise. If not, it might be better to limp in. You don't get kings or aces often, but when you do, you want to make money on them.

You can also play suited connectors, such as 6-7, 7-8, 8-9, and 10-J, if you can see the flop cheaply.

The Blinds

The blinds have the advantage of going last in the first round of play but the big disadvantage of going first in all other rounds. Play the blinds according to the advice in the early position strategy section.

If a late position bettor continually raises you out of the pot when you're the big blind, then you have to take a stand at some point to keep him in line. You'd like to have two big cards or ace-anything to reraise with, but you can also do this with garbage. If you read him correctly, he'll fold and you've got *his* chips. Do this once or twice and you'll get his attention and respect.

If everyone folds to you in the small blind and you can see the flop cheaply, it's not a bad play to call the big blind. You may flop something pretty or check to the showdown and win with better garbage than your opponent.

If there is no raise and you're in the big blind, and you're not in a raising situation, always see it for free— don't make the mistake of folding!

The Flop

If you came in raising preflop, you want to continue playing aggressively. If you're first, bet regardless of what flops. Your opponent will probably fold and you've got the pot. If he calls and you don't improve, you might consider checking on the turn. If he raises you, it's a tough call, but you'll have to consider giving up the hand unless you feel you've got better. Now, if you're second, and he checks, bet out at him.

What if he bets into you? If you miss the flop, give him the pot. Since you've shown strength preflop, his bet on the flop means you're probably second-best.

When you have what you think is the best hand, your goal is to take the pot immediately, particularly when there are straight and flush draws possible, for example, two cards of the same suit are on the board. You don't want opponents playing for another card cheaply, making it, and then destroying you on a hand that shouldn't have even seen another card. If opponents are going to beat you, make them pay to do so.

However, if you have an absolute monster like a full house or quads, you want to keep players in and extract more bets out of them. Often, that means checking and hoping a free card gives them a bigger hand.

The Turn

If you've played aggressively on the preflop and flop and your opponent hasn't budged, you have to figure him for possible strength. It's time for you to look at what you think *he thinks* you have. If you're representing strength and playing tight, you have to give him credit for a strong hand and slow down your betting unless you're confident that you've got a better hand. If he checks, you check, and if you're first, check to him and see how he reacts.

The turn is a time to put the brakes on a bluff that didn't work and possibly ease your way into the river with a hand that can't weather much more betting. If your opponent is weak, he may check along with you. This may be a clue that you can zap him out on the river or play it slow and see who shows down better. You can always push your bluff one more bet, but if your opponent saw you through on the flop, this could be dangerous.

You've felt your opponents out on the flop. How they played on the flop greatly influences the types of hands you think they may be playing. Use your best judgments and go with them. If you think a bet may push a weak opponent out of the pot, betting is a strong option. If you're not sure, checking is not a bad option. And if you think you have the best hand, get more chips into the pot.

The River

When you have a big hand that you're confident is the best, you want to get more chips into the pot. If you're last and there have been no bets, put the amount of chips in the pot you feel your opponent will call. If you're first, you have two options: check or bet. If your opponent is very aggressive or has been leading at the pot, you can consider checking and letting him bet, then going over the top of him with a raise to try and get more chips in the pot. You want to be careful not to move an opponent off a pot with a bet. Let your knowledge of how your opponent plays guide you.

When you have a strong hand but have doubts whether it's the best one out there, it's often better to check at the river, rather than bet and risk a big raise that you won't call. If your opponent checks, you'll see the showdown with no further cost. If he bets, you see what you want to do. Be careful about betting in an attempt to get an opponent to fold. He might raise you back or set you all in, and you'll be forced to muck your cards and give up your chips.

If you're going to bluff at the river, however, make sure it's for enough chips so that your opponent will be faced with a tough decision on whether to call.

CASH GAME STRATEGY

In cash games, you're not worried about blinds, because they're generally small, nor are you concerned with antes, because there aren't any. Your goal in a cash game is purely and simply to win chips. You don't care if you have more chips than other players, or less, as long as you finish playing with more of them than you started with. And then you have won money.

When you have a good session and win lots of chips, you can take them off the table and leave any time you want. The chips you play with can be converted to real profits at any time.

OMAHA

Omaha high, which is also called **Omaha**, is a high poker game that is played exactly like hold'em, except for two things:

1. Players get *four* cards to start with, as opposed to just two as in hold'em.
2. Each player *must* use exactly two of his pocket cards, not more, not less, together with three from the board, to form his final five-card hand.

Omaha is played with a button, which moves clockwise around the table after each deal, as well as a small blind and a big blind. The deal starts with each player getting four downcards, called pocket cards or hole cards. The first betting round proceeds exactly as in hold'em, with the player to the left of the big blind acting first.

When the betting action has been completed on the preflop round, the flop of three community cards is turned face-up in the center of the table. This is followed by a round of betting. The turn and river are similarly dealt, each followed by a betting round. At the showdown, the highest hand wins the pot.

In limit games, all bets in the first round must be in the lower increment: $3 in a $3/$6 game, $5 in a $5/$10 game, $15 in a $15/$30 game, and so on. If you were playing pot-limit, then you could bet up to the amount in the pot, and if no-limit were being played, your maximum bet would be limited only by the amount of chips you had on the table. Betting on the turn and the river must be at the higher level of the betting structure. For example, $6 in a $3/$6 game, $10 in a $5/$10 game, and $30 in a $15/$30 game.

It is easy to misread your hand in Omaha. For example, if you were dealt four aces in the hole, you wouldn't have quads because only two of the aces would count toward the final hand! The remaining three cards would have to come from the board.

Omaha can also be played as high-low in a variation called **Omaha high-low 8-or-better** or simply, **Omaha 8-or-better**. In this version, the best low hand and best high hand split the pot. However, if no hand qualifies for low—has five unpaired cards of 8 or lower—the best high hand scoops (wins the entire pot). Players can choose two different five-card combinations to make their final hands, one for the high hand and one for the low hand.

The best high hand and best low hand can be held by the same player; if so, that player also scoops.

HOW TO READ AN OMAHA HIGH-LOW HAND

Here is an example showing how a high and low hand is made in conjunction with the board. If you hold A-A-J-4 with a board of A-J-7-6-2, two aces from your pocket cards are used to form the high hand, A-A-A-J-7.

The ace and 4 would be combined with the 7-6-2 of the board to form a 7-6-4-2-A for low.

Note that in both instances, two of your downcards and three community cards are used to make the final poker hand.

Note that you don't have a full house of aces over jacks for the high hand because, again, you can only use two of your hole cards. If your opponent holds 3-3-3-J, he would lose on the high end since he only has a pair of jacks! Since he must use his jack as part of the hand, he does not have a 7-6-3-2-A low, so he would lose on the low end as well.

GETTING QUARTERED AND SIXTHED

In Omaha high-low 8-or-better, players often split the pot at the showdown. In fact, there can be multiple split pots. For example, if two low hands are tied for best and there is a high-hand winner, the high hand will take half the pot, and the two low players will get **quartered**—meaning each of them will split the low half, getting just one quarter each of the total pot.

If there happens to be three low winners, they would split the low end three ways, getting one-sixth of the pot each, with the high winner taking sole possession of the high half of the pot. Ties for the best high hand would be divided the same way—all winners get an equal portion from the high half of the pot or from the whole pot if no player qualifies for low.

For there to be a winner on the low end, that hand must be no worse than five unpaired cards of 8 or better. For example, the hand 8-7-5-3-A qualifies for low, but the hand 8-7-5-2-2 does not because of the paired deuces. A hand of 9-7-3-2-A would not qualify either, even though it may be the lowest hand, because the 9-high hand doesn't meet the 8-or-better qualifier. In this case, the high-end winner or winners would get all the spoils.

STRATEGY FOR OMAHA HIGH-LOW 8-OR-BETTER

With both a high half and low half to go after, many players stay interested in the pot, especially in low-limit "no fold'em" games, in which players will chase hands right to the river since the last card dealt can so dramatically change the complexion of a hand. Don't get sucked into the rampant betting that often occurs in 8-or better, not unless your hand is worthy of all the action. Speculation and loose play can lose you a bunch of chips in a hurry in this game.

General Strategy

The first four cards dealt in Omaha—your hole cards—are the only cards you alone can use, so they play an important role in defining your chances of winning. As in all poker variations, you must start out with solid cards to give yourself the best chances of winning.

There are great starting cards, good starting cards, and poor starting cards, but what appears to be a good or bad preflop hand may change in a flash when the flop throws three more cards into the mix. And the final two community cards open up even more possibilities that could make or break your hand.

With such a wide range of possibilities, hopes stay high and betting can be fierce. Unlike hold'em, where the starting hand combinations are fewer and it is less common for more than two players to see the flop, in Omaha 8-or-better, multiple players often bet and raise liberally. This will get expensive if you play hands that aren't good enough to stand the action. Thus, you must play solid poker to survive Omaha 8-or-better with your chips intact. Don't get sucked into rampant betting unless your hand is worthy of all the action. In this game, speculation and loose play can lose you a bunch of chips in a hurry.

Omaha is a flop game, in which the button stays constant in a hand, so your position at the table is a major factor in how you play your cards and which hands you choose to see the flop with. Before we touch on these important points, the four key winning concepts of Omaha 8-or-better must be emphasized.

1. Key Concept: Scooping

In high-low games of any type, there is one guiding principle that is the foundation of all winning strategies: play hands that have a chance to scoop the pot, that is, win both the high and low half of the pot. This is especially true in Omaha, particularly pot-limit versions.

2. Key Concept: Aces

The best card in Omaha 8-or-better is the ace, and generally speaking, if you don't have one, you're better off not even being involved in the pot. The cost of playing to see the flop, turn, and river is too expensive in this game for you to get involved in pots without an ace. And while there are ace-less hands that have good potential to make you money, if you're a beginner, you can still play a profitable game without playing any of them.

The ace is so important in Omaha 8-or-better because it is the best low card and the best high card, and your goal is to scoop the pot. When you hold an ace, you have a chance to improve to the top pair, top two pair, top set, top straight, top flush and top full house as well. An ace is a boss card that gives you a big edge over any opponent who doesn't have one. And since most of the cards get dealt in a full-handed Omaha game, if you don't have an ace, you can count on one of your opponents having one and holding that boss-card advantage over you.

3. Key Concept: Play Good Starting Hands

An ace, a 2, or a 3 and one more unpaired card 5 or below is a strong starting low. The best starters in Omaha 8-or-better have both high and low possibilities, so along with the ace plus 2 or 3 and third low card, you'd like another ace (A-A-3-5), or two suited cards, preferably led by the ace, so that you have a shot at a nut flush. A king is a good card to accompany the ace, for example A-2-5-K, because it's the top kicker to an ace hand with nut-high and nut-low straight possibilities.

Four low cards, like A-2-3-4, A-2-3-5, and A-2-4-5, with two suited cards, give you a decent chance of going low and wheeling (making a perfect low, a wheel—A-2-3-4-5) or flushing to a strong high hand.

When competing for the high end of the pot, hands with A-K and A-A have more strength against fewer players and less value against a larger field of opponents since straights, flushes, and full houses are more common as more people stay to the end. You can start with some high-only hands, but if you do, all four of the cards must be **coordinated**, that is, close in rank to one another. Thus, a hand like K-K-Q-J would be good, but K-K-Q-7 would not. That 7 is a **dangler**, meaning that it doesn't coordinate with the other cards.

4. Key Concept: Playing for the Nuts

With so many players seeing the flop and playing through to the river, it is important that you start out with hands that have the potential to be the **nuts**, the best hand possible given the cards on board. In other words, if you make a flush, it should be the best flush (one led by an ace), and if it's a straight, then you don't want the ignorant, or low, end of the straight. When you're going for low, your hand should have the potential to be the best possible low.

Starting Hand Requirements

You're dealt what you're dealt in Omaha 8-or-better, but if you had a choice, you'd rather have a low draw than a high draw for one very simple reason: a low hand can develop into a high hand (by forming a low straight, an ace-led nut flush, two pair, trips, full house, or quads) while still being the nut low. But a high hand can never develop into a low hand.

Three low cards give you a strong starting position in Omaha 8-or-better, so along with your ace, you'd like to have a 2 or a 3 and one more card 5 or below. You need the third low card because the three-card flop will often **duplicate** or **counterfeit** one of your good low cards, that is, pair it up, rendering it useless. For example, if you hold A-2-K-K, and the flop is 2-6-8, your 2 is counterfeited and useless to you since you must use two hole cards toward your low. You would need two more low cards that are not an ace or 2 to make a qualified low.

But if you held a third low card, say A-2-5-K, now your low draw contains four cards, since you'd use the A-5 from your hand toward a low. You only need one more non-pairing low card to be dealt to make your low hand. Thus, with a third low card, you stay very much in the hunt.

The best starters in Omaha 8-or-better have both high and low possibilities, so along with the ace plus 2 or 3 and third low card, you'd like another ace (A-A-3-5), or two suited cards, preferably led by the ace, so that you have a shot at a nut flush.

A king is a good card to accompany the ace, for example A-2-5-K, because it's the top kicker to an ace hand with nut-high and nut-low straight possibilities. Four low cards, like A-2-3-4, A-2-3-5, and A-2-4-5, with two suited cards, give you a chance of going low *and* wheeling (making a perfect low, a wheel—A-2-3-4-5) or flushing to a strong high hand.

When competing for the high end of the pot, hands with A-K and A-A have more strength against fewer opponents and less value against more opponents, since straights, flushes, and full houses are more common as more players stay to the end. You can start with some high-only hands, but if you do, all four of the cards must be coordinated, that is close in rank to one another. Thus, a hand like K-K-Q-J would be good, but K-K-Q-7 would not. That 7 is a **dangler**, meaning that it doesn't coordinate with the other cards.

The Flop and Beyond

When the three-card flop hits, it's important for you to reevaluate your situation. The more players remaining to see the flop, the better your hand must be. In particular, you either need to have the nuts or a draw to the nuts, because with the loose action common in many games, especially low-limit ones, that's what it's going to take to win.

When you're unsure of how to proceed with a hand, remember position. If you're early and vulnerable to raises behind you, you have an easy fold. If you're late, you can see what develops.

High starting hands of A-A-K-Q and A-A-K-K remain strong if the flop is all high cards, preventing low hands from taking half the pot, which would immediately devalue the pot by one half. This is a key concept that players going for the high end of the pot must consider in Omaha 8-or-better. Also, for any player to qualify for a low total, there would have to be *three* low cards (8 or below) on board.

 KEY TIP FOR THE HIGH END OF THE POT:
If two low cards or fewer are on board, there will be no low hand, and the high hand will take the whole pot.

When making your decision on how to play a high hand, you must consider that the pot is only worth *half* of what you might normally expect if a low possibility is on board. The dilution of the pot is something that regular high or low players often overlook, but it affects betting and playing strategy. That is why hands with the strength to go both ways are so valuable in high-low games.

If you don't connect with the flop, especially with high-only cards, drop your hand. If you do connect, make sure your hand is going toward the nuts and not second best. With more betting rounds to come, you don't want to be putting in a lot of chips unless you have a hand that can go all the way.

TOURNAMENT POKER

Tournaments are a great way to have fun and hopefully, win lots of money. They can be entered for as little as $10 to as much as $50,000 in the big events! Tournaments are set up as a process of elimination. As players lose their chips, the remaining competitors get consolidated into fewer tables. Eventually, only the **final table** will remain. This is where the prestige and big money is earned. Those last players will compete until one player holds all the chips—the **champion**.

Tournaments are divided into **levels** or **rounds**. Each level is marked by an increase in the blinds and after a few levels, the antes kick in, putting more pressure on players to make moves or lose their chips to inactivity. Levels may be as short as fifteen minutes in low buy-in events that are designed to be completed in as little as a few hours, or as long as ninety minutes to two hours for major multi-day events.

There are two types of tournaments—freeze-outs and rebuy tournaments. A **freeze-out tournament** is a do or die structure. Once you run out of chips, you are eliminated. In a **rebuy tournament**, you can purchase additional chips which is usually allowed only when your chip stack is equal to or less than the original starting amount and only during the first few rounds of play. Once the rebuy period ends, your tournament is over if you lose your chips.

TOURNAMENT PRIZE POOL

Most tournaments are set up so that approximately 10% to 15% of all players (and sometimes as high as 20%) will win cash prizes. The number of places paid, those who finish **in the money**, is decided in advance by the organizers.

For example, if the size of the starting field is 300 players, the organizers might limit the cash payouts to the top 10%. Often, the payout will be rounded down to the number of full tables remaining so if the 300 person tournament was being played nine-handed, the event may pay the top three tables, or twenty-seven players.

The worst feeling in a tournament is being caught on the **bubble**—that is, being the last player eliminated before the money payouts begin. So if you're player number twenty-eight in the example above, you're very unhappy going home empty when every other player remaining wins money.

The payout structure is usually posted soon after the tournament begins, as the organizers add up the total number of entrants and figure out the number of places and amount paid to each money-winner.

If the structure will affect your decision to play, or if your curiosity can't wait the few minutes to the start time, you can approach the tournament director, and he'll have a good idea of how many places will be paid. Most players simply wait, however, until the announcement is made by the tournament director or on the television monitors that are typically placed in a location easily visible to the players. The monitors will usually list the number of places paid and the amount of money each finisher will win.

You can determine if the event is right for you by the entry fee and the potential prize pool. The greater the number of players, the bigger the prize pool. When the events are large, such as the $10,000 buy-in events, the prize pool often gets into the millions. These tournaments draw the top players you see on television, along with the amateurs trying their hand at winning the big money.

STARTING CHIP COUNTS

Your starting chip total in a tournament is determined in advance by the tournament director. In low-limit events, a $30 buy-in might give you $500 in chips, though the tournament director could just as easily give you $200 or $1,000.

And in high-limit events, you'll typically receive the same number of chips as the amount of the buy-in. For example, in the main no-limit event of the World Series, players get $10,000 in chips for the $10,000 buy-in. And in WSOP preliminary events that cost, say, $1,000, players get $1,000 in chips. But there are exceptions. In the WPT championship event at the Bellagio in Las Vegas, players received $50,000 in chips for a $25,000 buy-in, and at another tournament, players were given $12,000 in tournament chips for the $10,000 buy-in. At yet another, a $10,000 buy-in netted players $20,000 in starting chips. So, as you see, there are many variations.

However, whether you are given $200 in chips, $1,000 in chips, or $10,000 in chips, you are on a level playing field with your competitors because in a tournament, everyone starts with the same amount of chips.

TOURNAMENT CHIPS

Unlike a cash game, where chips are the exact equivalent of money, tournament chips have no cash value. They may just as well be Monopoly money, because no one is going to give you anything for them outside the tournament. Thus, if you have accumulated $150,000 in chips and try to cash them out, all you'll get from the casino is strange looks and an explanation that all you have are tournament chips.

TOURNAMENT STRATEGY

Your Chip Stack

To be a winner in no-limit hold'em tournaments, you must quickly integrate the concept that every professional player intuitively understands: it is not how you play your cards, but how you play your chips! The number of chips you have relative to the big blind and your opponents is a factor in every decision you make. When you're short on chips, there is greater pressure on you to make moves to stay alive—and every opponent will be aware of this. And when you're awash in chips, you can exert greater pressure on opponents who want to stay out of confrontations with you that can take them out of the tournament. You have the luxury of being patient and choosing the spots that best suit your situation. A few rounds of attrition from blinds and antes won't make a serious dent in your stack.

 KEY TOURNAMENT CONCEPT
It is not how you play your cards, but how you play your chips!

Ideally, you would like your stack to be *at least* twenty-five times the size of the big blind. This is your **minimum ideal stack** size. You have enough chips to play pressure-free poker without worrying too much about being blinded out. Sometimes your chips get low and the pressure-cooker is on the stove. Or worse, your chips might get really low and the situation becomes critical. Other times, you'll be a big stack, with the advantage of leverage against smaller stacks just trying to survive.

Playing Short Stacks

If you have less than ten times the big blind in your tournament stack, then you have a **short stack** and must play more aggressively to grow your stack. You don't have the luxury of waiting for good cards forever. By doing nothing but folding, every set of deals around the table costs you the equivalent of about two big blind bets. And if you're starting with only ten big blinds, one round means you're down to about eight big blinds and in two rounds you're almost cut in half and down to about six big blinds!

Beginners make the mistake of limping in pots with low stacks or calling all-ins with inferior hands. As a low stack, you want to make the big move *first* and put the decision to your opponents. Limping in with a third of your chips allows opponents to call with hands they may have folded against a bigger bet. Make the big move when you have to make the big move. It's your only chance. And by moving with *all* your chips, you maintain enough leverage to give opponents pause when considering whether to call your hand.

Playing With an Emergency Short Stack

When your chip count is five-times the size of the big blind or less—what I call an **emergency short-stack**—you're in trouble, and must be ready to pounce with all your power at the very *first* decent opportunity. You have to pick up the blinds and antes to stay alive. It's your food for survival. To give yourself the best chance of getting those chips, you need to use all the leverage you have available. You cannot afford to play passive here—calling is not an option, nor is a standard raise—the all-in bet is your *only* move.

If the pot is unraised and you are dealt any pair, ace-any (an ace with any other card), or any two cards 10 or higher, push in all your chips and hope for the best. Quite often you'll get no callers and the blinds and antes that you win will give you enough fuel for another round of play. If you have to, you'll make your move with *any* two cards. Keep this in mind: if you have 7-2 and go head-to-head against an opponent with an A-K, you're only about a 2 to 1 underdog. So you always have a chance.

Playing Average Stacks

Having an **average stack**—about equal to the average amount of chips held by players—means you're right in the center of things. You have enough chips to be patient and wait for your opportunities. In other words, you can play your best poker without undue pressure. Just like the big stacks, you want to avoid major confrontations against other average stacks or big stacks unless you've got the best hand. Good players with chips will avoid confrontations with you as well so there will be bluffing opportunities, but don't lose chips to foolish moves.

As always, smaller stacks are your targets. Push them around and get chips from them. If bigger stacks play weak, don't be afraid to exert pressure on them as well. Look for chips wherever you can get them and from whomever will give them to you.

Playing Big Stacks

Having a **big stack** means you have more than double the average amount of chips in play. You have a big advantage as a big stack. You can afford to lose big pots and still have chips to play, particularly against small stacks. This doesn't mean you want to lose big pots—which can come as a result of a huge mistake or from a bad beat (and those can't be helped)—only that you can afford a bad break and still be alive. This is a luxury smaller stacks do not have.

As a big stack, you can pressure players trying to stay alive by betting aggressively, especially against players who are playing scared or are short-stacked. You want to avoid other big stacks unless you have the best hand. This goes for average stacks as well, because a big confrontation with an average stack can make him the big stack and you the average one—or smaller.

Players fear big stacks, especially aggressive big stacks who are willing to push chips into the middle. When you sense weakness in an opponent, pounce on it. Stealing blinds, aggressive flop betting, and reraising are very effective weapons. However, do not foolishly throw away chips just because you have a lot of them. Whatever good play got you the big stack, keep it going to maintain and increase your position. A big stack has leverage, but use that leverage wisely.

Stack Sizes

Chip Stack	Stack Size	Strategy
Emergency Short Stack	5 times big blind	All-in first good situation
Short Stack	10 times big blind	All-in is only bet
Medium (Average) Stack	Average chip stack	Play to style
Minimum Ideal Stack	25 times big blind	Play to style
Large Stack	2 times average stack	Step up aggression. Find opponents who play scared and pound them

THE FOUR STAGES OF A TOURNAMENT

Early Round Tournament Strategy

In the first few rounds of a tournament, the blinds are generally small, and the antes won't kick in until the third or fourth level. During these early rounds, there is little pressure on you to make any moves as the blinds won't make too much of a dent in your stack, at least not a critical dent. Your strategy here is to play conservatively, trying to win little pots when possible and avoiding big pots unless you're reasonably convinced that you have the winner. You don't want to risk your tournament on a foolish bluff.

Your goal is to increase your chips stack as the tournament progresses, hopefully to double up after three rounds.

Middle Round Tournament Strategy

The middle rounds of a tournament, around levels four to eight, is when players start getting eliminated at a more rapid pace. The blinds and antes are more expensive and this means you have to play more hands and take more chances.

If you're low-stacked, aggressive play and stealing blinds becomes more important to keep up with the costs of feeding blinds and antes into the pot. If you're big-stacked, you want to push around the weak players and small stacks and get more chips. You're looking to position yourself for the final table.

Late Round Tournament Strategy

If you've lasted into the later rounds, you've either made it into the money or are getting real close. Now you look forward, hoping to get to the final table and the bigger money. You want to pick up your game here and play your best poker. Avoid facing off in big pots or all-ins against stacks that can take you out—unless you've got the goods—but as always in a tournament, keep pushing your weight around against players that can be bullied.

Final Table

If you get to the final table, you have a real shot at winning, but you still have to get through the last players. If you're among the big stacks, avoid going to war against another big stack that can bust you or make you one of the small stacks. Use your big stack to put pressure on smaller stacks struggling to stay alive.

If you're low-stacked, the blinds and antes are exerting tremendous pressure, leaving you with little choice but to find your best opportunity and then go after it for all your chips. Calling is not an option here.

Think before you make your moves, keeping in mind that every player eliminated means a big jump in prize money.

ONLINE POKER

Playing poker on the Internet has become hugely popular. There are now millions of players from around the world competing against one another on hundreds of sites. With a few clicks of your mouse, you can get in on the action too.

It's easy to get started playing online. You begin by choosing a site and going to its homepage. From there, the instructions will guide you through all the basics: how to set up a unique account and password, how to play for free, and how to deposit funds into your account so that you can play for real money.

There are some good things about online poker. Let's take a look and see what they are.

SEVEN ADVANTAGES OF ONLINE POKER

1. It's Convenient

At any time of the day or night, all you have to do is go over to your computer, log on to your poker site of choice, and off you go. You're playing! There is nothing easier than that. It doesn't matter what you are wearing—or not wearing!—or how you look. You don't have to travel to a cardroom and search for the right game; with thousands of players online at any time, there is always a game with the stakes you want to play waiting for you.

2. It's Good Social Fun

Poker fires up that competitive spirit and is a great social outlet as well. You may not be able to see your opponents live, but that won't stop you from being able to communicate with them. Just as in a live game, you *can* interact with your tablemates. The chat windows in online sites allow you to type messages back and forth to your fellow players.

3. Make Friends Around the World

Internet poker is now a worldwide phenomenon and it is not uncommon to see players at your table from a variety of countries. Like everything else, you eventually strike up friendships and you never know, you may soon be visiting some of your internet poker buddies—or receiving them. Many great friendships have started online.

4. It's Great Practice

Online poker moves much faster than regular live games so you get to see lots of hands and situations. You can practice skills that you'll be able to apply to your regular tournament or cash game.

5. Play for Money or Play for Free

You can play poker for free on pretty much every site, a service online poker rooms offer their customers so they can get acclimated to the software. Or, if you prefer, you can sign up and play for real money.

6. It's Profitable

Online players are generally much weaker than competitors you'll find in regular cash games, especially at the low limit games. This makes it very profitable for good players. If you're a really skilled player, it's more than a good way to make money, it's a great way to make a living!

7. It's Generally Safe

The main Internet poker sites are already established businesses with hundreds of thousands of satisfied customers. It is generally accepted that major sites provide games as honest as any poker room, if not more so.

QUICK ONLINE STRATEGY TIPS

Online players tend to play too many hands and see too many showdowns. You can profit from this by playing solid straightforward poker, extracting maximum value from your good hands and minimizing losses with your weak and marginal hands. With more players seeing the flop on average, you want to tighten up a little on the selection of hands you play.

Aggressive betting becomes even more important online, especially in no-limit. You need to limit the field to protect your premium hands. Avoid bluffing—you can't bluff players who won't fold—and give loose opponents less credit for having strong hands.

Like poker played in any form and in any setting, learning how your opponents play and adjusting your strategy accordingly will bring you the most profits.

One unique feature of online poker sites is the option players have to make a playing decision in advance, before play reaches their position by using the **early-action buttons**. And while there are no physical tells in online poker, the frequent use of these early-action buttons can give you information about an opponents' hands. For example, if you see almost instant checks or raises when the action reaches a player, quite often, that indicates that the player has pre-selected his action. In the first case, the check probably means he is weak, and in the latter, he is either strong or he decided that he was going to bluff at the pot regardless of the action that preceded him.

They key element here is that the player decided in *advance* what his play was going to be, without even considering how the betting might go. So with garbage, a player may select the Check/Fold button, which will fold his hand if there is a bet or check if there is not.

Also look out for players who frequently use the pre-select options and then break the pattern by taking time in a situation. That could be useful information, but at the same time, it could also be indicative that the player was busy doing something else—on the phone, checking email, or in another game! But do pay attention to the timing of an opponent's reactions, and you can pick up online tells that you can use to your advantage. And pay attention to your own tendencies as well. You're not the only one watching!

Once you get comfortable online, you may find it profitable to play two games at the same time, which will allow for lots of hands and lots of possibilities. Some action junkies (and pros) looking to maximize the number of hands they receive, may play up to three or four games simultaneously! If you are considering playing multiple games, which can get confusing, remember one key tip: avoid playing tricky marginal hands that show little long-term profit! The concentration you need to finesse victories with these marginal hands will be difficult when you're flying back and forth between multiple games. Profits in the other games will suffer as your concentration is focused on the marginal hand.

If you're a tournament player, there are an endless number of choices, some of which are for straight prize money and some which award seats to the main events in the World Series of Poker and World Poker Tour tournaments as prizes for the top finishers.

PLAYING ONLINE SAFELY

For the most part, playing online poker is safe. Many new players are concerned with being cheated by the online software. While this is possible, and I certainly cannot guarantee or vouch for the integrity of anyone else's business practices, online poker rooms would enjoy no benefit in offering games where they manipulated the software or altered the random distribution of cards. This would be foolhardy and outright stupid on the part of the casinos. Online rooms make their money through the rake and want nothing more than the most honest game possible. And believe me, they make so much money dealing a legitimate game that there is no possible gain they could get from cheating.

This does not mean there isn't cheating. However, it's not the online poker rooms you need to be wary of—it's the players! There is collusion in certain games; sometimes by multiple players working together against unaware opponents, and sometimes an individual acts as more than one player at a table by having multiple online identities. In either case, this *is* cheating. Online poker rooms would have you believe that it never happens or that their software protects against this, but the truth is that it does occur. They do their best to prevent collusion, but they have not yet perfected the safeguards. Your best protection, as in any live face-to-face game, is to trust your instincts. If you're ever uncomfortable in a game, stop playing. Either switch tables, or if you feel uncomfortable playing on a particular site, then switch sites.

FIND OUT MORE

To find out more about playing on online poker sites, go to **www.cardozapub.com**.

MORE PRINCIPLES OF WINNING POKER

Following are a few more winning concepts you should have in your arsenal of poker knowledge.

POT ODDS

Pot odds is the amount of money in the pot *including* what your opponent has already bet—because that money is in the pot and he can't take it back—against what it will cost you to call the bet. For example, if $50 is in the pot, and you need to call a bet of $10 to play, you are getting pot odds of 5 to 1. So, in this situation, you can win $50. The question is: are your winning chances better than 5 to 1, which would be giving you good pot odds and make this a good bet, or worse than 5 to 1, which would be giving you bad pot odds and make this a bad bet?

Suppose there's $300 is in the pot and your opponent bets the size of the pot, another $300. Now there is $600 available to be won. It will cost you $300 to see the raise and have a chance to win that $600, so you are getting pot odds of 2 to 1. If you're on a flush draw or straight draw with one card to come and are figuring your hand to be about a 4 to 1 or 5 to 1 underdog, you are not getting enough of a return to make this a profitable call. But if you figure your hand has about an even-money chance of winning, then you're getting great odds to make the call.

Here's another way to look at pot odds: let's say you are offered a proposition where you would bet $20 on a coin toss but could only win a total of only $1. You'd turn it down. You'd be getting incorrect odds—and how! The risk isn't worth the reward. However, if you would get $20 for every win, you'd have an even-money shot—a fair proposition. But if you could win $40 on that same flip of the coin, then you'd be very happy to risk $20 to win $40. You have one chance in two of winning (1 to 1 odds)—the same as on the other two propositions—but you would be getting a 2 to 1 payoff. If you made this bet all day long, you would make a fortune, provided your host didn't wise up or run out of money.

Use pot odds to determine if going for the pot is justified by the amount you might win. If the bet will make you money in the long run, it's a good bet. Whenever you have a hand that is favored to win, the pot odds will always be favorable.

But it is also correct to play hands even though you are *not* favored to win—provided there is enough of a payoff for the risk! So when you do play second-best hands, it should be because they give you good value, because your long term expectation is to win money in that particular situation even though you may lose a majority of the times. If playing a hand gives you more profits than losses in the long run, you should play it. And that, in a nutshell, that is what pot odds is all about.

SEVEN PRINCIPLES OF WINNING POKER

Following are seven steps to success at poker.

1. Play with players you can beat. Don't be a patsy for players who are just too good for you.

2. Play at stakes you can afford. You can never go wrong playing at stakes within your means.

3. Fold when you're beat. Being an overall winning player has more to do with losing less when your cards don't come in the running than it has to do with the pots you win when you have the best hand!

4. Play with starting cards that can win. The object in poker is to have the best hand at the showdown, which means that to win you must enter into the betting with hands that have a reasonable chance of winning.

5. Play aggressive poker. Betting and raising often causes opponents to fold, giving you a "free" pot, or makes them more them cautious playing against you on further betting rounds or hands.

6. Respect position. Your position is an important consideration in whether and how to play your starting cards and then how to proceed in future betting rounds. The deeper your position, the more playable a marginal hand.

7. Vary your play. If you're unpredictable, opponents can't get a read on you, which gives you leverage that can be turned into profits.

BLUFFING

The bluff! The beauty, romance and drama of poker lies in the bluff. Bluffing is an integral part of poker and is an art which matures with experience. There are two advantages to successful bluffing.

The first and most obvious reason is that a player can "steal pots" from better hands and win money he otherwise would not have seen. The second reason is that when a player is caught bluffing, he is more likely to get called on the occasions when he does have the goods, and will therefore win bigger pots.

The more opponents are kept guessing, the better off we are. A player who is never known to bluff will win smaller pots, for when he's got a strong hand, players with weak and marginal hands will not challenge him for the pot.

Here are a few pointer on bluffing:

Five Pointers on Bluffing

1. Avoid bluffing in low limit games. The bluff may be too small to scare anybody out.

2. Don't bluff for small pots with overly large bets. The small gain possible isn't worth the large risk. (However, do bluff for small pots. There is money to be made by stealing the antes - just keep the bluffed bet within reason.)

3. It's easier to bluff a good player than a weak one. Good players respect scare cards, weak players tend to call on garbage and almost nothing will get them out of a pot.

4. Bluffs are most effective against one player. The more players in the pot, the greater the chance that at least one player will call the bet.

5. Pick your spots carefully. Successful bluffing is a matter of proper timing and circumstance.

A LAST WORD

Poker is one of the greatest and most exciting gambling games ever invented, and one sure to challenge you. In this section, we've given you a very brief introduction to the strategies of play; if you're interested in becoming a stronger poker player, we suggest you further your studies by reading more about the poker variations you enjoy playing.

To continue growing and improving as a poker player, you'll need to reevaluate your play at the tables on a constant basis, learning from both your mistakes and strong moves, and from the play of your opponents. Poker is a constant learning process for the good players; every hand a challenge and a classroom with gems of knowledge to be stored away for future hands. Be smart, and keep your eyes open, and you won't be able to help from being a better player every time you sit down at the poker table.

Blackjack

FIVE KEYS TO BLACKJACK

1 You must learn the Basic Strategies and make the correct plays every time.

2 Make all the aggressive double down and splitting plays.

3 Don't bust on your hand when the dealer shows a 2 or 3 (unless you have a 12).

4 If the dealer has a 7 or higher as an upcard, you must try to get 17 or better yourself.

5 If you want to increase your advantage against the casino, learn the correct strategies in this section, then move on to a professional card or non-card counting strategy.

INTRODUCTION

Blackjack can be beaten! Once you've finished reading this section and learned the skills presented, you'll find that there will be one major difference between you and 95% of the other players at the tables – you'll be a winner at blackjack!

We'll teach you to win without the blind memorization and boring tedium usually associated with learning blackjack. Our computer tested basic strategies are carefully explained so that every play you make is easily learned. In addition, all the winning strategies are presented in easy to read charts.

You'll learn how to beat the single deck game without counting cards. Also shown will be the best way to adjust your play for multiple deck games and variations whether you're a player in the major American gambling centers, Las Vegas, Northern Nevada, Laughlin or Atlantic City, or you're heading for play on cruise ships, in Europe, the Bahamas, the Caribbean or anywhere casinos are found.

You'll receive a wealth of information from this section. We cover the fundamentals of casino blackjack—the rules of the game, the player's options, the variations offered in casinos around the world, how to bet, casino vocabulary, how to play and everything else you'll need to know about playing winning casino blackjack.

So read this section carefully, and you'll be among those players that the casinos fear, and for good reason—you will be a consistent winner at blackjack!

BEGINNERS GUIDE TO CASINO BLACKJACK

OBJECT OF THE GAME

The player's object in casino blackjack is to beat the dealer. This can be achieved in two ways:

1. When the player has a higher total than the dealer without exceeding 21.
2. When the dealer's total exceeds 21 (assuming the player has not exceeded 21 first).

In casino blackjack, if the player and the dealer both hold the same total of 21 or less, the hand is a **push**, nobody wins.

BUSTING OR BREAKING – AUTOMATIC LOSERS

If the drawing of additional cards to the initial two cards dealt causes the point total to exceed 21, then that hand is said to be **busted**, an automatic loss. Busted hands should be turned up immediately. Once the player has busted, his hand is lost, even if the dealer busts as well afterwards. If the dealer busts, all remaining players automatically win their bets.

BLACKJACK – AUTOMATIC WINNER

If the original two card hand contains an ace with any 10 or face card (J,Q,K), the hand is called a **blackjack**, or **natural**, and is an automatic winner for the player whose bet is paid of at 3 to 2. If the dealer gets a blackjack, all players lose their bets. (The dealer wins only the player's bet, not the 3 to 2 payoff the player receives for a blackjack.) If both the dealer and the player are dealt a blackjack, the hand is a push. Blackjacks should be turned up immediately. Many single deck games now pay only 6 to 5 on blackjacks, which is worse for the player. When you can, find games paying 3 to 2, rather than the reduced 6 to 5.

PAYOFFS

All bets are paid off at even money ($5 bet wins $5), except in cases where the player receives a blackjack which is a 3 to 2 payoff ($5 bet wins $7.50) or when the player exercises an option that allows him to double his bet. In these instances (doubling and splitting), the payoff is equal to the new doubled bet. If a bet is doubled from $5 to $10, a win would pay off $10.

CARD VALUES

Each card is counted at face value. 2=2 points, 3=3 points, 10=10 points. The face cards, jack, queen and king, are counted as 10 points. The ace can be counted as 1 point or 11 points at the player's discretion. When the ace is counted as 11 points, that hand is called **soft**, as in the hand ace, 7 = *soft 18*. All other totals, including hands where the ace counts as 1 point, are called **hard**, as in the hand 10, 6, A = *hard 17*.

The dealer must count his ace as 11 if that gives him a hand totaling 17 to 21, otherwise he must count the ace as 1 point. In some casinos the rules dictate that the dealer must draw on soft 17. In these casinos the dealer's ace will count as 1 point when combined with cards totaling 6 points, and the dealer will have to draw until he forms a hand of at least hard 17.

DEALER'S RULES

The dealer must play by prescribed guidelines. He must draw to any hand 16 or below and stand on any total 17-21. As mentioned above, some casinos require the dealer to draw on soft 17. The dealer has no options and cannot deviate from the above-stated rules.

PLAYER'S OPTIONS

Unlike the dealer, the player can vary his strategy. After receiving his first two cards the player has the following options:

1. Drawing (Hitting)

If the player is not satisfied with his two card total he can draw additional cards. To draw a card, the player scrapes the felt surface with his cards, scraping toward his body. In a game where both the player's cards are dealt face up, he scratches the felt with his index finger or points toward the cards if he desires a hit. A player is not supposed to handle the cards when they're face up.

2. Standing

When a player is satisfied with his original two card total, and does not wish to draw additional cards, he signals this by sliding his cards face down under his bet. When the cards are dealt face up, the player indicates his decision to stand pat by waving is hand palm down over his cards.

3. Doubling Down

This option allows the player to double his original bet, in which case he must draw one additional card to his hand and cannot draw any additional cards thereafter. To double down, the player turns his cards face up, and places them in front of his bet. Then he takes an amount equal to his original bet and places those chips next to that bet, so that there are now two equivalent bets side by side. The dealer will then deal one card face down, usually slipping that card under the player's bet. The bettor may look at that card if he desires.

4. Splitting Pairs

If dealt a pair of identical value cards, such as 3-3, 7-7, 8-8 (any combination of 10, J, Q, K is considered a pair), the player can split these cards so that two separate hands are formed. To split a pair, the player turns the pair face up, separates them, putting each card in its own place in front of his bet. He then places a bet equal to the original wager behind the second hand. Each hand is played separately, using finger and hand signals to indicate hitting and standing.

If the first card dealt to either split hand has a value identical to the original split cards, that card may be split again (resplit) into a third hand, with the exception of aces. When the player splits aces, he can receive only one card on each ace and may not draw again, no matter what card is drawn.

5. Doubling Down After Splitting

The player can double down on one or both of the hands resulting from a split according to the normal doubling rules of the casino. This option is offered in all Atlantic City casinos and in certain Nevada casinos. Also found in Australia, Great Britain, various European and Asian casinos and southern Africa.

For example, if a pair of 8s are split, and a 3 is drawn to the first 8 for an 11, the player may elect to double down on that 11. He can place an amount equal to the original bet next to the 11, and will receive only one additional card. If a 2 is drawn to the second 8, the player may double down on that hand as well.

6. Surrender (Late Surrender)

The player can give up his original two card hand and lose one half on his bet after it has been determined that the dealer does not have a blackjack. To surrender, the bettor turns both his cards face up, puts them above his bet, and says "surrender." The dealer will collect the cards and take one half of the bet. This option is offered in only a few Nevada casinos.

7. Early Surrender

A player option to give up his hand and lose half his bet before the dealer checks for a blackjack. This option originally introduced in Atlantic City is no longer offered because of changes in Atlantic City rules.

8. Insurance

If the dealer shows an ace as his upcard, he will ask the players if they want insurance. If any player exercises this option, he is in effect betting that the dealer has a 10-value card as his hole card, a blackjack. To take insurance, he places up to one-half the amount of his bet in the area marked insurance. If the dealer does indeed have a blackjack, he gets paid 2 to 1 on the insurance bet, while losing the original bet. In effect, the transaction is a "standoff", and no money is lost. If the dealer does not have a blackjack, the insurance bet is lost and play continues.

If the player holds a blackjack and takes insurance on the dealer's ace, the payoff will be even-money whether the dealer has a blackjack or not. Suppose the player has a $10 bet and takes insurance for $5 on his blackjack. If the dealer has a blackjack, the player wins 2 to 1 on his $5 insurance bet and ties with his own blackjack. If the dealer doesn't have a blackjack, the player loses the $5 insurance bet but gets paid 3 to 2 on his blackjack. Either way the bettor wins $10.

INSURANCE STRATEGY

Insurance is a bad bet for the following reason:

Making an insurance wager is betting that the dealer has a 10 under his ace. Since the insurance payoff is 2 to 1, the wager will only be a profitable option for the player when the ratio of 10s to other cards is either equal to or less than 2 to 1.

A full deck has 36 non-tens and 16 tens, a ratio greater than 2 to 1. If the first deal off the top of the deck gives us a hand of 9,7, and the dealer shows an ace, then we know three cards, all non-tens. Now the ratio is 33 to 16, still greater than 2 to 1, still a poor bet. If you have two 10s for a 20, then the ratio is 35 to 14, an even worse bet.

In a multiple deck game, taking insurance is an even worse bet than in a single deck one.

Insuring a Blackjack

Taking insurance when you have a blackjack is also a bad bet, despite the well-intentioned advice of dealers and other players to always "insure" a blackjack. When you have a blackjack, you know three cards, your 10 and ace, and the dealer's ace. The already poor starting ratio of 36 non-tens to 16 tens gets worse, becoming 34 to 15 in a single deck game. Taking insurance when you have a blackjack gives the house an 8% advantage, a poor proposition for the player.

THE PLAY OF THE GAME

The dealer begins by shuffling the cards and offering the cut to one of the players. If refused, it is offered to another player. The dealer then completes the cut, and removes the top card, called the **burn card**. In single and double deck games, the burn card is either put under the deck face up, where all subsequent cards will be placed, or is put face down into a plastic case (procedures vary from casino to casino) to be followed similarly by future discards.

In games dealt out of a shoe, the burn card will be placed most of the way into the shoe and discards will be put in the plastic case.

Players must make their bets before the cards are dealt.

The dealer deals clockwise from his left to his right, one card at a time, until each player and the dealer have received two cards. The players cards are usually dealt face down in a single or double deck game, though it makes no difference if they are dealt face up as they usually are in a game dealt out of a shoe, for the dealer is bound by strict rules from which he cannot deviate. The dealer deals only one of his two cards face up. This card is called an **upcard**. The face down card is known as the **hole card** or the **downcard**.

If the dealer's upcard is an ace, he will ask the players if they want insurance. Players that decide to take that option place a bet of up to one-half their wager in front of their bet in the area marked insurance.

If the dealer has a blackjack, all players that did not take insurance lose their original bets. Players that took insurance break even on the play. If the dealer hasn't a blackjack, he collects the lost insurance bets and play continues.

The procedures vary when the dealer shows a 10-value card. In Nevada casinos the dealer must check his hole card for an ace. If he has a blackjack, it is an automatic winner for the house. All player bets are lost. (Players can't insure against a 10-value card.) If the dealer doesn't have a blackjack, he will face the first player and await that player's decision. Players that hold a blackjack push on the play.

In Atlantic City, the Bahamas and most European games, the dealer will only check the hole card after all the players have acted.

Play begins with the bettor on the dealer's left, in the position known as **first base**.

The player has the option to stand, hit, double down, split (if he has two cards of equal value) and surrender (if allowed). A player can draw cards until he is satisfied with his total or busts, or he can exercise one of the other options discussed previously.

Play then moves to the next player. If any player busts (goes over 21) or receives a blackjack, he must turn over his cards immediately. If a bust, the dealer will collect the lost bet. If a blackjack, the dealer will pay the player 3 to 2 on his bet.

After the last player has acted upon his cards, the dealer will turn his hole card over so that all players can view both of his cards. He must play his hand according to the strict guidelines regulating his play; drawing to 17, then standing. (In some casinos the dealer must draw to a soft 17.) If the dealer busts, all players still in the game for that round of play win automatically.

After playing his hand, the dealer will turn over each player's cards in turn, paying the winners, and collecting from the losers. Once the bettor has played his hand, he shouldn't touch his cards again. He should let the dealer expose his hand which he will do once the dealer has played out his own hand.

When the round has been completed, all players must place a new bet before the next deal.

CASINO PERSONNEL

The casino employee responsible for the running of the blackjack game is called the dealer. The dealer's duties are to deal the cards to the players, and play out his own hand according to the rules of the game. He converts money into chips for players entering the game or buying in for more chips during the course of the game, makes the correct payoffs for winning hands, and collects bets from the losers.

The dealer's supervisor—technically called the **floorman**, but more commonly referred to as the **pit boss**—is responsible for the supervision of between 4-6 tables. His job is to make sure the games run smoothly and to settle any disputes that may arise with a player. More importantly, his job is to oversee the exchange of money and to correct any errors that may occur.

ENTERING A GAME

To enter a blackjack game, sit down at any unoccupied seat at the blackjack table, and place the money you wish to gamble with near the betting box in front of you and inform the dealer that you would like to get some chips for your cash. Chips may be purchased in various denominations. Let the dealer know which chips or combination of chips you'd like.

The dealer will take your money and call out the amount he is changing so that the pit boss is aware that a transaction is taking place and can supervise that exchange.

CONVERTING TRAVELER'S CHECKS AND MONEY ORDERS TO CASH

The dealers will accept only cash or chips, so if you bring traveler's checks, money orders or the like, you must go to the area of the casino marked **Casino Cashier** to get these converted to cash. Be sure to bring proper identification to insure a smooth transaction.

CASINO CHIPS

Standard denominations of casino chips are $1, $5, $25, $100, and for the high rollers, $500 and even $1,000 chips can sometimes be obtained. Though some casinos use their own color code, the usual color scheme of chips are: $1=silver, $5=red, $25=green and $100=black.

BETTING

Casinos prefer that the players use chips for betting purposes, for the handling of money at the tables is cumbersome and slows the game. However, cash can be used to bet with, though all payoffs will be in chips. To bet, place your chips (or cash) in the betting box directly in front of you. All bets must be placed before the cards are dealt.

HOUSE LIMITS

Placards located at either corner of the table indicate the minimum and maximum bets allowed at a particular table. Within the same casino you will find minimums raging from $1, $2 and $5 to other tables that require the players to bet at least $25 or $100 per hand. At the $1, $2 and $5 tables, the house maximum generally will not exceed $500 to $1,000 while the $25 and $100 tables may allow the players to bet as high as $3,000 a hand.

There are casinos that will book almost any bet and give high rollers their own private table for large stakes games. If you catch the right night, you might find a *whale*, a high roller, making bets in $10,000 units!

CONVERTING CHIPS INTO CASH

Dealers do not convert chips into cash. When you are ready to cash in your chips, take them to the cashier's cage where they'll be changed into cash.

FREE DRINKS AND CIGARETTES

Casinos offer their customers unlimited free drinking while playing at the table. In addition to alcoholic beverages, a player can order milk, soft drinks, juices or any other beverages. Cigarettes and cigars are also complimentary. Both drinks and smokes can be ordered through the cocktail waitress.

THE DECKS OF CARDS

Nevada casinos use one, two, four, six and sometimes as many as eight decks of cards in their blackjack games. Often, within the same casino, single and multiple deck games will be offered. When one or two decks are used, the dealer holds the cards in his hand. When more than two decks are used, the cards are dealt from a rectangular plastic or wooden device known as a **shoe**. The shoe is designed to hold multiple decks of cards, and allows the cards to be easily removed one at a time by the dealer.

Outside of Nevada, multiple deck blackjack is the norm, and it is rare to see single deck play.

Each deck used in blackjack is a standard pack of 52 cards, consisting of 4 cards of each value, ace through king. Suits have no relevance in blackjack. Only the numerical value of the cards count.

STANDEES

In some areas around the world, most notably Europe and Asia, **standees**, players not occupying a seat and betting spot at the table, are allowed to place bets in the boxes of players already seated. Standees must accept the seated player's decision and are not allowed to advise or criticize the play made.

NO HOLE CARD RULE

The predominant style of play in casinos outside the United States is for the dealer to take his second card after all the players have acted upon their hands. In some cases, the dealer may deal himself the card as in the U.S. casinos, but will not check a 10 or ace for blackjack until after the bettors have finished playing their hands. The disadvantage to the player is that on hands doubled or split, the additional moneys bet will be lost if indeed the dealer has a blackjack. As you'll see, we adjust our strategies accordingly when playing in no hole card games so as to minimize the effect of this rule.

(In Atlantic City, the game is played in this style, except that when the dealer has a blackjack, the player's additional bets on doubles and splits are returned. Only the original bet will be lost. Thus, it is not a disadvantage to Atlantic City players and playing strategies need not be adjusted for this factor.)

RULES AND VARIATIONS OF THE CASINO CENTERS

Blackjack can be found all over the world, and though basically the same wherever played, the rules and variations vary from country to country, from casino to casino within a country, and sometimes, they even differ within a casino itself.

NEVADA RULES

The Las Vegas Strip rules are advantageous to the player and gives one a slight edge on the single deck game if our strategies are followed. The rule exceptions noted in Downtown Las Vegas and in Northern Nevada games are slightly disadvantageous to the player, but these can easily be overcome by using the winning techniques presented later.

Las Vegas Strip Rules
- Dealer must draw on all totals of 16 or less, and stand on all totals of 17-21.
- Player may take insurance on a dealer's ace.
- Insurance payoffs are 2 to 1.
- Player receives a 3 to 2 payoff on his blackjack (in some games only 6 to 5).
- Player may double down on any initial two card combination.
- Identical pairs may be split, resplit, and drawn to as desired with the exception of split aces, on which the player is allowed only one hit on each ace.

Downtown Las Vegas

The same rules as the Las Vegas Strip rules with one exception:

• Dealer must draw to soft 17.

Northern Nevada

Same as Strip rules with two exceptions:

• Dealer must draw to soft 17.
• Doubling is restricted to two card totals of 10 and 11 only.

ATLANTIC CITY RULES

The New Jersey Casino Control Commission regulates the rules and variations allowed in Atlantic City casinos, and all Atlantic City clubs must abide by the following guidelines:

• Dealer must draw to all totals 16 or less, and stand on all totals of 17-21.
• Player may take insurance on a dealer's ace. Insurance payoffs are 2 to 1.
• Player receives a 3 to 2 payoff on his blackjack (in some games only 6 to 5).
• Player may double on any initial two card combination.
• Identical pairs may be split but not resplit.
• Doubling after splitting allowed.
• Multiple deck games are standard

EUROPEAN RULES

Blackjack is offered in numerous countries around Europe with the rules and variations changing slightly from place to place. However, the following conditions apply in a good many of these places.

• Dealer must draw to all totals 16 or less, and stand on all totals of 17-21.
• Player may take insurance on a dealer's ace.
• Insurance payoffs are 2 to 1.
• Player receives a 3 to 2 payoff on his blackjack.
• Doubling down on 9-11 only
• Standees permitted
• No hole card rule
• 4-6 decks standard
• If player draws a 2 on a A8 double down hand, the total counts as 11, not 21

RULES AROUND THE WORLD

The general variations we present under the European Rules above is probably the most prevalent style of play in casinos around the world. Sometimes you may find double after split permitted as in Great Britain, southern Africa, many European casinos and other places; in Asian and Caribbean casinos, surrender is often allowed—just ask the particular rules before you enter a game.

In our strategy section, we'll show you the best way to play no matter the variation used.

GENERAL STRATEGIC CONCEPTS

THE DEALER'S ONLY ADVANTAGE

Before we examine the correct strategies of play, it would be instructive to look at a losing strategy. In this strategy, the player will mimic the dealer; he'll draw on all totals 16 or less, and stand on all totals 17-21.

The player doing this figures that, since this strategy wins for the dealer, it must be effective for the player as well. After all, the dealer and the player will get the same number of good hands and the same number of poor hands. And if we draw just as the dealer draws, we must come out even, mustn't we?

No. As a matter of fact, the player will be playing at about a 5 1/2% disadvantage to the house. The "Mimic the Dealer" strategy overlooks one important thing. The player must act upon his hand first.

The dealer's only advantage lies in the fact that once the player has busted, the player's bet is automatically lost, regardless of the outcome of the dealer's hand. While both the dealer and the player will bust equally following these drawing-to-17 guidelines (about 28% of the time), the double bust, where both the dealer and the player bust on the same round, will occur approximately 8% of the time (28% of 28% of the time or 28 x 28). And since the player acted first, this 8% of the time (the double bust) will be the house advantage.

When we adjust for the 3 to 2 bonus the player receives on blackjacks, a bonus the house does not enjoy, we find the house enjoying a 5 1/2% edge over the player that follows the "Mimic the Dealer" strategy.

OVERCOMING THE DISADVANTAGE OF ACTING FIRST

In the "Mimic the Dealer" strategy we played our hands as if our goal was to get as close to 21 as reasonably possible by using 17 as a cut-off point for drawing. But this losing strategy misstates the goal of the player. In blackjack, the object is to beat the dealer. Our chances of winning are not determined by how close our total approaches 21 as the other strategy assumed, but on how good our total is compared to the dealer's.

We can overcome the disadvantage of having to act first by making judicious use of the options available to us as a player. Not only should we double down, split pairs, hit, stand and surrender (if allowed), but we can use our knowledge of the dealer's exposed upcard to fully capitalize on these options. Needless to say, adjusting our strategy according to this knowledge of the dealer's upcard will vastly improve on the "Get as Close to 21 - Mimic the Dealer" strategy, and completely eliminate the house edge.

TO BEAT THE DEALER

There are two factors that affect our chances of winning; the strength of our total and the strength of the dealer's total. To beat the dealer, we must know how strong our total is compared to the dealer's total so that we know if drawing additional cards or exercising a player option is a viable consideration. In addition, we must be aware of the factors that influence the final outcome of these totals so that we can determine the optimal way to play our hand.

In determining the best way to play our hand, we must know how good our total is as it stands. Do we have the expectancy of winning by standing? If so, can we increase this expectancy by drawing additional cards or by exercising a doubling or splitting option when applicable? If we do not have the expectancy of winning by standing, will the drawing of additional cards or the employment of the doubling or splitting option increase our chance of winning?

Since our object is to beat the dealer, to answer the question "how strong is our total?" We need to ask ourselves if the dealer's expectancy, judged by the information we get from his exposed card, is greater than our total.

Being able to see the dealer's upcard gives us a great deal of information about the strength of the hands that the dealer is likely to make, and we can use that information to our advantage.

UNDERSTANDING THE DEALER'S UPCARD

Being able to see the dealer's upcard is of great value to the player, for there are two factors—the rules governing the dealer's play of his hand, and the number of tens in a deck of cards (ten factor)—that tell us a great deal about the potential strength of the dealer's hands, and the frequency with which those hands will bust.

TEN FACTOR

The most striking feature of blackjack is the dominant role that the 10-value cards (10, J, Q, K) play. Each ten and face card is counted as 10 points each in blackjack. Thus, the player is four times more likely to draw a 10 than any other individual card since all the other cards, aces through nines, consist of only four cards each as opposed to sixteen 10s. Collectively, the 10s constitute just under 1/3 of the deck (16 out of 52 cards).

Because the 10s are such a dominant factor in a deck of cards, it's correct to think of the dealer's hand *gravitating* toward a total 10 points greater than his exposed upcard. When I speak of a hand as gravitating toward a total, I am referring to the tendency of that hand to increase in value by 10 points as a result of the 10 factor. Thus, starting out with an upcard of 9, the dealer will make a hand of 19 thirty-six percent of the time and 19 or better 52% of the time.

THE DEALER'S RULES AND THE TEN FACTOR

Our strategy is based on the fact that the dealer must play by prescribed guidelines from which he cannot deviate. He must draw to all totals 16 or below, and stand on all totals 17-21 (except in casinos that require the dealer to draw to soft 17). All hard totals that exceed hard 21 are automatic dealer losses.

By combining our knowledge of the 10 factor with the above mentioned dealer rules gives us a natural separation of the dealer's upcard into two distinct groupings: 2s through 6s, the dealer "stiff" cards, and 7s through aces, the dealer "pat" cards.

2s through 6s – Dealer Stiff Cards

Whenever the dealer shows a 2, 3, 4, 5 or 6 as an upcard, we know that he must draw at least one additional card regardless of the value of his hole card (unless the dealer has an ace under his 6 and is playing Las Vegas Strip, Atlantic City or European style rules which require the dealer to stand on soft 17). The high concentration of 10s in the deck make it likely that the dealer will expose a 10 as his hole card, giving him a stiff total of 12-16.

Since the dealer must draw to all hard totals 16 or below, the drawing of a 10 (and in some instances, smaller totaled cards) will bust any of these stiff totals. For example, if the dealer shows a 6 and reveals a 10 in the hole, any card higher than a 5 will bust his hand.

Thus, the high concentration of 10 value cards in the deck tells us that the dealer has a good chance of busting when his upcard is a 2, 3, 4, 5 or 6.

7s through As – Dealer Pat Cards

Whenever the dealer shows a 7, 8, 9, 10 or A as an upcard, we know, because of the large number of 10s, that he has a high likelihood of making pat totals 17-21, and conversely, a smaller chance of busting than when he shows a stiff card. This high concentration of 10s makes it likely that the dealer will expose a 10 for an automatic pat hand (17-21). Even when he hasn't a 10 in the hole, combinations such as 89; A7; 99 and so forth, give him an automatic pat hand as well.

UNDERSTANDING THE DEALER'S UPCARD

Dealer Stiff Cards	Advantageous for Player
2 3 4	5 6
Less Advantageous	More Advantageous

Dealer's Upcard of 2 and 3

Though it is favorable for the player when the dealer shows a 2 or 3 as an upcard, we will need to be cautious against these stiff cards, for the dealer will bust less often with these than when he shows the 4, 5 and 6.

Dealer's Upcard of 4, 5 and 6

The dealer is showing the upcards you always want him to hold. The dealer will bust about 42% of the time with these upcards (5% more than the 2 and 3 and about 18% more than with the pat cards). We will take advantage of these weak dealer upcards by aggressive splitting and doubling.

Dealer Pat Cards	Disadvantageous for Player
7 8 9	10 ace
Moderately Disadvantageous	Very Disadvantageous

Dealer's Upcard of 7 and 8

While the dealer will not bust often with these upcards, they also indicate to us that the dealer's hands gravitate toward the weaker totals of 17 and 18. It is interesting to note that of all the dealer upcards including the stiff cards, the 7 will form the weakest totals.

Dealer's Upcard of 9, 10 and Ace

The 9 and 10 gravitate toward totals of 19 and 20 respectively—tough hands to beat. The ace is also a powerful dealer upcard, for in addition to forming strong hands, the dealer will bust less with an ace than with any other upcard.

Against these powerful upcards, we will be very cautious in our doubling and splitting strategies.

UNDERSTANDING THE PLAYER'S HAND – HARD TOTALS

The player's totals can be divided into three distinct groupings: 11 or less, 17-21 and 12-16. We will look at each in turn to see how they affect our strategy.

Player's Hand of 11 or Less – (Hard Totals)

We should always draw to any hard total 11 or less (unless a doubling or splitting option is more profitable). By hitting this hand we have no risk of busting, no matter what we draw, and the drawing of a card can strengthen our total. There is no question about the correct decision; drawing is a big gain.

Player's Hand of 17-21 – (Hard Totals)

We should always stand on these hard totals (17-21), for the risk of busting is too high to make drawing worthwhile. It should be obvious that the chances of improving these high totals are minimal, and the risks of busting very probable. In addition, totals of 19, 20, 21, and to a lesser extent, 18, are already powerful hands. While hard 17 is a poor player total, the risk of busting by drawing is way too costly to make drawing a viable option. Stand on hard totals of 17-21 against any dealer's upcard.

Player's Hand of 12-16 – (Hard Totals)

With these hands the bulk of our decision making will be exercised, for on these hard totals there are no automatic decisions as on the other player totals. Our hand is not an obvious draw (such as the 11 or less grouping) for the risk of drawing a 10 or other high card and busting is substantial. Our hand is not an obvious stand decision either (such as the 17-21 grouping), for the only times we will win with these weak totals of 12-16 are the times that the dealer busts.

For the Cardoza Non-Counter winning strategies to be effective, you must first know the correct way to play your hands. (The same applies to any player who moves on to any professional counting or non-counting strategy.) Therefore, make sure you understand these basic strategies before going on to the winning techniques of play.

THE OPTIMAL BASIC STRATEGIES

HITTING AND STANDING – HARD TOTALS

These strategies are applicable for single and multiple deck games in all casino centers.

General Principles

- When the dealer shows a 7, 8, 9, 10 or A, hit all hard totals of 16 or below (unless doubling or splitting is more profitable—in any case, you will always draw a card).
- When the dealer shows a 2, 3, 4, 5 or 6, stand on all hard totals of 12 or more. Do not bust against a dealer stiff card. Exception - Hit 12 vs. 2, 3.

Hitting and Standing - Hard Totals
All Casino Centers

	2	3	4	5	6	7	8	9	10	A
11/less	H	H	H	H	H	H	H	H	H	H
12	H	H	S	S	S	H	H	H	H	H
13	S	S	S	S	S	H	H	H	H	H
14	S	S	S	S	S	H	H	H	H	H
15	S	S	S	S	S	H	H	H	H	H
16	S	S	S	S	S	H	H	H	H	H
17-21	S	S	S	S	S	S	S	S	S	S

H = Hit   S = Stand

(In all our charts, the dealer's upcard is indicated by the horizontal numbers on the top row, and the player's hand is indicted by the vertical numbers in the left column. The letters in the matrix indicate the correct strategy play.)

Conceptual Hitting and Standing Strategy

In the "Understanding the Player's Hand" section we discussed the strategy for hard totals of 11 or less, and for hard totals 17-21.

They will be reiterated briefly here.

11 or less – Draw against all dealer upcards.

17-21 – Stand against all dealer upcards.

Hard Totals 12-16

It is when we hold hard totals 12-16 (stiffs) that the player's big disadvantage of having to go first (the only built-in house advantage) is a costly proposition. If we draw to hard totals and bust, we are automatic losers. But, on the other hand, if we stand, we will win with these weak totals only when the dealer busts.

It is important to realize that the decision to hit or stand with hard totals 12-16 is a strategy of minimizing losses, for no matter what we do, we have a potentially losing hand against any dealer upcard. Do not expect to win when you hold a stiff. However, in order to maximize the gain from our overall strategy, we must minimize the losses in disadvantageous situations (as above), and maximize our gains in advantageous one.

Player Totals of 12-16 vs. Dealer Pat Cards 7, 8, 9, 10, A

When the dealer's upcard is a 7 through an ace, you should expect the dealer to make his hand, for he will bust only about one time in four, a mere 25% of the time. If we stand on our hard totals 12-16, we will win only the times that the dealer busts.

Thus, for every 100 hands that we stand with our stiff totals 12-16 against dealer pat cards, our expectation is to lose 75 of those hands and to win only 25, a net loss of 50 hands. Not an exciting prognosis.

On the other hand, drawing to our stiff totals 12-16 against the dealer pat cards gives us a big gain over standing. By drawing, we will gain an average of 15%. The dealer makes too many hands showing a 7, 8, 9, 10 or ace, to allow us to stand with our stiffs.

You will bust often when drawing to your stiffs, but do not let that dissuade you from hitting your stiffs against pat cards. The strategy on these plays is to minimize losses. We cannot afford to stand and sacrifice our hand to the 3 out of 4 hands that the dealer will make.

When the dealer shows a 7, 8, 9, 10, or ace, hit all hard totals 16 or below.

Player Totals of 12-16 vs. Dealer Pat Cards 2, 3, 4, 5, 6

The greater busting potential of the dealer stiff cards makes standing with hard player totals of 12-16 a big gain over drawing. While we will win only 40% of these hands (the times that the dealer busts), standing is a far superior strategy to drawing, for we will bust too often drawing to our own stiffs against upcards that will bust fairly often themselves. The times that we would make pat totals by drawing wouldn't guarantee us winners either, for the dealer will often make equal or better totals.

On these plays, our disadvantage of having to go first makes drawing too costly, for once we bust, we automatically lose. Though the dealer will make more hands than bust, our strategy here is to minimize losses so that when we get our good hands, we'll come out an overall winner.

Exception – Hit Player 12 vs. 2, 3

Hitting 12 vs. 2, 3 is the only basic strategy exception to drawing with a stiff total against a dealer's stiff upcard. The double bust factor is not as costly on these plays, for only the 10s will bust our 12. Similarly, the dealer will bust less often showing a 2 or a 3 than with the other stiff cards, 4, 5 and 6.

This is in contrast to the play 13 vs. 2 where the correct strategy is to stand. The additional player busting factor of the 9 makes the player slightly better off by standing, even though the dealer will bust less with a 2 as an upcard. This clearly illustrates the greater importance of the player's busting factor (compared to the dealer's busting factor) when deciding whether to stand or draw with a stiff total 12-16 vs. a dealer stiff upcard.

The combination of the player being less likely to bust (more likely to make his hand) and the dealer being more likely to make his hand (less likely to bust) makes drawing 12 vs 2, 3 the correct strategy play.

HITTING AND STANDING – SOFT TOTALS

The strategy for hitting and standing with soft totals in Northern Nevada and Europe is identical to the Atlantic City and Las Vegas strategies for both single and multiple deck, except that the Atlantic City and Las Vegas basic strategy players can take advantage of the more liberal doubling rules and will double down on hands that Northern Nevada and European Style rules players cannot.

Hitting and Standing - Soft Totals
Northern Nevada & Europe • Single and Multiple Deck

	2	3	4	5	6	7	8	9	10	A
A2-A6	H	H	H	H	H	H	H	H	H	H
A7	S	S	S	S	S	S	S	H	H	H
A8-A9	S	S	S	S	S	S	S	S	S	S

H = Hit S = Stand

Hitting and Standing - Soft Totals
Atlantic City & Las Vegas • Single and Multiple Deck

	2	3	4	5	6	7	8	9	10	A
A2-A5	H	H	D*	D	D	H	H	H	H	H
A6	D**	D	D	D	D	H	H	H	H	H
A7	S	D	D	D	D	S	S	H	H	H
A8	S	S	S	S	S	S	S	S	S	S
A9	S	S	S	S	S	S	S	S	S	S

H = Hit   S = Stand   D = Double

*Do not double A2 or A3 vs. 4 in a multiple deck game.
**Do not double A6 vs. 2 in a multiple deck game.

Conceptual Hitting and Standing –
Soft Totals Player's Hand of A2, A3, A4, A5

Unless the player is able to double down, he should always draw a card to these hands. Standing is a poor option, for these totals will win only when the dealer busts. The player has nothing to lose by drawing (no draw can bust these totals), and may improve his total. Players that stand on these hands might just as well give the casinos their money. Draw on A2-A5 against all dealer upcards.

Player's Hand of A6, A7, A8, A9

The decision to hit or stand with soft totals 17 or higher necessitates a closer look at the strength of these totals. Unlike hard totals of 17 or more, drawing is a viable option with these soft totals. Since we have the option of counting the ace as 1 point or 11 points, the drawing of a 10, or for that matter, the drawing of any other card, will not bust our soft totals. While we have no risk of busting, we do have the risk of drawing a weaker total, and therefore must ask the question, "How strong is our total?"

For Soft Totals, We Want to Know:
- What are our chances of winning by standing?
- What are the chances of improving our hand by drawing additional cards?

Player's Hand of Soft 17 (A6)

A standing total of 17 is a weak hand against all dealer upcards, including the dealer stiff cards, and in the long run is a losing total. The only time we will win with this total is when the dealer busts. Otherwise, at best we have a push.

Always draw on soft 17 no matter what the dealer shows as an upcard. (In Las Vegas, Atlantic City, and other locations where allowed, the correct strategy may be to double down. See doubling section.) This standing total is so weak that attempting to improve our hand by drawing is always a tremendous gain against any upcard.

When a casino requires the dealer to draw to soft 17, it is a disadvantageous rule to the player. Though the dealer will sometimes bust by drawing to a soft 17, in the long run he will make more powerful totals and have more winners. It affects the player the same way.

Player's Hand of Soft 18

Against dealer stiff totals of 2, 3, 4, 5 and 6, standing with our 18 is a smart strategy move (unless playing Las Vegas or Atlantic City doubling rules where doubling will often be a big player gain). We have a strong total against these weak dealer upcards.

Stand against dealer upcards of 7 and 8, for our 18 is a solid hand. Against the 7, we have a winning total, and against the 8, we figure to have a potential push, as these dealer upcards gravitate toward 17 and 18 respectively. We do not want to risk our strong position by drawing.

Against the powerful dealer upcards of 9, 10, ace, our standing total of 18 is a potentially losing hand. Normally you would think that hitting a soft 18 is only a fair total. We are not chancing a powerful total but rather attempting to improve a weak situation.

As a matter of fact, for every 100 plays (at $1 a play) that we draw rather than stand on soft 18 vs. 9 and 10, we will gain $9 and $4 respectively. You must realize that 18 vs. 9, 10, ace is not a winning hand and since our 18 is a soft total, we have a chance to minimize losses by drawing.

Player's Hand of Soft 19 and 20

These hands are strong player totals as they stand.

DOUBLING DOWN

Doubling down is a valuable option for it gives the player a chance to double his bet in advantageous situations. The only drawback to the doubling option is that the player must receive one card and gives up the privilege to draw additional cards should that card be a poor draw. To determine if the doubling option will be profitable, we must weigh the benefits of doubling our bet against the drawbacks of receiving only one card.

One of the most important factors to consider when contemplating the doubling option is the 10 factor. We are more likely to draw a 10 on our double than any other card value. Thus, doubling on a total of 11, where the drawing of a 10 gives us an unbeatable 21, is a more powerful double than an initial two card total of 9, where the drawing of 10 gives us a strong total of 19, not as powerful as the 21.

On the other hand, we would not double any hand of hard 12 or more, for the drawing of a 10 would bust our total, and we would have an automatic loser at double the bet.

The 10 factor is also an important strategic consideration, for it affects the dealer's busting potential. We double more aggressively against the weakest of the dealer stiff cards, the 4, 5 and 6, and less aggressively against the other stiff cards, the 2 and 3. The only times we will double against the dealer pat cards are when our doubling totals of 10 and 11 are powerful themselves.

Doubling Down – Single Deck Basic Strategy

A. Northern Nevada – The player is restricted to doubling down on two card totals of 10 and 11 only.

Doubling Down
Northern Nevada • Single Deck

	2	3	4	5	6	7	8	9	10	A
10	D	D	D	D	D	D	D	D		
11	D	D	D	D	D	D	D	D	D	D

D = Double Down   Blank = Do Not Double Down

B. Las Vegas – The player may double down on any initial two card combination.

Doubling Down
Las Vegas • Single Deck

	2	3	4	5	6	7	8	9	10	A
62										
44/53				D	D					
9	D	D	D	D	D					
10	D	D	D	D	D	D	D	D		
11	D	D	D	D	D	D	D	D	D	D
A2				D	D	D				
A3				D	D	D				
A4				D	D	D				
A5				D	D	D				
A6		D	D	D	D	D				
A7			D	D	D	D				
A8										
A9										

D = Double Down   Blank = Do Not Double Down

Multiple Deck Basic Strategy

A. Northern Nevada – The player is restricted to doubling down on two card totals of 10 and 11 only.

Doubling Down
Northern Nevada • Multiple Deck

	2	3	4	5	6	7	8	9	10	A
10	D	D	D	D	D	D	D	D		
11	D	D	D	D	D	D	D	D	D	

D = Double Down   Blank = Do Not Double Down

B. European Style – The player may double down on totals of 9, 10 and 11 only. The no hole card rules accounts for the less frequent doubling against the dealer's 10 than you see with the Atlantic City and Nevada casinos.

Doubling Down – European Style Rules • Multiple Deck

	2	3	4	5	6	7	8	9	10	A
9		D	D	D	D					
10	D	D	D	D	D	D	D	D		
11	D	D	D	D	D	D	D	D		
A8										

D = Double Down   Blank = Do Not Double Down

C. Atlantic City and Las Vegas – The player can double down on any initial two card combination. These strategies are good for all multiple deck games in Atlantic City and Las Vegas.

Doubling Down – Atlantic City & Las Vegas • Multiple Deck

	2	3	4	5	6	7	8	9	10	A
8										
9		D	D	D	D					
10	D	D	D	D	D	D	D	D		
11	D	D	D	D	D	D	D	D	D	
A2				D	D					
A3				D	D					
A4			D	D	D					
A5			D	D	D					
A6		D	D	D	D					
A7		D	D	D	D					
A8										
A9										

D = Double Down   Blank = Do Not Double Down

Conceptual Doubling - Hard Totals (11, 10, 9, 8)

These strategies are applicable to single and multiple deck games in all casino centers. Where multiple deck strategies differ from the single deck, an asterisk will denote the strategy change, and that change will be indicated.

Doubling 11*

This is the strongest doubling hand for the player and should be doubled against all the dealer upcards in a single deck game. If we draw a 10 value card on our double, we will have a 21, the strongest hand we can have. At best, the dealer can tie us.

*Do not double 11 vs. ace in multiple deck games. In no hole card rules games, do not double against the 10 or ace. Hit instead.

Doubling 10

This is the second strongest doubling hand for the player and should be doubled against the dealer's 2 through 9. Our hard 10 gravitates toward a 20, an overwhelmingly strong hand against these dealer upcards.

Do not double 10 against the dealer's 10 or ace. Doubling our hard 10 against the dealer's 10 is not a potential winner as before (against the dealer's 2 through 9), for the dealer's hand gravitates toward a 20 as well, and our possible 20 is not powerful enough to compensate for the low busting probabilities of the dealer's ace. Giving up the option to draw an additional card should the first card be a poor one is too costly on these plays.

Note: In Northern Nevada, only hard 10 and 11 can be doubled down.

Doubling 9

Double 9 against 2 through 6 only*. The high busting potential of the dealer stiff cards (2-6) makes the 9 a profitable double down. We cannot double down against any of the pat cards (7-ace) for our win potential when we do draw the 10 (for a total of 19) is not strong enough to compensate for the times when we when we draw a poor card and cannot draw again.

*Do not double 9 vs. 2 in a multiple deck game.

Doubling 8

Doubling 8 vs. 5, 6 is a valid play in a single deck game*. Our 8 gravitates toward an 18, only a fair total. However, the very high busting potential of the dealer 5 and 6 make this double a slight gain. Our 8 is not strong enough to make doubling against the other dealer upcards a good play.

* Do not double 8 against any upcard in a multiple deck game.

Conceptual Doubling - Soft Totals

The high concentration of 10s play a different role in soft doubling than in hard doubling, for instead of having a positive effect on our chances of making a good total, the drawing of 10 will not even give us a pat hand on many of these doubles.

Doubling with soft totals is generally a gain against the weak dealer upcards. The 10 factor will figure strongly in the dealer's chances of busting, while the drawing of small and medium cards will often improve our hand to a competitive total.

Doubling A2, A3, A4, A5

Double A2, A3, A4 and A5 against the dealer's 4, 5 and 6*. The very high busting probabilities of the dealer 4, 5 and 6 makes doubling with our A2 to A5 profitable for the player. Again, the drawing of a 10 value card does not help our total, but the high dealer busting factor gives us an edge.

We do not double against the 2 and 3, because the dealer will make just too many hands with these upcards. The same is more strikingly true with the dealer pat cards, 7 through ace.

* Do not double A2 vs. 4, A3 vs. 4 in a multiple deck game.

Doubling A6

Double A6 vs. dealer 2, 3, 4, 5 and 6*. The A6 is a more powerful double than the A2-A5, for the drawing of a 10 to the A6 will at least give us a pat total and a potential push against a dealer's 17. This "push" factor enables us to gain by doubling against the dealer's 2 and 3 despite the fact that they will make more dealer pat totals than with the weaker upcards 4, 5 and 6.

* Do not double A6 vs. 2 in a multiple deck game.

Doubling A7

Double A7 vs. 3, 4, 5 and 6. Our soft 18 is only a fair total and drawing an additional card won't risk the destruction of a powerful total such as a 19 or 20. Soft 18 is a strong double against the weaker dealer stiffs 4, 5 and 6, but differs from the soft 17 in that we do not double against the 2. A standing total of 18 vs. a 2 is a stronger winning hand and we do not want to risk the weakening of this hand by doubling and having to draw a card.

Doubling A8, A9

We have two very strong totals here and do not want to risk our excellent chances of winning by attempting to double.

SPLITTING PAIRS

Splitting does two valuable things. It can turn one poor hand into two stronger hands, such as splitting a 16 (8-8) into hands of 8 each. It also doubles the bet. The decision to split requires a closer look at our hand vs. the dealer's hand, for we must balance the our hand's standing total against the two proposed split hands to see if the split and resultant doubling of the bet increases the winning expectation. Here's our thought process:

1. **How strong is our total as it stands?**
   Is the hand too powerful a total as it stands to risk breaking up? If not, we can consider the split.
2. **How strong are the two proposed split totals?**
   Thinking in terms of the 10 factor, we want to see if our split totals gravitate toward strong totals relative to the strength of the dealer's upcard, or if the split totals represent an improvement over the hard standing original hand.
3. **Does splitting either increase our chances of winning or reduce our rate of loss?**

These three factors are our guides in seeing if a split produces a gain for us.

Splitting Pairs - Single Deck Basic Strategy

These strategies are applicable to all Northern Nevada and Las Vegas single deck games. Note that single deck blackjack is rare or nonexistent outside the Nevada casinos. Multiple deck blackjack is the predominant style of play in casinos around the world.

Splitting Pairs
Northern Nevada & Las Vegas • Single Deck

	2	3	4	5	6	7	8	9	10	A
22		spl	spl	spl	spl	spl				
33			spl	spl	spl	spl				
66	spl	spl	spl	spl	spl					
77	spl	spl	spl	spl	spl	spl				
88	spl	spl	spl	spl	spl	spl	spl	spl	spl	spl
99	spl	spl	spl	spl	spl		spl	spl		
AA	spl	spl	spl	spl	spl	spl	spl	spl	spl	spl

spl = Split   Blank = Do Not Split

Do not split 44, 55, 10s. Always split 88, AA.

Splitting Pairs – Multiple Deck Basic Strategy

A. Las Vegas and Northern Nevada Multiple Deck – The standard game allows pair splitting on any two cards but does not allow doubling after splitting. (If the particular game allows doubling after splitting, use the chart following this one.)

Splitting Pairs
Las Vegas & Northern Nevada • Multiple Deck

	2	3	4	5	6	7	8	9	10	A
22			spl	spl	spl	spl				
33			spl	spl	spl	spl				
66		spl	spl	spl	spl					
77	spl	spl	spl	spl	spl	spl				
88	spl	spl	spl	spl	spl	spl	spl	spl	spl	spl
99	spl	spl	spl	spl	spl		spl	spl		
AA	spl	spl	spl	spl	spl	spl	spl	spl	spl	spl

spl = Split   Blank = Do Not Split

Do not split 44, 55, 10s. Always split 88, AA.

B. Atlantic City (and selected Nevada casinos where doubling down after splitting is permitted) – Because of the doubling after splitting rule, the player will split pairs more aggressively so that he can take advantage of good doubling situations that may arise as a consequence of the split.

Splitting Pairs
Atlantic City • Multiple Deck

	2	3	4	5	6	7	8	9	10	A
22	spl	spl	spl	spl	spl	spl				
33	spl	spl	spl	spl	spl	spl				
44				spl	spl					
66	spl	spl	spl	spl	spl					
77	spl	spl	spl	spl	spl	spl				
88	spl	spl	spl	spl	spl	spl	spl	spl	spl	spl
99	spl	spl	spl	spl	spl		spl	spl		
AA	spl	spl	spl	spl	spl	spl	spl	spl	spl	spl

spl = Split   Blank = Do Not Split
Do not split 55, 10s. Always split 88, AA.

C. European Style – Players will split less aggressively than the Atlantic City (and certainly the Nevada) casinos due to the no hole card rule. This chart assumes that doubling after splitting is not allowed.

D. European Style with Doubling After Splitting Allowed – Many international casinos allow doubling after splitting, and in those instances the player will double more aggressively than Nevada, but less aggressively than Atlantic City due to the no hole card rule.

Splitting Pairs
European Style Rules • Multiple Deck

	2	3	4	5	6	7	8	9	10	A
22			spl	spl	spl	spl				
33			spl	spl	spl	spl				
66		spl	spl	spl	spl					
77	spl	spl	spl	spl	spl	spl				
88	spl	spl	spl	spl	spl	spl	spl	spl		
99	spl	spl	spl	spl	spl		spl	spl		
AA		spl	spl	spl	spl	spl	spl	spl	spl	spl

spl = Split   Blank = Do Not Split
Do not split 44, 55, 10s.

Splitting Pairs
European Style Rules • Doubling After Splitting Allowed

	2	3	4	5	6	7	8	9	10	A
22	spl	spl	spl	spl	spl	spl				
33	spl	spl	spl	spl	spl	spl				
44				spl	spl					
66	spl	spl	spl	spl	spl					
77	spl	spl	spl	spl	spl	spl				
88	spl	spl	spl	spl	spl	spl	spl	spl		
99	spl	spl	spl	spl	spl		spl	spl		
AA		spl	spl	spl	spl	spl	spl	spl	spl	spl

spl = Split   Blank = Do Not Split
Do not split 55, 10s.

Conceptual Splitting

We will examine the decision to split 99 first, for it is a good example of the thinking process involved in splitting. First of all, we should note that this hand totaling 18 is only "fair," not a powerful total like a 19 or 20.

Splitting 99 – Dealer shows a 2, 3, 4, 5, 6

Split 99 against these dealer stiff cards. Our 18 is a winner, but splitting the hand into two halves of 9 each is a big gain. Each starting hand of 9, because of the 10 factor, gravitates toward strong player totals of 19. The high busting potential of the dealer stiff cards gives us an excellent opportunity to maximize our gain in an advantageous situation.

Splitting 99 – Dealer shows a 7

Stand with 99 vs. dealer 7. We figure the dealer for a 17. Our standing total of 18 is a stronger total and a big potential winner. While splitting 9s will also produce a positive expectation of winning, the risking of our fairly secure 18 against the 7 for two strong but chancy totals reduces the gain. We have the dealer beat. Stand.

Splitting 99 – Dealer shows an 8

Splitting 99 against the dealer's 8 is a big gain. Against the dealer's 8, we figure our 18 to be a potential push. However, by splitting the 18 into two separate hands of 9 each, we hope to turn our potential push into two possible winners. (Each 9 gravitates toward a total of 19, one point higher than the dealer's 18.)

Splitting 99 – Dealer shows a 9

Splitting 99 vs. the dealer's 9 is also a big gain. Against the 9, our 18 is a losing total, but splitting the 18 into two totals of 9 each reduces our potential loss. Rather than one losing total of 18, we will have two hands gravitating toward potential pushes.

Splitting 99 – Dealer shows a 10 or Ace

Do not split 99 against the dealer's 10 or ace. Our split hands of 9 each gravitate toward good totals, but against these more powerful dealer upcards, splitting would be a poor play. We do not want to make one loser into two.

Splitting 22 and 33

Split 22 vs. dealer 3 through 7*
Split 33 vs. dealer 4 through 7*
The high busting probabilities of the dealer 4, 5 and 6 makes the 22 and 33 good splits. We split 22 vs. 3 and not 33 vs. 3, because of the lower player busting factor of our split hands of 2 each. The drawing of a 10 gives us another chance to improve on our 2, for correct basic strategy is to draw 12 vs. 3, while the drawing of a 10 on our 3 forces us to stand.

We do not split 22 or 33 vs. the dealer's 2, because the dealer's 2 does not bust often enough to make splitting a profitable play.

Splitting 22 and 33 vs. 7 seems unusual at first, for this play seems to exceed our normal strategic boundaries of making aggressive plays against the weak dealer stiff cards. Though the 7 is a pat card and will make a lot of pat hands, the 7 will also make the weakest totals, only gravitating toward a total of 17. Our starting totals of 2 and 3 will make hands of 18 or better about one-half the time. Splitting 22 and 33 against the dealer's 7 will not make us money (because of the high busting factor of our hands), but they will produce a moderate gain over drawing to these hands.

Do not split 22 and 33 against the 8, 9, 10 or ace. We do not want to make one loser into two losers.

> *Nevada multiple deck exception - Do not split 22 vs. 3.
> *Atlantic City multiple deck exception (and games with doubling after splitting allowed) – Split 22 and 33 vs. 2 through 7.

Splitting 44

Do not split 44*. The hard total of 8 gravitates toward a total of 18, a far better position than two weak starting totals of 4 each. Against the dealer stiff cards, 2 through 6, we have a big gain by drawing to our 8. While the drawing of 10 will not give us an overwhelmingly strong total, an 18 is far better than drawing the same 10 to a split 4. We do not want to hold two weak hands of 4 each against the dealer pat cards, especially the dealer's 7 and 8, where we have a good starting total of 8.

> *Atlantic City exception (and games with doubling after splitting allowed) – Split 44 vs. 5 and 6.

Splitting 55

Never split 55. 55 by itself is an excellent starting total of 10. You do not want to break up this powerful player total into two terrible hands of 5 each. (Our 10 is an excellent doubling hand against dealer upcards of 2 through 9.)

Splitting 66

Split 66 against dealer stiff cards 2 through 6 only*. Our hard total of 12 is not very favorable, nor are the split hands of 6 and 6 too promising either. We have a losing hand either way against all dealer upcards. However, we want to minimize our losses.

Against the dealer stiff cards 2, 3, 4, 5 and 6, our split hands of 6 and 6 will sometimes draw cards to give us some pat totals 17-21.

Of course, we will often end up with stiff totals on the split pair (by the drawing of a 10 or other sufficiently large card) and be forced to stand. But the high dealer busting factor makes splitting 66 against the dealer stiffs a slight gain.

Obviously we will not split 66 against the dealer pat cards. We don't need two hands of 16 against a card that will bust only one time in four.

*Nevada multiple deck exception – Do not split 66 vs. 2.
*Atlantic City multiple deck (and games with doubling after splitting allowed) – No exceptions. Split 66 vs. 2-6.

Splitting 77

Split 77 against dealer upcards of 2, 3, 4, 5, 6 and 7. Against the dealer stiff cards 2 through 6, two playable hands of 7 and 7 are preferable to one stiff total of 14. Splitting 77 is not a strong split, for these totals only gravitate toward a 17, but the high busting rate of the dealer stiff cards makes this split a big gain.

Splitting 77 against the dealer's 7 is also an excellent split, for we are taking one losing total of 14 into two potential pushes of 17 each.

We do not split 77 vs. the dealer's 8, 9, 10, ace, for we do not want to take one poor total of 14 into two hands gravitating toward a second best total of only 17.

Splitting 88

Split 88 against all dealer upcards. Against the dealer's 2 through 8, we are taking one terrible hand of 16 into two playable totals of 8 each. There is a tremendous gain on all these plays.

Splitting 88 against the dealer's 9, 10, A are the strangest of the basic strategy plays. Using all of the intuitive knowledge we have developed, at first glance we would reason that this is a poor split, for we are making two losers out of one. However, more is involved in this play.

First, you must realize that the player hand of 16 is the worst total possible. While splitting this 16 into two hands of 8 and 8 is not a winning situation against the strong dealer upcards of 9, 10 and A, it is an improvement over our very weak total of hard 16. Bear with this unusual play, for computer simulation studies have played out the hand millions of times for both drawing and splitting, and found that the player loses less by splitting 88. Realize that although the split is weak, it does produce a gain over drawing to our easily bustable 16.

In games employing the no hole card rule, do not split 8s against the dealer's 10 and ace. With the possibility of the dealer getting a blackjack, we don't need more money out on this hand. Hit instead.

Splitting 10,10

Do not split 10s. The hard total of 20 is a winning hand against all dealer upcards. Splitting 10s against any dealer upcard is a terrible play, for you are taking one "solid" winning hand into two good but uncertain wins. Too often, the splitting of 10s will draw low cards, in effect destroying a great hand.

Splitting AA

Split AA against all dealer upcards. Each ace is a powerful starting total of 11 points. If we draw the 10, our 21 can't be beat. Splitting AA is a tremendous gain against all dealer upcards.

In no hole card rule games, we will not split aces when the dealer shows an ace. The high likelihood of the dealer getting a blackjack when he already has an ace is too costly for us to double our bet. Draw instead.

Master Chart
Northern Nevada • Single Deck

	2	3	4	5	6	7	8	9	10	A
7/less	H	H	H	H	H	H	H	H	H	H
8	H	H	H	H	H	H	H	H	H	H
9	H	H	H	H	H	H	H	H	H	H
10	D	D	D	D	D	D	D	D	H	H
11	D	D	D	D	D	D	D	D	D	D
12	H	H	S	S	S	H	H	H	H	H
13	S	S	S	S	S	H	H	H	H	H
14	S	S	S	S	S	H	H	H	H	H
15	S	S	S	S	S	H	H	H	H	H
16	S	S	S	S	S	H	H	H	H	H
A2	H	H	H	H	H	H	H	H	H	H
A3	H	H	H	H	H	H	H	H	H	H
A4	H	H	H	H	H	H	H	H	H	H
A5	H	H	H	H	H	H	H	H	H	H
A6	H	H	H	H	H	H	H	H	H	H
A7	S	S	S	S	S	S	S	H	H	H
A8	S	S	S	S	S	S	S	S	S	S
A9	S	S	S	S	S	S	S	S	S	S
22	H	spl	spl	spl	spl	spl	H	H	H	H
33	H	H	spl	spl	spl	spl	H	H	H	H
66	spl	spl	spl	spl	spl	H	H	H	H	H
77	spl	spl	spl	spl	spl	spl	H	H	H	H
88	spl	spl	spl	spl	spl	spl	spl	spl	spl	spl
99	spl	spl	spl	spl	spl	S	spl	spl	S	S
AA	spl	spl	spl	spl	spl	spl	spl	spl	spl	spl

H = Hit   S = Stand   D = Double   spl = Split
Do not split 44, 55 (double on 55) and 10s. Always split 88 and AA.

Master Chart
Las Vegas • Single Deck

	2	3	4	5	6	7	8	9	10	A
7/less	H	H	H	H	H	H	H	H	H	H
62	H	H	H	H	H	H	H	H	H	H
44/53	H	H	H	D	D	H	H	H	H	H
9	D	D	D	D	D	H	H	H	H	H
10	D	D	D	D	D	D	D	D	H	H
11	D	D	D	D	D	D	D	D	D	D
12	H	H	S	S	S	H	H	H	H	H
13	S	S	S	S	S	H	H	H	H	H
14	S	S	S	S	S	H	H	H	H	H
15	S	S	S	S	S	H	H	H	H	H
16	S	S	S	S	S	H	H	H	H	H
A2	H	H	D	D	D	H	H	H	H	H
A3	H	H	D	D	D	H	H	H	H	H
A4	H	H	D	D	D	H	H	H	H	H
A5	H	H	D	D	D	H	H	H	H	H
A6	D	D	D	D	D	H	H	H	H	H
A7	S	D	D	D	D	S	S	H	H	H
A8	S	S	S	S	S	S	S	S	S	S
A9	S	S	S	S	S	S	S	S	S	S
22	H	spl	spl	spl	spl	spl	H	H	H	H
33	H	H	spl	spl	spl	spl	H	H	H	H
66	spl	spl	spl	spl	spl	H	H	H	H	H
77	spl	spl	spl	spl	spl	spl	H	H	H	H
88	spl	spl	spl	spl	spl	spl	spl	spl	spl	spl
99	spl	spl	spl	spl	spl	S	spl	spl	S	S
AA	spl	spl	spl	spl	spl	spl	spl	spl	spl	spl

H = Hit   S = Stand   D= Double   spl = Split

Do not split 44, 55 (double on 55) and 10s. Always split 88 and AA.

We just looked at the strategies for single deck blackjack in Nevada. Let's now see how the multiple deck game is different.

THE DIFFERENCE BETWEEN SINGLE AND MULTIPLE DECK BLACKJACK

The greater number of cards used in a multiple deck game makes the removal of particular cards less important for composition change purposes and, as a result, our doubling and splitting strategies are less aggressive.

For example, the removal of three cards (5,3,5) creates a favorable imbalance for the player in a single deck game and makes a 53 double vs. the dealer's 5 a profitable play. Not only will these cards be poor draws for the player's double but they're three cards the dealer needs to improve his hand. The effective removal of these three cards gives the player a better chance of drawing a 10 on his 8 and, at the same time, increases the dealer's chance of busting. In a single deck game, 53 vs. 6 is a favorable double.

However, the removal of these three cards are barely felt in a multiple deck game. There are 29 other 3s and 5s in a four deck game as compared to only five in a single deck. Thus, no favorable imbalance has been created, and the double down is not a correct play. This lack of sensitivity to particular card removal accounts for nine strategy changes in the multiple deck game from the single deck strategies we just presented.

Except for these nine changes in the doubling and splitting strategies, multiple deck basic strategy is identical to the single deck basic strategy.

In a multiple deck game:

1	Do not double hard 8 vs. 5	hit instead
2	Do not double hard 8 vs. 6	hit instead
3	Do not double hard 9 vs. 2	hit instead
4	Do not double hard 11 vs. ace	hit instead
5	Do not double A2 vs. 4	hit instead
6	Do not double A3 vs. 4	hit instead
7	Do not double A6 vs. 2	hit instead
8	Do not split 22 vs. 3	hit instead
9	Do not split 66 vs. 2	hit instead

Master Chart
Northern Nevada • Multiple Deck

	2	3	4	5	6	7	8	9	10	A
7/less	H	H	H	H	H	H	H	H	H	H
8	H	H	H	H	H	H	H	H	H	H
9	H	H	H	H	H	H	H	H	H	H
10	D	D	D	D	D	D	D	D	H	H
11	D	D	D	D	D	D	D	D	D	H
12	H	H	S	S	S	H	H	H	H	H
13	S	S	S	S	S	H	H	H	H	H
14	S	S	S	S	S	H	H	H	H	H
15	S	S	S	S	S	H	H	H	H	H
16	S	S	S	S	S	H	H	H	H	H
A2	H	H	H	H	H	H	H	H	H	H
A3	H	H	H	H	H	H	H	H	H	H
A4	H	H	H	H	H	H	H	H	H	H
A5	H	H	H	H	H	H	H	H	H	H
A6	H	H	H	H	H	H	H	H	H	H
A7	S	S	S	S	S	S	S	H	H	H
A8	S	S	S	S	S	S	S	S	S	S
A9	S	S	S	S	S	S	S	S	S	S
22	H	H	spl	spl	spl	spl	H	H	H	H
33	H	H	spl	spl	spl	spl	H	H	H	H
66	H	spl	spl	spl	spl	H	H	H	H	H
77	spl	spl	spl	spl	spl	spl	H	H	H	H
88	spl	spl	spl	spl	spl	spl	spl	spl	spl	spl
99	spl	spl	spl	spl	spl	S	spl	spl	S	S
AA	spl	spl	spl	spl	spl	spl	spl	spl	spl	spl

H = Hit   S = Stand   D= Double   spl = Split

Do not split 44, 55, 10s. Always split 88, AA.

Master Chart
Las Vegas • Multiple Deck

	2	3	4	5	6	7	8	9	10	A
7/less	H	H	H	H	H	H	H	H	H	H
8	H	H	H	H	H	H	H	H	H	H
9	H	D	D	D	D	H	H	H	H	H
10	D	D	D	D	D	D	D	D	H	H
11	D	D	D	D	D	D	D	D	D	H
12	H	H	S	S	S	H	H	H	H	H
13	S	S	S	S	S	H	H	H	H	H
14	S	S	S	S	S	H	H	H	H	H
15	S	S	S	S	S	H	H	H	H	H
16	S	S	S	S	S	H	H	H	H	H
A2	H	H	H	D	D	H	H	H	H	H
A3	H	H	H	D	D	H	H	H	H	H
A4	H	H	D	D	D	H	H	H	H	H
A5	H	H	D	D	D	H	H	H	H	H
A6	H	D	D	D	D	H	H	H	H	H
A7	S	D	D	D	D	S	S	H	H	H
A8	S	S	S	S	S	S	S	S	S	S
A9	S	S	S	S	S	S	S	S	S	S
22	H	H	spl	spl	spl	spl	H	H	H	H
33	H	H	spl	spl	spl	spl	H	H	H	H
66	H	spl	spl	spl	spl	H	H	H	H	H
77	spl	spl	spl	spl	spl	spl	H	H	H	H
88	spl	spl	spl	spl	spl	spl	spl	spl	spl	spl
99	spl	spl	spl	spl	spl	S	spl	spl	S	S
AA	spl	spl	spl	spl	spl	spl	spl	spl	spl	spl

H = Hit   S = Stand   D= Double   spl = Split
Do not split 44, 55, 10s. Always split 88, AA.

ATLANTIC CITY MULTIPLE DECK

The blackjack games offered in Atlantic City differ from the Nevada games in several ways. For one thing, all the Atlantic City games are dealt as multiple deck games. They do not offer single deck games as in Nevada. Doubling allowed after splitting is standard in Atlantic City as opposed to Nevada, where only a few casinos offer this option. Resplitting of pairs is not allowed in Atlantic City. Nevada casinos generally allow the player to resplit pairs as often as they wish.

To protect against collusion between the player and the dealer, the dealer does not check his hole card for a blackjack (as is standard in Nevada) until all the players have finished playing their hands. This safeguard does not affect the player's chances of winning, for if the dealer does indeed have a blackjack, any additional money the player wagered on a doubled or split hand will be returned. Only the original bet loses.

Another difference is that all player hands are dealt face up in Atlantic City. No casinos allow the player to physically handle the cards. The player must employ hand signals to convey his strategy intentions to the dealer. (Single and double deck games in Nevada are generally face down games where the player can handle his cards, while multiple deck games are played similarly to the Atlantic City face up game.)

The Atlantic City basic strategy is the same as Nevada multiple deck strategy except for more frequent pair splitting due to the player being allowed to double after splits.

EUROPEAN NO HOLE CARD RULES

These strategies are for multiple deck play and take into account that players may only double on totals of 9, 10 and 11, and also will double and split less aggressively when the dealer shows a 10 or ace due to the no hole card rule. In games that allow doubling after splitting, the player will split more aggressively to take advantage of this favorable option. We'll also show that strategy in a master chart.

Master Chart
Atlantic City • Multiple Deck

	2	3	4	5	6	7	8	9	10	A
7/less	H	H	H	H	H	H	H	H	H	H
8	H	H	H	H	H	H	H	H	H	H
9	H	D	D	D	D	H	H	H	H	H
10	D	D	D	D	D	D	D	D	H	H
11	D	D	D	D	D	D	D	D	D	H
12	H	H	S	S	S	H	H	H	H	H
13	S	S	S	S	S	H	H	H	H	H
14	S	S	S	S	S	H	H	H	H	H
15	S	S	S	S	S	H	H	H	H	H
16	S	S	S	S	S	H	H	H	H	H
A2	H	H	H	D	D	H	H	H	H	H
A3	H	H	H	D	D	H	H	H	H	H
A4	H	H	D	D	D	H	H	H	H	H
A5	H	H	D	D	D	H	H	H	H	H
A6	H	D	D	D	D	H	H	H	H	H
A7	S	D	D	D	D	S	S	H	H	H
A8	S	S	S	S	S	S	S	S	S	S
A9	S	S	S	S	S	S	S	S	S	S
22	spl	spl	spl	spl	spl	spl	H	H	H	H
33	spl	spl	spl	spl	spl	spl	H	H	H	H
44	H	H	H	spl	spl	H	H	H	H	H
66	spl	spl	spl	spl	spl	H	H	H	H	H
77	spl	spl	spl	spl	spl	spl	H	H	H	H
88	spl	spl	spl	spl	spl	spl	spl	spl	spl	spl
99	spl	spl	spl	spl	spl	S	spl	spl	S	S
AA	spl	spl	spl	spl	spl	spl	spl	spl	spl	spl

H = Hit   S = Stand   D = Double   spl = Split
Do not split 55, 10s. Always split 88, AA.

Master Chart
European No Hole Card Style • Multiple Deck

	2	3	4	5	6	7	8	9	10	A
7/less	H	H	H	H	H	H	H	H	H	H
8	H	H	H	H	H	H	H	H	H	H
9	H	D	D	D	D	H	H	H	H	H
10	D	D	D	D	D	D	D	D	H	H
11	D	D	D	D	D	D	D	D	H	H
12	H	H	S	S	S	H	H	H	H	H
13	S	S	S	S	S	H	H	H	H	H
14	S	S	S	S	S	H	H	H	H	H
15	S	S	S	S	S	H	H	H	H	H
16	S	S	S	S	S	H	H	H	H	H
A2	H	H	H	H	H	H	H	H	H	H
A3	H	H	H	H	H	H	H	H	H	H
A4	H	H	H	H	H	H	H	H	H	H
A5	H	H	H	H	H	H	H	H	H	H
A6	H	H	H	H	H	H	H	H	H	H
A7	S	S	S	S	S	S	S	H	H	H
A8	S	S	S	S	S	S	S	S	S	S
A9	S	S	S	S	S	S	S	S	S	S
22	H	H	spl	spl	spl	spl	H	H	H	H
33	H	H	spl	spl	spl	spl	H	H	H	H
66	H	spl	spl	spl	spl	H	H	H	H	H
77	spl	spl	spl	spl	spl	spl	H	H	H	H
88	spl	spl	spl	spl	spl	spl	spl	spl	H	H
99	spl	spl	spl	spl	spl	S	spl	spl	S	S
AA	spl	spl	spl	spl	spl	spl	spl	spl	spl	H

H = Hit   S = Stand   D = Double   spl = Split
Do not split 44, 55, 10s.

Master Chart
European No Hole Card: Doubling After Splitting Allowed

	2	3	4	5	6	7	8	9	10	A
7/less	H	H	H	H	H	H	H	H	H	H
8	H	H	H	H	H	H	H	H	H	H
9	H	D	D	D	D	H	H	H	H	H
10	D	D	D	D	D	D	D	D	H	H
11	D	D	D	D	D	D	D	D	H	H
12	H	H	S	S	S	H	H	H	H	H
13	S	S	S	S	S	H	H	H	H	H
14	S	S	S	S	S	H	H	H	H	H
15	S	S	S	S	S	H	H	H	H	H
16	S	S	S	S	S	H	H	H	H	H
A2	H	H	H	H	H	H	H	H	H	H
A3	H	H	H	H	H	H	H	H	H	H
A4	H	H	H	H	H	H	H	H	H	H
A5	H	H	H	H	H	H	H	H	H	H
A6	H	H	H	H	H	H	H	H	H	H
A7	S	S	S	S	S	S	S	H	H	H
A8	S	S	S	S	S	S	S	S	S	S
A9	S	S	S	S	S	S	S	S	S	S
22	spl	spl	spl	spl	spl	spl	H	H	H	H
33	spl	spl	spl	spl	spl	spl	H	H	H	H
44	H	H	H	spl	spl	H	H	H	H	H
66	spl	spl	spl	spl	spl	H	H	H	H	H
77	spl	spl	spl	spl	spl	spl	H	H	H	H
88	spl	spl	spl	spl	spl	spl	spl	spl	H	H
99	spl	spl	spl	spl	spl	S	spl	spl	S	S
AA	spl	spl	spl	spl	spl	spl	spl	spl	spl	H

H = Hit   S = Stand   D = Double   spl = Split
Do not split 55, 10s.

PLAYER'S OPTIONS

Use these strategies where the following variations are permitted:

Doubling Down Permitted After Splitting

A standard option in Atlantic City, Great Britain and many casinos around the world, but offered only in a few Nevada casinos. It allows the player to double down on one or more of the hands resulting from a split according to the standard doubling rules of the casino. This option allows us to split more aggressively so that we may take advantage of good doubling situations that can arise as a consequence of the split. This option is favorable to the player.

Our Hand		Single Deck	Multiple Deck
22	split against	2-7	2-7
33	split against	2-7	2-7
44	split against	4-6	5-6
66	split against	2-7	2-6
77	split against	2-8	2-7

Late Surrender (Surrender)

A player option to forfeit his hand and lose half his bet after it has been determined that the dealer does not have a blackjack. This option is favorable to the player.

Our Hand		Single Deck	Multiple Deck
16*	surrender against	10, A	9,10, A
15	surrender against	10	10
77	surrender against	10	—

* Do not surrender 88 (split)

Early Surrender

A player option to forfeit his hand and lose half his bet before the dealer checks for a blackjack. An extremely valuable option for the player. No longer offered in Atlantic City.

Dealer's Upcard		Player's Totals
A	early surrender with	5-7, 12-17
10	early surrender with	14-16
9	early surrender with	16*

*Do not early surrender 88 (split). Do not surrender soft totals.

THE WINNING EDGE

The removal of cards during play and the continued dealing from a deck depleted of these used cards creates a situation in blackjack where the odds of receiving particular cards or combinations of those cards constantly change during the course of the game. Computer studies have found that the removal of certain cards during play gives the player an advantage over the house, while the removal of others gives the house an advantage over the player.

Therefore, as cards are removed from play, the player's chances of winning constantly change. Sometimes the depleted deck of cards will favor the house and sometimes the player. By learning to analyze a depleted deck of cards for favorability, and capitalizing on this situation by betting more when the remaining cards are in your favor, you can actually have an edge over the casino.

The heart of all winning systems at blackjack is based on this theory—bet more when you have the advantage, and less when the house has the advantage. This way, when you win, you win more, and when you lose, you lose less. Beginning with an even game (playing accurate basic strategy), this "maximize gain, minimize loss" betting strategy will give the player an overall edge on the house.

How do we determine when we have the edge? Computer studies have determined that 10s and aces are the most valuable cards for the player, while the small cards, 2 through 7, are the most valuable cards for the house, 8s and 9s being relatively neutral. Off the top of the deck, with all cards still in play, the player has an even game with the house—neither side enjoys an advantage.*

The odds shift in favor of the player when there is a higher ratio of 9s, 10s and As in the deck than normal, and shift in favor of the house when there is a higher ratio of small cards, 2 through 7, than normal. All counting systems base their winning strategies on keeping track of the ratio of high cards to low cards. The systems vary in complexity from the very simple to the very complicated, all being based on the same principle—betting more when there is a higher proportion of high cards in the deck.

*Assuming the player plays perfect basic strategy, and that the game is a single deck game with the favorable Las Vegas Strip rules. If the particular game has less liberal rules (Northern Nevada) or is a multiple deck game, the house will enjoy a slight initial edge.

However, there are many blackjack players that wish to have an edge over the house but are loathe to learn counting systems. For the player that desires to win without counting cards, the Cardoza School of Blackjack has developed some simple but effective techniques.

THE CARDOZA NON-COUNTER'S EDGE

The system is simple. All you need to know is that high cards favor us and the small cards favor the house. When there are more high cards in the deck than normal, you will bet more. But you need not count cards. All you need to do is to keep your eyes open and watch the cards, just as you probably do anyway.

Here are 5 easy guidelines for the non-counter to have an edge:

1. When a great many small cards have been played in the first round, it is to the player's advantage. Bet 3 or 4 units instead of your normal 1 or 2 unit bet. (If $5 is your standard bet, then $15 is considered a 3 unit bet.) Example: The following cards have been played. You had an 8, 5, 6, one player had 10, 6, 2, another player had 10, 6, 5 and the dealer had a 10, 7. A disproportionate number of small cards have been played, meaning the remaining cards are richer in high cards—to the player's advantage. So you bet more.

2. If on succeeding rounds, you estimate that there are still a disproportionate number of high cards remaining, continue to bet at a higher level than your minimum or neutral bet. Through practical experience, you will be able to improve on your estimation abilities.

3. If the cumulative distribution of cards seems to be fairly normal after a round of play, bet your neutral or minimum bet (1 or 2 units, whatever your preference is). If, however, you notice that no aces have appeared, increase your bet by one unit. Your potential to get a blackjack has increased. While the dealer's chances of getting a blackjack has increased as well, he only gets paid even-money; you get paid 3 to 2.

4. On the other hand, if a disproportionate number of high cards appear in the first round, then place your minimum 1 unit bet, for the house has an edge. And if on succeeding rounds you judge that there is still a disproportionate number of small cards remaining, continue to place your minimum bets.

5. If the cumulative distribution of cards appears to be normal and you notice that more aces have appeared than what you normally would expect (one ace for every 13 cards is the normal composition), you want to downgrade your bet to one unit if you had been making 2 unit bets.

To sum up, when there are more 10s and aces remaining in the deck than normal, increase your bet. When there are fewer 10s and aces than normal (meaning more small cards than normal), decrease your bet. Every time the deck is shuffled, start your estimation of favorability over again.

The Power of Your Advantage

The Cardoza Non-Counter strategy gives the player an advantage powerful enough to give the $5-$20 bettor close to a $100 profit expectancy in a heavy weekend of play in a single deck game, and the $25-$100 bettor a $500 expectancy of winning. Now that you have the winning edge on the house, time will work to your advantage. The longer you play, the more money you can expect to make.

The Cardoza Non-Counter strategy is most effective in single deck games, and less so in double decks, due to the fewer number of cards compared to four deck or more games. The advantage of this strategy is that you can win with much less mental effort than the counting systems require. Obviously we cannot win as much without counting cards, but we will win.

The strategy is less effective in four, six and eight deck games where the overall number of the cards is less susceptible to composition changes from just a few cards being removed.

For multiple deck players, the news is not all bad though, for the basic strategies that we have presented in this book will bring you very close to an even game against the casino. Should you ever decide to improve your game further by learning a professional strategy, you must know these basic strategies anyway. They are 100% correct for single and multiple deck games, and the absolute best available.

Readers desiring to further their edge over the house and make more money playing blackjack, must learn a professional counting or non-counting system. We have developed several casino-tested strategies for use under actual playing conditions. The first and most powerful, the Cardoza Base Count Strategy is surprisingly easy to use, but for those players intimidated by counting, we have developed a new strategy that gives non-counting players the mathematical edge over the casino in multiple deck games. This strategy, more than 15 years in development, is our own research and is only available through Cardoza Publishing. (See the ads in the back of the book for information on buying these pro-level strategies.)

Getting the Most Out of the Cardoza Non-Counter Strategy

For those players that will be playing in Nevada, or other areas where there is a choice, it will be to your advantage to play in a single deck game rather than a multiple deck one for the following two reasons:

1. The single deck game is inherently more favorable.

2. The Cardoza Non-Counter strategy is most effective in a single deck game because the single deck game is highly sensitive to composition changes.

For those players who are accessible only to multiple deck games, you have two choices if you want to have the mathematical advantage over a multiple deck game. Choice number one is to purchase the *Cardoza Non-Counter Multiple Deck* Strategy discussed above. This will give you an edge of about 1/2 - 1%. Serious players who want to work just a little harder for the maximum edge possible, 1-3% over the casino, must learn the *Cardoza Base Count Strategy*. *(See back pages.)* However, before anything else, you must learn the material in this book. These basic strategies are the foundation for any winning approach.

BET RANGE

I recommend a bet range of 1-4 units. Thus, if $5 is your standard bet, your maximum bet should not exceed $20. This is an important guideline to adhere to for several reasons:

- Your advantage will rarely be large enough to warrant a bet larger than 4 units. We have bankroll limitations to consider, and do not want greed to be our downfall. Keep in mind that blackjack is a slow grind for the good players.
- Raising your bets in advantageous situations to a range greater than 1-4 will attract undue attention to you as a skillful player, and the casino may begin to shuffle every time you make a large bet, in effect shuffling away advantageous situations.
- You do not want to have one extremely large losing bet destroy an otherwise good session at the table.
- The losing of a huge bet will generally have a very detrimental effect on your confidence, your concentration and your ability to think clearly. You will be surprised at how fast this can affect your physical and psychological frame of being.
- The ranging of your bets from 1 unit in disadvantageous situations to 4 units in highly advantageous situations is a wide enough bet spread to maximize your gains while at the same time minimizing your risk.

TIPPING

Tipping, or **toking**, as it is called in casino parlance, should be viewed as a gratuitous gesture by the player to a dealer he feels has given him good service. Toking is totally at the player's discretion, and in no way should be considered an obligation. It is not the player's duty to support casino employees.

If you toke, toke only when you're winning, and only to dealers that are friendly and helpful to you. Do not toke dealers that you don't like or ones that try to make you feel guilty about not tipping. Dealers that make playing an unpleasant experience for you deserve nothing.

The best way to tip a dealer is to place a bet for the dealer in front of your own bet, so that his chances of winning that toke are tied up with your hand. If the hand is won, you both win together; if the hand is lost, you lose together. By being partners on the hand, you establish camaraderie with the dealer. Naturally, he or she will be rooting for you to win. This is the best way to tip, for when you win, the dealer wins double—the tip amount you bet plus the winnings from that bet.

CHEATING

It is my belief that cheating is not a problem in the major American gambling centers, though I would not totally eliminate the possibility. If you ever feel uncomfortable about the honesty of a game, stop playing. Though you probably are being dealt an honest game, the anxiety of being uncomfortable is not worth the action.

Do not confuse bad luck with being cheated, or a dealer's mistake as chicanery. Dealers have a difficult job and work hard. They are bound to make honest mistakes. If you find yourself shorted on a payoff, bring it immediately to the dealer's attention and the mistake will be corrected.

BANKROLLING

The following bankroll requirements have been prepared to give the player enough capital to survive any reasonable losing streak, and be able to bounce back on top.

In the following table, flat betting refers to betting the same amount every time. When ranging bets from 1-4, the player needs a larger bankroll, for more money is bet.

Bankroll Requirements

Hours to Play	Bet Range	Bankroll Needed
10	Flat	50 units
20+	Flat	100 units
10	1-4	150 units
20+	1-4	200 units

If you plan on playing for an extended weekend's worth of play (20 hours or more) at $5-$20 a hand, you should bring $1,000 with you, while if you are only planning to play 10 hours at those stakes, $750 will give you a fairly safe margin.

This does not mean that you will lose this money playing $5-$20. Using the Cardoza Non-Counter betting strategy, you will have an edge on the house in a single deck game, and your expectancy is to win money every time you go.* However, it is important that the reader be aware that losing streaks occur, and the losing of $500-$600 is a possibility, though admittedly small. If the thought of losing amounts comparable to this during a downswing scares you, then you should not play $5-$20 a hand, for you are betting over your head.

Again, bet within your financial and emotional means, and you will never regret a single session at the tables.

If you have a definite amount of money to play with and want to figure out how much your unit size bet should be, simply take your gambling stake and divide it by the amount of units you need to have.

Thus, if you bring $500 with you, and plan to play for 10 hours ranging your bets from 1-4, divide $500 by 150 units (see chart: bankroll needed column) and you will wager about $3 a hand. Betting more than $3 as a unit would be overbetting, and leaving yourself vulnerable to the risks discussed earlier.

---

* If playing a multiple deck game, the house will enjoy only a slight advantage over the player if following our strategies. You must learn the Cardoza Non-Counter Multiple Deck Strategy (for non-counters) or The Cardoza Base Count Strategy (for counters) to enjoy an edge over the casino in a multiple deck game.

Table Bankroll

How much money should you bring to the table?

My recommendation is that your bring 30 units to the table each time you play. If playing $5 units, bring $150; if $2 units, bring $60. $25 bettors should bring $750. $100 bettors should sit down with $3,000.

You can bring less if you want. If flat betting, 15 units will suffice. If your bet range is from 1-4, 20 units will do the trick. However, do not bring more money to the table. 30 units is enough to cover normal swings, and you never want to lose more than that in any one sitting.

SUMMARY

Blackjack is a game of skill that can be beat. However, to win, you must learn the game properly. Take you time reading this section and practicing your skills at home.

In a nutshell, here's the winning formula: Learn your basic strategies perfectly, apply the Cardoza Non-Counter betting strategy and pay careful attention to the advice offered in the money management section. This will give you the knowledge and skills to be a consistent winner at the blackjack tables and the basic strategy skills needed to move on to the professional level strategies advertised in the back of this book, strategies which will make the casinos fear your play.

If nothing else however, get the Basic Strategies down cold and get ready to win the casino's money!

Spanish 21

FIVE KEYS TO SPANISH 21

1 Though Spanish 21 is similar to blackjack, it is not blackjack, so be sure to learn the proper strategies for this game.

2 Be aware when you are eligible for a five, six, or seven card bonus.

3 Always make the aggressive doubling and splitting plays when it is correct to make those moves, regardless of what happened the last time you put the extra money on the felt. Playing scared will hurt your chances of winning.

4 Remember that you can surrender your extra chips even after doubling down—but do so only when it is the right play.

5 Learn the strategies to get the best chances of winning.

INTRODUCTION

Spanish 21 was introduced to Nevada casinos as a way to spice up the traditional blackjack game and get more action to the tables. At first glance, this blackjack variant looks like the same game except with a host of attractive and favorable options. It is played on a standard blackjack table in the same type of setting and typically dealt out of a six or eight deck shoe.

But there's a rub: all the tens have been removed from the deck! After the aces, the tens cards are the most valuable cards in the deck for a player. The other ten-value cards—the jacks, queens, and kings—are still there, but taking four tens out of every fifty-two cards is a tremendous disadvantage to the player that is only partially made up for by the favorable player options.

THE BASICS

Spanish 21 is played just like regular blackjack. Each player gets dealt two cards to start and has the following options:

Stand: Take no more cards

Hit: Draw additional cards one at a time

Split: Take two cards of equal value into two hands which are played separately, with an additional bet of equal value to the original one placed on the new hand.

Double down: To double the bet on a hand and receive one and only one additional card.

Hands may also be resplit, even aces. So if you split A-A, and get a third ace, you can split the hand one more time, playing each of the hands separately.

The dealer also gets two cards, one face down and hidden from the players, the other face up and exposed. Players make decisions based on their two cards and information they gleam from the dealer's upcard.

All cards are counted at face value, for example, a two of clubs is equal to 2 points and a nine of hearts is equal to 9 points. The picture cards are equal to ten points. aces can count as 1 point or 11. A hand of A-5 is called soft 16 since the ace can count as 11 points or one point. If a king is drawn, the ace would count as one point giving the player a hard 16. If a player gets more than 21 points, he busts and is an automatic loser, even if the dealer busts out afterwards. So if one more king or jack or even a 6 is drawn to the 16, the hand would bust and be an automatic loser.

When the players have finished taking their turns, it is the dealer's turn to play. He must take cards according to the prescribed rules of the game: draw cards up to a hand of 17 points and then stand. In most jurisdictions, if the dealer makes a hand of soft 17, that is, when the ace is used as an 11 to make 17, then the dealer must continue drawing to get to at least a hard 17 points. For example, if the dealer has an ace and a 6 for a soft 17, he would have to draw when the rules of the table require it. If a queen is then drawn, he must stand as he has a hard 17. If the dealer busts, all players left in the hand automatically win.

If both the player and the dealer have the same total, the hand is a push—a tie—and the player gets to keep his bet. There is one exception to this and it works in favor of the player. If both the player and the dealer have a multiple card 21, the player wins. (If either side has a natural, then the one holding that natural is an automatic winner. However, if both the player and the dealer hold a natural, the player will win.

Won bets are paid at even money, 1 to 1; for every $1 bet, the player wins $1. Or if the hand is lost, a player loses only what was bet. However, if the player gets a natural—an ace with a jack, queen, or king—on the first two cards, he gets paid 3 to

2. If the dealer has a natural at the same time, the player *still* gets the 3 to 2 payoff. (In regular blackjack, the hand would be a push instead.)

BONUS OPTIONS

There are some great options in Spanish 21 that make it exciting for regular blackjack converts. First, you can double down on any number of cards, not only on your first two cards. So if you start out with a 5 and a 3 and get dealt another 3, you can double down! Or if you're dealt a 3 and a 2, get dealt another 2, and then a 4, you can still double down. You can also double down after splitting. For example, if you've split 8-8 and get dealt a 2 on your first 8 for a total of 10, you can put additional chips on the felt and double down on that split hand. You can also double down on the other split hand if you so choose.

An additional attractive feature is the late surrender option. You can not only surrender your hand and forfeit half your bet if you don't like your initial two cards, but even *after* doubling down! Let's say you double down on an 11 and receive a 5. You may exercise the surrender option by forfeiting your hand and taking the doubled bet back, losing only the original wager.

Bonuses

In addition to the favorable options shown above, you'll receive bonus payouts for five, six, and seven card 21s

Following are the extra payouts that can be won in Spanish 21:

Bonus Hand	Payout
Five-Card 21*	3 to 2
Six-Card Hand*	2 to 1
Seven-Card 21*	3 to 1
6-7-8 Same Suit	2 to 1
6-7-8- All Spades	3 to 1
6-7-8 Mixed Suits	3 to 2
Three 7s Same Suit	2 to 1
Three 7s All Spades	3 to 1
Three 7s Mixed Suits	3 to 2

*Bonuses are not paid if the hand was doubled down on.

There is also a Super Bonus if you get a 7-7-7 hand all of the same suit and the dealer also holds a 7 (provided that it is not reached through a split or doubled play). The super bonus will be $1,000 if the original bet is $5 up to $24.50 and $5,000 if the original bet is $25 or more. In both cases, other players at the table who placed a bet that round will receive an envy bonus of $50. Some casinos have a different super bonus. In these cases, they'll pay $1,000 for every $5 bet up to a $25 bet ($5,000 maximum).

You'll see that pretty much all of the bonuses are on high risk hands, ones that the player can bust on with a draw.

STRATEGY

With perfect play, you can get the house edge between 0.4% and 0.8%, depending upon the particular rules in play. When the dealer stands on all 17s, the edge will be closer to the .4%, and when he hits soft 17 (which is unfavorable for the player—you would rather he stands), than it is closer to 0.8%. However, unless you really dig into a complicated playing strategy, you should figure an edge of around 1% to be more likely as a casual player.

In this chapter, I'm going to recommend a simplified strategy because the full-on correct strategy is very complicated, well beyond what the average player will want to digest just to get a good game against the house. The problem is that the correct strategy varies depending upon the number of cards drawn and it gets so complicated that few players would want to go through all that effort just to get the edge down an additional few tenths of a percentage point. For example, with a two-card soft 17, you would double down against a dealer's 4, but if it's a three card 17, correct strategy would be to only hit.

These kinds of complexities occur for all sorts of hitting, standing, doubling, splitting, and surrender situations and would make the entire task of memorizing complicated. If you're going to put all that effort in, you may as well do so at blackjack and learn a card counting strategy which can actually give you the edge.

Keeping that in mind, here is a simplified strategy set of strategy plays to give you a relatively solid game against Spanish 21.

The Simplified Strategy

The removal of the four 10s from the deck makes it a lot harder to draw a card valued at ten points. Rather than sixteen ten-value cards per deck (four each of the 10 through king), there are now only twelve of them, 25 percent fewer than a regular deck. Due to the altered balance of tens—which are good cards for the player to have in the deck—you'll see that the strategy you use at regular blackjack games does not apply at Spanish 21.

As a result of fewer tens, basic strategy calls for less aggressive play in doubling down and splitting situations than you would exercise in standard blackjack games. But at the same time, with fewer tens to bust hands, you'll be more aggressive with stiff hands (hard 12-16) since there are fewer tens to bust with.

Note that there are fewer blackjacks drawn in Spanish 21 than in blackjack (one in every twenty-four hands as opposed to one in every twenty-one).

There are some similarities between Spanish 21 and blackjack as you'll see, but you'll have to learn the specific strategies as applies to this game.

Following is the simplified strategy:

Hitting and Standing
Draw on hard 5 to 9
Hit on 10 and 11 versus 9 through ace
Hit 12, 13, 14 versus all upcards
Hit 15 and 16 versus 7 through ace
Stand on 15 and 16 versus 2 through 6
Stand on hard 17 through 21
Stand on 14 to 16 versus 2 through 6, hit against 7 and higher

Double Down Hard Totals
Double down on 10 and 11 vs. 2 through 8

Soft Totals (when the ace counts as 1 point)
Hit on all soft hands 17 or less
Stand on all soft hands 18 to 21

Splitting
Always split As and 8s
Never split 4s, 5s, 10s
Split 2s, 3s, 6s, 7s versus 2 through 7
Split 9s versus 2 through 9

Surrender
Surrender hard 16 and 17 versus ace
Surrender after doubling with 12 to 16 versus 8 to ace

Special Plays
Hit suited 7s against all upcards (go for the big bonus)
Never take insurance

Five or More Card Hands
Hit five-card plus hard 14 and 15 against all cards
Hit five-card plus soft 17 and 18 against all cards

Master Chart
Simplified Spanish 21 Strategy Chart

Hard Hands	2	3	4	5	6	7	8	9	10	A
5-9	H	H	H	H	H	H	H	H	H	H
10-11	D	D	D	D	D	D	D	H	H	H
12-14	H	H	H	H	H	H	H	H	H	H
15	S	S	S	S	S	H	H	H	H	H
16	S	S	S	S	S	H	H	H	H	X
17	S	S	S	S	S	S	S	S	S	X
18-21	S	S	S	S	S	S	S	S	S	S

Soft Hands	2	3	4	5	6	7	8	9	10	A
A2-A6	H	H	H	H	H	H	H	H	H	H
A7-A9	S	S	S	S	S	S	S	S	S	S

Splitting Situations	2	3	4	5	6	7	8	9	10	A
22-33	spl	spl	spl	spl	spl	spl	H	H	H	H
66-77	spl	spl	spl	spl	spl	spl	H	H	H	H
88	spl	spl	spl	spl	spl	spl	spl	spl	spl	spl
99	spl	spl	spl	spl	spl	spl	spl	spl	S	S
AA	spl	spl	spl	spl	spl	spl	spl	spl	spl	spl

After Doubling	2	3	4	5	6	7	8	9	10	A
12-16	S	S	S	S	S	S	X	X	X	X

H = Hit   S = Stand   D = Double   spl = Split   X = Surrender
Never split 4-4, 5-5, 10-10 (play as hard hands). Always split 8-8, A-A.

Craps

FIVE KEYS TO CRAPS

1 Get a good understanding of the different bets possible at the game.

2 Avoid *all* the proposition bets in the center of the table. The odds are awful and they can quickly delete your chips.

3 Stick to the best bets at the house—the pass, don't pass, come, don't come, and free odds bets.

4 Always protect yourself by playing conservatively. Craps is a fast game and money can be lost at a dizzying pace.

5 Money management is essential. Protect your wins when you're ahead by pocketing extra profits and restrict losses when the dice are against you.

INTRODUCTION

Craps is the most exciting of the casino games, one perfectly tuned to the temperament of action players. The game offers you opportunities to win large sums of money quickly. However, big money can be lost just as fast unless you are conversant with the best bets available and know how to use them in a coordinated strategy.

You'll learn everything you need to know about craps – from the rules of the game, how to bet and how to play, to the combinations of the dice and the casino vocabulary. You'll learn the best percentage bets to make and how to use them in winning strategies, and how to bankroll and handle your cash so that you'll manage your money like a pro.

We present winning strategies for players betting with the dice, and for players against the dice, and show the best ways conservative and aggressive players alike can bet their money so that losing streaks are kept to the bare minimum and winning streaks can be taken all the way to the bank!

You'll learn 11 winning strategies in all, enough to keep the excitement level high, and when things are going right, the profits rolling. So whether you're a beginner, new to craps, or an experienced player with decades of experience under your belt, you'll find this chapter to be an indispensable guide on how to play and win at craps!

So let's get on with it, and let the dice roll!

BEGINNER'S GUIDE TO CASINO CRAPS

THE TABLE

The standard casino craps table is rectangular in shape and depending upon the particular size of the casino's table, is built to accommodate between 15 to 24 players. The sides of the table are several feet above the layout where the bets are made, giving the players an edge to lean on, and giving the dice walls to carom off.

THE LAYOUT

The craps layout is divided into three distinct sections. The two end sections, which are identical, are areas around which the players cluster, and where the majority of bets are made. Each end area is run by one of the standing dealers.

The middle area is flanked on either side by a boxman and stickman. This area contains the proposition, or center bets, and is completely under the jurisdiction of the stickman.

The layout is a large piece of green felt with various imprints marking the plethora of bets possible. All action is centered on the layout. Bets are placed, paid off and collected on this felt surface. And, of course, it is on the layout where the dice are thrown.

Layouts around the world are basically the same, though some clubs may have slight variations, but none of these need concern us, for the game of craps is basically the same whatever casino you play in. The minor variations that do occur, concern bets whose odds are so poor that we wouldn't want to make them anyway.

THE DICE

The game of craps is played with two standard six sided dice, with each die numbered from 1 to 6. The dice are manufactured so that they fall as randomly as possible, with a 5 being just as likely to fall on one die as a 3. However, we'll see later that combining two dice together creates some combinations that are more likely to appear than others, and this is the basis of the odds in craps.

PLAYERS

Only one player is needed to play craps, while as many as can fit around a craps table are the maximum. When the action is hot and heavy, bettors will be lined up shoulder to shoulder, screaming, yelling and cajoling, for the dice to come through and make them winners.

Below is a standard craps layout.

THE LAYOUT

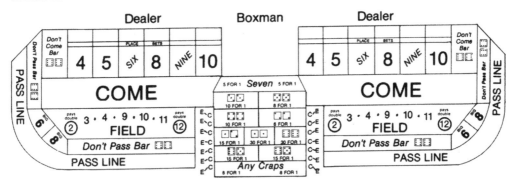

CASINO PERSONNEL

The average craps table is manned by a crew of four casino employees—one stickman, who stands at the center of the table, two dealers, who stand on the opposite side of the stickman at either end of the table, and a boxman who is seated between the two standing dealers and directly across from the stickman.

Let's look at the function of each crewman in turn.

The Stickman

The **stickman's** main responsibility is the handling of the dice, a task he performs with a flexible, hooked stick. When a new shooter is coming-out, the stickman will offer him a cache of dice to choose from, and after two have been selected, will return the remaining dice to his box.

After each roll of the dice, the stickman will announce the number thrown and bring the dice back to the center of the table. Usually, he will supply additional information about its consequences.

If a 7 is thrown on the come-out roll, he may announce, "7, winner on the pass line."

If instead, a 2, 3 or 12 is rolled on the come-out, he may say, "Craps, line away." When a shooter sevens-out, the stickman might exclaim, "7 out, line away."

A good stickman is a show in himself, and by the excitement he generates, makes the game more lively and colorful for both the players and the dealers. And from the casino's standpoint, happy players tend to bet heavier and wilder than they normally would.

The dice will be returned to the shooter after the dealers have finished making payoffs.

The stickman is also responsible for the proposition, or center bets made in the middle of the layout. He will place all proposition bets directed his way into their proper location on the layout.

If these bets are winners, the stickman will direct the dealers to pay off the winning players, and if the bets are losers, he will collect the lost bets and push them over to the boxman.

The Dealers

There is a dealer located on either side of the boxman, and his main responsibility is to handle all the monetary transactions and betting on his end of the table. He pays off winning bets and collects losing ones, converts cash into chips, and will change chips into higher or lower denominations for the player.

Though the player can make many of the bets himself, there are wagers such as the place bets and certain free-odds bets which must be given to the dealer to be placed.

Each standing dealer has a **marker buck**, a plastic disk used to indicate the established point. If a player is coming-out, beginning his roll, the marker buck will be lying on its black side, labeled "**off**," and if a point is established, the dealer will flip the marker buck to the white side, marked "**on**," and place it in the appropriately numbered box to indicate the point. It is with the dealers that the player will have most of his contact and to whom he can address his questions.

The Boxman

The **boxman** sits between the two dealers and across from the stickman, and from this central position, supervises the running of the craps table. His job is not only to watch over the casinos bankroll, most of which sits right in front of him in huge stacks, but to make sure the dealers make the correct payoffs so that neither the player nor the house gets shorted.

He is responsible for settling any disputes that may arise between the players and the dealers. Generally, the benefit of the doubt will be given to the player on any disputed call. If the dice leave the table for any reason, the returned dice are brought directly to the boxman for inspection. He will check the logo and coded numbers on the dice to make sure they haven't been switched, and will inspect the surfaces for imperfections that may influence the game. If, for any reason, the boxman feels suspicious of the returned dice, he will remove them from play and have the stickman offer the shooter a new pair.

When one boxman is on duty, he will supervise one end of the table while the stickman watches the other.

However, when the action is fast, and stacks of chips are riding on each roll of the dice, a second boxman will often be added to the crew to help watch the table. In these cases, the boxmen will sit next to each other behind the chips, each being responsible for one end of the table.

In addition to the boxmen, there are other supervisors, called floormen and pit bosses, who watch over the action from behind the boxman in the area known as the pit.

Floormen

The **floormen** spend their entire shift on their feet, and are responsible for supervising a particular table or group of tables in the pit.

In addition to these supervisory capacities, they deal with players that have established credit lines. If a player requests credit, the floorman checks to see if his credit is good, and if verified, authorizes the dealer to give the requested chips. At the same time, or soon afterwards, he will bring the player an IOU to sign, acknowledging the credit transaction.

The Pit Boss

The **pit boss**, under whose authority the floormen work, is in the charge of the entire craps pit. He's rarely in contact with the players, unless a high roller is playing, whereby he may come over and introduce himself or offer the roller some comps.

THE PIT

Craps tables are arranged in a pattern so that a central area, known as the **pit**, is formed in the middle. The tables are arranged around the pit so that the boxmen and standing dealers have their backs to the pit area, and so that the floormen, standing inside the pit, can easily watch over all of the craps tables.

ENTERING A GAME

To enter a craps game, slip into a space by the rail of the craps table. After catching the dealer's attention, place your cash on the layout and inform him of the denomination of chips you would like. The dealer will take your money, and give it to the boxman who will supervise the exchange.

CONVERTING TRAVELER'S CHECKS AND MONEY ORDERS TO CASH

The dealers will accept only cash or chips at the table, so if you bring traveler's checks, money order or the like, you must go to the area of the casino marked **Casino Cashier** to get these converted to cash. Be sure to bring proper identification to insure a smooth transaction.

CASINO CHIPS

Chip denominations run in $1, $5, $25, $100 and $500 units. $1 chips are generally referred to as **silver**, $5 chips as **nickels**, $25 chips as **quarters**, and $100 chips as **dollars**. Unless playing at a 25¢ minimum craps table, $1 chips are the minimum currency available.

BETTING

Casinos prefer that the player uses chips for betting purposes, for the handling of money at the tables, is cumbersome and slows the game. However, cash can be used to bet with, though all payoffs will be in chips.

HOUSE LIMITS

The house limits will be posted on placards located on each corner of the table. They will indicate the minimum bet required to play and also the maximum bet allowed.

Minimum bets range from $1 and $5 per bet, to a maximum of $500, $1000 or $2,000 a bet. Occasionally, 25¢ minimum craps tables may be found as well. If special arrangements are made, a player can bet as much as he can muster in certain casinos. The Horseshoe Casino in Las Vegas is known to book any bet no matter the size.

In 1981, a man walked into the Horseshoe and placed a bet for $777,777. He bet the don't pass, and walked out two rolls later with one and a half million dollars in cash!

CONVERTING CHIPS INTO CASH

Dealers do not convert your chips into cash. Once you've bought your chips at the table, that cash is dropped into a drop box, and thereafter unobtainable at the table. When you are ready to convert your chips, take them to the cashier's cage where they'll be changed into cash.

FREE DRINKS AND CIGARETTES

Casinos offer their customers unlimited free drinking while gambling at the tables. In addition to alcoholic beverages, a player can order milk, soft drinks, juices or any other beverages. This is ordered through and served by a cocktail waitress.

Cigarettes and cigars are also complimentary and can be ordered through the cocktail waitress.

TIPPING

Tipping, or **toking**, as it is called in casino parlance, should be viewed as a gratuitous gesture by the player to the crew of dealers he feels has given him good service. Tipping is totally at the player's discretion, and in no way should be considered an obligation.

If you toke, toke only when you're winning, and only if the crew is friendly and helpful to you. Do not toke dealers that you don't like or ones that try to make you feel guilty about not tipping. Dealers that make playing an unpleasant experience for you deserve nothing.

Tips are shared by the crew working the craps table. Though the usual tip is to make a proposition bet, with the exclamation "one for the boys," a better way to toke the crew would be to make a line bet for them, so they can have a good chance of winning the bet. Dealers prefer this type of tip for they too are aware how poor the proposition bets are. This is also better than just handing over the toke, for if the bet is won, the dealer wins double for the tip—the amount bet for him plus the winnings from that bet.

PLAY OF THE GAME AND THE COME-OUT ROLL

When a new player is to throw the dice, the stickman will empty his box of dice and push them across the layout with his stick. After this player, known as the **shooter**, selects two dice of his choice, the stickman will retrieve the remaining dice and return them to his box. In a new game, the player closest to the boxman's left side will receive the dice first, and the rotation of the dice will go clockwise from player to player around the craps table.

The shooter has no advantage over the other players except perhaps the psychological edge he may get throwing the dice himself. He is required to make either a pass or don't pass bet as the shooter, and in addition, can make any other bets allowed.

There are a wide variety of bets the players can make, and these bets should be placed before the shooter throws the dice. Players can bet with the dice or against them at their preference, but in either case, the casino will book all wagers.

Play is ready to begin. The shooter is supposed to throw the dice so that they bounce off the far wall of the table. If the throw does not reach the far wall, the shooter will be requested to toss harder on his next throw, and if he persists in underthrowing the dice, the boxman may disallow him from throwing further. This policy protects against cheats that can manipulate unobstructed throws of the dice.

The first throw is called the **come-out roll**, and is the most significant roll in craps. It marks the first roll of a shoot, and can either become an automatic winner or loser for players betting with the dice, called **right bettors**, or those betting against the dice, called **wrong bettors**, or establish a point with which the shooter hopes to repeat before a 7 is thrown.

The come-out roll works as follows. The throw of a 7 or 11 on the come-out roll is an automatic winner for the pass line bettors, players betting that the dice will win, or *pass*, while the throw of a **craps**, a 2, 3 or 12 is an automatic loser. For the don't pass bettors, those betting against the dice, the come-out roll works almost exactly opposite to the pass line bet. A come-out roll of a 7 or an 11 is an automatic loser, a 2 or a 3 an automatic winner, while the 12 (in some casinos a 2 instead) is a standoff.

If the come-out roll is an automatic decision, a 2, 3, 7, 11 or 12, the affected players will have their bets paid or collected, and the following roll will be a new come-out roll.

Any other number thrown, a 4, 5, 6, 8, 9 or 10, becomes the **point**, and the dealers will indicate this by flipping their respective marker bucks to the white side marked "on," and move the disk into the rectangular numbered boxes corresponding to the point number thrown.

The shoot will continue until either the point is repeated, a winner for the pass line bettors and a loser for the don't pass bettors, or until a seven is thrown, known as **sevening-out**, a loser on the pass line and winner on the don't pass. In either case, the shoot will have been completed, and the following roll will be a new come-out roll, the start of a new shoot.

Once a point is established, only the 7 and the point are consequential rolls for the pass and don't pass bettors, also called **line bettors**. All other rolls are neutral throws for these bets.

There are many other bets available to the player as we will discuss later, some that can be made only after a point is established, and others that can be made at any time during a shoot. So while the line bettors may not be affected by a particular throw, the dealers may be paying off or collecting chips on other affected wagers while the shoot is in progress.

The shooter can continue throwing the dice until he sevens-out, whereupon, after all the bets are settled on the layout, the stickman will present his collection of dice to the next player in a clockwise rotation. Even though the shooter may **crap-out** (the throw of a 2, 3 or 12) on his come-out roll, a losing roll for the pass line bettors, the shooter does not have to yield the dice. It is only when he throws a 7 before his point repeats, sevens-out, that the dice must be relinquished.

The Come-Out Roll Encapsulated

The come-out roll occurs when:
A new shooter takes the dice.
The shooter throws a 2, 3, 7, 11 or 12 on the come-out roll, an automatic winner or loser for the line bettors.
After a point is established, the shooter either repeats that point or sevens-out.

BETTING RIGHT OR WRONG

Betting right or wrong are only casino terms used to designate whether a player is betting with the dice, **betting right**, or betting against the dice, **betting wrong**, and are in no way indicative of a correct or incorrect way of playing. As we shall see, both ways of betting are equally valid.

UNDERSTANDING THE ODDS

Knowing how to figure the possible combinations that can occur when two dice are thrown is essential to understanding the basics of craps—the bets, the odds and the payoffs. You'll be surprised at how simple the odds really are, and will find craps to be a more rewarding experience once you learn these fundamentals.

Craps is played with two dice, individually called die, and each die is a near perfect six sided cube, guaranteed to be within 1/10,000 of an inch accurate.

Each die has six equally possible outcomes when thrown—numbers one through six. The two dice thrown together have a total of 36 possible outcomes, the six combinations of one die by the six combinations of the other. The chart below shows these combinations. Notice how certain totals have more possibilities of being thrown, or are more probable of occurring by the random throw of the two dice.

COMBINATIONS OF THE DICE

NUMBERS   COMBINATIONS

NUMBERS	COMBINATIONS
2...	ONE
3...	TWO
4...	THREE
5...	FOUR
6...	FIVE
7...	SIX
8...	FIVE
9...	FOUR
10...	THREE
11...	TWO
12...	ONE

You can see by the chart that the 7 is more likely to be thrown than any other number, having six possible combinations. Next in frequency are the 6 and the 8, five outcomes each, then the 5 and the 9, four outcomes, the 4 and the 10, three outcomes apiece, the 3 and the 11, two outcomes, and finally, the 2 and the 12, one combination each.

A SHORTCUT TO REMEMBERING THE ODDS

Notice the symmetry of combinations on either side of the 7. The 6 and 8 have equal possibilities of being thrown, just as the 5 and 9, 4 and 10, 3 and 11, and 2 and 12 do.

If you take rolls of 7 and below and subtract one from that number, you arrive at the correct number of combinations for that roll. Thus, there are four ways to roll a 5 (5-1), six ways to roll a 7 (7-1) and one way to roll a 2 (2-1).

For numbers greater than the 7, match that number with the corresponding symmetrical number on the other side of the 7, and subtract one. Thus, to find the combinations of the 8, you match it with the 6 (which has an equal likelihood of occurring), and subtracting one, you get five combinations.

FIGURING THE ODDS OF ROLLING A SPECIFIC NUMBER

To figure the odds of rolling any particular number, divide the number of combinations for that particular number into 36, the total number of combinations possible.

Let's say the 7. There are six ways to roll a 7. Dividing the six combinations into 36, the total number of combinations, we find the odds of rolling a 7 on any one roll is one in six (6/36 reduced to 1/6), or equivalently, 5 to 1. The chart below shows the odds of rolling a number on any one roll.

Odds of Rolling the Numbers

	Combinations	Chance of Being	Expressed in Odds
2 or 12	1	1/36	35 to 1
3 or 11	2	2/36	17 to 1
4 or 10	3	3/36	11 to 1
5 or 9	4	4/36	8 to 1
6 or 8	5	5/36	6.2 to 1
7	6	6/36	5 to 1

The listing of two numbers together such as the 5 or 9 is done to abbreviate. The odds apply to either the 5 or the 9, not to both together.

UNDERSTANDING THE TERMINOLOGY –
CORRECT ODDS, HOUSE PAYOFF AND EDGE

The house advantage or edge is the difference between the player's chances of winning the bet, called the **correct odds**, and the casino's actual payoff, called the **house payoff** or simply, the **payoff**. For example, the correct odds of rolling a 7 are 5 to 1. Since the house will pay only 4 to 1 should the 7 be thrown, they maintain an edge of 16.67 percent on this wager.

To play craps intelligently and better understand the choices available to him, the player must first and foremost be aware of the house advantage on every bet he will ever make, for that, in the long run, determines the player's chances of winning.

Five for One, Five to One

Sometimes on a layout you will see payoffs represented as *for* instead of the usual *to*, such as 9 for 1. This means that the payoff will be a total of nine units, eight winning chips along with your original bet, a house subterfuge to increase its edge over the player. The usual 9 to 1 payoff means nine winning chips and your original bet returned, for a total of 10 units.

Beware of any payoffs with the *for*. As a rule, this type of bet has poor odds to begin with and we wouldn't want to make it anyway, with the to or the for.

The Bets

Craps offers the player a wide variety of possible wagers, with each bet having its own characteristics and inherent odds. Some bets, which we will refer to as **sequence bets**, may require a series of rolls before the outcome is determined, while the outcome of others, called **one-roll bets**, is determined on the very next roll.

Some bets are paid off by the house at **even-money**, for every dollar wagered, the player wins a dollar, while other bets have payoffs as high as 30 to 1. However, as you will see, generally the higher the house payoff, the worse the odds are for the player.

And the odds of the bet, that is, the mathematical house return on every dollar wagered, is the most important concern of the player. To have the best chances of winning, the player must avoid all the sucker bets, and make only the best bets available to him.

MOST ADVANTAGEOUS BETS

The bets presented in this section have the lowest built-in house edge of all the bets in craps, and one bet, the free-odds bet, gives the house no advantage whatsoever. These bets, the pass, don't pass, come, don't come and the free-odds bets, are the most important bets a player can make, and are the foundation of our winning strategies.

THE LINE BETS - PASS AND DON'T PASS

These even-money bets can only be made on a come-out roll, before a point is established, and give the house an edge of only 1.4 percent. And when backed by the free-odds wagers, the overall house edge drops to 0.8 percent in a single odds game and to 0.6 percent in a double odds game.

Pass Line

Players making pass line bets are wagering that the dice will **pass**, or win, and are called right bettors. Pass line bets are also referred to as **front line bets**, and are made by placing the wager in the area marked *pass line*.

On the come-out roll, a throw of a 7 or 11 is an automatic winner for the pass line bettors while the throw of a craps, a 2, 3 or 12 is an automatic loser. If any other number is thrown, the 4, 5, 6, 8, 9 or 10, then that number is established as the point, and the shooter must repeat the point before a 7 is thrown for pass line bettors to win. The throw of a 7 before the point repeats is a loser for pass line bettors, called **sevening-out**, and the dealers will collect the lost bets.

Once the point is established, only the 7 and the point number affect the pass line bettor. All other numbers have no bearing on the bet and can be considered neutral throws.

Let's look at three progressions to see how the pass line bet works.

1. The come-out roll is a 5, establishing 5 as the point. The following roll is a 2, a neutral throw, for a point has already been established. An 8 is then thrown, still having no bearing on the outcome, and then a 5. The point was repeated, or made, before the seven was thrown, and the pass line bettors win their bets.

2. The come-out roll is a 7, an automatic winner for the pass line bettors, and they are paid off by the dealers. Since the progression has been completed, the following roll will be another come-out roll.

3. Here is a losing proposition. The come-out roll is a 9, establishing 9 as the point. The shooter then rolls a 6, then a 12, and then an 11. All three rolls are neutral since a point is already established. The following roll is a 7. Since the 7 was rolled before the 9, the shooter's point repeated, pass line bettors lose and the dealer will collect their bets. A new come-out roll will ensue.

Pass Line Encapsulated

Payoff	House Edge	Automatic Winners	Automatic Losers
Even-Money	1.4%	7 or 11 on the come-out roll	2,3, or 12 on the come-out roll

If a point is established on the come-out roll, the pass line bettor:
Wins – by the point repeating before the 7 is thrown.
Loses – by the roll of a 7 before the point repeats.

Don't Pass

Players betting don't pass are called wrong bettors, and are betting against the dice. Don't pass bets are also called **back line bets** and are made by placing the wager in the area marked *don't pass*.

On the come-out roll, a throw of a 2 or 3 is an automatic winner for the don't pass bettors, while a 7 or an 11 is an automatic loser. The 12 is a standoff between the back line bettor and the house. (In some casinos the 2 is the standoff and the 12 is the automatic winner. Either way it makes no difference, for there is only one way to throw the 2 or 12.)

Once the point is established, don't pass bettors win by having the 7 thrown before the shooter repeats his point, and lose by the point being repeated before the shooter sevens-out. Here are some progressions to illustrate the don't pass wager.

1. The come-out roll is a 6, establishing 6 as the point. The following rolls are a 5 (no bearing on the outcome), then a 12 (still no bearing) and then a 7. Since the 7 was rolled before the 6 repeated, don't pass bettors win.

2. The come-out roll is a 3, an automatic winner for the don't pass bettor.

3. The come-out roll is a 4, establishing 4 as the point. A 3 is then rolled (neutral), and then a 4, a loss for the back line bettors since the point repeated before the 7 was rolled.

Don't Pass Line Encapsulated

Payoff	House Edge	Automatic Winners	Automatic Losers	Standoff
Even-Money	1.4%	2 (or 12) and 3 on the come-out roll	7 or 11 on the come-out roll	12 (or 2 in some casinos) on the come-out roll

If a point is established on the come-out roll don't pass bettors:
Win – by the throw of a 7 before the point repeats.
Lose – by the point repeating before the 7 thrown.

COME AND DON'T COME BETS

The come and don't come bets work according to the same rules as the pass and don't pass bets except that the come and don't come bets can only be made after a point is established. The line bets, on the other hand, can only be placed on a come-out roll, before a point is established.

The advantage of these bets are that they allow the player to cover more points as a right or wrong bettor at the same low 1.4% house edge. And like the line bets, the overall house edge drops to 0.8% when backed by single odds, and 0.6% when backed by double odds.

Come bets are made by putting the chips into the area marked *come*, while don't come bets are placed in the *don't come* box. Won bets are paid at even-money.

Come Bets

We follow the play of the come bets just as we would with the pass line bets. A 7 or 11 on the first throw following the placing of the bet is an automatic winner, while a 2, 3 or 12 in an automatic loser.

Any other number thrown, the 4, 5, 6, 8, 9 or 10, becomes the point for that come bet, called the **come point**, and the dealer will move the bet from the come box into the large rectangular numbered boxes located at the top of the layout to mark the come point.

Once the come point is established, the bet is won if the come point repeats before the shooter sevens-out, and lost if the 7 is rolled before the point repeats. All other throws are inconsequential on this bet. Won bets will be paid off and removed from the layout.

The bettor can make continuous come bets until all the points are covered if he desires. Thus, it is possible for the throw of a 7 to simultaneously wipe out several established come bets. On the other hand, a hot shooter rolling point numbers can bring frequent winners to the aggressive come bettor.

Let's follow a progression where the right bettor makes both pass line and come bets.

Player Bets: $5 on the pass line.
The come-out roll is a 5, establishing 5 as the point.

Player Bets: $5 on the come.
The roll is an 8, establishing 8 as the come point. The dealer moves the $5 come bet to the rectangular box marked 8 to indicate that 8 is the point for that come bet. In effect, the player has two points working, the 5 and the 8, and decides to make another come bet.

Player Bets: $5 on the come.
The roll is a 6. The dealer moves this new come bet to the 6, the come point for this bet. The other two points are not affected by this roll.

Player Bets: The player has three points established, the 5, 6 and 8, and makes no more bets at this time.
The roll is a 5, a $5 winner on the pass line. It is paid off and removed from the layout, leaving the player with two come points, the 6 and 8.

Player Bets: $5 on the pass line. Since the next roll is a come-out roll and the player wants to cover another point, he bets the pass.
The roll is a 10, establishing 10 as the point.

Player Bets: No additional bets at this time.
The roll is a 2 (neutral on all established bets), then an 8 is thrown, a $5 winner on the come point of 8, and that bet is paid off and removed. The following roll is not a come-out roll, for the come point was made, not the pass line point, the 10.

Player Bets: Wishing to establish a third point, $5 is bet on the come.
The roll is a 7. While the 7 is a $5 winner for the new come bet, it is a loser for the two established points, and they are removed from the layout by the dealer. The roll of the 7 cleared the layout, and the following roll will be a new come-out roll.

Don't Come Bets

Like the don't pass wager, a 7 or 11 on the first roll following a don't come bet is an automatic loser and the 2 and 3 are automatic winners, 12 being a standoff. (In casinos where the 2 is a standoff and the 12 a winner on the don't pass, the same will hold true for the don't come bets.)

If a 4, 5, 6, 8, 9 or 10 is thrown, establishing a point for the don't come bet, the dealer will move the chips behind the appropriate point box to mark the don't come point. Don't come bettors now win by having the 7 thrown before that point is made. Other numbers, as with the don't pass bets, are neutral rolls. Only the 7 and the come point determine the bet.

Let's follow a progression where the wrong bettor makes both don't pass and don't come bets.

Player Bets: $5 on the don't pass.
The roll is a 10, establishing 10 as the point.

Player Bets: Continuing to bet against the dice, the player now makes a $5 bet on the don't come.
The roll is a 2, a $5 winner on the new don't come bet, and that bet is paid off and removed.
Player Bets: $5 on the don't come.
The roll is a 6. The dealer moves the bet from the don't come area to the upper section of the box numbered 6 to indicate that 6 is the point for this don't come bet. The player now has two points working, the 10 and 6, and decides to establish a third point.

Player Bets: $5 on the don't come.
The roll is a 10, a $5 loser on the don't pass since the point repeated before a 7 was thrown. The don't come point of 6 is unaffected, and the new don't come bet is moved to the 10 box, since 10 is the come point for the new don't come wager.

Player Bets: The player decides not to make any more bets, being content with his bets on points 6 and 10, unwilling to place more bets on the layout. If he were to make another bet against the dice, he would bet don't pass for the next throw is a come-out roll.
The roll is 7, winner on both established come points; they are paid off and removed. The next roll will be a new come-out.

FREE-ODDS BETS

Though not indicated anywhere on the layout, the free-odds bets are the best bets a player can make at craps, and are an indispensable part of the winning strategies. The **free-odds** bets are so named, for, unlike the other bets at craps, the house has no advantage over the player. Hence, the term *free-odds*.

However, to make a free-odds bet, the player must first have placed a pass, don't pass, come or don't come wager, and in a sense, is backing those bets, for the free-odds bet can only be made in conjunction with these wagers. When backed by single odds, the overall odds of the pass, don't pass, come and don't come bets drop to 0.8%, and where double odds are allowed and utilized, the overall odds drop to only 0.6% against the player. These are the best odds a player can get at craps.

Free-Odds – Pass Line

Once a point is established on the come-out roll, the pass line bettor is allowed to make an additional bet, called a **free-odds bet**, that his point will be repeated before a 7 is thrown. This bet is paid off at the correct odds, giving the house no edge, and is made by placing the chips behind the pass line wager and just outside the pass line area.

Pass Line and Free-Odds Bet

When single odds are allowed, the player can bet up to the amount wagered on his pass line bet, and in certain instances he can bet more. And when double odds are allowed, the player can bet twice his pass line bet as a free-odds wager.

Though the player can bet less than the permissible amount on the free-odds wager and is allowed to reduce or remove this bet at any time, he should never do so, for the free-odds bets are the most advantageous bets in craps, and should be fully taken advantage of.

Following is a table which shows the correct odds of the point repeating before a 7 is thrown and the house payoff. Note how the house takes no percentage advantage on these bets since the payoff is identical to the correct odds.

Odds of Point Repeating Before a Seven

Point Number	Correct Odds	House Payoff
4 or 10	2 to 1	2 to 1
5 or 9	3 to 2	3 to 2
6 or 8	6 to 5	6 to 5

The odds presented in this table are easy to figure for the only numbers that affect the free-odds bet are the point number, which is a winner, and the 7, which is a loser. All other throws are inconsequential.

There are three ways to roll a winning 4 or 10, and six ways to roll a losing 7, thus 2 to 1 is the correct odds on points 4 or 10. A 5 or 9 can be rolled four ways each against the same six ways of rolling a 7, thus the correct odds are 3 to 2 against the 5 or 9. A 6 or 8 can be made by five combinations, and again, since there are six ways to roll a losing 7, the correct odds are 6 to 5 against the 6 or 8.

Special Allowances – Single Odds Game

To make the payoffs easier, most casinos will allow the player to make a single odds bet greater than his pass line (or come) bet in the following instances.

a. With a pass line bet such as $5 or $25 and the point being a 5 or 9, the casino will allow the player to make an odds bet of $6 and $30 respectively behind the line. If the bet is won, the 3 to 2 payoff on the $6 free-odds bet would be $9, and on the $30 bet, $45.

If the player wasn't allowed this special allowance, he would be unable to get the full correct odds on the $5 or $25 free-odds bet since the $1 or more minimum craps tables do not deal in half dollars.

b. With a three unit bet such as $3 or $15, and the point being a 6 or 8, the casino will allow a five unit free-odds bet behind the line. This allows the player to take full advantage of the 6 to 5 payoff on points 6 and 8. In the above examples, $5 and $25 free-odds bets would be permitted, and if won, would pay the player $6 and $30 respectively.

A three unit bet translates to $3 for the $1 bettor, $15 for the $5 bettor, $30 for the $10 bettor, and so on. Any bet that can be divisible by three can be considered a three unit bet and be backed by the special allowance single odds bets.

A $30 bet on the pass line can be backed by only $30 if the point is a 5 or 9 since the 3 to 2 payoff can be made on this amount, but if the point is a 6 or an 8, can be backed by $50 (five unit special allowance).

If uncertain about the amounts you are allowed to back your pass line bet with, check with the dealer, and he will let you know the permissible wager.

Three Unit Bet • Single Odds Special Allowance

Basic Three Unit Bet	6 or 8 as Point
$3	$5 ($6)
$15	$25 ($30)
$30	$50 ($60)
$45	$75 ($90)
$75	$125 ($150)
$300	$500 ($600)

The first column, Basic Three Unit Bet, is what our standard pass and come bet is, while the second column shows the special allowance permitted when the point is 6 or 8. Numbers in parenthesis indicate the amount paid if the single odds bet is won.

Note that this is only a partial listing of the basic three unit bets, and many more are possible for the player that wants to bet in different ranges than shown.

No special allowances are allowed when the 4 or 10 are points for they are easily paid off at 2 to 1, no matter the amount wagered.

On bets smaller than $5 with the point being a 6 or 8, single odds bets will not be able to receive the full 6 to 5 payoff, and will be paid off at even-money only, for again, the craps tables do not stock units smaller than $1 chips.

On bets larger than $5 but in unequal multiples of $5, the free-odds bet will be paid to the highest multiple of $5 at 6 to 5, and the remainder will be paid at even-money. Thus, a $12 odds bet on the 8 will yield a payoff of only $14, $12 on the first $10 (at 6 to 5), and even-money on the unequal remainder of $2.

When the free-odds bets do not receive their full payoff, the bet works to the disadvantage of the player. Therefore, we recommend that pass and come wagers be made in multiples of $3, for this allows the player to take full advantage of the special allowances and lowers the overall house edge for the single odds game below 0.8 percent.

Double Odds – Pass Line

Double odds work just like single odds except that the player is allowed to bet double his pass line bet as a free-odds wager. If $10 was bet on the pass line and a 5 was established as the point, the double odds game would allow the player to bet $20 as a free-odds wager and receive the same correct 3 to 2 odds on that point, instead of only being allowed a $10 free-odds bet as in the single odds game.

When combined with the pass line bet, double odds brings the overall house edge down to only 0.6%, the best odds a player can get at craps. Therefore, when there is a choice of playing a single or double odds game, choose the latter, for you should take advantage of every favorable option allowed.

If you're uncertain whether double odds are allowed, just ask the dealer, and he will let you know.

Special Allowances – Double Odds Game

One special allowance to keep in mind on the double odds game. With a two unit bet on the pass line and the point a 6 or 8, double odds casinos will allow the player to wager five units as a free-odds bet. Thus, with a $10 bet (two $5 unit chips), and the point a 6 or 8, a $25 double odds bet would be allowed. If won, the 6 to 5 payoff would bring $30 in winnings (six $5 chips, an easier payoff for the casino).

We recommend that players bet in multiples of two for it permits us to take advantage of the special five unit allowance when the point is a 6 or an 8. Any bet that can be divisible by two can be considered a two unit bet and be backed by the special five unit allowance if the point is a 6 or an 8.

Two Unit Bet • Double Odds Special Allowance

Basic Two Unit Bet	6 or 8 as Point	4, 5, 9 or 10 as Point
$2	$5 ($6)	$4
$10	$25 ($30)	$20
$20	$50 ($60)	$40
$30	$75 ($90)	$60
$50	$125 ($150)	$100
$200	$500 ($600)	$400

*The Basic Two Unit Bet is our standard pass and come bet. The third column is the normal double odds allowance for points 4, 5, 9 and 10.

Numbers in parenthesis indicate the amount paid if the double odds bet is won at 6 to 5 payoff). Other two unit bets than the ones shown in this chart are possible.

Let's see how this would work.

$15 is bet on the pass line, and the come-out roll is a 6. Taking advantage of the special five unit allowance, $25 is wagered as a free-odds bet behind the line. (This bet is placed by the player.)

If the shooter throws a 7 before the point repeats, the player loses the $15 pass bet and the $25 free-odds bet, but should the point be rolled before the 7, $15 will be won on the pass line bet and $30 on the odds bet ($25 paid at 6 to 5).

If the game was a double odds game, the player could have backed the $15 pass bet with a $30 free-odds bet. And if the point was a 6, the free-odds bet would pay $36 if won ($30 at 6 to 5 = $30).

Free-Odds – Don't Pass

Once the point is established, don't pass bettors are allowed to make a free-odds bet that a 7 will be rolled before the point repeats. The bet is paid off at correct odds, the house enjoying no edge, and is made by placing the free-odds bet next to the don't pass wager in the don't pass box.

Don't Pass and Free-Odds Bet

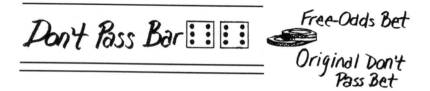

Since the odds favor the don't pass bettor once the point is established, there being more ways to roll a winning 7 than any point number, the don't pass bettor must *lay odds,* that is, put more money on the free-odds bet than he will win.

Let's say the point is a 4. The don't pass bettor's chances of winning the bet are now 2 to 1 in his favor. There are only three ways to roll a 4, a loser, against the six combinations of a 7, a winner. Therefore, the don't pass bettor must bet $20 to win $10 when the point is a 4 (or 10).

(On the other side of the bet, pass line bettors are receiving 2 to 1 odds, for their bet is the underdog, having only three winning chances against six losing combinations.)

To lay odds as a don't pass bettor, the allowable free-odds bet is determined by the *payoff*, not the original bet. Using the above example of a $10 bet on the don't pass with 4 established as the point, the don't pass bettor in a single odds game is allowed up to a $10 win on the free-odds bet. Since the odds are 2 to 1 in his favor, the don't pass bettor must lay $20 to win $10. If it was a double odds game, meaning the player could win $20 on his original $10 bet, than at 1 to 2 odds, $40 would have to be staked for a potential win of $20.

The odds the don't pass bettor must lay are exactly opposite the odds pass line bettors take on the same points. Below is a table showing the free-odds bets from the wrong bettors position.

Odds of Rolling a Seven Before Point Repeats

Point Number	Correct Odds	House Payoff
4 or 10	1 to 2	1 to 2
5 or 9	2 to 3	2 to 3
6 or 8	5 to 6	5 to 6

Note how the house has no percentage advantage on these bets since the payoff is identical to the correct odds.

Like the free-odds bets for right bettors, don't pass free-odds wagers can be removed or reduced at any time, but since these are the player's best bets, it should not be done.

Let's look at a quick example to see how the free-odds bet works for the don't pass bettor.

$10 is bet on the don't pass, and the come-out roll is a 9. The wrong bettor bets $15 behind the line as a free-odds bet, the maximum allowed in a single odds game. He stands to win $10 on the free-odds bet if the 7 is rolled before the 9 repeats, in addition to $10 on his don't pass bet.

Should the point be rolled before the 7, the $15 free-odds bet and $10 don't pass bet will be lost. If double odds were allowed, $20 would be the maximum allowable free-odds win. At 2 to 3 odds, the don't pass bettor would have to lay $30 to win $20.

Wrong Bettors Special Allowances – Single Odds Game

The casino makes a special provision for don't pass bettors when the point is a 5 or 9 and an odd figure such as $5 is wagered. Since the craps tables do not deal in half dollars, the player is allowed to make a free-odds bet of $9 behind the line in this instance, and if the bet is won, will get paid $6 ($9 at 2 to 3).

Whenever the point is 5 or 9 and the original bet is unequal, the house will allow the player to bet more than the straight single odds. Ask the dealer the exact amount allowed in those instances; the rules may vary from casino to casino.

Free-Odds: Come and Don't Come

Once a come point is established, the bettor can take odds (or lay odds for don't come bettors) and get the same advantageous payoffs, 2-1 on points 4 and 10 (1-2 for wrong bettors), 3-2 on the 5 and 9 (2-3 for wrong bettors), and 6-5 on the 6 and 8 (5-6 for wrong bettors).

The house has no advantage on these free-odds wagers, and like the line bets, the overall house edge on the come or don't come bets teamed with single odds drops to 0.8%, and with double odds, to 0.6%.

The same special allowances apply for the come bets. In a single odds game; a three unit bet can be backed by five units if the point is 6 or 8, while a free-odds bet on points 5 and 9 can be backed by additional chips if the original come bet is uneven. In the double odds game, a two unit wager can be backed by five units if the point is a 6 or 8.

However, the odds bets on the come and don't come bets are placed differently than line bets. Rather than being made by the player, the odds bets are given to the dealer with the instruction, "odds on the come," or "odds on the don't come."

The dealer will place the odds bet in the appropriate box atop the come point, but slightly offset, so that the odds bet can be differentiated from the come bet.

Come, Don't Come and Free-Odds Bets

Dealer will place free-odds bet atop original bet but offset to distinguish from come or don't come bet.

The only other difference is with the come bet. While the come bet itself is working on the come-out roll, the odds bet on that come bet is not. Let's say the player had $15 bet on the come point of 6 and had that bet backed by $25 free-odds.

A come-out roll of a 7 would of course be a loser for the $15 come bet, as that bet is always working, but since the free-odds bet was off, the $25 single odds wager would be returned to the player.

If a 6 was rolled instead, a winner for the come bet, the player would only win the $15, and be returned the $25 odds bet.

Though it is standard procedure for the free-odds bet backing the come wager to be off on the come-out roll, the player can request the odds bet to be "on" by informing the dealer that the "odds are on for the come bet," and then, of course, the odds bet is subject to the normal rules.

The odds on the don't come bets, as with the pass and don't pass wagers, are always working.

Let's look at some betting sequences to illustrate how the free-odds bets on come and don't come wagers work in conjunction with the line bets.

Right Bettors (Pass and Come Bets)

Player A is a right bettor, he likes betting with the dice. His standard betting unit is $15 (3 units of $5) and this allows him to take advantage of the special free-odds allowances when the points are 5 and 9, and 6 and 8.

Single Odds Game

Player Bets: $15 on the pass line.
The come-out roll is an 8, establishing 8 as the point.

Player Bets: $25 odds bet behind the 8 (5 unit special allowance bet). $15 on the come.
The roll is a 4, establishing the 4 as a come point. Dealer moves Player A's bet from the come line to the box marked 4.

Player Bets: $15 odds bet on the 4. The dealer places the wager on the come bet but at a tilt to show it's an odds bet. Player A decides to make another $15 come bet.
The roll is an 11. The new come bet is an automatic winner for $15. The other bets are unaffected.

Player Bets: $15 more on the come.
The roll is a 4, a winner on that come point. Player A wins $15 on the come bet and $30 (2 to 1 payoff) on the free-odds bet. The new $15 come bet is moved to the place box of 4, to indicate that it's a come point.

Player Bets: $15 odds on the come point of 4. $15 more on the come. Player A now has a $15 pass line bet backed by $25 odds on the point of 8, a $15 come bet backed by $15 odds on the point of 4, and a new $15 come wager.

The roll is an 8, a winner on the pass line. Player A gets paid $15 on the pass line bet and $30 on his odds bet (6 to 5 odds) and these bet are removed from the layout. The new come bet is moved to the 8 box, the come point for that last bet. A new come-out roll will follow since the point was made.

Player Bets: $15 on the passline. $25 odds bet on his come point of 8.

The roll is a 7, a $15 winner on the new passline bet, but a loser for the two come points of 4 and 8. Since the odds bets were off on the come-out roll, the $15 odds on the 4 and $25 odds on the 8 are returned to the player, leaving the player with only a $30 loss on the come points themselves, but a $15 winner on pass line bet.

Player A won $120 in bets and lost only $30 for a net win of $90.

Wrong Bettors (Don't Pass and Don't Come Bets)

Player B is a wrong bettor, he prefers to bet against the dice. His standard betting unit is $20 because it's easier to figure the laying of odds with bets in multiples of $10.

Single Odds Game

Player Bets: $20 on the don't pass.

The come-out roll is a 6, establishing the 6 as a point.

Player Bets: $24 free-odds bet behind the 6 (laying 5 to 6 odds). $20 on the don't come.

The roll is a 3, craps, a winner on the new don't come bet. The other bets are unaffected. The winning bet is removed from the layout.

Player Bets: $20 on the don't come again.

The roll is a 10, and the dealer moves the don't come bet above the box marked 10 to indicate the come point for the don't come bet.

Player Bets: $40 free-odds on the come point of 10 (laying 1 to 2 odds). The dealer places the odds bet atop the original bet but at a tilt so the bet can be a distinguished from the don't come bet. $20 bet in the don't come box.

The roll is a 9, establishing 9 as the come point for the new don't come bet. Player B now has bets against three points, the 4, 9 and 10. The roll of any of those point numbers is a loss for Player B on that particular number rolled, while the throw of a 7 will be a winner on all.

Player Bets: $30 free-odds on the 9, and decides not to make any more come bets.

The roll is a 6, a loser on the don't pass. Player B loses that $20 bet and the $24 odds bet behind it. Since the point was made, the next roll is a new come-out roll. All bets for the wrong bettor will be working.

Player Bets: $20 on the don't pass.

The roll is an 8, establishing 8 as the come point on the new don't pass bet.

Player Bets: $24 odds on the come point of 8, and decides not to make any further bets at this time.

The roll is a 7, a simultaneous winner on all the don't pass, don't come and odds bets. Player B wins $20 per wrong bet plus the $20 odds behind each bet for a $40 win per point. With three points covered, the total win on that 7 was $120.

Player B won $140 in bets and lost only $44 for a net win of $96.

THE REST OF THE BETS

With the exception of the place bet of 6 and 8, none of the bets presented in this section, which include the remainder of the bets possible at craps, are recommended for play. The house edge over the player on these bets is too large to be incorporated into a winning strategy, and the bettor making these bets will soon find himself drained of significant portions of his bankroll.

In fact, the majority of bets listed here are sucker bets, wagers that give the house an edge so exorbitant that the player stands no more than a slim chance of winning. Just because a bet is exotic looking and available doesn't mean that it should be bet on. To do well at craps, all bets with prohibitive odds must be avoided.

The bets listed in this section are discussed anyway so that the player has a full understanding of all the bets possible at craps, and so that the player is never tempted to make these poor wagers.

PLACE BETS

The **place bets** are among the most popular wagers in craps, and are a bet that a particular point number, whichever is wagered on, the 4, 5, 6, 8, 9 or 10, is rolled before a 7 is thrown. The player can make as many place bets as he wants, and some players do, covering all the numbers with place bets.

However, this is not recommended strategy, for as we will see, with the exception of the place bets of 6 and 8, the other place bets, the 4, 5, 9 and 10, are poor wagers, and will have no role in our winning strategies.

Place bets are made by giving the dealer the desired wager, and telling him, for example, "to place the 9," or any such statement that indicates the player wants to make a place bet on the 9.

Though place bets can be made at any time, they are not working, or are "**off**" on the come-out roll, unless the player requests them to be "**on**" (working).

The player can also request his place bets to be off for a limited series of throws, and may increase, reduce or remove them at any time prior to a roll.

House Payoffs on Place Bets

Bet	Payoff	Correct Odds	House Advantage
4 or 10	9 to 5	2 to 1	6.67%
5 or 9	7 to 5	3 to 2	4.00%
6 or 8	7 to 6	6 to 5	1.52%

To get the full payoffs on the place bets, the player should make his bets in the proper multiples. On place bets of 4 and 10, and 5 and 9, the bets should be made in multiples of $5 since the payoffs are 9 to 5 and 7 to 5 respectively. On the 6 and 8, the bet should be in multiples of $6 (7 to 6 payoff).

Excess bets in unequal multiples will be paid off at even-money only and work to the disadvantage of the player. For example, a $10 bet on the 6 will be paid as follows. The first $6 will get the full 7 to 6 odds for $7, while the remaining $4 gets paid at even-money, or $4, for a total win of $11. The last $4, paid off at only even-money, is a terrible payoff, and makes the entire bet a poor one.

Unless the player makes the place bets of 6 or 8 in multiples of $6 to insure full payoffs, the bet should not be make. Also, bets less than $5 on the 4, 5, 9 and 10, and less than $6 on the 6 and 8, will be paid of at only even-money.

To summarize, do not make place bets of 4 or 10, or 5 and 9, for the house edge is too high.

The place bets of 6 and 8 have playable odds of 1.52 percent and can be used in an aggressive maximize gain strategy, though some players may prefer to stick with the line, come and don't come bets backed by free-odds, the best bets of all.

BIG 6 AND BIG 8

The **Big 6** and **Big 8** are bets that a particular number bet on, the 6 or 8, is thrown before a 7 is rolled. These bets can be made at any time, and are bet by putting the wager into the box marked Big 6 or Big 8.

These bets work just like the place bets of 6 and 8 except that the house only pays even-money on a won bet as opposed to the 7 to 6 payoff he would receive had he made the superior place bet on 6 or 8 instead.

Let's look at the correct odds. There are five ways to throw a winning 6 (or 8, if that is bet), and six ways to throw a losing 7, making the correct odds 6 to 5. The house pays only even-money on a won bet in Nevada, giving them a whopping 9.90% advantage. This makes the Big 6 and Big 8 terrible bets in Nevada, especially when they are compared to the 1.52% odds of the 6 and 8 place bets.

(The Big 6 and Big 8 bets were formerly offered in Atlantic City and were paid off at 7 to 6, like the place bets of 6 and 8. However, the New Jersey gaming commission approved the removal of the Big 6 and Big 8 wager, and they are no longer offered there.)

BUYING THE 4 OR 10

This is an option the casino gives the player when betting on a place number, and though it reduces the odds on the 4 or 10 from 6.67 percent to 4.76 percent, the buy bet is still a poor one and should not be made.

But here's how it works.

To **buy** the 4 or 10, you must give the house a 5% commission on your bet. Once you've bought a number, the house will pay off the bet at the correct odds. Thus, your payoff will be 2 to 1, the correct odds, rather than 9 to 5 as is usually the payoff for these place bets.

A five percent commission on $20 would be $1. For any bet smaller than $20, the commission would still be $1 since the craps tables generally carry no smaller units. In these cases, the house edge on your buy bet would be much larger than 4.76 percent. If you buy the 4 and 10 at $10 each, for a total of $20, the commission would only be 5 percent of the two bet total, or $1.

Like the place bets, buy bets are not working on the come-out roll, unless you instruct the dealer that the bet is on. They are also similar to the place bets in that they can be increased, reduced or removed at any time prior to the roll. Note that an increased buy bet is subject to the 5 percent commission on the additional wager.

Some casinos will keep the 5 percent commission if you decide to remove an established bet or charge an additional 5 percent if you win your bet and decide to let it ride.

BUYING THE 5, 6, 8, 9

Theoretically, you can buy these numbers as well, but since the commission is 5 percent, and the house edge on all these place bets is less than that, there is no advantage in buying these numbers.

LAY BETS

The **lay bet** is the opposite of a buy bet, and is used by wrong bettors who are wagering that the 7 will be thrown before the point or points they bet against is rolled. While the bet is paid off at correct odds, it costs the bettor 5 percent commission on the projected win to get this payoff, and is therefore, a poor bet.

Lay bets, which can be bet at any time, are made by giving the dealer your chips along with the required 5 percent commission on the projected win. The dealer will place the bet above the point number covered (in the area where the don't come bets are placed) and place a buy button on top to distinguish the lay bet.

To receive the full value on the lay bet of 4 or 10, the bettor would have to wager at least $40 to win $20 (1 to 2 odds). The 5 percent commission on the projected win of $20 would be $1. Any bet smaller than the $40 lay bet on the 4 or 10 would still be charged the minimum $1 commission (craps tables do not generally deal in currency smaller than $1 chips) making the house edge greater than the 2.44% advantage already built into this wager.

The 5 and 9 lay bets would require a minimum wager of $30 for the player to get the maximum value. The potential $20 win (laying odds at 2 to 3) would be charged $1 commission. Again, a bet smaller than the projected win of $20 would still be charged the minimum $1 commission, and raise the overall house edge on the bet.

The 6 and 8 bets would require a wager of $24 at 5 to 6 odds on a projected win of $20 to get full value from the commission.

House Allowance on Lay Bets

Points	House Advantage
4 or 10	2.44%
5 or 9	3.23%
6 or 8	4.00%

The lay bet can be added to, reduced or removed altogether at any time.

The player is advised not to make lay bets. We get much better odds with the wagers in the previous section, "The Most Advantageous Bets."

FIELD BET

The **field bet** is a one roll wager that the next throw of the dice will be a number listed in the field box, the 2, 3, 4, 9, 10, 11 or 12. If one of the numbers not listed is rolled, the 5, 6, 7 or 8, then the bet is lost.

The field bet can be made at any time and is done by placing the wager in the area marked "Field".

At first glance, the bet seems attractive. There are seven winning numbers listed in the field box, and two of these numbers, the 2 and the 12, pay double if they are rolled. In some casinos, the 2 or 12 pays triple. The other winning numbers, the 3, 4, 9, 10 and 11 pay even-money. But let's look closer.

The losing numbers, the 5, 6, 7 and 8, are the most frequently rolled numbers, and make up a total of 20 losing combinations. (Four ways to roll a 5, five ways to roll a 6, fives ways to make an 8, and six ways to roll a 7 = 20). Adding up all the other numbers gives us a total of only 16 winning combinations. The 2 to 1 bonus on the 2 and the 12 is actually worth one more combination each for a total of 18 winning units, and where the 12 (or 2) is paid at 3 to 1, we get a total of 19 winners.

However, there are 20 combinations that will beat us, giving the house an edge of 5.55% when the 2 and 12 are paid at 2 to 1, and 2.7% when one is paid at 2 to 1 and the other at 3 to 1.

In either case, the house advantage is much larger than other bets available at craps, and the player should not make field bets.

PROPOSITION OR CENTER BETS

The **proposition**, or **center bets**, as they are sometimes called, are located at the center of the layout, and are made by either giving the chips to the dealer who will pass them along to the stickman, or, as with the hardways bet or craps-eleven bet, can sometimes be tossed directly to the stickman.

The central area of the layout is under the complete domain of the stickman, and though he will physically handle the placing and removing of bets in this area, it is with the dealer that the player will generally make his bets and receive his payoffs.

The proposition bets are the worst bets a player can make at craps and should never be made. The house advantage rages as high as 16.67 percent on some of these wagers. However, these bets are listed and their odds explained so that the reader will be fully conversant with all the wagers possible at craps.

Any Seven

This bet, which is that the following roll of the dice will be a 7, is paid off by the house at 4 to 1 (5 for 1), and is among the worst bets a player can make.

There are six ways to throw a 7 out of 36 possible combinations, making the odds one in six of throwing a 7 on any one roll, or equivalently, 5 to 1. Since the player is paid off at only 4 to 1, the house maintains an exorbitant edge of 16.67 percent over the player.

Don't even make this bet in your dreams.

Any Craps

This bet, located at the bottom of the center layout and along its sides, is a bet that the following roll will be a craps—a 2, 3 or 12.

There are four ways to roll a winner. The 2 and 12 account for one way each, while there are two ways to roll a three. The other 32 combinations are losers, making the correct odds 8 to 1. The house only pays 7 to 1; an 11.1 percent house edge.

2 or 12

This is a bet that the next roll of the dice will come up a 2, or a 12 if you bet that number, and is paid off by the house at 30 to 1.

Of the 36 possible combinations of the dice, there is only one way of rolling a 2 or a 12, making the correct odds 35 to 1 against rolling either number. With only a 30 to 1 payoff, the house enjoys a hefty 13.69 percent advantage.

Sometimes a casino may only pay off at 30 for 1 (29 to 1), giving them an edge of 16.67 percent. This should make no difference to us for we won't go near that bet in either case.

3 or 11

This is a wager that the following roll will be a 3, or an 11, whichever you place your money on, and the house payoff is 15 to 1.

Since there are only 2 ways to roll either number out of a possible 36 combinations, the correct odds are 17 to 1 (34 losers, 2 winners). The house edge is 11.1 percent. Where the payoff is 15 for 1 (14 to 1), this edge jumps to 16.67 percent.

Horn Bet

It takes four chips or multiples thereof to makes this bet. The horn bet is a four way bet that the next roll will be a 2, 3, 11 or 12, in effect combining four poor bets together. The house pays off the winning number at the normal payoffs (15 to 1 for the 3 or 11, and 30 to 1 for the 2 or 12), and deducts the other three losing chips from the payoff.

This sucker bet combines four losing wagers for a combined house edge of 11.1 percent, or 16.67 percent with the poorer payoffs discussed earlier. Never make this bet.

Hop Bet

This one roll wager, which does not appear on the layout, is generally made on a combination of the dice not otherwise offered on the one roll bets, such as 2, 3. If the bet is a pair such as 5, 5, the player will get the same payoff as the casino gives on the 2 or 12 bet (30 to 1 or 29 to 1). If the bet is a non-pair, such as 4, 5, which has two ways to win (4, 5; 5, 4), the payoff will be the same as on the 3 or 11 bet (15 to 1 or 14 to 1).

To make a hop bet, give your bet to the dealer or stickman, and call out for example "Hop 54", if the 5, 4 is the hop bet you wish to make.

With the more generous payoff, hop bets give the casino an edge of 13.39%; otherwise the edge is 16.67%. In either case, consider the bet a donation. Never make these bets.

Craps-Eleven (C-E)

The stickman will constantly exhort the player to make this horrendous bet, which is an appeal to bet the Any Craps and 11 bet simultaneously—the circles with the "C" and "E" on the layout. We don't want to go near either bet by itself let alone together. Save your money for the show.

Hardways

Whenever the numbers, 4, 6, 8 or 10 are rolled as doubles, the roll is said to be thrown **hardways** or **hard**. A throw of 22 is said to be *4, the hardway* or *hard 4*, and similarly with 33, 44 and 55 for hard 6, 8 and 10 respectively.

Rolling the 4, 6, 8 and 10 in other combinations is called **easy** such as 6, 4; *10 the easy way.*

Betting hardways is betting that the particular number you choose comes up hard before it comes up easy or before a 7 is thrown. Let's look at the odds involved.

Hard 4 and Hard 10

There is only one way to throw a hard 4 (22) or hard 10 (55), and eight ways to lose—six ways to roll a seven, and two ways to throw a 4 or 10 the easy way (13, 31, 64 and 46).

The correct odds should be 8 to 1 but the house only pays 7 to 1 for an advantage of 11.1 percent. As with the other center bets, this bet is greatly disadvantageous to the players and should never be made.

Hard 6 and Hard 8

There are a total of 10 losing combinations—the 6 ways to roll a 7, and 4 ways to roll a 6 or an 8 the easy way. (There are a total of 5 ways to throw the 6 or 8, and subtracting the hardway, it leaves 4 other combinations). There is only 1 way to throw the 6 or 8 the hardway.

The correct odds of this hardway bet is 10 to 1 but the house only pays 9 to 1, giving them a commanding edge of 9.09% percent. Don't make this bet.

WINNING STRATEGIES

The underlying principle of all our winning strategies is to make only the best bets available, those with the lowest odds, for this gives us the best chances of winning. When used as we suggest, the overall house edge will be only 0.8 percent in a single odds game and 0.6 percent in a double odds one. We will never make any bet which gives the house an advantage greater than 1.52%, and in fact, the majority of our money will be placed on bets in which the house has no advantage whatsoever!

We'll play aggressively when winning, so that our winning sessions will be big, and when the dice go against us, we'll reduce our bets or even stop betting altogether. This will maximize our profits and minimize our losses, a smart money management technique that can put winnings in our pocket. And we'll follow the guidelines in the money management chapter, so that once we're winning big, we'll leave big winners.

This winning strategies chapter is divided into two main sections, one for right bettors, and the other for wrong bettors. The reader is reminded that betting right or wrong are equally valid approaches to winning, with equivalent odds, and that the choosing of either method is merely a matter of personal style.

Within each approach, right and wrong betting, we'll present the best strategies for the single and double odds game, and also the best methods for conservative and aggressive bettors to follow.

The **Basic Conservative** methods presented are formulated for the cautious bettor, one who wants to get the best odds possible, but not risk substantial sums, while the **Aggressive** methods are more suited for the heavier bettor, one who is willing to risk more to win more.

The two methods, Basic Conservative and Aggressive, though, are equally powerful. The choice of one or the other depends solely on a player's bankroll considerations and financial temperament.

WINNING STRATEGIES: BETTING WITH THE DICE

In this section we're going to show how the right bettor, using sound principles of play can lower the house edge to the lowest possible figure, 0.8 percent in a single odds game and 0.6 percent in a double odds one.

Using our methods, the majority of the right bettors wagers will be made on the free-odds bets, wagers that the house not only has no advantage whatsoever, but which if won, will pay the player more than he bet!

We'll use only the best bets in our basic strategies—the pass line, come and free-odds wagers, bets which give the player the best chances of winning. Built-in to the strategies are methods to turn winning sessions into big winning sessions without any risk of big losses.

Basic Conservative Method – Right Bettors Single Odds Strategy

Our standard bet will be in increments of three units so that we can take advantage of the special free-odds allowances should the points be 6 or 8, whereupon we can back our pass line or come bet by five units, or points 5 or 9, where we can bet extra if the original bet is uneven such as $15, where $20 would be permitted as a free-odds wager.

This allows maximum usage of the free-odds bets, wagers the house has no edge on, and brings the overall house advantage down to the barest minimum possible in a single odds game.

These are the guidelines of our basic conservative strategy:

- We will make three unit pass line and come bets until we have two points established, and back both those bets with the maximum single odds allowed.
- Every time a point repeats, whether as a come or pass line point, we will make another three unit pass line or come bet so that we continue to have two points working for us. If a 2, 3, 11 or 12 declares a winner or a loser on the new pass line or come bet, we will follow with another bet until we get that second point established and then take the maximum single odds allowed on that point.

- If the shooter sevens-out, clearing the board of all bets, we'll begin the progression again with a new pass line bet.

Aggressive Method – Right Bettors/Single Odds Strategy

Rather than playing only two points as in the Basic Conservative method, this strategy immediately attempts to establish three points. Otherwise, the strategies are equivalent.

We begin by making a pass line bet. After a point is established, we will make a free-odds bet behind the pass line and a three unit come bet. When the come point is established, we will back that point with the maximum single odds allowed, and place yet another come bet backing that too with free-odds.

Once three points are established, we'll stop betting. Every time a point repeats and is paid off, we'll make another bet, so that at all times during a shoot we strive to have three points working for us. If the come point is made, we'll place another come bet. If it's the pass line, then we'll make another pass line bet. Like always, we'll back all our bets with the maximum single odds allowed.

If the shooter sevens-out, we'll start the sequence over again.

With three points covered, the bettor using this Aggressive method can make a lot of money when the shooter starts rolling numbers, especially when he utilizes our strategies for maximizing winning sessions.

Maximizing Profits – Methods For Right Bettors

The way to win big at craps is to play winning streaks aggressively so when points start repeating, our profits will mount quickly. The beauty of these strategies is that, while we give ourselves the opportunity of making huge profits, we never incur the risk of taking a devastating loss, for we'll only increase our bets when winning.

We won't start playing more aggressively until we're ahead by at least 20 units as Basic Conservative players and 25 units as Aggressive players. For $1 bettors making standard bets of $3, that means $20 and $25 respectively, for $5 bettors making standard bets of $15, that means $100 and $125, while for $25 chip players betting $75 a play, it means $500 and $625 respectively.

Theoretically, we could increase our bet size before this time, but that leaves or bankroll vulnerable to bad runs of luck. The concept is to play aggressively on their money, not ours.

We wait until all our points are established and working before increasing our bets.

Let's say we're betting $15 as our basic three unit bet ($5 units), and have already established the pass line point with single odds on the 8, and two come points with single odds on the 5 and 10. We now have three points working for us, the basic plan for the Aggressive Method, and see that we're already ahead 27 units.

Our strategy now works as follows. Every time a point repeats and we get paid off, instead of re-establishing an additional come or pass line point at the basic three unit bet, we increase that bet by three units to six units, and back the new bet with maximum single odds. Thus, on a six unit bet, points 4 and 10 can be backed by six units, 5 and 9 by six units, and 6 and 8 by ten units.

(If the bet is uneven on points 5 and 9, more than six units can be bet as a free-odds wager, but if the bet is even and can be paid at 3 to 2, the special allowance wouldn't apply.)

Let's say points 8 and 10 have repeated and we have made six unit bets on the new pass and come wagers. The new points thrown are 9 on the come bet and a 10 on the pass line. So as it stands, we have six unit bets on the 9 and 10 (both bets backed by the full odds) and three units on the come point of 5. Should the 10, our pass line point repeat, our new bet would be six units, for our other point, the 5, still has only a three unit bet on it. Do not increase bets to higher levels (in this example, above 6 units) until all the points have been brought up to the same bet size.

If the streak continues and all the basic pass and come bets have been brought up to six unit bets, begin to reestablish won points by making pass and come bets in units of nine, and of course, backing all these bets with the maximum single odds allowed. Increase bets in this fashion for as long as the streak continues.

This steady progressive increase of bets allows us to maximize the profits resulting from a hot roll while protecting us against a sudden seven-out making serious inroads into our winnings.

Maximizing Profits: The Texas Roll Method

As an alternate and more aggressive way of increasing won bets, the bettor could increase each won bet by three units regardless of how many units were already placed on the other points. Thus, a bet that repeated twice in a row, could have a nine unit bet on it while the other points were covered by only three units each.

Our bet increases are in units of three so that we can continue to take advantage of the special three unit single odds allowances.

Do not begin new progressions (once a shooter sevens-out) at a level higher than three units. This is very important. A bettor that continues to bet in amounts higher than his initial standard three unit wager is susceptible to a short losing streak wiping out his hard earned gains in a matter of a few bad shoots. We will only bet more aggressively during a hot streak, and will not try to anticipate one occurring.

Once we've had our one great shoot we'll never give the casino a chance to get our winnings back. We'll return to our basic three unit bet. If things go poorly, we'll call it quits soon afterwards, a huge winner. If the shooter gets hot again, we'll start increasing our bets and winnings, always ready for the next big kill.

This is smart money management, the key to success for winners.

Double Odds Strategies

Whenever the bettor has a choice, he should always choose a double odds game over a single odds game, for the additional allowance of the free-odds bet drops the overall house edge from 0.8 percent to 0.6 percent when using our methods.

The playing strategies we will pursue in the double odds game are identical to the single odds game except that we will bet in units of two instead of three as recommended in the single odds game to take advantage of the special five unit free-odds allowance when the point is 6 or 8. Basic Conservative bettors should establish two points with maximum double odds on each, while Aggressive bettors will want to cover three points.

Follow the procedures for the single odds methods substituting only the two unit basic bet for the three unit bets, and making double odds bet instead of single odds.

Maximizing Profits – Double Odds Game

Again our strategy here will follow that of the single odds game except we'll be increasing our bets by two units instead of three. Basic Conservative bettors will not begin increasing bets until they've accumulated 20 units in profits, and Aggressive bettors will need 25 units.

Remember to take advantage of the special allowances when the point is a 6 or 8. A four unit bet can be backed by 10 units in the double odds game, and a six unit bet by 15.

When eventually the shooter sevens-out, ending our winning streak, we'll start the next progression again at two units, ready to capitalize on another hot roll should one develop.

WINNING STRATEGIES: BETTING AGAINST THE DICE

Though the odds of winning are equivalent to the right betting strategies, 0.8 percent in a single odds game and 0.6 percent in a double odds game, very few craps players bet against the dice. Many bettors feel uncomfortable about having to lay odds, putting more money on their free-odds bet than they will win should the bet be won, but as stated earlier, the free-odds wagers give the house no edge betting right or wrong.

However, players that bet wrong don't mind giving the odds, for the roll of a 7, their winner, will occur more often than any point number, and they'll have frequent winners. In addition, should a point be repeated, a losing roll for wrong bettors, only one bet will be lost. The other points covered by the wrong bettor are still in play.

On the other side of the dice, the right bettors fear the 7, for when it is thrown, all their established points and free-odds bets are lost.

We will apply the same principles of play as right bettors. We'll make only the best bets available to us, those that reduce the house edge to the lowest possible figure—the don't pass, the don't come and free-odds bets.

Basic Conservative Method – Wrong Bettors/Single Odds Strategy

Our standard bet will be in even increments of two units. Bets such as $15 or $25 are difficult to work with when the point is a 5 or 9 and 2 to 3 odds should be laid. Betting in other unit sizes is equally valid, but the player will find it easiest to work in multiples of $10.

These are the guidelines of our Basic conservative strategy:

1. We will make two unit don't pass and don't come bets until we have established bets against two points, and back both those bets with maximum free-odds.
2. Should a point repeat, a loser for us, we will make another don't come or don't pass bet, so that we can continue to have bets working against two points. If a 2, 3, 11 or 12 determines a winner or loser on a new don't pass or don't come bet, we will follow with another bet until we get that second point established, and then we'll play the maximum single odds against that point.
3. Stop establishing don't pass and don't come bets if a second point repeats. This is an important safeguard to protect us against bad losing streaks.
4. If a 7 is thrown, a winner on all our bets, we'll begin the progression again with our two unit don't pass bet.
5. Follow the recommendations in the Maximizing Profits section for advice on how to increase winnings when the dice are going our way.

As cautious bettors, we'll limit ourselves to a coverage of only two points and strictly follow the safeguard recommended in step three.

Aggressive Method – Wrong Bettors Single Odds Strategy

Our Aggressive strategy follows the same guidelines as the Basic-Conservative method except that we will cover three points during a shoot instead of two, and will stop making additional don't pass and don't come bets if three points repeat, instead of two as advised in the Basic Conservative method. We'll use the same bets—the don't pass, don't come and free-odds bets, and enjoy the same low 0.8 percent house edge in a single odds game.

We begin by making a don't pass bet, and backing that with the maximum single odds once the point is established. Then, we'll make two successive don't come wagers, or as many as necessary, until two points are established, and will back those bets with maximum single odds as well. Once we have bets established against three points, we'll stop betting.

Should a 2, 3, 11 or 12 be rolled before all the points are established, we'll make another don't come bet until that third point is set. And we'll strictly adhere to our safeguard. If a third point repeats, we'll stop making additional bets during the cycle, and just ride out the unlucky streak. We never want to bet into a losing streak.

When the shooter sevens-out, a winner on all our bets, we'll start our cycle again, establishing three points with the maximum single odds.

Maximizing Profits – Methods for Wrong Bettors

The safest and most effective way of winning big at craps is to increase bets only during cold runs*, when the dice are going *our* way. The concept is to parlay winnings into big winnings. We do this by increasing bets only during a winning cycle, when the dice have already won for us, and never after a losing bet. Players and systems that attempt to regain lost money by increasing their bets only court disaster, for this type of desperate betting leaves one vulnerable to huge losses, and that's bad money management.

We won't start playing more aggressively until we're ahead by at least 20 units as a Basic-Conservative player and 25 units as an Aggressive method player. This gives us the opportunity to make big profits when the dice are with us, while protecting us against ever getting hurt by a bad run. And as a matter of fact, if the basic wrong betting safeguards and the stop-loss advice in the money management section are adhered to, we'll never take a crippling loss. But we're always ready to win big.

Unlike the right bettors strategies where bets are increased during a cycle, we will wait until the shooter sevens-out, a winner for us, before we begin to play more aggressively. Once you're ahead the aforementioned amounts, and the previous betting cycle was a winning one, increase the basic bet by two units.

If all our points were covered by two unit basic bets, we'll now cover the points by four unit basic bets, and if after the shooter sevens-out, we have emerged winners again, we'll continue to bet into the winning streak, and up our bet by another two units, to six units. We'll continue to increase bets by two units as long as the streak continues, all the time backing the bets with the maximum single odds allowed.

If the basic bet was $10 (two units of $5), the next basic bet will be $20, and then $30 and so on.

Anytime a sequence has been a losing one, begin the following shoot at the original two unit basic bet. In the example above, we would begin again at $10. Smart money management dictates that we only increase bets during a winning streak.

All the time during a shoot, we'll follow the safeguards outlined in the strategies. Basic Conservative method bettors will stop establishing points should two points be repeated, and Aggressive method bettors will hold their bets if a third point repeats.

Double Odds Strategy – Wrong Bettors

Whenever possible, the wrong bettor should play a double odds game over a single odds game, for it lowers the overall house edge from 0.8% to 0.6%. And we always want to play with the best odds we can get—the lower the house edge, the greater our chances of winning.

By nature, the double odds strategies are more aggressive than the single odds games, and are more in tune for players whose temperament demands hotter action. For example, if the point is a 4 and $10 is bet on the don't pass, the single odds bettor would wager $20 (laying 1 to 2) as a free odds bet while the double odds bettor covers that some point with a $40 wager (also laying 1 to 2).

The double odds bettor lays more to win more and therefore needs a larger bankroll than his single odds counterpart. Therefore, to play this strategy, the double odds bettor must feel comfortable with the larger bet levels.

Our double odds strategies are identical to the single odds methods, except that we're playing double odds instead of single odds. We'll begin by making a two unit don't pass bet, and backing that bet by double odds once a point is established. If $10 is the line bet, $40 will be the double odds bet if the point is 4 or 10 (laying 1 to 2), $30 if the point is 5 or 9 (laying 2 to 3), and $24 if the point is 6 or 8 (laying 5 to 6).

Basic Conservative bettors will follow with a don't come bet and lay double odds on both points while Aggressive Strategy bettors will make two more don't come bets backed by the full double odds, or as many don't pass or don't come bets as needed until three points are covered and then backed by free odds bets.

Like the single odds strategies, the Basic Conservative players attempt to keep two points working at all times while the Aggressive Strategy players strive for three working points. When points repeat, new don't pass or don't come bets are made to reestablish another, but should a second point repeat for Basic Conservative players or a third point for Aggressive Strategy players, then we'll curtail all new betting until the shooter sevens-out, a winner on our remaining bets.

We employ this stop-loss as a safeguard to protect against one really bad shoot wiping out our table stakes. However, should the dice start blowing profits in our direction, we're immediately ready to capitalize on the situation.

We start the next come-out roll fresh, with a two unit don't pass wager, always ready for the streak that will mint chips for us.

Double Odds Strategy - Maximizing Gains

It is recommended that the bettor increase his wagers cautiously when playing a double odds game. The mushrooming effect of double odds can rapidly increase the outlay of money on the table, so we want to be conservative in our increases. For example, a $10 bettor may want to increase bets by only $5, since each $5 increase could call for an additional double odds bet of $20 if the point were a 4 or 10. The player must use his own discretions for bet increases, possibly one unit per winning cycle.

We'll use the same principles outlined in the single odds Basic Conservative strategy for increasing bets. We'll increase only during a winning streak and not before we're up at least 20 units, and for Aggressive Strategy players, we'll leave ourselves a cushion of 25 units before increasing our wagers.

BANKROLLING

The amount of money necessary to withstand the normal fluctuations common to craps vary according to the type of strategy you employ (right or wrong betting), the aggressiveness of your approach (Basic Conservative or Aggressive), and your expected playing time.

We'll discuss the single session bankroll first for the various strategies, and then present the type of bankroll the player will need for longer sessions at the craps table.

Single Session Bankroll • Right Bettors
Single & Double Odds Game

Approach (Points Covered)	Units Needed for a Single Cycle	Table Bankroll Needed
Basic-Cons. (2 Points)	14	100
Aggressive (3 points)	21	150

BANKROLL NEEDED: BASIC CONSERVATIVE STRATEGY

In the single odds game, Basic Conservative bettors will cover two points through pass and come bets and back both points with the maximum single odds allowed.

Since the standard line bet will be three units, and the single odds bet backing the pass and come wagers will be between three to five units, we can expect each point to require a total of six to eight units to be fully covered, or about 14 units to fully cover each cycle of two points.

In the double odds game, our standard line bet of two units will be backed with the maximum double odds allowed, or about four to five units for a total of six to seven units per point. Fully covering a cycle of two points will require about 14 units, the same as the single odds game.

BANKROLL NEEDED: AGGRESSIVE STRATEGY

Aggressive strategy bettors will need roughly 21 units to fully cover their three points in a single or double odds game.

To play safe, and give himself sufficient funds, the bettor should have enough of a table stake for about seven betting cycles. The Table Bankroll Needed columns in the above charts are computed by multiplying the units needed for a single cycle by seven, and then adding a few units as extra padding.

Single Session Bankroll • Wrong Bettors
Single Odds Game

Approach (Points Covered)	Units Needed for a Single Cycle	Table Bankroll Needed
Basic-Cons. (2 Points)	10	75
Aggressive (3 points)	15	115

Single Session Bankroll • Wrong Bettors
Double Odds Game

Approach (Points Covered)	Units Needed for a Single Cycle	Table Bankroll Needed
Basic-Cons. (2 Points)	16	125
Aggressive (3 points)	24	175

BANKROLL NEEDED:
SINGLE ODDS GAME – WRONG BETTORS

The standard bet size for both Basic Conservative players and Aggressive Strategy players is two units in our strategies*. Our free odds wager in the single odds game will be two units on the 6 or 8 (laying 5 to 6), three units on the 5 or 9 (laying 2 to 3), and four units on the 4 or 10 (laying 1 to 2) for an average of about three units per

*For players that bet in unit sizes other than two units, they can figure the table stake needed by estimating the number of units needed for one full cycle of play, and multiplying that number by seven.

single odds bet. In addition to the two unit don't pass or don't come bet, that adds up to five units per point.

Basic conservative bettors will need 10 units, two points times five units, for each betting cycle, while Aggressive Strategy bettors will need 15 units for a round, three points each covered by approximately five betting units.

BANKROLL NEEDED:
DOUBLE ODDS GAME – WRONG BETTORS

The standard betting size for either strategy here is two units, and we'll back each point by about six units, for a total of about eight units needed to fully cover each point in a double odds game. Basic Conservative bettors playing two points will need 16 units for a betting cycle while Aggressive Strategy players, who cover three points, need about 24 betting units.

In a double odds game, a two unit bet on the 4 or 10 gets backed by eight units, on the 5 and 9 gets backed by six units, and on the 6 or 8 gets backed by a little under five units, for an average of six units per double odds bet.

TOTAL BANKROLL

The longer one plans on playing craps, the larger one's bankroll must be to cover the inevitable fluctuations. The following bankroll requirements have been formulated to give the player enough capital to survive any reasonable losing streak, and be able to bounce back on top.

Total Bankroll Requirements • Right Bettors
Single and Double Odds Games

Approach (Points Covered)	Single Session Stake	One Day Bankroll	Weekend Bankroll
Basic-Cons. (2 points)	100	300	500
Aggressive (3 Points)	150	450	750

Total Bankroll Requirements • Wrong Bettors
Single Odds Games

Approach (Points Covered)	Single Session Stake	One Day Bankroll	Weekend Bankroll
Basic-Cons. (2 points)	75	225	375
Aggressive (3 Points)	115	350	675

Total Bankroll Requirements • Wrong Bettors
Double Odds Games

Approach (Points Covered)	Single Session Stake	One Day Bankroll	Weekend Bankroll
Basic-Cons. (2 points)	125	375	625
Aggressive (3 Points)	175	525	875

The bankroll needed for a full day's session should be about three times that of a single session, and the weekend's bankroll should be about five times that of a single session. Players should never dip into their pockets past these levels for we never want to get beat bad at the tables.

These bankroll levels give us sufficient room to take some losses and still have enough of a bankroll to play confidently and wait for a hot streak to turn the tables on the casino and make us winners.

This does not mean the player must have all the money out on the table when playing, but that that money should be readily available in his pocket in case it's needed.

As you will see later in the minimizing losses section, we will never use all our table stake in any one session but will restrict our losses should luck go against us. This way we'll never get hurt by an unlucky session.

If you arrive at the casinos with a definite amount of money to gamble with, and want to figure out how much your unit size bet should be, simply take your gambling stake and divide it by the amount of units you need to have for the particular strategy you want to play.

If you bring $1,000 with you and were to spend a day using the right bettors Basic Conservative strategy in a single odds game, you would divide $1,000 by 300 units, the number in the *Total Bankroll* column, for a basic unit bet of roughly $3 ($3,33). Since right bettors wager in units of three in our single odds strategy, the standard pass or come bet would be about $10.

If you were to play the Aggressive Strategy, you would divide $1,000 by 450 units, for a basic unit bet of $2 ($2.22). Three unit bets would come out to the rough equivalent of betting $5 or $6 on the pass line or come bet, $5 being a good choice in the single odds game for we could use the special odds bet allowance when the point is a 6 or an 8.

Similarly, a player who likes to bet against the dice and has brought $1,500 for a single day's gambling would bet in $10 units if playing the Aggressive Strategy in a single odds game. We divide $1,500 by 350 for the rough equivalent of $5 ($4.29), and since our strategies call for bets in increments of two units, the standard don't come or don't pass wager will be $10.

However, we advise against the player overdoing it at the craps tables, for though we have reduced the house edge to the lowest possible amount, and give the player the best chances of winning, that small house edge can grind out the bettor over extended sessions of play.

MINIMIZING LOSSES

Here are some simple guidelines that, if followed, will save you a lot of money. You'll notice that our stop-loss limits are less than the recommended single session table stakes.

STOP-LOSS LIMITS

Right bettors: Limit your table losses to 70 units for Basic Conservative bettors, and 100 units for Aggressive bettors. If betting $5 chips ($15 standard line bet), never lose more than $350 and $500 respectively in any one session; if $1 chips ($3 standard line bet), then $70 for Basic Conservative bettors and $100 for Aggressive bettors.

Wrong bettors: Wrong bettors should limit their table losses to the same levels as right bettors in single and double odds games.

Do not dig in for more money, and you can never be a big loser. Take a break, try again later. You never want to get into a position where losing so much in one session totally demoralizes you.

BET WITHIN YOUR MEANS

Never increase your bet range beyond your bankroll capabilities. In other words, always bet within your means.

DO NOT INCREASE BETS WHEN LOSING

Never increase your bet size to catch up and break even. Raising it will not change the odds of the game, nor will it change your luck. What it will do is make your chances of taking a terrible beating frighteningly high. Do not get into a position where losing so much in one session destroys any reasonable chance of coming out even. You can't win all the time. Rest a while, you'll get them later.

PROTECTING WINS

Once winning, the most important thing in craps is to walk away a winner. Read the money management section carefully so that you can use the strategies here to maximum advantage.

Baccarat

FIVE KEYS TO BACCARAT

1 Don't be intimidated by the tuxedos. The game has a "classy" veneer, but in reality, the only decision you make in baccarat is how much to bet.

2 For average players, the house edge at baccarat is one of the best in the casino whether betting Player or Banker.

3 Get familiar with the third card drawing rules. Baccarat will be more fun if you know the rules as well as the dealer.

4 Do not make the Tie bet. This terrible bet gives the casino a big 14.1% edge.

5 Card counting strategies can be used to take advantage of altered decks at baccarat of a professional strategy.

INTRODUCTION

This glamorous game is steeped in centuries of European tradition and while a mainstay and important game on the continent, is only just beginning to catch on in the American casinos.

Bettors are not only attracted to baccarat's leisurely style of play and the very low casino odds the game offers the player, but to the exciting new winning approach, card counting, which has proved so successful for blackjack players.

In its different varieties, baccarat can be found in casinos around the world. The version played in the United States originated in Cuba in the 1950s and is called **American** or **Nevada style baccarat** though U.S. casinos simply refer to it as **baccarat**. Elsewhere in the world this version is known as **punto banco**.

In Europe, **chemin de fer** and **baccarat banque** are quite popular, while **mini-baccarat**, a smaller version of punto banco is found more and more in casinos in the U.S. and around the world.

Baccarat is a simple game to play even for beginners, for the dealer or croupier, directs all the action according to fixed rules. As you'll see, the game is quite easy to play and in no time at all, you'll be ready to take your place at the tables and enjoy all that baccarat has to offer.

Let's move on now and see what the game is all about!

THE BASICS OF BACCARAT

THE LAYOUT

Baccarat is played on a specially constructed layout which allows players to choose either of the two betting spots, **Banker** or **Player** to make their wager. The regulation tables normally have betting spots for 12-14 players, with each player having a corresponding number spot, 1 through 12, or 14 as the case may be, to place his or her bets.

Bets on the Player position can be placed immediately in front of the player, in the numbered area, while bets on the Banker position, go in the numbered slots indicated by "**bank**."

The mini-baccarat layout has space for about seven players. As on the regulation table, each spot is numbered, and bets on either of the betting positions are placed in front of the bettor.

The Baccarat Layout

CASINO PERSONNEL

The game is generally manned by three dealers. One dealer is in charge of the game and his function is to run the show. He or she will direct the play, telling players what to do—when they need a draw and when the cards should be dealt. The other two dealers handle the betting, collecting lost bets from the losers, making payoffs on won hands and keeping track of the commissions owed.

CARD VALUES

Cards valued 2 to 9 are counted according to their face value, a 2 equals 2 points, an ace equals one point, and a 7 equals 7 points. The 10, jack, queen, and king, have a value of 0 points. They have no effect when adding up the points in a hand. Points are counted by adding up the value of the cards. However, hands totaling 10 or more points, have the first digit dropped so that no hand contains a total of greater than 9 points. For example, two nines (18) is a hand of 8 points and a 7 5 (12) is a hand of 2 points. A hand of a 3 and a 4 would simply be valued at 7 points.

The suits have no value in baccarat.

THE OBJECT OF BACCARAT

A player has the choice of betting Banker or Player, and the object of the game is for the position chosen to beat the other hand. The hand closer to the total of 9 is the winner. The worst score is zero, called **baccarat.** A tie is a standoff or push, neither hand wins.

BETTING LIMITS

The casino limits on minimum and maximum bets will be posted by the table, and as long as these guidelines are followed, a player may bet whatever desired. Higher limits than those posted can often be arranged.

TABLE DE BANQUE CARD

Like roulette, serious baccarat players like to keep track of the winning progressions and can do so on cards provided by the casino and called, a **Table de Banque** card. These cards provide a convenient place to record wins by either the Banker or Player position, and keep the systems players on track for the game.

THE PLAY OF THE GAME

Baccarat is normally played with eight decks of cards dealt out of a shoe, though a mini-baccarat table may use only six decks. Each deck is a standard 52 card deck containing thirteen cards, ace through king, in each of the four suits, though as we mentioned above, the suits have no bearing in the game.

There are two opposing sides, the Player and the Banker, and no matter how many players are betting in a game, only two hands will be dealt; one for the Banker position and one for the Player position, except in the baccarat banque version, where there are two Player positions instead of one.

A bettor may choose either side to bet on and does so by placing the wager in the Banker or Player's position, whichever is chosen, corresponding to his or her numbered seat. After the betting is done, each side will be dealt two cards.

In Nevada style baccarat (punto banco), the players deal the cards. The shoe rotates counterclockwise around the table with each player having his or her turn at it. There is no advantage in dealing and a player may refuse the deal, in which case the shoe will be offered to the next player in turn.

The player acting as dealer will slide the first card face down to the **caller**, the dealer who controls the pace and runs the game, and slip the second card, also face down, under the front corner of the shoe. Likewise, the third card will go face down to the caller, and the fourth one, like the second, goes face down under the shoe.

Each side now, the Player position represented by the caller's cards, and the Banker position, represented by the two cards under the shoe, has two cards.

The caller will pass the two cards dealt to him to the bettor with the highest wager on the Player's position. After examining the cards, the bettor will flip them back to the caller who then will announce the total.

The dealer will now take the Banker's cards from under the shoe and pass them along to the caller who will announce their total as well.

HAND VALUES

A dealt total of 8 or 9 points is called a **natural**, and no additional cards will be drawn. It is an automatic win unless the opposing hand has a higher natural (a 9 vs. an 8), or the hand is a tie.

A natural of 8 points is called **le petit**, a total of nine, **le grande.**

On all other totals, 0 through 7, the drawing of an additional card depends strictly on established rules of play. There is never more than one card drawn to a hand in any case.

The player need not be familiar with the rules for drawing on the third card for the caller will direct the action and request that a third card be drawn if the rules require it. Just follow the caller's instructions—as easy as that!

The Player's hand will be acted upon first, and then the Banker's. Despite the different variations of baccarat, the third card rules for draw are consistent for games around the world.

The two card total of the Player's hand determines whether a third card should be drawn and is regulated by the following rules:

PLAYER RULES

Two Card Total	Player's Action
0-5*	Draw a Card
6 or 7	Stand
8 or 9	Natural. Banker cannot draw.

*In chemin de fer and baccarat banque, the player has the option to stand or draw on a point total of 5 points only.

After the Player's hand has been acted upon, it is the Banker's turn. Whether the Banker position receives a card depends upon two variables. In some cases, it depends upon his two card total, and other times, it depends upon the card that the Player position has drawn.

If the Banker hand is 0, 1 or 2, a card is drawn, while with hands of 7, 8 and 9, no cards are drawn. The other Banker totals of 3, 4, 5 and 6 are drawn upon depending upon what card the Player position has drawn.

Rules for drawing or standing can be broken up as follows.

Situation 1 – Either the Player or the Banker has a natural 8 or 9. It is an automatic win for the hand with the natural. If both hands have naturals, the higher natural wins. (A natural 9 beats a natural 8.) If the naturals are equal, the hand is a tie.

Situation 2 – If the Player has a 0-5, Player must draw another card; if a 6-7, the Player must stand.

Situation 3 – If Player stands, than Banker hand follows the same rules as the Player—it must draw on totals of 0-5, and stand on 6-7.

Situation 4 – If Player draws, Banker must draw or stand according to the value of the third card dealt as show below in the Banker Rules chart. (Note that the banker always draws on totals of 0-2, unless of course, the Player has a natural.)

Banker Rules

Banker Total	Bank Draws When Giving Player This Card	Bank Does Not Draw When Giving Player This Card
0-2	0-9	
3	0-7, 9*	8
4	2-7	0-1, 8-9
5	4*, 5-7	0-3, 8-9
6	6-7	0-5, 8-9
7	Banker Always Stands	
8-9	A Natural – Player Can't Draw	

*In punto banco and mini-baccarat, the drawing of a third card is mandatory, while in chemin de fer, it is an optional draw or stand.

PAYOFFS AND ODDS

The winning hand in baccarat is paid at 1 to 1, **even money**, except in the case of the Banker's position where a 5% commission is charged on a winning hand. Commission is charged because of the inherent edge the Banker position has over the Player position.

During actual play, this commission is kept track of on the side by use of chips and won bets at the Banker position are paid off at even money. This avoids the cumbersome 5% change-giving on every hand. The commission is collected later at the end of every shoe or before the player parts from the game.

With the commission, the average Banker edge over the bettor is only 1.17%, quite low by casino standards. The average house edge over the Player position is only slightly more, 1.36%. These percentages can vary though as cards are removed during the course of play.

BACCARAT AROUND THE WORLD

Let's now look at the differences in the main versions of baccarat as played around the world.

AMERICAN OR NEVADA STYLE BACCARAT (PUNTO BANCO)

In this version of play, usually referred to as simply baccarat in the U.S. casinos, the bettor has a choice of betting the Player (Punto), or the Banker (Banco). He plays against the house which books all bets and pays winning hands. There are no third card drawing options for either the Banker (Banco) or Player (Punto) position.

The bettor may wager on a **tie bet**—a poor wager that pays off at 9 *for* 1 (8 to 1) and gives the casino an edge of 14.10%. (This bet is not offered in chemin de fer and baccarat banque.)

In this variation of baccarat, the only decisions a player makes are whether to bet Banker or Player, and how much to bet.

CHEMIN DE FER

The bettor who plays the Banker position deals the cards and books all bets. The other players oppose the Banker. The Player position has one third card drawing option, and is controlled by the bettor with the highest bet placed. The Banker has two drawing options and plays the hand himself. (See Player and Banker Rules charts.) No tie bet is offered.

The casino acts only in a supervisory capacity and collects its fee as a percentage levy or as an hourly rate charged to the players.

The Banker is decided by either **auction**, where the highest bidder takes the Banker position and puts up his or her bid as the bank, by lot, or by acceptance as the bank moves its way around the table.

A bettor plays Banker until he loses a hand or voluntarily gives it up. The next player, clockwise or counterclockwise, according to the house rules, can play Banker, and set his own limit on the bets he will book. A bettor may refuse the bank and pass it on to the next player.

The total amount of money bet against the Banker in a hand is limited by the amount of money in the bank. Any player who wishes to bet against the entire bank, calls out "**banco**," thus nullifying the other bets.

BACCARAT BANQUE

The casino deals all cards and books all bets. There are two player (punto) positions on this two-sided layout. These spots are manned by bettors who oppose the banker (banco) position which is always taken by the house. Bettors may wager on either Player position or both. The Player has one third card drawing option.

The Banker is not bound by third card drawing restrictions as in other variations and may stand or draw one card. (Some casinos apply restrictions on the banker.)

BACCARAT A TOUT VA

Everything goes baccarat in the two-sided style of Baccarat banque. No maximum limit on bets.

MINI-BACCARAT

The same game as Nevada Style/Punto Banco except that it's played on a miniature blackjack-type table, and that the casino deals the cards.

GAME COMPARISONS

The following chart shows the positions a bettor may wager in the various versions of baccarat.

Players Betting Guide

Game	Player	Banker
Punto Banco	Yes	Yes
Mini-Baccarat	Yes	Yes
Chemin De Fer	Yes	Only the bettor playing the Banker may bet Banker.
Baccarat Banque	Yes*	No

* Can wager on either or both of the player hands.
Yes – Indicates a player may bet the position. No – Indicates a player may not bet the position.

The odds vary slightly among the various version of baccarat and the following chart will outline this for you.

House Edge at Baccarat

Wager	Payoff	House Edge
Nevada Style/Punto Banco		
Player	1 to 1	1.36%
Banker	1 to 1	1.17%
Tie	9 for 1	14.10%
Chemin de Fer		
Player	1 to 1	1.23%
Banker	1 to 1	1.06%
Baccarat Banque		
Average Edge		0.92%

WINNING STRATEGIES

TRADITIONAL BETTING STRATEGIES

There is very little decision making in baccarat, thus winning strategies were traditionally confined to betting systems and money management techniques. These strategies are based on winning streaks and won/lost trends, going with the positions that are hot and adjusting bets according to whether the last hand won or lost.

There are many interesting approaches available for players who enjoy betting systems. Just keep in mind that these systems don't change the odds of the games they attempt to defeat.

WINNING WITH CARD COUNTING

Card counting techniques, which proved so effective at winning at blackjack, have been attracting a lot of study lately as a winning method at baccarat. Here's how they work.

In baccarat, just like blackjack, the removal of cards from play creates situations where the chances of receiving particular cards or combinations of cards change. The removal of certain types of cards favor the Player while others favor the Banker.

A good count strategy shows you how to recognize situations that favor betting Banker and others where Player is the better bet. By judiciously altering bets with the count, a card counter can improve his or her chances at the table and win money at baccarat.

The basic theory is that low cards favor the Player position, and high cards favor the Banker. Certain cards have little effect and are considered neutral. Counters track the removal of these cards, betting the Player position when there is a higher ratio of low cards in the deck, and the Banker position when there is a higher ratio of the high cards remaining.

For players interested in winning with card counting methods, we recommend the excellent advanced strategy, the Baccarat Master Card Counter, advertised at the end of the book.

BACCARAT SUMMARY

Baccarat combines the allure and glamour of European tradition with relatively low house odds for the average player, 1.17% in the Banker's position and 1.36% in the Player's spot.

One advantage of baccarat, especially for high rollers, is that one cannot make mental mistakes which will give the casino an added edge. Compare this to games such as blackjack, craps or poker, where poor decisions in the heat of the game can cause the bettor to make costly errors and you can understand one of the allures of the game.

Despite the exclusive look of the game though, baccarat can be played by anyone. There's no need to bet mini-fortunes to play. It is a leisurely game, and in the version played in the American casinos, an easy one as well. There are no decisions to make save for how much to bet and which position, Player or Banker, to back.

The low casino edge and the exciting winning possibilities available makes baccarat a perfect place to wager in style, surrounded by elegant decor, playing this centuries-old game in the grand tradition.

Roulette

FIVE KEYS TO ROULETTE

1 When possible, always play a single zero game over a double zero game. The better house odds makes your chances of winning much greater.

2 Get familiar with all the bets and payouts so you have the full arsenal at your command.

3 Have fun with betting systems but realize that roulette is a negative expectation game and no betting system will overcome this.

4 Except for the 5-number bet, all bets at American roulette offer equal odds.

5 Money management is essential. Be smart with your money.

INTRODUCTION

Roulette offers players a huge variety of bets, more than any other casino table game, and the constant possibilities of winning and the different payoffs of the wagers, ranging from even-money payoffs to returns of 35 to 1, keeps the game exciting and suspenseful.

The game is set up for systems players, and it is not unusual to find tables full of bettors armed with pencil and pad, plying their favorite winning systems. The systems sometimes fail and sometimes win but we'll discuss their virtues and shortcomings, so that you'll be able to approach the game fully prepared to play the best way possible.

The attraction of making fortunes with the spin of the wheel has made roulette the oldest and most famous gambling game in European casinos where roulette is king. Roulette is enormously popular there and is a game favored by royalty and celebrities as well as regular gamblers looking for the thrill of action. Roulette is much less popular in America, and as opposed to the crowded and noisy tables prevalent over on the other side of the Atlantic, tables in the U.S. casinos remain comparatively quiet.

We'll show you how the two styles of play differ, American and European, and why roulette games are so popular in Europe yet play second fiddle to the other table games in American casinos.

We'll also show you how to make all the different bets possible, their designations in French and in English, and the odds involved, so that you'll be ready to play roulette anywhere in the world and be fully prepared to have the best chances of winning!

THE BASICS OF ROULETTE

THE ROULETTE SETTING

Roulette is played with a circular wheel containing 36 grooved slots numbered from 1 to 36, half the numbers of which are black and the other half red, a tiny ball which is used in conjunction with the wheel, and a betting layout where players can place their wagers.

The American Wheel

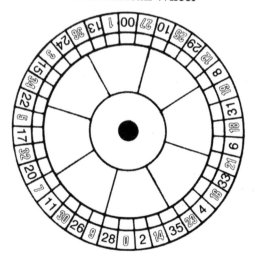

In addition to the 36 numbers on the roulette wheel, the American game has a 0 and 00, while the European game has but one 0. The zero slots are neither red nor black as are the other numbers but are green in color.

The wheel is cut into tiny pockets, one for each number—37 total on a European wheel and 38 on an American—so that the ball, when spun around the wheel, will eventually fall into one of these slots, that number being the winning spin.

The European game generally has the wheel flanked on two sides by a betting layout, so that the busy tables can accommodate players on both sides of the wheel, while the less popular American games typically use but one layout to the side.

THE LAYOUT

1to18	1st 12	0		00
		1	2	3
		4	5	6
EVEN		7	8	9
		10	11	12
◇	2nd 12	13	14	15
		16	17	18
		19	20	21
◆		22	23	24
ODD	3rd 12	25	26	27
		28	29	30
		31	32	33
19to36		34	35	36
		2-1	2-1	2-1

THE DEALER

The American game typically employs just one dealer who handles all of the functions at the table. He changes money into chips, spins the wheel, collects losing bets and pays off the winners. In between he finds time to stack and restack collected chips from the layout into neat, colorful piles, so that payoffs from the next spin will proceed smoothly and rapidly.

If a table is exceptionally busy, the dealer may have an assistant to help run the game.

European style games have one to as many as three or four **croupiers**, the French term for dealers, paying and collecting bets on the two adjacent layouts, and a **tourneur**, whose main responsibility is to spin the wheel and call the result. Often, a supervisor will be present as well.

Thus, when things get rolling and the tables crowded, one might find as many as six casino personnel manning a roulette game—a tourneur, four croupiers and a supervisor.

THE PLAY OF THE GAME

Once players have placed their bets on the layout, choosing from the myriad possibilities available in front of them, the game is officially ready to begin. The roulette wheel will be spun by the dealer or tourneur who immediately afterwards, will throw the ball in the opposite direction from which the wheel is spinning so that both ball and wheel are racing in opposite directions on the wheel itself.

Players must now get in their last minute wagers for when the ball is about to leave the track, the dealer will announce that bets are no longer permitted. The call of *Faites vos jeux*, *messieurs* (Make your bets gentlemen) or *Rien ne va plus* (Nothing more goes) are classic in the French speaking casinos.

Once the ball has stopped, the dealer or tourneur will call out the outcome, and a marker will be placed on the number just spun so that all players and dealers can clearly see the winning number.

The dealers or **croupiers**, as they're called in French, will now settle the wagers. Lost bets are collected first by the dealers, and after this is done, all the winning bets will be paid off.

THE CHIPS

Keeping track of one's bets are easy in American roulette games, for each player is issued special chips applicable only to the roulette game at that casino, and these chips are colored, a different color for each player. Ten different players may be represented by, for example, yellow, red, pink, blue, green, black, white, beige, purple and grey chips.

The colored chips are valid and can be used only at the roulette table which issues them. If the table is crowded and no more colors are available, a player may use regular casino chips for his or her bets.

There is no confusion in ownership of the chips this way. Color coding makes life easy at these tables. When a player approaches the roulette table, he exchanges cash or casino chips for an equivalent value in the colored chips, called in the parlance of the game, **wheel checks**. The value assigned to those colored chips, be it 25¢, $1.00, $5.00 or whatever, is set by the player. Thus, if the player wants to value the chips at 25¢, more chips will be issued from the dealer than if the chips were valued at $1.00.

The dealer will place a coin or **marker button** on top of the colored chips and place these on the stationary outer rim of the wheel, so that the value of that wheel check is clearly marked.

When a player is ready to leave, he converts the wheel checks back into the regular casino checks with the dealer at that table.

Life is a bit more complicated in the European style game where color coding is not used and bettors simply use casino chips or cash to make their bets. Sometimes, in the confusion of a crowded game, vociferous arguments ensue as players lay identical claim to chips on the felt.

THE BASIC ODDS

The primary difference in the popularity of European and American roulette lies in the simple fact that the European game gives the player much better odds of winning, and this is where the 0, 00 difference of the two wheels comes into play.

Let's see how the odds are figured.

There are slots numbered from 1 to 36 on the roulette wheel—a total of 36. There is only one way to win for each number chosen. That leaves 35 other numbers, which if they come up, are losers for the bettor. True odds of 35 to 1 against—35 ways to lose, one way to win.

And that is exactly what the casino will pay on a single number bet.

So where is the casino's profit?

It is the zeros added to the wheel that give casinos their edge, for now there are a total of 37 possibilities on a European wheel (single zero added) and 38 possibilities on an American one (double zero added). The casino's payoff is still 35 to 1, being based on the true odds of a 36 number wheel. However, with the added zeros, the true odds on a single number bet are now 36 to 1 on a single zero wheel (the European game) and 37 to 1 on a double zero wheel (the American game).

Those zeros give the casino its edge on all bets made. Unless the zero (and in American roulette the 00 also) are bet directly, the spin of either on the wheel causes all other wagers to lose.

The sole exceptions are the even-money bets in a European style game (and Atlantic City), for the spin of a zero gives the red-black (rouge-noir), high-low (passe-manque) and odd-even (impair-pair) bettors a second chance, and reduces the house edge on these bets to 1.35% (2.63% in Atlantic City)—the best odds one can receive in roulette.

The zeros represent the house advantage and that is why the 00 in American roulette makes that game a worse gamble for the player than its European counterpart. Atlantic City makes up for this a little by offering surrender on even-money bets, bringing the casino's edge on these wagers down to 2.63%.

Let's sum up the odds for you in chart form so that you can clearly see them in one spot.

Casino Edge in Roulette

American Roulette (Double Zero)	House Edge
The 5-Number Bet	7.89%
All Other Bets	5.26%
Atlantic City – Even Money Bets	2.63%

European Roulette (One Zero)	House Edge
Even-Money Bets – *En prison* Rule	1.35%
All Other Bets	2.70%

The difference between the 1.35% of European style roulette and 5.26% of the American style is significant, almost a four-fold increase, which calculates directly to a loss rate four times as fast.

Now you can see why roulette with a single zero and *en prison* rule is the rage of Europe, and double zero American roulette is not popular at all.

THE BETS

Roulette offers the player a multitude of possible wagers, more than any other casino table game. All in all, there are over 150 possible combinations to bet. And a player may make as many bets in whatever combinations desired as long as the bets fit within the minimum and maximum limit of the casino.

Let's now examine the bets one by one. (The French names for the bets are listed in parenthesis.)

COMBINATION OR INSIDE BETS

These bets are made within the numbers on the layout, and hence, are termed **inside bets**.

Single Number Bet – (En Plein)

A **single number bet** can be made on any number on the layout including the 0 and 00. To make this wager, place your chip within the lines of the number chosen, being careful not to touch the lines. Otherwise you may have another bet altogether.

The winning payoff is 35 to 1.

The Single Number Bet

Split Bet (A Cheval)

Place the chip on the line adjoining two numbers. If either number comes up, the payoff is 17 to 1.

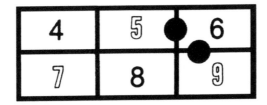

Trio Bet (Transversale)

The chip is placed on the outside vertical line alongside any line of numbers. If any of the three are hit, the payoff is 11 to 1.

Trio Bet (Transversale)

4-Number Bet (Carre)

Also called a square or corner bet. Place the chip on the spot marking the intersection of four numbers. If any of the four come in it is an 8 to 1 payoff.

4-Number Bet (Carre)

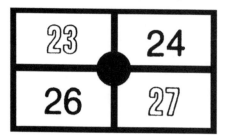

Quatre Premiere

Only in European roulette. The bet covering the 0, 1, 2 and 3. An 8 to 1 payoff.

5-Number Bet

Only in American roulette. Place the chip at the end of the intersection where the 0 and 1 overlaps to cover the 0, 00, 1, 2, and 3 five number bet. If any of these five come home, the payoff is 6 to 1. In American roulette, it is the only bet not giving the house an edge of 5.26%. It's worse—7.89%!

5-Number Bet

0   00
1   2   3

6-Number Bet (Sixaine)

Also called a **block bet**. The chip should be put on the outside line of the layout while intersecting the line separating the sets of numbers chosen. The payoff is 5 to 1.

6-Number Bet (Sixaine)

28	29	30
31	32	33

OUTSIDE BETS

The *outside bets* are outside the 36 numbers on the layout. They include the columns, dozens and even money bets—red-black, high-low and odd-even.

Outside Bets

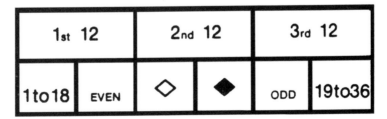

Columns Bet (Colonne)

A chip placed at the head of a column, on the far side from the zero or zeros, covers all 12 numbers in the column and has a winning payoff of 2 to 1. The 0 and 00 are not included in this bet and would make this bet a loser if they come up.

Columns Bet (Colonne)

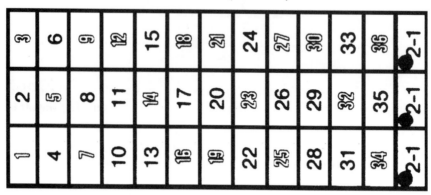

Dozens Bet (Douzaine)

This is another way to bet 12 numbers, either numbers 1 to 12, 13 to 24 or 25 to 36. On the American layout they're called the **first**, **second** and **third dozen** respectively, and on the French layout, they're known as **P12**, **M12** and **D12**. The winning payoff as in the column bet is 2 to 1.

Dozens Bet (Douzaine)

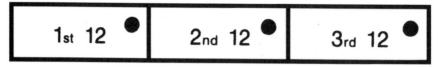

Even-Money Bets

There is one final type of bet, the even money bets: Red-Black (Rouge-Noir), High-Low (Passe-Manque) and Odd-Even (Impair-Pair). Spots for these bets are found outside the numbers, thus these are still classified as outside wagers. These wagers are clearly marked in large boxes.

In Atlantic City and European style roulette, these bets are the best at the roulette table, for they offer the player additional features which are greatly advantageous to the player. In Europe, the features are called *en prison* and *partage*, and in Atlantic City, surrender.

First we'll go over the bets, and after, we'll examine how the *en prison*, *partage* and surrender rules work and how they affect the player.

Even-Money Bets

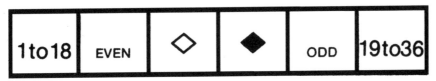

Red-Black (Rouge-Noir)

There are 18 black and eighteen red numbers. A player may bet either the **red** or the **black** and is paid off at 1 to 1 on a winning spin.

Red-Black (Rouge-Noir)

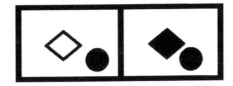

High-Low (Passe-Manque)

Numbers 1-18 may be bet (**low**) or 19-36 (**high**). Bets are paid off at 1 to 1.

High-Low (Passe-Manque)

Odd-Even (Impair-Pair)

A player may bet on the 18 even numbers, **even**, or **odd**, the 18 odd numbers. Winning bets are paid at 1 to 1.

Odd-Even (Impair-Pair)

EN PRISON AND PARTAGE

It is on these even number bets (above) where the American and European games really differ. In American roulette, the house automatically wins on these bets when the 0 or 00 is spun (except in Atlantic City).

However, in Europe, if the 0 is spun, the *en prison* rule comes into effect. The player has two choices now.

He or she can either surrender half the bet, called *partage*, or elect to allow the bet to be "imprisoned" one more spin. If the spin is won, the bet stays intact and is "released" for the player to do what he or she will. If the spin is lost, so is the bet.

This rule is greatly advantageous to the player, and brings the odds down on these bets to 1.35% in favor of the casino as opposed to the 2.70% on the rest of the bets in the single zero game.

SURRENDER

In an attempt to get more gamblers to play roulette, the game in Atlantic City helps make up for the 00 of the American wheel by offering **surrender**, which is really *partage* by another name.

When a 0 or 00 is spun, players with bets on any of the even-money propositions lose only half the bet, "surrendering it," and keep the other half. This brings the house edge down to 2.63% on these bets.

AMERICAN AND EUROPEAN ROULETTE

The European and American game is pretty much the same besides the use of the French terms in Europe, and of course the American terms in the U.S. casinos. However, there are two significant differences.

1. In addition to the 36 numbers on the roulette wheel, the American game has a 0 and 00, while the European game has but one 0.
2. The European game offers *en prison* and *partage*, rules greatly beneficial to the player. *En prison* and *partage* is not offered in American casinos, with the exception of Atlantic City where surrender (*partage*) is used.

The end result, as we showed earlier, is that the casino edge in the European game is but 1.35% as opposed to American roulette where the player has to overcome a hefty 5.26% house edge (or 2.63% on even-money bets in Atlantic City).

Roulette Payoff Chart
Bets in Roulette

American Name	#	French Name	Payoff
Single Number	1	En Plein	35-1
Split Bet	2	A Cheval	17-1
Trio	3	Transversale	11-1
4-Number (Corner)	4	Carre	8-1
(Not Applicable)	4	Quatre Premiere	8-1
5-Number	5	(Not Applicable)	6-1
6-Number or Block	6	Sixaine	5-1
Columns Bet	12	Colonne	2-1
Dozens Bet	12	Dozaine	2-1
Red or Black	18	Rouge ou Noir	1-1
High or Low	18	Passe ou Manque	1-1
Odd or Even	18	Impair ou Pair	1-1

 # column is the amount of numbers covered by the bet.

THE WINNING STRATEGIES

First it must be stated clearly, that like most other casino games, the casino has the mathematical edge over the player, and that no betting strategy or playing system can overcome those odds unless the wheel is a biased one—which we'll cover.

That edge is 5.26% in American roulette, with the exception of even-money bets in Atlantic City where the edge is 2.63%, and 2.70% in European roulette, unless the even-money wagers are made, where the house edge drops to 1.35%.

Based on the above facts, one must develop a lucid picture on how to approach a winning strategy. The key words here are casino edge or advantage.

It must be understood that in the long haul, the casino's edge will grind out the player—but that doesn't mean the player can't show a profit in the short run. Fluctuations are normal to gambling, whatever the game, and with a little luck, a player can ride a hot streak into some healthy profits.

There are many betting systems that have been devised to overcome the casino's edge in roulette, but you must keep these in perspective. Systems cannot alter or change the reality of the house edge any more than one constantly calling a tree a river will change that tree to a river or calling blue red will change that blue to a red. One may convince oneself, but irrefutable facts are cemented in reality and only a distortion or departure from that reality will change the appearance of what one perceives—but not the reality.

This is not to say that some of the betting strategies don't look good—some of them are brilliant in concept so that they "appear" nearly foolproof. (Note the key word, "appear.") However, these systems don't change the short or long term house edge at roulette and the player must view them as no more than a fun approach.

The beauty of these systems is that they entrance the player with such beautiful, though slightly tainted logic, that one actually sees how they can work and how they can beat the odds. And they can work—in the short run—and provide the player with that age-old smoke cloud attempt that makes one feel that he's beating the odds. But again, don't be too much entranced with the fun ideas of these systems; the house edge is the house edge.

Man will never give up attempting to overcome the odds, that is one of the beauties of life. And that's why we are so attracted to gambling.

Let's look at one of the most famous systems first, The Martingale.

THE MARTINGALE

This dangerous system can dig you into a deep hole quick should you have a long string of losses—if not, like other systems, you'll be sitting pretty.

The system is easy. You attempt to win $1.00 on every sequence of the dice, a sequence being defined as either one spin when you have won, or a number of spins, ending when there is a winner.

Your first bet is $1.00. If the bet is won, you start again, betting $1.00. If you lose, the bet is doubled to $2.00. Should that bet be won, you have won $1.00 on the sequence, a $1.00 loss on the first spin but a $2.00 win on the second. If the second bet is lost, the next bet is again doubled, and is now $4.00. A winner here again brings a $1.00 profit, $1.00 + $2.00 in losers for $3.00, and a $4.00 winner— still $1.00 over the top.

And so the system works. Every won bet is followed by a $1.00 wager, the beginning of a fresh cycle. Every lost bet is followed by a doubling of that bet. And here is the danger of the Martingale. As consecutive losses mount, so does the size of your bet, where the end result is only a $1.00 win!

This is what happens if you lose seven in a row.

Martingale Progression

Loss	Initial Bet	Total Loss
1st	$1.00	$1.00
2nd	$2.00	$3.00
3rd	$4.00	$7.00
4th	$8.00	$15.00
5th	$16.00	$31.00
6th	$32.00	$63.00
7th	$64.00	$127.00
8th	$128.00	—

Now suddenly, you're faced with a $128.00 bet with $127.00 worth of losses behind you. That's a lot of sweat and aggravation just to win $1.00 on the sequence. And we all know that seven losses in a row is not that strange of an occurrence.

What happens on the next spin? Surely you're due for a winner now after seven consecutive losses. If you're pregnant or expecting a raise or some such thing, you may be due.

In gambling, you're never due for anything. There are expectations based on the odds, but the fact that seven times the wheel spun black when you've been betting red, has no bearing on the eighth spin. The odds don't change—it's still an 18 out of

37 (European wheel) or 38 (American wheel) shot for your winning red on the next spin.

Remember, it's only a wheel. It has no memory, no brain. It doesn't know who you are, what you're betting, or that seven times in a row, black came up on it.

So back to the game. Heaven forbid that two more spins should go against you, for then you're faced with the following:

Martingale Progression Continued

Loss	Initial Bet	Total Loss
8th	$128.00	$255.00
9th	$256.00	$511.00
10th	$512.00	—

Add up these numbers then get out the Pepto-Bismol. Think twice before using this classic system. Do you really want to risk a situation where you'll need to bet over five hundred dollars just to win $1.00?

THE GRAND MARTINGALE

If you liked the above example, you'll love this system. The rallying point of the **Grand Martingale** is to attempt to win more than $1.00 on a losing progression by adding $1.00 to the bet after each loss. We'll spare ourselves the anguish of adding up these numbers, but you can see they'll add up even faster than the Martingale, and seriously, who needs that?

THE PYRAMID SYSTEM

This system is far more appealing to the player for its winning approach doesn't entail the kind of deep ditch digging that the Martingale and Grand Martingale do.

In this system, also called the **D'Alembert**, we'll look at each bet it terms of units, and to make life easy, we'll use $1.00 as our unit bet. The first bet will be $1.00. If we win, the sequence is ended, and we'll begin a new one.

If the bet is lost, our next bet becomes $2.00. Each subsequent loss adds $1.00 to the bet, so that five consecutive losses would produce a $6.00 bet on the following play. (Compare this to the Martingale, where you'd be watching a $32.00 bet gracing the tables for your $1.00 win, and the first tinges of a headache beginning to pound your skull.)

This system is interesting for after every win, you will decrease your bet by one unit! The end result of this system is that every win (as opposed to every progression) produces a win of $1.00, or if you prefer to think in terms of units, every win produces a one unit gain.

Every won bet is $1.00 more than the previous lost bet. Let's follow a progression to see how this works.

Pyramid Progression

Bet	Result	Total
$1.00	Win	+$1.00
$1.00	Loss	$0.00
$2.00	Loss	−$2.00
$3.00	Win	+$1.00
$2.00	Win	+$3.00
$1.00	Loss	+$2.00
$2.00	Loss	+$0.00
$3.00	Loss	−$3.00
$4.00	Loss	−$7.00
$5.00	Loss	−$12.00
$6.00	Win	−$6.00
$5.00	Loss	−$11.00
$6.00	Win	−$5.00
$5.00	Win	$0.00

TOTAL – 14 Plays: 6 Wins, 8 Losses

You can see the attractions of this system, for despite sustaining five straight losses and eight overall as against only six wins, the sequence where we left off showed the player dead even. A win on the next play would forge a profit of $4.00, with the next bet being $3.00, so the bettor's position looks pretty good overall.

This is all well and good on a short run look. However, in the long run, this system like all others trying to fight a game where the house has an edge, will ultimately lose.

As the progression continues, there will be more losses than wins and the downward dips will be deeper and more frequent than wins.

As long as this is kept in mind, the immovable house edge, than one might play this system to great enjoyment, and in the short run, maybe some profit!

BIASED WHEELS

There is a way to beat the casino at roulette, but this involves finding an unbalanced wheel, presumably old and rickety, more likely in a smaller casino, or perhaps at a fair where the mechanics of the wheel are far from state of the art.

It is impossible to make a perfectly balanced wheel, one where each number has exactly the same chance of coming up as any other number. A slight imperfection in the material, normal wear and tear, a warp, a tiny tilt, an unlevel floor, a slightly larger or shorter slot—these possibilities or any of a number of others can cause an imbalance of a wheel and favor some numbers to be spun more than others.

Wheels are made with such tremendous precision nowadays that it is extremely unlikely to find a wheel with a bias significant enough to make this theory interesting.

However, you may find an older wheel in use, one that's been subjected to enough wear and tear of normal usage that a bias is created, or one with faulty mechanics, and until the casino has figured out that you've got something going on and shuts down the wheel, you can make a lot of money—with the odds.

First you must determine if the wheel is biased and how large the bias is. To do this requires a lot of work and patience, but if indeed you're hunch is right and the wheel is significantly biased, you will have made the effort worthwhile. There are many stories of dedicated players patiently clocking wheels, finding a bias, and winning enormous sums of money until the game is shut down on them.

To properly track a wheel, you'll need a partner or an associate or two for every spin of the wheel will need to be recorded for at least 24 hours and ideally two or three times that much to get a fair sampling. A sampling taken for less than 24 hours will only show short run deviations (unless the wheel is incredibly biased) and will not be an accurate look at numbers which may be biased.

The expectation of any single number being spun is 1 in 38 on an American wheel (1 in 37 on a European one).

For a strategy to be effective and show profits, a single number's bias must not only be greater than the 1/38 (1/37 in Europe) expected result, but be sufficient enough to overcome the inherent casino's edge of 5.26% on an American wheel and 2.70% on a European one for single zero betting.

You may find one number or several that stand out on a wheel as being biased and base your winning strategy on those numbers (or number). The superior odds inherent in single zero roulette make those games much better to track for if a bias is found, the smaller house edge is easier to overcome and the profits will be greater.

WINNING WITH BETTING SYSTEMS

Roulette is a fun way to relax and try your luck at calling and betting the numbers that will come up winners on the wheel. We've presented some basic winning systems for beginning players that you can try at the tables plus the very interesting biased wheel strategy.

There are all sorts of interesting betting systems available—different number parlays, single and multiple number cycle plays, alternate betting systems, jump plays and more. Many of these systems are quite creative, some, in fact are very good.*

With a run of luck, money can be made at roulette if your numbers come up winners and your other wagers ride a streak. However, no matter what bets are made or what system is used, always keep sound money management principles in mind. That is the key to winning at roulette.

Good Luck!

*For serious players, GRI has developed advanced winning systems specially designed for winning at roulette (including advanced multiple number cycle plays and other systems). These are available through our mail order ads in the back.

Slots

FIVE KEYS TO SLOTS

1 Look for casinos catering to slots players. They are likely to have the loosest machines and therefore give you the best chances of winning.

2 Join slots clubs in every casino you play in.

3 Avoid mega-progressives. While the "one in a million" payday is really remote, these machines will grind you up with lousy payoffs and few wins.

4 Find the better paying machines and put your money. Similarly, avoid cold ones that don't seem to payoff for you.

5 Don't play adjacent machines. Loose slots are rarely put next to each other.

INTRODUCTION

There is a reason that more space is devoted to slots than any other gambling game in the casinos. Slots is easy to play, it is fun, and best of all, if you get a lucky spin on the reels, you could win a jackpot worth thousands of dollars or even millions of dollars!

Playing the slot machines is easy, literally no more complicated than getting your money in the machine and either pulling the slots handle or pressing the "SPIN REELS" button to activate the reels. There are, of course, more aspects to the game, and we will cover these in this chapter.

Your goal is quite simple. You want the symbols on the reels to line up directly behind the payline in one of the winning combinations listed on the machine. The higher ranked the combination, the greater the payout will be.

Bing! Bing! Bing! That's what you want to hear. Jackpot! Let's see now how to increase your chances.

BASICS OF SLOTS

THE "NEW" SLOT MACHINE

Putting coins into a slot machine is fast becoming a relic of the past. While there are machines that can still be played by coins, the new models being manufactured for the US market will take only paper money. You read that right. These machines cannot be played by coins! But that's not the only change brought by modernization to the industry.

The old term for slot machines, "one armed bandits," so named because the reels were activated by the slots handle on the side of the machine, is no longer appropriate. For one, most players don't even use the handles anymore – that is, if the machine even has a handle! A simple press of the button gets everything going.

For another, where the reels will stop is not a mechanical function, as before, but is calculated by computer chips using random number generators. The function of the mechanical device that spins the reels now is only to *display* the result calculated by the computer, not to *determine* it.

In fact, the modern day slot machine is essentially a fancied up computer device. We have come a long way, baby.

PLAYING THE SLOTS

The easiest way to play the slots is by inserting bills directly into the machine and playing off the credits. The device that accepts your money is called a **bill acceptor**. The machines will normally accept $1, $5, $20, $50 and even $100 bills.

These bills get converted directly into credits on the machine and allow you to play carefree as long as you still have credits available. There are still older machines on the floors that will accept coins, but as I implied earlier, they are fast becoming a relic of the past. Let's take a closer look at paying by credits.

PLAYING BY CREDITS

Once you have credits, playing slots couldn't be easier. On every machine, you'll see a play button marked "PLAY MAX COINS," "PLAY THREE COINS," "PLAY FIVE CREDITS," or similar buttons. The buttons might also be marked as "PLAY MAX CREDITS," "BET MAX COINS" or "PLAY ALL CREDITS."

Pressing the play button automatically spins the reels if you have credits available. That is it! Unlike the older generations of slot machines, you have no fuss with constantly putting in coins or pulling handles. Once you have established credits on a machine, all you need to play is one finger! Now that is easy.

Experienced slots players love the play button for its ease of play and speed use that button as if it were a speed dial. They'll run through multiple plays faster than a player on an old machine could get off even one spin of the reels. The casinos love this feature as well for it allows gamblers nonstop play at speeds not possible before. And this means more action per hour.

The play button is typically found on the right side of the machine, the area most convenient for easy play. You can expect this button to be large and easily visible.

COIN DENOMINATIONS

You have various choices on how much you want to risk on every spin of the reels. Slot machines come in a variety of coin denominations with larger coin amounts available at casinos attracting high rollers and smaller coin amounts available in sawdust and grinder joints.

The most popular machines are the 25¢ and $1 machines, found in most locations. Smaller casinos will also feature 5¢ and 10¢ machines, while high roller locations, such as Caesar's Palace, Bellagio, and the Venetian in Las Vegas, feature machines of $5, $25, $100 and even $500 coin amounts. How about that!

THE SLOT MACHINE

Slot machines are comprised of various components. Let's take a look at them.

REELS

The symbols on a slots machine are printed on spinning mechanisms called **reels**. Typical slot machines contain three reels, though there are also four reel machines and novelty-type slots with as many as eight or ten reels, monster machines often referred to as *Big Berthas*.

Reels contains 20-24 **steps** or **stops**. Each step is a place where the reel can end up when it is spun. This step may contain a **symbol**, such as a cherry or lemon, or a **blank**, a step with no symbol, just a blank.

PAYLINE

The glass window in front of a slot machine's reels is marked by one or more horizontal or diagonal lines, called **paylines**. Essentially, this is the visual display that shows if you have scored a winning spin or not. Winning combinations must line up directly behind a payline to be considered a winner.

When there are three paylines on a machine, they will generally be lined up as three horizontals, one in the middle, and one each above and below that middle line.

Usually, it takes one coin for each payline to be activated. Thus, on a three payline machine, you'll need to play all three coins to activate all three paylines, one coin for each line. If you only put in one coin on a three payline machine, it will probably count only for the middle payline. If you hit a winning combination on the bottom line for example, with only one coin played, it won't be a winner, since a coin for that line wasn't inserted. You would have had to insert three coins.

Machines with five paylines generally add two diagonal paylines so you have five directions that can win. Again, you will typically need the full five coins for all these paylines to be active.

WINNING HINT
When playing a slot with multiple paylines, make sure to insert the full number of coins so that all paylines get activated.

SYMBOLS

Cherries, lemons, 7's, and liberty bells, have been basic slot machines symbols dating back more than 50 years! Bars in various forms is another popular symbol found on many machines. While you'll see a wide variety of symbols from the many slot manufacturers, the most successful machines always come back to the basics.

Wild Symbols

Some machines designate a particular symbol as "wild." The wild symbol can be used as any symbol on the machine to create a winning combination. For example, BAR BAR Wild might payout for three bars, and LEMON Wild LEMON and 7 7 Wild might give you winning combinations as well, to be paid according to the payout schedule on the front of the machine.

Some machines use symbols to multiply a payout line. For example, the diamond on IGT's Double Diamond machine, when lined up to form a winning combination, will double the payout. Two diamonds are even better. They will double each other for four times the payout.

The "Any Bar" Symbol

You'll sometimes see a winning combination noted as *Any Bar*. What this means is that any one of the single, double or triple bar symbols on the reels can work as a paying symbol for the combination listed. Thus, you might have Cherry Cherry Any Bar as the three symbols needed for a winner.

WINNING TIP

Never, ever leave a machine that owes you money. Wait for the attendants to come by no matter how long it takes. You should just as soon leave your wallet on a New York City street corner as walk away from a machine that's stacked with winning credits.

DIFFERENT TYPES OF MACHINES

There are basically two types of slot machines. The first type, the **Straight Slots**, pays winning combinations according to the schedule listed on the machine itself. These payoffs never vary. The second type, the **Progressive**, features a jackpot that gets progressively larger as every coin is played. This jackpot total is posted above the machine and can accumulate to enormous sums of money!

SLOT DISPLAYS

There are various displays on the machine that give you information about what is happening on your machine. We'll take a brief look at some of the more relevant ones.

Payout Display

This is the most important display on the machine because it shows you what combinations are needed to have a winning spin and how much each of these winners will pay. On a straight slot machine, all winning amounts will be posted on the display itself.

These are typically expressed in number of coins to be won as opposed to dollar amounts. (Now and then, some displays will give you a dollar amount that can be won for a specific combination.)

For example, a winning combination might show a payment of 50 coins or 100 coins.

On progressive machines, "Progressive" might be indicated next to the payout for the big jackpot hand. That progressive jackpot total won't be posted on the machine itself but on a lighted display above the bank of machines.

You'll notice that the progressive jackpot amount constantly rises when machines in a bank of progressive slots are getting heavy play.

Credits Played or Coins Played

The **Credits Played** or **Coins Played** display shows how many coins are being wagered on the current spin. If three coins are played, the display would indicate the number "3" in the area provided.

Credits

The **Credits** indicator shows how many credits you have accumulated either through winning spins or through money entered into the machine. For example, placing a $20 bill into a 25¢ machine will enter eighty 25¢ credits into your account. The indicator in Credits will display the number "80."

Playing the PLAY ONE CREDIT or PLAY MAX CREDITS button will automatically deduct one credit in the first case, or the max credit amount, whatever that might be on the particular machine being played, from your credits.

You can use your credits by either playing them through until the total is down to 0 (which means you've lost them all!), or hitting the CASH OUT button, which will convert credit into actual coins and send them tumbling into the well below. Be prepared for lots of noise when the coins start dropping. But that's part of the fun!

Winner Paid

The **Winner Paid** indicator displays the amount won on the current spin. For example, if three liberty bells align for a winning combination paying 40 coins, the Winner Paid area will display the number "40."

PLAY BUTTONS

There are a few buttons that you will interact with at the machine. We'll take a brief look at them here.

Play Max Credits/Bet Max Coins

Pressing the PLAY MAX CREDITS button bets the maximum amount of coins allowed and automatically spins the reels. Thus, if the machine accepts five coins as a bet, pressing PLAY MAX CREDITS will deduct five coins from your credits. Similarly, if three coins were the maximum bet, then three coins would be played and that amount would be deducted.

This button may also read as BET MAX COINS or PLAY ALL CREDITS, or may have another similar designation which would amount to the same thing.

The PLAY MAX CREDITS button only activates the reels if you have credits available.

Play One Credit

You can also play one coin at a time by depressing the PLAY ONE CREDIT button. In this case, the reels will not spin until the handle is pulled or the SPIN REELS button is pressed.

You can also play two credits by pressing the PLAY ONE CREDIT button twice, or three coins by pressing it three times, or the maximum number of credits by pressing this button until the full allowance of coins is reached.

This button may also read as BET ONE COIN or PLAY ONE CREDIT or some similar designation which would amount to the same thing.

Cash Out Button

The Cash Out button, when pressed, cashes out your credits and deposits them as coins into the well below. If you have more credits than the machine will pay out, then you will have to wait for an attendant to pay out the rest of the coins.

Change Button

There is a change button on every machine, that when depressed, turns on a red light atop the machine, a signal for the changeperson to give you service.

HOUSE PERCENTAGES ON SLOTS

Slots is the only game offered in the casino where you can't figure out the house edge. The payback percentage could be 93%, 99%, 96%, or any other percentage, but you would have no way of knowing this as a player. The percentages are not posted anywhere nor is the frequency of occurrence of any one symbol made available.

So how do you figure out the casino's edge on a particular slot machine? You don't!

You may see a casino advertise 99% return on slots, but the question is: Which machine or machines have that return? There is no way to *know* where a good machine might be, however, in the strategy section, we'll show you ways to locate the better-paying machines just the same.

SLOT CLUBS

Slots clubs are a relatively new marketing program that allows players to earn credits for slot and video poker machine play and use those credits to earn a whole range of comps. The programs vary from casino to casino, but almost all of them give you a chance to earn comps for buffets and meals, rooms, shows, and sometimes, even cash rebates!

This innovative program has greatly added to the popularity of the slots and given players more ways to win. Best of all, there is no charge to become a member!

The concept is simple. Once enrolled as a member, the casinos will issue a card with your name and card number. These cards get inserted into the machines prior to play and automatically track your betting action. The more action you give the casino, the greater the benefits you enjoy just for playing the machines. What could be better?

Each casino has their own slots program, some with greater benefits than others. But all are worth joining if you plan to play slots at various casinos, especially if you plan to play a lot of slots.

JOINING A SLOTS CLUB

To become a member, first you have to register. The slots host is usually located in the rear of the casinos, but if you can't find the slots host desk, ask any of the personnel to point you in the right direction.

The application process for joining a slots club is simple and will take but a few minutes to fill out. The casino will require a valid ID to complete the application. Keep in mind that this application is simply a formality – you are not going to get turned down. The casinos have no interest in your credit history or how much money you make. They just want you to play slots in their casino.

The first thing that happens when you sign up for a slots club is that you'll get issued a card. This card identifies you as a player and member of the casino's slots club and allows you to immediately earn credits at the machines. And then you're ready to go. The casinos will have you on file and in the system. Armed with this card, you'll earn rewards credits every time you play.

Just make sure that before you begin playing, you insert the card into the card reader on the machine itself. The card is programmed to identify you as the player and register the action you give the machine. Note that you cannot earn credits if your card is not in the machine! Every slot and video poker machine in the casino will have a card reader for this purpose. The cards readers are typically found in the front of the machines, though they may be on the sides.

Casinos that really value you as a customer will let you know up front how much action you need to generate for their awards programs to kick in. Some casinos though, keep their rewards programs, for whatever reasons, a mystery. Typically, and again this varies completely from one program to another, approximately one hours' worth of action at the $1 slots or 2-3 hours at the 25¢ machines will kick in the first tier of bonuses and comps.

Faster players may reach these levels a little faster, slower players may take a little longer. The critical element the casinos are looking for is the amount of action and how much money is wagered into the machines, not how long you happen to be sitting in front of a machine warming a chair. The casinos want *action*. You give it to them, and they'll kick back in with their incentives.

The more coins per hour you play (not how much you win or lose), the faster you will accumulate the points required by a casino to reach activation levels.

WINNING STRATEGIES AT SLOTS

Surprisingly, there are lots of strategies you can pursue for such a simple game. And following our advice, you'll do much better than the average player and at times, under the right conditions, you may actually find yourself with an edge.

There is only room to briefly touch upon a few ideas here, but for those players serious about their slots play, I recommend my book, *Secrets of Winning Slots* (available from our website at www.cardozapub.com), which is loaded with information about slots strategies and the machines in general.

The first rule is to concentrate your action at casinos that cater to serious slots players. If a casino is looking to attract serious slots business, it's got to give these players something to whoop about so that it can keep them as steady players. In the old days, this meant having machines with a good payback. Nowadays, it also means having an aggressive slots club rich with rewards for their good players. With all else equal, you would much rather play at a casino with a more aggressive slots club program, one that will get you to the slots rewards quicker. And of course, you would rather play at a casino that has better paying machines.

So how do you get a sense of when a casino is good for slots players? If the casino is buzzing with slots players, that's a good sign. On the other hand, an empty mausoleum-like atmosphere doesn't bode well. Regular players will return to places where they win and avoid places that seem to suck their bankrolls dry.

There is another principle which is true as well. Play in places that *cater* to slot players and avoid places that do not. Do not play slots in places where the slots business is incidental to the main business. Why? Because the customers that play slots in these establishments are there to do something else. These places can get away with horrific odds because their customers did not come to play slots and won't be the most demanding of clients – another way of saying that they are not sophisticated players needing the best odds possible.

What kinds of places are these? If you want to get good odds, avoid playing slot machines in the following places like the plague: laundromats, bars, grocery and convenience stores, gas stations, and the like, places whose slot machines will swallow your money as fast as you can feed them.

Choosing the right location within a casino is often important as well. That slot machine in the bathroom can be counted on to have the worst payback in the entire casino. Think about it: Who is going to be hanging around a bathroom very long for the purpose of gambling? (If you can think of someone that might, well, what can I tell you?) Slots lining a restaurant or buffet line are generally set with lower percentages to catch the impulse coins that go into these machines.

Slot machines pay proportionately more on their jackpots if the maximum coins are played, thus a very important principle to keep in mind is to play the maximum number of coins allowed. The big jackpot payouts in slots only earn out to their full potential when all coins are played, so you don't want to miss losing a big payday because you weren't playing the machine properly.

On non-progressive machines, there is often a payout difference as well on the bigger money payout. For example, one coin might pay 800, two coins 1600, and three coins, 4,000. That's a big difference.

WINNING TIP – DON'T EVER LEAVE A WINNING MACHINE
Unless you really had enough play for a day, or need to go elsewhere, don't ever leave a winning machine. When you got a hot one, ride it for all it's worth. But once it stops paying well, back off, and then take a break—with all your profits.

FINDING THE LOOSEST AND TIGHTEST SLOTS IN A CASINO

The placement of loose and tight slot machines, and the actual paybacks of a casino's slot machines are about the closest kept secrets in a casino. While the slots hosts, change girls, and slots manager will not *know* the percentages of any of the machines, or where the best ones are located, the slots girls themselves will notice which machines pay the most often.

Ask a change girl nicely and she may give you a great tip that will put you real close to a 99% payback. That really is the best way to find a good slots machine.

WINNING TIP

Rarely will loose machines be set side by side. Casinos are aware that slots players often play in pairs, and know that the excitement from one machine can carry over to the player in the adjacent machine. Thus, machines adjacent to loose machines tend to be tight. When you do discover a loose machine, you'll want to avoid the machines on either side.

Video Poker

FIVE KEYS TO VIDEO POKER

1 Shop around where possible to get the best paying machines, and on progressives, the highest jackpot total.

2 Learn the correct playing strategies and never deviate from them.

3 Make sure to hold all five cards when dealt a pat winning hand. You don't want to throw away a big payer because of carelessness.

4 Never leave the machine while waiting for an attendant to pay a big winner.

5 Always, always play five coins on a standard video poker machine. The royal only pays the big jackpot when all five coins are being played.

INTRODUCTION

Since video poker was originally introduced to the casinos, it has caught on like wildfire. Players love the fact that not only can they play the game at their leisure and without hassle, just themselves and the video poker machine, but that decision-making and skill are involved.

Video poker is loosely based on draw poker. You get five cards to start and can keep or exchange any or all of these cards to form a new five card hand. Your goal is to get a five card poker hand in the combinations listed on the front of the machine. The higher ranked the poker hand, the greater the payout.

The game is simple to play, but you must make the right decisions on which cards to hold to maximize your winning chances. That is the skill element in video poker. The fun element comes in when your good play turns into winnings.

You have a wide variety of variations to choose among, from the standard jacks or better machines found in most places, and the popular deuces wild games, to a widening choice of spin-offs and variations off the original jacks or better theme.

GETTING STARTED

The typical video poker game uses a 52 card deck which is dealt fresh after each hand. There are other variations that use multiple decks and extra cards such as wild cards, but the principles are the same.

To start, you need to insert anywhere from one to five coins into the machine or use credits that are already established in the machine. As we discussed in the slots section, playing machines by coin is fast becoming a thing of the past. In fact, many new machines made by manufacturers will not even accept coins anymore!

Almost all modern machines have bill acceptors, devices that accept $1, $5, $10, $20, $50, and $100 bills. Once the bills are accepted into the machine, the equivalent amount of credits will be posted on the machine for your bankroll. For example, if you insert a $20 bill into the bill acceptor on a quarter machine, 80 credits will be posted.

Wins and losses will be added or deducted from your credits. If you start out with 80 credits and bet five coins, then five credits will be deducted from your total credits and the machine will show "75" credits. A win of 45 credits will boost your total to 120 credits and "120" will appear in the credits area.

CREDITS AND COINS

You will typically play off credits on the video poker machine. In fact, on the latest machines, you will always play off credits since the only way to get started is by inserting a bill into the machine and getting credits posted.

PLAYING BY CREDITS

With credits on the machine, getting your cards dealt is as easy as hitting a button. On every machine, you'll see a button marked "PLAY MAX COINS," "PLAY FIVE CREDITS," or a similar play button. Pressing this button deals five cards to you and deducts five credits from your credit total. Thus, if you had 100 credits to start, pressing PLAY FIVE CREDITS would reduce your total to 95 credits. You now have your initial five card hand.

There is also a button on the machine that allows you to play one credit at a time. This button may be marked "PLAY ONE CREDIT," "PLAY ONE COIN," or the like. Since the maximum number of coins are not being played, you also have to hit the DRAW/DEAL button for the cards to be dealt.

PLAYING BY COIN

There are still machines that accept coins for play and the principles are exactly the same as playing by credits. If five coins are inserted (which would be the same as PLAY MAX CREDITS or PLAY MAX COINS), your five card hand will automatically be dealt and appear on the screen.

If less than the maximum amount of coins are inserted, you'll need to press the button marked **DRAW/DEAL** to receive your cards.

Once you have established credits on the machine (by winning hands), until you hit the CASH OUT button, you will be playing by credits anyway and using the "PLAY MAX COINS" or "PLAY FIVE CREDITS" to deal cards.

YOUR INITIAL FIVE CARD HAND

You start out with a five card hand. You may keep one, some, all, or none of these cards. It's your decision. There are five hold buttons, one underneath each card. To keep a card, press the button marked "**hold**" underneath the corresponding card you wish to keep. Thus, for each card you want to keep, you must press the hold button.

"**HELD**" will appear on the screen underneath each card or cards so chosen. The other cards, the ones you wish to discard, will not be kept by the machine.

What happens if you press the wrong hold button by accident or change your mind? No problem. Press the corresponding button again. If the card indicated "HELD," the "HELD" will disappear and the card will not be held by the computer. If you change your mind, press the button one more time and again "HELD" will appear on the screen indicating that the card will be kept on the draw.

Until you press the draw button, it is not too late to change your strategy decision.

KEEPING/DISCARDING ALL 5 CARDS

You may keep all five original cards by pushing the hold button under each card, or discard all five original cards by pressing the DRAW/DEAL button without having pressed any of the hold buttons.

Discarding all your cards is often the correct strategy in video poker and we'll discuss when to do so in the winning strategies section.

THE FINAL HAND

To discard the cards you don't want to keep and receive your new ones, you now press the DRAW/DEAL button again. Cards that had "HELD" underneath will remain, while those cards not chosen to be held will be replaced by new ones. This set of cards is your final hand.

WINNING HINT

If you get dealt a great five card hand that you want to keep, such as a straight or even a royal flush, you must remember to press the hold button underneath each and every one of the card before pressing the DEAL/DRAW button or you will lose the hand on the card exchange!

If your hand is a winner, the machine will flash "**WINNER**" at the bottom of the screen. Winning hands are automatically paid according to the payoffs shown on the machine and will be added to your total number of credits.

THE CASH OUT BUTTON

When you are finished playing and want to leave the machine, you'll want to take your money with you of course. You can retrieve your credits at any time by pressing the CASH OUT button. Your winnings will be sent tumbling into the well below in a noisy racket as metal meets metal.

IMPORTANT TIP

If you have won more money than is in the machine or more than it can pay out, sit tight and do not leave the machine until an attendant comes to pay you off the rest of the money you've won.

THE WINNING HANDS

Typically, the minimum winning hand in video poker is jacks or better, though that varies by machine type. For example, deuces wild machines require at least a three of a kind for a payout and Pick Five machines pay out for hands as low as a pair of sixes.

The chart below describes the winning hands for the jacks or better based variations. Hands are listed from weakest to strongest.

Winning Video Poker Hands

Jacks or Better	Two cards of equal value are called a pair. Jacks or better refers to a pairing of jacks, queens, kings or aces.
Two Pair	Two sets of paired cards, such as 3-3 and 10-10.
Three of a Kind	Three cards of equal value, such as 9-9-9.
Straight	Five cards in numerical sequence, such as 3-4-5-6-7 or 10-J-Q-K-A. The ace can be counted as the highest card or the lowest card in a straight, however,
Flush	Any five cards of the same suit, such as five hearts.
Full House	Three of a kind and a pair together, such as 2-2-2-J-J.
Four of a kind	Four cards of equal value, such as K-K-K-K.
Straight Flush	A straight all in the same suit, such as 7-8-9-10-J, all in spades.
Royal Flush	10-J-Q-K-A, all in the same suit.

On wild card machines, you will see additional listings for five of a kind hands (made possible because of the wild cards) and two types of royal flushes.

The more valuable royal flush is the natural royal flush which doesn't use any wild cards to form it. The natural is harder to get and will pay more. The other type of royal flush is the wild royal flush, which uses at least one wild card to form the five card royal flush.

There are also payouts for other types of hands, such as the bonus quad machines where specified four a kind hands will receive a higher payout amount than other types of four of a kinds hands, but these will be clearly listed on the machines themselves.

TYPES OF VIDEO POKER MACHINES

PROGRESSIVES/NON-PROGRESSIVES

Video poker machines can be played as either **Flat-Top** (or **Straight**) machines, where there are set payoffs on all the hands won, or as **Progressives**, where the progressive jackpot constantly increases until the royal flush is hit.

On both type of machines, all the payoffs are proportionate for the winning hands. Thus, a winning payoff on two coins played will be exactly double that for the same winning hand with one coin played.

The one exception is for the royal flush, where a winning payoff on a non-progressive machine typically gives you a 4,000 coin return when all five coins are played. One, two, three and four coins pay respectively, 200, 400, 600 and 800 coins for the royal. The progression would normally take you to a 1,000 coin payoff, but there is a bonus for playing the full five coins and that is the 4,000 coin payoff. It is the same on a progressive machine, where to get the full benefit of the royal flush jackpot, you need to play the full five coins.

That is why it is always important to play all five coins whether playing the straight machines or the progressives.

 WINNING HINT
Always insert the full five coins to get the best odds at video poker.

FIVE VIDEO POKER CATEGORIES

Following are five general categories of video poker machines that you may find.

1. **Jacks or Better** – The original of the video poker machines, these games are based on the player receiving a hand of jacks or better to get the minimum payout.

2. **Tens or Better and Two Pair** – Tens or better is similar to jacks or better except that the minimum payout on a hand is tens, not jacks. On the two pair hands, two pair is the minimum payout.

3. **Wild Card** – Wild card machines add the element of the wild card, a card which can be used as any card to form the most valuable hand possible.

4. **Multiple Deck** – These variations use multiple decks of cards (as opposed to one deck) in their games.

5. **Specialty** – These are the video poker machines that don't quite fit into the other categories.

Jacks or Better

The minimum hand needed to win in this game is a pair of jacks; any lesser pair or lesser hand pays nothing. On the other hand, the greater the strength of the hand, the larger the payout will be. For example, as you see in the 9-6 paytable below, for a full five coins being played, a flush will pay 30 coins as opposed to five coins for a pair of queens.

The following chart shows typical payoffs for video poker on a jacks or better machine in a competitive market such as Las Vegas. I use the term *competitive*, since there are locations where video poker games are offered, such as bars in Louisiana, where the payout tables are so horrific, I wouldn't advise anyone to play them

Machines using the paytable below are known as **9-6 machines**, so named for the payoffs on the full house and flush respectively.

Paytable on Jacks or Better
9-6 Machine

Coins Played	1	2	3	4	5
Royal Flush	250	500	750	1000	4000
Straight Flush	50	100	150	200	250
Four of a Kind	25	50	75	100	125
Full House	9	18	27	36	45
Flush	6	12	18	24	30
Straight	4	8	12	16	20
Three of a Kind	3	6	9	12	15
Two Pair	2	4	6	8	10
Jacks or Better	1	2	3	4	5

Bonus Quads

These jacks or better variations, which come in a number of flavors, offer extra bonus payouts for specified four of a kind hands, called **quads**. For example, a bonus quad machine may pay more for four 2s, 3s and 4s, than the other four of a kind hands.

There are many types of quads available but they all work according to the same principle – a higher payout for getting the listed four of a kind hands.

The jacks or better bonus quads are found in increasing numbers as they have become popular among players.

Deuces Wild and Jokers Wild

Some video poker machines are played with wild cards that can be given any value or suit with the machine interpreting those cards in the most advantageous way for the player.

For example, the hand 2-2-5-6-8 in deuces wild would be a straight. One 2 would be used as a 7 and the other as either a 9 or 4. The deuces could also be used as eights to give three of a kind, but since the straight is more valuable, the machine will see it as a straight.

Wild card machines have different minimum payouts than the jacks or better machines. For example, in deuces wild, payoffs only start with hands of at least three of a kind hand. A pair of jacks wins you nothing in deuces wild.

Following is a typical payoff schedule for deuces wild:

Payoffs on Deuces Wild
9-5 Machine

Coins Played	1	2	3	4	5
Natural Royal Flush	250	500	750	1000	4000
Four Deuces	200	400	600	800	1000
Wild Royal Flush	25	50	75	100	125
Five of a Kind	15	30	45	60	75
Straight Flush	9	18	27	36	45
Four of a Kind	5	10	15	20	25
Full House	3	6	9	12	15
Flush	2	4	6	8	10
Straight	2	4	6	8	10
Three of a Kind	1	2	3	4	5

Natural Royal Flush – No wild cards as part of the royal flush.
Wild Royal Flush – The royal flush uses at least one wild card (deuce).

There are also progressive machines with nice jackpots. All payoffs, like the straight machines are fixed except in the case of a royal flush, where this fortuitous draw pays the accumulated total posted above the machine on the electronic board.

The jackpot total slowly and constantly rises, and on a quarter machine in Las Vegas can rise into the thousands of dollars.

WINNING STRATEGY

The big payoff in video poker on the jacks or better machines is for the royal flush—4,000 coins are paid for this score when all five coins are played. You always want to keep yourself in a position to take advantage of this win if the right cards are drawn and that is why I keep stressing the importance of playing the full five coins when you sit down at the video poker machine.

On progressive machines, if the full five coins are played, the total could be a great deal higher, possibly as high as $3,000 (12,000 coins) on a quarter machine. Again, the key phrase is "if the full five coins are played."

Of course, the royal doesn't come often. With correct strategy, you'll hit one every 30,000+ hands on the average. This doesn't mean, however, that you won't hit one in your very first hour of play! Meanwhile, you'll be collecting wins for straights, full houses and the like, and with proper play, you can beat the video poker machines.

To collect the full payoff for a royal flush, proper play dictates that you always play the full five coins for each game. Of course, you can play any amount of coins from 1 to 5, but that would negate the main goal of video poker—getting the royal flush and the big jackpot.

(The 9-6 charts are not applicable to the 8-5 progressives. For full strategy charts on all video poker games including progressives, jokers wild, deuces wild and more, you should order the professional strategy in the back.)

JACKS OR BETTER STRATEGY – 9-6 MACHINES

1. Whenever you hold <u>four cards to a royal flush</u>, discard the fifth card, even if that card gives you a flush or pair.

2. Keep a <u>jacks or better pair</u> and any higher hand such as a three of a kind or straight over three to the royal. Play the <u>three to a royal</u> over any lesser hand such as a low pair or four flush.

3. With <u>two cards to a royal</u>, keep four straights, four flushes, and high pairs or better instead. Otherwise, go for the royal.

4. Never break up a <u>straight or flush</u>, unless a one card draw gives you a chance for the royal.

5. Keep <u>jacks or better</u> over a four straight or four flush.

6. Never break up a <u>four of a kind</u>, <u>full house</u>, <u>three of a kind</u> and <u>two pair</u> hands. The *rags*, worthless cards for the latter two hands, should be dropped on the draw.

7. The <u>jacks or better pair</u> is always kept, except when you have four cards to the royal, or four to the straight flush.

8. Keep <u>low pairs</u> over the four straight, but discard them in favor of the four flushes and three or four to a royal flush.

9. When dealt <u>unmade hands</u>, a pre-draw hands with no payable combination of cards, save in order, four to a royal flush and straight flush, three to a royal flush, four flushes, four straights, three to a straight flush, two cards to the royal, two cards jack or higher and one card jack or higher.

10. Lacking any of the above, with no card jack or higher, discard all the cards and draw five fresh ones.

Simplified Basic Strategy Chart

This chart sums up the simplified basic strategy for jacks or better on a 9-6 machine. Keep the hands listed higher in preference to hands listed lower. For example, you'll keep a high pair over a three to a royal, but throw it away in favor of a four to the royal.

Jacks or Better Strategy
9-6 Machine

Hand to Be Held	Cards Held	Draw
Royal Flush	5	0
Straight Flush	5	0
Four of a Kind	5	0
Full House	5	0
Four to a Royal	4	1
Flush	5	0
Three of a Kind	3	2
Straight	5	0
Four to a Straight Flush	4	1
Two Pair	4	1
High Pair	2	3
Three to a Royal	3	2
Four to a Flush	4	1
Low Pair	2	3
Four to a Straight	4	1
Three to a Straight Flush	3	2
Two to a Royal	2	3
Two High Cards	2	3
One High Card	1	4
Garbage Hand	0	5

DEUCES WILD STRATEGY

There is no payoff for hands less than three of a kind, so if you're coming from a jacks or better game, you'll need to adjust your strategy accordingly.

The key in deuces wild is to go for the big payouts – the royal flush. Therefore, when you have three cards toward a royal flush discard the other two and go for it.

Of course, the same holds true when you have four to the royal. Thus, if you have two deuces and a 10 or higher along with two sub-10 cards of no value, go for the royal.

If you hold one or two deuces with nothing else, dump the junk and hang onto the deuces. With five unrelated cards, get rid of them all and go for five fresh ones.

Three card flushes or straights and unmatched high cards are worthless in this game and you should discard them.

With two pair hands (which don't pay), hang onto only one of the pairs and go for three new cards. If one of the pairs is teamed with a wild deuce, keep the three of a kind. If the deuce forms a pair with a high card, it does no good at all so keep only the deuce and draw four cards.

Keep a pair unless you've got a three card royal flush, in which case you'll dump the pair and go for the gold.

WINNING HINT
Deuces are gold in this game so make sure you never discard them by accident.

You'll find that many of the hands dealt will contain nothing worth saving and you'll be drawing for five fresh cards. Three card straights and flushes fit in this category along with some of the others we've mentioned. In any case, don't be afraid to discard your original five cards if they hold nothing of value.

It will take a little while getting used to wild card video poker after playing the non-wild versions, but once you get accustomed to the different payouts and strategies, you should have lots of fun at these machines.

Deuces Wild Strategy • 9-5 Machine
No Deuces

Hand to Be Held	Cards Held	Draw
Royal Flush	5	0
Four to a Royal	4	1
Straight Flush	5	0
Four of a Kind	4	1
Full House	5	0
Flush	5	0
Straight	5	0
Three of a Kind	3	2
Four to a Straight Flush	4	1
Three to a Royal	3	2
One Pair (Discard 2nd Pair)	2	3
Four to a Flush	4	1
Four to a Straight	4	1
Three to a Straight Flush	3	2
Two to a Royal	2	3
Garbage Hand - Draw Five	0	5

One deuce

Hand to Be Held	Cards Held	Draw
Royal Flush	5	0
Five of a Kind	5	0
Straight Flush	5	0
Four of a Kind	4	1
Four to a Royal	4	1
Full House	5	0
Three of a Kind	3	2
Four to a Straight Flush	4	1
Flush	5	0
Straight	5	0
Three to a Royal	3	2
One Deuce	1	4

Two deuces

Hand to Be Held	Cards Held	Draw
Royal Flush	5	0
Five of a Kind	5	0
Straight Flush	5	0
Four of a Kind	4	1
Four to a Royal	4	1
Two Deuces	2	3

Three deuces

Hand to Be Held	Cards Held	Draw
Royal Flush	5	0
Five of a Kind	5	0
Three Deuces	3	2

Four deuces

Hand to Be Held	Cards Held	Draw
Four Deuces	4	1

I have presented strategies in this chapter for two of the most popular video poker variations, jacks or better: 9-6 machines and deuces wild. If you are a serious video poker player and want to learn the important differences in strategy between the 8-5 progressive and 9-6 jacks or better machines plus receive the full professional strategy charts for the many other variations, I highly recommend the professional video poker strategy advertised in the back.

Cho Dai Di

FIVE KEYS TO CHO DAI DI

1 This is a great game, however, don't play for money until you get comfortable with the rules of the game and the skill level of your opponents.

2 The goal is to gain points versus your opponents, not necessarily to go out of a round first.

3 Keep track of the aces and deuces – you always need to know what the controlling cards are.

4 Don't get caught with 10 or more cards and a double penalty.

5 Generally speaking, get rid of your weaker cards first, and hold the strong ones to control rounds.

INTRODUCTION

This exciting card game combines all the elements of a great game—skill, luck and a little of that ever-so-fun backstabbing, with skill being the overriding factor. Cho Dai Di is tremendously popular with the Chinese, and for some reason has not caught on in other cultures yet. This can't last too much longer for the game is not only a lot of fun but is perfectly suited to gamblers as well.

Cho Dai Di is closely related to both poker, in that poker hands and values are used in the play of the game, and to other card game variations where players attempt to rid their hand of all its cards. The game is simple to play, as you'll soon see, but where strategy comes in, there's much to learn.

So, while Cho Dai Di may sound foreign, you'll find this unique game uses element of play you're already familiar with, and thus will be fairly easy to learn.

Take the time to go through this chapter for this great card game is worth knowing. You and your friends will soon be hooked on Cho Dai Di (the Cantonese D is pronounced like a td together) and will find yourself counting the days until the next game begins!

So let's get on with the game!

THE BASICS OF CHO DAI DI

It takes four players to play Cho Dai Di, with each participant playing for themselves against all the others. A standard 52 card pack is used, containing four suits of 13 cards each, the ace through king of diamonds, clubs, hearts and spades.

THE OBJECT OF THE GAME

The object of Cho Dai Di is to discard all 13 cards initially received by a player before his opponents do so, or if another player goes out first, to gain points by having fewer cards remaining than the other players.

For all intents and purposes, each card a player is stuck with when the first player goes out counts as one point regardless of the cards' suit or value, and one gains points from any player who is left with more cards than he.

HAND AND CARD VALUES

The hands valid in Cho Dai Di are similar to standard poker hands with the main difference being that the 2 is the highest value card in Cho Dai Di and not the ace (which is next in ranking). The other difference is that two pair is not a playable hand in Cho Dai Di.

ORDER OF SUITS

Suit values play a role in Cho Dai Di, and are in order of strength, the highest listed first, spades, hearts, clubs and diamonds. The first order of ranking in a card is its numeric value, thus a four of diamonds is higher than a three of spades.

However, when both cards are of equal numeric value, such as two fours, the suit order determines the higher ranking card. Thus, a four of spades is superior to a four of any other suit, spades being the strongest suit, while a 10 of clubs is higher ranked than a 10 of diamonds.

CHO DAI DI RANKINGS

For the benefit of players not familiar with poker, we'll list the hands here, beginning with the lowest ranking hands and going on up to the highest ranking. Cards will be abbreviated by the commonly accepted abbreviations such that a three will be 3, a jack=J, queen=Q, king=K, ace=A, two=2 and so on.

You'll see that the rankings pretty much approximate poker rankings with the noticeable exception that the 2 is the highest ranking card and not the ace, and that two pair is not considered a Cho Dai Di hand. Also, though four of a kind is a valid hand, it must be played as a five card hand with any other card thrown in to make the fifth card.

Thus, legitimate Cho Dai Di hands consist of 1, 2, 3 or 5 cards.

Legitimate Hands by Card

One Card	Any card may be led.
Two Cards	The only valid two card hand is a pair.
Three Cards	Three of a kind is the only valid three card hand. A pair with an odd card is not a valid hand for three of a kind.
Five Cards	In order of strength, lowest to highest, straight, flush, full house, four of a kind with an odd card, straight flush and royal flush are valid five card hands.

High Card – The high card in Cho Dai Di is the 2, followed by the A, K, Q, J, 10, 9, 8, 7, 6, 5, 4 and then the 3, the weakest card. Equivalent high card hands are decide by suit order.

One Pair – Two cards of identical value, such as 4-4 and K-K from a pair. The highest pair is 2-2, the lowest 3-3. When two pair of equal value, such as 7-7 and 7-7, are in competition, the pair with the spade, the highest ranking suit, is the stronger one.

Three of a Kind – Three cards of equal value, such as 9-9-9 from three of a kind. When two players hold a three of a kind, the hand with the higher raking triplets is stronger. 2-2-2- is a higher ranking hand than A-A-A.

Straight – Five cards in numerical sequence, such as 3-4-5-6-7 or A-2-3-4-5. The ace can be counted as the highest card (A-K-Q-J-10) in a straight, or the lowest card, however, it may not be in the middle of a five card run, such as Q-K-A-2-3, which is not a straight.

When two or more straights are in competition, the highest ranking card determines the stronger hand. K-Q-J-10-9 is higher than J-10-9-8-7. A straight containing a 2 is higher than any other straight. Thus, A-2-3-4-5 is a higher straight than Q-J-10-9-8. However, if the straights are identical in value, such as K-Q-J-10-9 and K-Q-J-10-9, than the strongest suit of the high card, in this example the king, determines the higher ranking hand. A king of hearts straight is higher than a king of clubs one.

Flush – Any five cards of the same suit, such as five hearts. When two players have flushes, the highest card in the flush determines the stronger hand, regardless of suit. If both hands have the same high card, than the next highest card determines the stronger hand and so on down to the fifth card. Thus, a 2-A-K-6-4 of clubs is stronger than a 2-K-Q-J-9 of spades. It is only when all five cards are identical that the higher ranking suit makes one flush a higher ranking hand than the other.

Full House – Three of a kind and a pair together, such as 2-2-2-J-J. When two players have a full house, the higher ranking full house is the hand with the higher three of a kind.

Four of a Kind – Four cards of equal value, such as K-K-K-K. When two players hold a four of a kind, the higher ranking four of a kind is represented by the higher foursome. J-J-J-J is higher than 3-3-3-3. The four of a kind is played as a five card hand in Cho Dai Di with any other card thrown in to make the fifth card.

Straight Flush – A straight all in the same suit, such as 7-8-9-10-J, all in spades. If two players hold a straight flush, the highest ranking card determines the more powerful straight flush. If the straight flushes are led by an equivalent high card, than the higher ranking suit of the competing straight flushes determines the stronger hand.

Royal Flush – 10-J-Q-K-A, all in the same suit. In the unlikely event two players hold a royal flush, the higher ranking suit is the dominant hand.

THE FIRST ROUND DEAL

The dealer for the first round will be decided by the random drawing of a card from the deck. Beginning with the person picking the card and going counter-clockwise, right to left, one place is counted off for each number value on the card. For this purpose only, the jack equals 11 places, the queen 12 and the king 13. All other cards are at face value.

Thus, if a 7 is picked, the person picking the card counts off his place as 1, to his right, 2, opposite will be 3, to his left, 4, back to himself again, 5, to his right, 6, and again opposite, 7.

Now we have the dealer for the first round—the player opposite the one who picked the card.

Thereafter, the dealer will always be the winner of the previous round, but as we'll see in a minute, we still use the traditional draw to determine which player gets dealt to first.

THE TRADITIONAL DEAL

Cards are always dealt counterclockwise in Cho Dai Di.

Before the cards are dealt, the traditional draw to determine which player will be dealt the cards occurs first. Though it has no bearing on the game, since the dealer will play first anyway (except for the very first game), this tradition probably arose, like the cut, as a safeguard to the players.

As we did above, the dealer randomly picks a card and counts off one place for each number on the card, starting with himself and proceeding counterclockwise, right to left, around the table.

The cards should now be dealt one at a time, counter-clockwise (right to left), beginning with the player chosen by the traditional draw, and continuing until all players have received 13 face down cards.

Since there are four players in the game, the deck should now be exhausted of all cards.

THE DIRECTION OF PLAY

The first round in Cho Dai Di is played in the counterclockwise direction.

Thereafter, each round's play will alternate in direction so that on all odd rounds (first, third, fifth, etc.), play will be from right to left, counterclockwise. And all even rounds (second, fourth, sixth, etc.) will be dealt and played clockwise, left to right.

So if the previous hand was played left to right, than the following one will be played right to left.

THE PLAY OF THE GAME

The winner of the previous game is always the dealer of the following game and except for the first round in the very first game, which we'll cover after, the dealer will always be the first to lead in a game.

He has a choice of whether to play one, two, three or five cards as his opening hand. If he leads with one card, it can be any card he wants, but if he leads with more than one card, it must be a legitimate Cho Dai Di hand to be a valid discard.

(There is no valid four card lead or hand in Cho Dai Di as two pair is not a valid hand and four of a kind hands are played as five card hands with an extra card thrown in.)

After deciding his move, the dealer lays his hand of 1, 2, 3 or 5 cards face up on the table so that all can see what he has played.

The second player to act, the one to the dealer's right, now has two options: he may either pass by announcing **"Dai,"** the Cantonese equivalent for pass, or simply say **"pass,"** which may also be indicated by rapping one's knuckles on the table, waving one's hand vertically across the table or some such understood expression just as one would do in poker; or the player may lay down cards in response to the dealer's play.

For this next player to be able to play a hand, he must lay down the same number of cards, no more and no less than what the lead player threw, and the card or cards that he plays must not only be a legitimate Cho Dai Di hand but must be of greater value than the previously played hand.

This is true at all times in Cho Dai Di.

For example, if the dealer leads with a pair of fours, the next player, to be able to lay down cards, must play a higher pair than the fours. If he cannot beat the pair of fours by either throwing a higher suited pair of fours or a higher pair, or chooses not to, he may not lay down cards and must pass.

His play must be a two card throw since two cards were led. Thus, a hand of a straight or three fives may not be played for these are not two card hands.

After the second player acts upon his hand, play then moves to the next player in turn who faces the same options; either discarding a higher hand of the same number of cards, or passing.

If, for example, the second player played a pair of nines, which he places face up in the middle, on top of the fours, the third player must throw a higher suited pair of nines or higher pair to lay down cards.

Any time a hand is played within a round, the following player must lay down a higher valued hand of the same number of cards to be able to play.

The action in any round, like poker, does not end until three passes in a row are called and the last player to throw cards has had his play unanswered by his three opponents.

When a player's throw goes unanswered by three succeeding players, he now has the advantage, for he or she gets to lead the next round and may lay off any legitimate hand of 1, 2, 3 or 5 cards.

And so the game goes, with one player leading 1, 2, 3 or 5 cards, and the other players answering his lead until three passes in a row have occurred. The last to throw, gets to lead now, and another round ensues.

The game is over when any player gets rid of his last card. And then its time to tally the score.

THE FIRST GAME ONLY

In the first round of the first game only, the player holding the three of diamonds goes first and must lead that card. The card may be led by itself, or as part of a 2, 3 or 5 card Cho Dai Di hand.

Thereafter, the winner of each game leads first in the following game, as we showed previous (and is also the dealer).

SCORING

Every card that a player has remaining when an opponent goes out counts as one point against him. Players gain points from any other player who is left with more cards than they. Thus, strictly speaking, there's usually more than one winner in a round.

However, should a player get stuck with 10 cards or more when an opponent goes out, he must pay double the points to the other players. Even worse, should a player be unable to get rid of any cards at all, and be stuck with the original 13 cards, the penalty is triple points to every player, even those stuck with more than 10 cards themselves.

Should two players have more than 10 points, let's say 10 and 11 points, than they would both pay the double penalty to the other players, though the one having 11 cards pays just one point to the player having 10 cards.

There is one other scoring rule and that is the four deuce bonus. If any player is dealt four deuces, he should immediately turn over his hand. The four deuce bonus nets the lucky player 39 points from each player—the triple penalty times the 13 cards each player holds. Then a new game is dealt.

KEEPING SCORE

Cho Dai Di, like poker, can be played with chips, coins or cash. After each game is played out, players settle with each other. The Chinese generally prefer this method, for like poker, the instant gratification of touching the winnings is more fun.

If, on the other hand, you're playing just for the challenge of the game or simply prefer using a scorepad to keep track of accounts, Cho Dai Di is best played to a set amount of points—say 150, though you can play for less or more points as you find appropriate. Once any player goes over 150 points or whatever amount is set, the game is over, and for those playing for more than the points, accounts can be settled.

Of course, the idea of the game is not to get points, so the player over the point total first will obviously be the big loser and will have to pay off the difference in the scores to the other three players.

Likewise, the second highest score pays off the two lower scores and the second lowest score pays off only the low point total while collecting from the two players with more points. The player with the low point total, the one who went out first and has no cards remaining, is in the money, for all three of his opponents owe him the difference in their scores.

However, either way, keeping score or settling after each game, works equally well and is just as valid as the other.

OTHER STYLES OF PLAY

There are different styles of play in Cho Dai Di, however, whatever the style, it is still basically the same game. For example, some players play that when there is only one card left, opponents must play their highest cards, and may not "feed" a small card to the "Bo Do" player and let him go out.

Some games use a different bonus schedule as well. They may penalize a player double penalties when he's stuck with but 8 cards (as opposed to 10) and triple penalties for any point total above 10 (as opposed to 13). They may also disallow the four deuce instant 39 point bonus from each player, and instead, the game will be played out according to the normal conventions.

You may find games where play always goes in the counterclockwise direction, instead of alternating as we have shown, but whatever the particular rules, you can see that Cho Dai Di, for all intents and purposes, is the same game, and once you know how to play, the nuances of a different style of play are no trouble at all to adjust to.

SAMPLE GAME OF CHO DAI DI

Let's go through a sample game so you can get a feel of how the game is played.

We'll pick up our example earlier where the dealer led a pair of 4s to start the game and was followed by the next player who threw 9s. Let's put some names on the players to make the game easy to follow. Going counter-clockwise, the direction of play for this round, we have Phil, the dealer, who played the 4s, then Quilo, who threw the 9s, Marta and finally Chang.

Marta now plays a pair of 10s; Chang passes. Play comes back to the dealer, Phil, who also passes and then on to Quilo who plays two queens. Marta calls "Dai," pass, as does Chang and Phil, neither of whom have a higher pair or at least don't want to play one if they do.

Since his pair of queens went unanswered by three passes, Quilo wins the round and gets to lead the play for the following round.

Quilo looks around at his opponents: Phil, looking like a preacher needing his prayer to get answered; Marta wearing a thinly-veiled smile ready to burst into flower should the cards prove fertile; and Chang cool as night, unreadable, but wearing some strange green socks.

Quilo now leads with a four of clubs and places it atop the other cards in the center of the table. In Cho Dai Di, cards are played out in the center of the table, and there is no need to collect them until the game is over and the cards are ready to be shuffled.

Quilo looks again and notices that Chang's socks don't match, the left one close in color, but more blue in it. Stoneface notices and lets loose with an uncharacteristic golden grin, but he's looking somewhere else, and Quilo can't figure if it's this world he sees.

Proceeding counterclockwise, the direction of the game, it is Marta's turn, and since one card is led, she may only play one card as well. She throws a four of spades, which is a higher suited four. "Your play, Chang."

Play continues as before, with each player, in turn, laying down higher ranking hands or passing.

Chang, very softly and very quietly, plays a 5. Phil throws a 9, then Quilo a higher suited nine, followed by Marta's king and Chang's ace of diamonds. Phil passes and Quilo, still bothered by something about Chang's socks, puts down the 2 of spades.

He has no need to wait for his opponents response, for the 2 is the highest ranking card and no card can outrank that deuce.

Now, that if the 2 of spades is out of play, the highest ranking unplayed card is the 2 of hearts. Continuing on, Quilo leads with a five card diamond flush and promptly announces **"Bo Do,"** the Cantonese expression signifying that he has one card left.

Whenever a player is down to one card, he must announce that fact to the other players.

It is Marta's turn and she must have a higher five card hand than the flush to play, and if she does have it she better play it, for Quilo is one card away from going out. Marta doesn't and passes, but Chang does and plays a full house. Nobody answers that play, and after three consecutive passes, Chang, as the winner of this round, gets the lead.

Chang sees that the Quilo has but one card left and would like to feed him that one card and let him go out. For if Quilo does go out, they will both collect points from Phil, stuck with 10 cards and Marta, loaded with 9.

The problem is that Phil plays first, and if he plays a controlling card, or at least one higher than Quilo holds, Quilo won't be able to go out and Phil will take control of the lead and maybe turn the game to his own advantage.

In any case, the play is clear-cut for Chang has a pair and plays them, sevens. All three opponents rap their knuckles on the table, pass. Nobody has a higher pair, and in Quilo's case, he can't play against two cards with a one card hand anyway. Chang leads with another pair, eights this time, and again takes the round.

Chang leads again, and more softly than before, leans forward, plays a 10, and announces in a whisper, "Bo Do." Chang also has but one card left. He looks over at Quilo, then coolly at the money in front of his place, and dreamily, awaits the next play.

Phil, holding the 2 of hearts, the highest ranking card now that the spade two is gone, immediately plays it and takes the round. With 10 cards in his hand, he can't play games, not with two players one card away from going out.

He leads a small straight which no player can answer, then leads again with the 2 of clubs which also takes the round without response. It is the highest ranking card remaining, and with its removal, the ace of spades is king. (The diamond two had been played earlier in a flush).

Normally, the correct strategy is to save a **controlling card**, the highest ranking card remaining, to win a round and gain the lead, but if a smaller card is led, Phil will never see the chance, not with two players one card away.

Phil is down to three cards, and having little other choice plays a queen of hearts. Continuing around, right to left, Quilo can't go out with his 10 and passes. Marta plays the queen of spades, a higher ranked queen.

Chang hesitates for a few seconds and bowing his head ever so slightly, plays the king of hearts and goes out.

SCORING OF THE SAMPLE ROUND

After Chang went out, players were left with the following cards.

Chang	0 Cards
Quilo	1 Card
Phil	2 Cards
Marta	8 Cards

For Chang, who went out first, it's a good win, for the three other players owe him points, one for each card they have remaining. Thus, he wins 8 points from Marta, 2 from Phil and 1 from Quilo.

Quilo doesn't fare so bad at all, for while he loses 1 point to Chang, the winner of the round, he collects points from the other two players, 1 from Phil and 7 from Marta, an overall gain of 8 points.

Phil loses 2 points to Chang and 1 point to Quilo but gains 6 from Marta. Despite paying off two opponents, Phil wins enough from Marta for an overall win of 3 points.

Marta, on the other hand, uncharacteristically quiet, didn't have the best luck this round, and winds up paying 8 points to Chang, 7 to Quilo and 6 to Phil for a total loss this round of 21 points. (The next round however, the rest of the players will pay their dues, for Marta will steam in with a big victory and a big gloating smile.)

In the round above, we saw three winners, of varying degrees, and one loser. Let's see how it works when a player gets caught with penalty points.

In this round, Marta goes out first, and with a flourish of knowing looks, particularly at Phil, who mutters about her luck in return.

Marta	0 Cards
Quilo	4 Cards
Chang	4 Cards
Phil	11 Cards

In this game, Marta collects 4 points from both Quilo and Chang, plus a big 22 (2 x 11) from Phil. A pretty good round, she wins 30 points.

Quilo loses four points to Marta, is dead even with Chang, but gains a hefty 14 points (7 point difference x 2) from Phil thanks to the double penalty Phil is paying, and comes out ahead 10 points for the round.

Having the same number of cards remaining, Chang and Quilo neither win or lose from each other, and Chang's total is also +10 points for the round.

Phil bites the big one this round. After losing 10 points to both Chang and Quilo and 22 to Marta, who was screeching with delight at the victory, he finds himself with a 42 point loss for the round.

If you're keeping score on paper, this is how the first two games would look.

Quilo	Chang	Marta	Phil
1	0	8	2
4	4	0	22
5	4	8	24

STRATEGY

The dealer enjoys a distinct advantage over the others for he gets to play the first hand, and thus, controls the initial tempo of the game. And since the goal is to get rid of cards, the player who acts first certainly has that head start as well.

The worst position in a round is the fourth to act, for sometimes, by the time play comes around to his or her position, the cards already played may be stronger than what is held, and this player will be forced to pass without getting to play any cards at all.

LAYING CARDS

Generally speaking, a player will lay down cards whenever possible. However, there are times when a player may find it advisable not to put down playable cards, either because it may break up a bigger hand for example, or because of future positioning.

CONTROL

Making the first discards in a playing round is advantageous, for the player laying down cards first not only controls the number of cards to be played in the round but also dictates the initial strength of the cards that must be beat for others to lay down cards as well. This player controls the tempo of the round and may play into his own strengths in an attempt to rid himself of all cards.

The name of the game in Cho Dai Di is *control* and a lot of your strategy is worked around that. For, if you can control a round by playing the final cards, then you get to lead the next round and that's a big advantage. For example, if you hold the 2 of spades, the most powerful card in the deck, and the lead is a single card, you know you can control that round because nobody has a higher ranking card.

PLAYING FIRST

The player going first in the game will usually, though not always, want to play a five card hand, especially if it's a low ranking one such as a 10 high straight. The straight is unlikely to control the round, but it does quickly get rid of five cards and prevents the player from being blocked out of playing the straight later on because another player plays a higher five card hand.

GAINING POINTS

In Cho Dai Di the strategy is not so much to be the first one to go out in a round, but to gain points overall against the other players. This could be done by having the next fewest number of cards or even sometimes, as we saw in the sample game, having the third largest number of cards with only one player having more.

Thus, if the player to go next has one card remaining and it's your lead, you might not mind throwing a small one card lead if a third player will get caught with 10 cards or more and you'll win double. Of course, you would rather be the player going out first, for the wins are larger, but that is not always possible, and as we have just shown, not always necessary.

Let's outline some other important winning concepts.

Try to Lead with Smaller Cards First – Generally speaking, you want to play your low cards first, and get rid of these weaker cards. The weaker the card, the less playable that card is. For example, if a player has two cards remaining, a four and a three, he'll have great difficulty in going out. For one thing, he will have difficulty in gaining the lead with a small card, if he can even play it at all, and even if he is lucky enough to get rid of one of them, it is doubtful that it will be enough to control a round and permit the unloading of the second small fry.

On the other hand, if one of two remaining cards is high, one may be able to maneuver that card into a controlling position and win the round. The small card can now be led, and since that's the last card, the game is over.

Don't Get Caught with 10 or More Cards – If the game progresses and a player comes within striking distance of going out, the wise move is to break up a good hand so that you don't get caught with a double penalty. It's better to be stuck with eight cards and have to pay three players their dues, than to risk being caught with 10 or more cards and a double penalty to all three opponents.

If you can't control the game, don't take chances if a player gets close to going out—break up your hand and play the game safe.

Keep Track of the High Cards – It's extremely important to know what twos and aces have been played. When it gets near the end, you need to know if the single lead you play can be followed later by a card you hold and know to be the highest, thereby giving you control over the next rounds start. You always need to know what the current controlling card is at all times.

(Remember, the 2 of spades is the initial controlling card, and when it's played, the 2 of hearts becomes the controlling card, then the 2 of clubs, the 2 of diamonds, the ace of spades and so on.)

Knowing how many aces and deuces played also clues you in to the highest possible pairs that can be made. If you know that three aces and all four deuces have already been used, your pair of kings rules as the largest pair left. Or if you hold the remaining ace, you've got the highest card left and can control with it.

Defensive Play – If an opposing player has but one card left, do not lead with one card unless you lead with the highest single card remaining, which means that player cannot go out in his turn and also that you'll control the round, or that, by his going out, you'll benefit, for you have few cards remaining and the other players have many cards to go.

This strategy also applies when opposing players have two, three, four or five cards remaining before they go out. If you're stuck with a lot of cards and one player has but two to go, a two card lead is dangerous, for a pair gives that player an opportunity to go out.

SUMMARY

We hope you enjoy this exciting game. There's a lot of strategy in Cho Dai Di and therefore lots of challenges. Write in to us here and let us know if you enjoyed Cho Dai Di.

Until then, "Jhoy King"—see you later.

CJOK LAY HO WAN
(Good Fortune)

Horseracing

FIVE KEYS TO HORSERACING

1 The best straight bets for your money are win and show.

2 If betting to win, stick with horses that give you odds of 5-1 or better; if betting to place, stick with odds of 5-1 or less.

3 If you really like a horse, go with your instincts and make a play on it. Don't bet horses you don't really like.

4 Avoid horses moving up in class. It's one thing to beat up on lesser horses, quite another, to beat up on better ones.

5 Your best bets are often with horses that have some winning background, not with ones that are chronic losers and have never tasted the finish line first.

INTRODUCTION

Horseracing is the largest spectator sport in the United States, drawing countless fans every year at tracks across the country. It is also quite popular in numerous other countries around the world. The thrill of competition and the challenge of analyzing all the relevant data to pick a winner, continues to enthrall fans everywhere.

The tracks are fervid with the excitement, color and anticipation of the race. Men and women, buried deep into their racing forms, analyze and handicap the races, figuring which horse going off at what odds presents them the best bet. They look at various factors, discuss the possibilities and watch the tote board to see how the odds are moving.

Others, out to the track for the first time, or simply less handicapping-minded, may choose the horse with a name that strikes their fancy—perhaps its similar to the name of a person they know, a place they've been or it just sounds good to them. Or maybe they like the color associated with that horse.

This section will show the language of the track, the various wagers available to the bettor, the different philosophies and strategies of winning, the odds you face every time you wager on a horse and 11 suggestions for winning at the track!

THE BETS

STRAIGHT BETTING

The win, place and show bets, called **straight bets**, are the most popular wagers at the horsetrack, and we'll discuss them first.

The **win** bet, is a wager that a horse will finish first in the race. Any other finish, second, third or whatever is irrelevant. It is only the first place finish that counts with a win bet.

The **place** bet is a wager that the horse will come in first or second—either way the bet is a winner.

A bet to **show** allows the bettor even more leeway, for the horse may come in first, second or third for the bet to be a winner.

Finishing either first, second or third is called **being in the money**, a classic term used outside the track as well.

Of the straight bets, win tickets will pay the best, for they are hardest to pick. Place and show bets pay less than win bets for more horses share the betting pool, two in the case of place bets and three in the case of show bets.

EXACTA BETS

The **exacta** is a bet that the two horses chosen in a race come in first and second, in exact order. Many bettors like this type of wager for if the exacta is a winner, the payoffs can be pretty good.

QUINELLA BETS

On this wager you're betting on the top two finishers in a race, like the exacta, only with the **quinella**, you don't care about the order of finish—you only care that your two horses are the first and second place finishers in that race.

The quinella bet is easier to win than the exacta, and consequently pays less.

DAILY DOUBLE

This popular bet is a wager on the winners of the first two races. If you picked the winner of one race only, it counts for nothing. To win a daily double, both the first and second races must be picked correctly.

TRIPLES

This bet is similar to the Daily Double except that with the **triple**, you must choose the winner of the three consecutive races designated by the track.

PICK SIX

You can make a fortune correctly picking this ticket but it's not easy—you must pick the winner of six races! Good luck on this one. Usually there is a smaller payoff if five winners are chosen as well.

OTHER EXOTIC BETS

There are other exotic bets offered at some tracks but these should be clearly explained on their programs. You may find bets like a **Pick Nine**, where you have to choose the winners of nine races! Win that one and all your money troubles are over.

SOME TRACK BASICS

THE TOTE BOARD

The big computerized board at the track, called the **Totalizer** or **Tote Board**, displays the amount of money bet on each horse to win, place and show, and the resultant odds that constantly change as wagers come in on particular horses.

The lines listed on the tote board, reflect the betting at the track—the more money bet on a horse, the lower its odds will be. Thus, if many people favor a particular horse to win and back that horse with more bets than any other horse, that horse will be the **favorite**, and will have the smallest payoff of any horse in the race.

Horses that get little action, are considered **longshots** , and will go off at high odds, 10 -1 or 17-1 for example.

The tote board is important to watch for it shows the odds of each horse and lets you know which horse is the current favorite and which horse is the **longest shot** (the horse with the least amount of money bet on it and consequently, the highest odds).

The odds continually change as more betting money comes in and this will be reflected on the tote board for all to see. Sometimes a favorite will become a bigger favorite or even become supplanted by another horse as the favorite as late money comes in.

When the race is ready to begin, no more bets will be accepted and the posted odds become the actual odds of the race on which all payoffs are based. If you were lucky enough to pick the winner, it will be the final odds at post time that determines your payoff, not the odds at the time you placed your bet.

THE MORNING LINE

The initial line at which the odds on competing horses are quoted is set by the track handicapper and is his estimation of how the horses might be bet by the public. This line is called the **morning line** and has no final bearing on the actual payoff on a horse if it wins.

Once bets start coming on, the odds on the tote board will change to reflect the amounts bet on each horse.

Many bettors use the morning line as a rough guide to the comparative strengths of the horses. Horses listed at low odds, say 2 to 1, probably have a good chance of winning the race, while those going off at 25 to 1, considered high odds, probably have little chance of finishing in the money.

BETS AND PAYOFFS

The minimum bet in horseracing is generally $2.00. The amount of money a bettor receives back will reflect the winning odds as listed on the tote board plus the original $2.00 bet. For example, if your horse goes off at 5 to 2 odds and is a winner, you'll receive $5.00 for the win plus the original $2.00 bet for a total of $7.00.

The results posted are always based on the $2.00 bet so if you have a larger bet, say $10.00, you simply multiply the $2.00 results by 5 ($10.00 is five $2.00 wagers) to come out with the total won. In the above example, a $10.00 bet would pay off $25.00 in winnings plus the original bet of $10.00 for a total $35.00 return.

The tote board will read $7.00 on the 5-2 win anyway, already reflecting the $2.00 bet placed.

Let's say that in a particular race, horse #2, **Liberty Charles** wins the race at 3 to 1 odds, horse #5, Skidmore Jones comes in second, and horse # 1 **Begboke Vindaloo** comes in third.

This is how it may be listed:

Order of Finish	Win	Place	Show
2 Winning Horse	8.00	4.80	4.00
5 Second Horse		11.60	4.80
1 Third Horse			2.60

Only those who bet horse #2 (**Liberty Charles**) to win collect the $8.00 to $6.00 in winnings for the 3-1 odds plus the $2.00 bet. Players who bet **Liberty Charles** to place collect only $4.80 and ones who bet to show get back $4.00.

Players who bet either the #5 or #1 horse to win are losers, for those horses didn't win, though place and show bets on #5 and show bets on #1, in this example, will pay as shown on the chart.

HOW TO BET

Horses are identified by post position in the racing program as well as on the tote board and the tickets you will buy at the betting windows. Thus, a horse sporting a 1 in the program, will be running out from the first post position, and a horse identified by a 7 will be exiting from the seventh post position.

The tote board uses the post position numbers as well to identify horses. To follow the betting line as it progresses, simply track your horse by the number.

Let's say that you've added up the pros and cons of each horse and are now ready to place your bet. The horses on your program are listed as follows:

Squarebacks	1
Bongo Player	2
Rubics	3
Ted the T.	4
Chess	5
Octogon	6
Woodstock	7
Bird in the Cage	8

If you want to bet on **Bongo Player** to show and **Octogon** to win, you would identify #2 as the place and #6 as your win bet. Similarly, if you want to pick **Octagon** (post position 6) and **Bird in the Cage** (post position 8) as your 1-2 horses in an exacta, you'll identify the ticket as a 6-8 exacta.

THE PARI-MUTUEL POOL

The total amount of money on a race is collected into what is called the **Pari-Mutuel pool**, and after the government and track take are pulled from the total, the rest is proportionately divided among the winners.

The higher the odds of a winning horse, the greater the payoff will be should the horse win or come into the money, and likewise, the lower the odds, meaning more bettors wagered on the horse, the smaller the winning payoff will be.

(Keep in mind that historically, the higher the odds against a horse, the less chance this horse has of winning.)

Let's see just how big a cut is taken from the Pari-Mutuel pool before the bettors get their share.

THE PERCENTAGES

Betting is as embedded in horseracing as the horses themselves, but it is one of the tougher gambling pursuits to beat. The racing fan faces a stiff tax at the mutuels in America, and he must overcome this albatross to come ahead a winner. Few do.

Here is why.

Most U.S. states levy at least a 17% tax on every dollar bet at the horsetrack, a gargantuan percentage to try and beat. Additionally, fans who make such exotic bets as the Pick Six and Triple, get taxed at an even greater rate—25%!

There is one additional price the horse bettor must pay, and that is called **break-age**. The track pays out winnings to the dime only, and keeps whatever odd pennies left over. For example, if the mutuel payoff figures to be $5.78, the bettor would receive only $5.70 back, or a $3.56 win would pay off at $3.50.

Some tracks pay out only to the 20¢, and on the above $5.78 mutuel would return only $5.60, at even greater cost to the winner.

So what's the big deal, a few pennies here or there? Plenty. On average, this costs the bettor about another 2% per dollar wagered—more straws on the camels back.

And may the betting gods help you if you happen to be a New York OTB bettor, for their commission runs you another 5%.

Where this leaves the serious horseracing fan is in a big ditch if he's got profits on his mind. You have to be a very good handicapper to overcome these percentages.

It's a lot of fun to watch the horses and jockeys compete, to be part of the colorful track atmosphere, and to study the racing form and figure the winning horses. However, keep the races and the heavy odds in perspective when you hit the mutuels for a little action.

A Word on Horserace Betting

Keep in mind that you're bucking big odds when you take on the track, so we heartily recommend that one pursue betting on the horses as strictly recreational.

If you decide you want to play the track on a more serious level, than you should first test your skills on a small scale and be sure to win at that level before putting out the big bucks.

Don't jump up in bet size until you've proven your skills for the difference between betting small dollars and betting big dollars, might only be that the losses will be bigger. Bigger bets won't necessarily change your luck.

THE CLASS OF RACES

There are five basic classes of horseracing, and while there is some overlap between the groupings, these classifications will give you a good idea about the relative strength of horses in one group as compared to another.

CLAIMING RACES

Out of the nine or so races you'll see featured in a racing program, the **claiming race** will be the type of race most frequently encountered. The purses for winning horses are the smallest of any of the races, and consequently the horses entered are the lowest in quality.

The concept of the claiming race is really quite interesting. Any horse entered in a claiming race can be bought, in the jargon of the track, **claimed**, by anyone for the **claiming price** listed in the program. Generally, another stable or horseman will be the buyer, but now and then, an amateur out of the stands might pick one up.

A horse must be claimed prior to a race, in writing, and once claimed, is fully the property of the new owner. The purse for that race, however, will still belong to the previous owner.

It is more difficult to handicap these types of races for the horses entered, being of the lowest quality, are more inconsistent, and therefore more difficult to predict.

There are varying claiming prices on these horses, and you can figure that a higher claiming price generally indicates a better class of horse. Sometimes you'll see a horse **going down in class**, being entered at a lower claiming price than previous.

This might indicate that the horse was unable to successfully compete at the higher level, and has therefore dropped down, the owner perhaps hoping to catch some purses against lesser class horses, or maybe hoping to unload the horse with the cheaper price. Horses cost a lot of money to maintain, and the owners, being businessmen or businesswomen, need to keep the ship afloat.

The claiming system is clever and is a deterrent against higher class horses, clearly superior, from entering the race and stealing the purse, for once the horse is entered, it is open market for another buyer who feels the horse is worth the price.

Some trainers and owners are real good evaluators of talent, and make a good little business out of claiming horses. They are referred to as **claiming trainers** or **claiming owners**.

MAIDEN RACES

These races are clearly a cut above the claiming races, and sometimes the best of horses start out at this level. Horses are entered in these races who have not yet won a race and are too valuable to the owner to run in a claimer.

Within this category is the **Maiden Special Weight** race, for two year old horses who also, have not won a race.

ALLOWANCE RACES

In these races a variety of elements are factored in, such as amount of races run and money won previously, and the horse is assigned a **weight allowance** to help offset the differences between it and the other contestants in a race.

For example, a seemingly superior horse may be assigned five extra pounds on the theory that those extra pounds will equalize its talents with lesser horses in the race.

There are all sorts of allowance races, run for different ages of horses and run for different size purses. There are class levels within the allowance category. You can figure a horse running a $25,000 allowance to be superior to a horse running a $15,000 one.

HANDICAP RACES

These races are for near top level horses, offering high purses and game horses going for the winners spot. The track handicapper examines each horses credentials carefully and assigns weights to each one, in an attempt to equalize the speeds and skills, so that each horse has a fair shot at winning the race.

STAKES RACES

These races feature the cream of the talent, the top thoroughbreds competing for the top prizes. Races such as **The Preakness**, **The Kentucky Derby** and **The Belmont Stakes**, the events of horseracing's famous **Triple Crown**, are all stakes races.

Here is where famous horses such as Secretariat and Seattle Slew cement their fame in horseracing's hall of fame.

These races create the most excitement of all the thoroughbred events for it is the top contenders in the world competing horse to horse in a thrilling spectacle that is discussed long before the race is ever run, and glorified long after.

HANDICAPPING PHILOSOPHIES

FORM HANDICAPPING

A horse's current form, how it has fared in the last few races, is what racetrackers call **form handicapping**. The proponents of this type of handicapping argue that horses, like humans, are conditioned athletes—they reach peaks of high performance at times, and other times, are just not as good.

If a horse has not run well lately, form handicapping says that all the other handicapping factors just don't make sense. Plainly, the horse is not in good enough form to win the race.

Form handicappers attempt to back the horse that, according to recent past performance charts, is in the peak of its form, and on that basis, has the best chances of winning the race.

TRIP HANDICAPPING

Trip handicappers are looking for inconsistency in a horse caused by a track mishap which caused an otherwise strong contender to perhaps finish out of the money. The final result may show that the horse didn't fare so well, but the trip handicapper, noting that the horse started fast, suddenly lost a bunch of lengths, but then finished strong, may conclude that the horse got tripped-up, and is really a better horse than the order of finish in the past race might indicate.

CLASS HANDICAPPING

This form of handicapping proposes that there is no more important factor than a horse's class. Horseplayers define **class** as a comparison of the quality of a race a horse has competed in as judged by the level or claiming price of the race, the importance of the race or the stakes involved.

A better horse will compete at better levels they feel, and will look for opportunities where a superior horse, judged on class, will race against inferior horses.

There are many formulas used to judge class. One of the more popular ones is to judge the amount of money earned by a horse over a specified period of time, divide the earnings amount of the horse by the number of races run, and come up with a figure that could be used for comparison.

For example, when a horse attempts to move up in class, the class handicappers will look carefully at the horses credentials, and if they conclude it's racing out of class, they would consider this horse a poor bet. But on the other hand, a horse moving down in class enjoys a marked advantage over the lesser horses, and given the right odds, may indeed be a very good bet.

SPEED HANDICAPPING

This method specifies that the speed with which the horse has run its races is the most important variable in picking winners. A general rule of thumb at the track is to assign one second to every five lengths at the track. Thus if a horse finished 10 lengths behind the winner's time of 1.11 in a six furlong race, you would call the speed 1.13.

Horses run races under different conditions and speed handicappers would adjust times or give weighting to these factors so that horses with different racing backgrounds can be compared to each other. Some tracks are faster than others, some horses carried different weights, some may have run on an off track (not a fast track), some may have ran at different track lengths.

Once these variable have been adjusted, the speed handicapper finds the horse which shows the greatest speed and would back that horse for the race.

PACE HANDICAPPING

Pace handicappers believe that it's not so important how fast a horse can run per se, but how well the horse paces itself during a race that is the crucial element in winning route races.

A pure speed horse can have the edge in a sprint race, but when the race is a route, other elements such as pace come into play.

On the theory that a horse cannot run a route at absolute full speed for the length of the track, but must pace itself against the others and save its maximum energy for the stretch run, the pace handicappers spot the horses they feel can run the distance at the best pace. Fast sprint horses may be avoided by the pace handicappers, instead opting for horses that have a proven record in routes.

OTHER HANDICAPPING ELEMENTS

There are numerous other ways that horseplayers figure an angle on the race, not the least on which is to judge a jockey's abilities and a trainer's abilities. Some jockeys and trainers are proven winners with records far exceeding their peers and this is an element bettors may factor into their analysis.

And that is what makes horseracing so interesting, all the various theories of why a horse should be better than another, the tangibles and intangibles that when added up, make the analysis of a horserace so mysterious and elusive. There are people who spend their lives figuring the horses and constantly refining and updating their techniques to get a better edge.

There are many theories on beating the track, and we'll leave that up to you to figure the best way to approach the horses to fit your style of thinking.

However, let's present some standard percentages that have held true over many years and then give you some winning techniques to get you started on the road.

STANDARD WINNING PERCENTAGES

It is interesting to note that over the long run, a horse's winning percentage is in direct correlation to its **send-off position**, the relative listing of odds on the horse at race time.

Over the years, horses going off as favorites will win approximately 33% of the time, while **second choices**, horses with the next lowest odds after the favorite, will win about 20% of the time, and **third choices**, the next down in send-off position, will win the race about 15% of the time.

Similarly, **fourth choices**, **fifth choices** and lesser will win a smaller proportion of the races in order of send-off position.

Altogether, the top three choices account for just below 70% of all wins.

Favorites will place a bit over 50% of the time, while second choices place around 40% and third choices 30%.

Keep in mind that these figures have stayed fairly constant over the years, but that doesn't mean that they'll hold true over a limited period of time at a particular track. Short run anomalies are normal in horseracing as in all forms of gambling but certainly, these figures are good guideposts to go by when formulating your winning approach at the track.

WINNING STRATEGIES

Following are some general guidelines followed by many pros which will give you a leg up on many other horse bettors.

1. When betting straight, restrict your bets to win and show only.

2. As a general rule, bet horses you like with odds of 5-1 or greater to win and odds of 5-1 or less, to place.

3. Pay close attention to a horses recent performances. Form handicapping has a lot of merit, and you face your best chances with a horse in top condition.

4. Horses backed heavily by touting services and computer handicappers may win more, but so many bettors are placing their dollars on them, they give poor value for the money. Try to find the **"dark horse,"** one that has a good shot at the tape but is not overly backed.

5. Be wary of the "smart money," bets placed at the last minute by supposedly, those in the know. There isn't much smart money at the tracks.

6. Go with you gut feelings. If there's a horse you like, by all means bet that horse. There's no worse feeling than not doing what you felt you should have done, and it working out—without you. And if it doesn't work out, no big deal.

7. Pay special attention to fast starters on off tracks. It's more difficult to maneuver on a muddy or slow track, and these conditions will favor the horse that takes the early lead.

8. Avoid horses moving up in class. They may have looked good against lesser horses, but now the move to better competition may reveal some different colors.

9. Avoid horses that have not raced in the past four weeks. They may be recuperating from illness and the owners are using the race as a tune-up. The winning percentages of long-idled horse are way below the average.

10. Bet only winners. If you see a horse that has been around but has never won a race, why figure that today's race will be a reversal of past performance? Instead, choose a horse that has some background of winning.

11. Bet only horses you feel have a good chance of winning. If you had eliminated all the horses you've bet in the past but have not really believed in, you would be sitting with a much higher winning percentage. If you don't like a horse, don't bet it.

Keno

INTRODUCTION

The origins of this fun game go back some 2,000 years to the Han Dynasty in China—quite a long history, and quite a long distance to travel to make it to casinos as far away as Nevada, halfway across the globe.

Keno is quite popular and one of the attractions of the game is that it's easy to play. The only decisions a player need be concerned with are which numbers he or she will play, and how much to bet. Once the bet is placed, the fun begins as number upon number appear on the board, and the player waits to see if indeed, enough lucky numbers were hit to bring in the big fish.

And there's always that attraction of the giant win—that a 70¢ or $1.00 or $1.40 wager, whatever is played, may catch the right numbers and land the lucky bettor a $50,000 bonanza.

Keno has that lure, the big win, the myriad possibilities of numbers that can land, the almost wins, the "if I had played those numbers," and bettors keep coming back for more.

Let's move on now, see how the game is played, and how best to make yourself a winner.

THE BASICS OF KENO

HOW TO PLAY

All bets in keno are made and recorded on a **keno ticket**, a pre-printed form where a player indicates the choices he or she will make. The tickets are readily available in the keno lounge and are kept in generous supply on the counters and next to every seat in the keno area.

Situated near the tickets will be the thick, black crayons which are used to mark keno tickets, and the casinos **rate card**, showing the exact payoffs for tickets played and won.

There are 80 numbered squares on a keno ticket which correspond exactly to the 80 numbered balls in the keno cage. A player may choose anywhere from one to fifteen numbers to play, and does so by marking an **"x"** on the keno ticket for each number or numbers he or she so chooses.

You'll notice on the keno ticket, "KENO LIMIT $50,000, To aggregate players each game." This means that if you do hit the big $50,000 prize in the same game as another player, that you'll have to split the jackpot. However, the likelihood of this occurring stretches the imagination into far off places, in other words, don't worry about it.

Twenty balls will be drawn each game, and will appear as lighted numbers on the keno screens. As the game progresses, each number will be lit as it is drawn, so that the player can easily keep track of the numbers drawn and see how his or her ticket is faring.

Winnings are determined by consulting the payoff chart each casino provides. If enough numbers have been correctly picked, you have a winner, and the chart will show the payoff. The more numbers that come up, the greater the winnings.

BETTING

Bets are usually made in 70¢ or $1.00 multiples, though other standard bets may apply. A player may bet as many multiples of this bet as he desires. For example, a player may bet $5.00 on a $1.00 ticket, giving him or her in fact, five games with the same combinations.

HOW TO MARK THE TICKET

The amount being wagered on a game should be placed in the box marked **Mark Price Here** in the upper right hand corner of the ticket. Leave out dollar or cents signs though. $1 would be indicated by simply placing **"1-"** and 70 cents by **".70-"**. Of course, any amount up to the house limit can be wagered.

Underneath this box is a column of white space. The number of spots selected for the game is put here. If six spots were selected on the ticket, mark the number **"6"**, if fifteen numbers, mark **"15"**.

Let's show a five spot ticket that we've marked for a $1 game.

This type of ticket, which is the most common one bet, is called a **straight ticket**, or more precisely, in this example, a **five-spot straight ticket**. Similarly, if 11 numbers were chosen, it would be called an **11 spot straight ticket**.

PAYOFF CHARTS

Let's look at typical Las Vegas payoff charts for $1.00 and $1.40 games. You'll notice that there are payoff schedules for any amount of numbers picked, 1 through 15, and that each one has its own minimum set of numbers needed to win.

For example, if you play a 9 spot game with a $1.00 bet, you'll need to **"catch"** a minimum of five numbers for a payoff. In this case, $4.00 would be returned—your original $1.00 bet plus the $3.00 in winnings. If all nine numbers are caught, however, a cool $25,000 perfumes your senses.

RATE CARD: 1-15 SPOTS • $1.00, $3.00, $5.00, $1.40 WAGERS

MARK 1 SPOT

Winning Spots	$1.00 Ticket Pays	$3.00 Ticket Pays	$5.00 Ticket Pays	$1.40 Ticket Pays
1	3.00	9.00	15.00	4.20

MARK 2 SPOTS

Winning Spots	$1.00 Ticket Pays	$3.00 Ticket Pays	$5.00 Ticket Pays	$1.40 Ticket Pays
2	12.00	36.00	60.00	17.00

MARK 3 SPOTS

Winning Spots	$1.00 Ticket Pays	$3.00 Ticket Pays	$5.00 Ticket Pays	$1.40 Ticket Pays
2	1.00	3.00	5.00	1.40
3	42.00	126.00	210.00	60.00

MARK 4 SPOTS

Winning Spots	$1.00 Ticket Pays	$3.00 Ticket Pays	$5.00 Ticket Pays	$1.40 Ticket Pays
2	1.00	3.00	5.00	1.40
3	4.00	12.00	20.00	5.40
4	112.00	336.00	560.00	160.00

MARK 5 SPOTS

Winning Spots	$1.00 Ticket Pays	$3.00 Ticket Pays	$5.00 Ticket Pays	$1.40 Ticket Pays
3	1.00	3.00	5.00	2.40
4	14.00	42.00	70.00	30.00
5	720.00	2,160.00	3,600.00	680.00

MARK 6 SPOTS

Winning Spots	$1.00 Ticket Pays	$3.00 Ticket Pays	$5.00 Ticket Pays	$1.40 Ticket Pays
3	1.00	3.00	5.00	1.20
4	4.00	12.00	20.00	6.60
5	88.00	264.00	440.00	120.00
6	1,480.00	4,440.00	7,400.00	2,200.00

MARK 7 SPOTS

Winning Spots	$1.00 Ticket Pays	$3.00 Ticket Pays	$5.00 Ticket Pays	$1.40 Ticket Pays
3				60
4	1.00	3.00	5.00	2.40
5	20.00	60.00	100.00	30.00
6	380.00	1,140.00	1,900.00	460.00
7	8,000.00	24,000.00	40,000.00	7,000.00

MARK 8 SPOTS

Winning Spots	$1.00 Ticket Pays	$3.00 Ticket Pays	$5.00 Ticket Pays	$1.40 Ticket Pays
5	9.00	27.00	45.00	12.00
6	80.00	240.00	400.00	120.00
7	1,480.00	4,440.00	7,400.00	2,300.00
8	25,000.00	50,000.00	50,000.00	25,000.00

MARK 9 SPOTS

Winning Spots	$1.00 Ticket Pays	$3.00 Ticket Pays	$5.00 Ticket Pays	$1.40 Ticket Pays
4				60
5	4.00	12.00	20.00	4.60
6	44.00	132.00	220.00	60.00
7	300.00	900.00	1,500.00	400.00
8	4,000.00	12,000.00	20,000.00	5,600.00
9	25,000.00	50,000.00	50,000.00	25,000.00

MARK 10 SPOTS

Winning Spots	$1.00 Ticket Pays	$3.00 Ticket Pays	$5.00 Ticket Pays	$1.40 Ticket Pays
5	2.00	6.00	10.00	2.80
6	20.00	60.00	100.00	28.00
7	136.00	408.00	680.00	196.00
8	960.00	2,880.00	4,800.00	1,400.00
9	4,000.00	12,000.00	20,000.00	5,320.00
10	25,000.00	50,000.00	50,000.00	25,000.00

MARK 11 SPOTS

Winning Spots	$1.00 Ticket Pays	$3.00 Ticket Pays	$5.00 Ticket Pays	$1.40 Ticket Pays
5	1.00	3.00	5.00	1.20
6	8.00	24.00	40.00	12.00
7	72.00	216.00	360.00	100.00
8	360.00	1,080.00	1,800.00	500.00
9	1,800.00	5,400.00	9,000.00	2,400.00
10	12,000.00	36,000.00	50,000.00	15,000.00
11	28,000.00	50,000.00	50,000.00	40,000.00

MARK 12 SPOTS

Winning Spots	$1.00 Ticket Pays	$3.00 Ticket Pays	$5.00 Ticket Pays	$1.40 Ticket Pays
5				1.20
6	5.00	15.00	25.00	6.00
7	32.00	96.00	160.00	40.00
8	240.00	720.00	1,200.00	300.00
9	600.00	1,800.00	3,000.00	800.00
10	1,480.00	4,440.00	7,400.00	2,000.00
11	12,000.00	36,000.00	50,000.00	10,000.00
12	36,000.00	50,000.00	50,000.00	50,000.00

MARK 13 SPOTS

Winning Spots	$1.00 Ticket Pays	$3.00 Ticket Pays	$5.00 Ticket Pays	$1.40 Ticket Pays
6	1.00	3.00	5.00	2.40
7	16.00	48.00	80.00	24.00
8	80.00	240.00	400.00	100.00
9	720.00	2,160.00	3,600.00	950.00
10	4,000.00	12,000.00	20,000.00	5,000.00
11	8,000.00	24,000.00	40,000.00	9,000.00
12	25,000.00	50,000.00	50,000.00	20,000.00
13	36,000.00	50,000.00	50,000.00	50,000.00

MARK 14 SPOTS

Winning Spots	$1.00 Ticket Pays	$3.00 Ticket Pays	$5.00 Ticket Pays	$1.40 Ticket Pays
6	1.00	3.00	5.00	4.40
7	10.00	30.00	50.00	11.00
8	40.00	120.00	200.00	44.00
9	320.00	960.00	1,600.00	350.00
10	1,000.00	3,000.00	5,000.00	1,000.00
11	3,200.00	9,600.00	16,000.00	4,000.00
12	16,000.00	48,000.00	50,000.00	15,000.00
13	25,000.00	50,000.00	50,000.00	30,000.00
14	40,000.00	50,000.00	50,000.00	50,000.00

MARK 15 SPOTS

Winning Spots	$1.00 Ticket Pays	$3.00 Ticket Pays	$5.00 Ticket Pays	$1.40 Ticket Pays
6				2.00
7	8.00	24.00	40.00	10.00
8	28.00	84.00	140.00	30.00
9	132.00	396.00	660.00	150.00
10	300.00	900.00	1,500.00	400.00
11	2,600.00	7,800.00	13,000.00	3,000.00
12	8,000.00	24,000.00	40,000.00	10,000.00
13	25,000.00	50,000.00	50,000.00	30,000.00
14	32,000.00	50,000.00	50,000.00	40,000.00
15	40,000.00	50,000.00	50,000.00	50,000.00

Keno runners are available for your convenience. Since they must transport your tickets to the main counter for validation, please have the tickets ready as early as possible. We cannot accept responsibility if tickets are too late for the current game.

THE DUPLICATE TICKET

Now you have your ticket filled in and are ready to play the game. You ta~~ original~~ or **master ticket** to the keno writer at the window and hand it in with th~~ amount for which you'll be playing.

The writer will retain your original ticket and hand back a **duplicate ticket**. This ticket will show the same numbers you have chosen, which are generally marked in thick black strokes from the brush they use, the dollar amount of the game and the total numbers played, just like your ticket did.

It will also show some things that were not on your original. The duplicate will have printed on it, the date and time of the game, the game's number, and a particular code number used by the casino. You'll also see the printing, "Winning tickets must be paid immediately after each keno game," or some such writing.

Take this piece of writing very seriously.

If you have a winning ticket, you must present your duplicate before the next game resumes, or you will forfeit that payoff. There is a quirk in the legal structure of the game which differentiates keno from a lottery in that the immediate payoff prevents the keno game from being called a lottery.

Remember, if you have a winning ticket, cash it in immediately.

THE KENO RUNNER

Many casinos offer players the luxury of playing keno from virtually anywhere in the casino. One can play the game while at the slots or while luxuriating over a meal in the restaurant.

This is done through the services of a keno runner, casino employees, usually women, whose sole job is to take keno bets from patrons in various parts of the casino, return to them a duplicate ticket and collect their payoff should the ticket be a winner.

Ah, the easy life! If you do win, it is customary to tip a little something to the runner (the bearer of good tidings).

THE PUNCH-OUT TICKET

To make life easy, the casinos employ what is called a **punch-out ticket or draw**, to verify if a player's ticket is a winner. The 20 called numbers are "punched-out" of a ticket, and by placing this ticket over a player's, it allows one to see the amount of winning numbers at a glance.

Since the tickets are identical in size and alignment, only marked off numbers will appear in the spaces. This clever method clears up any doubts about the number of winning spots hit.

When in doubt about whether you've won, request that a punch-out ticket be placed over your duplicate, and the result will clearly show through.

REPLAYING A TICKET

You may have a lucky set of numbers you like to play, or a particular set that either just won for you, or which you've just played, and feel that the same numbers are ripe to score.

In any case, the casino allows you to replay the same numbers again, and to save you the trouble of rewriting your ticket, you simply need to hand in your duplicate, which now becomes your original ticket, and the keno writer will issue you a new duplicate.

Easy as that. You can do this all day long if you like, exchanging duplicate as original for a new duplicate.

OTHER TICKETS

SPLIT TICKETS

Players are not limited to just straight tickets but may also play as many combinations as they choose. A **split ticket** allows a player to bet two or more combinations in one game.

This is done by marking two sets (or more) of 1-15 numbers on a ticket and separating them by either a line, or by circling the separate groups. Numbers may not be duplicated between the two sets.

On split tickets, in which several games are being played in one, the keno ticket should be marked as follows. In addition to the x's indicating the numbers, and the lines or circles showing the groups, the ticket should clearly indicate the amount of games being played.

For example, a split ticket playing two groups of six spots each would be marked 2/6 in the column of white space. The 2 shows that two combinations are being played, and the 6 shows that six numbers are being chosen per game.

If $1 is being bet per combination, we would put a **"1-"** and circle it underneath the slashed numbers to show this, and of course, in the Mark Price Here box, we would enter **"2"**, to show $2 is being bet—$1 on each combination.

We'll show two examples of a split ticket, one separated by a line, and the other, separated by circles.

Split Ticket • Line Separated

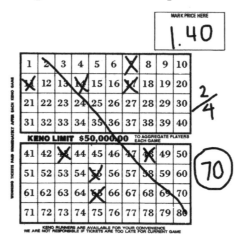

Split Ticket • Circle Separated

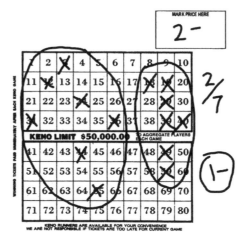

A player could theoretically play 80 one spots on one split ticket, or 40 two spots or 10 five spots—as long as numbers aren't duplicated.

Remember that on split tickets, each split game, for all intents and purposes, is played separately and counts as a separate game. Numbers cannot be combined among different groups to create a winner, the winning numbers must be among one group.

Any odd combination of split groups is allowed on a split ticket. If a player desires, for example, he or she could play two groups of five spots, one seven spot, one four spot and one three spot on the same ticket. Different amounts of money can be wagered on each group. In the above example, $1.00 could be bet on the five, seven and four spot groups, while $2.00 could be wagered on the three spot.

The only restriction to the different dollar amounts allowed to be bet on one split ticket is that equal groupings of numbers, in the above example, the two five spots, must be bet with the same amount of money. Otherwise, bet what you will on each grouping as long as it conforms to the minimum and maximum amounts permitted by the casino.

COMBINATION TICKETS

Combination tickets allow the player to combine groups of numbers in all sorts of ways with the player betting one unit for each combination possible.

For example, a player can indicate groups of two, three and four numbers on a ticket. Using all possible combinations, he can play the game as a 2-spot, 3-spot, 4-spot, 5-spot (2 + 3), 6-spot (2-spot + 4 spot), 7-spot (3-spot + 4 spot) and 9-spot (2-spot, 3-spot and 4-spot) for a total of a seven unit bet.

Whew—lots of combinations!

The groups bet on combination tickets should all be clearly marked in the white space on the right of the keno ticket. In the above example of a combination ticket, we would mark 1/2, 1/3, 1/4, 1/5, 1/6, 1/7 and 1/9, showing that one combination is being played on each of these groupings.

If $1 was bet per grouping, we would circle a **1-** underneath, just like on the way ticket. Seven combinations by $1 per group, and we have a total bet of $7. This gets marked as 7- in the Mark Price Here area.

Let's show one more example, this time a simpler combination ticket. This time the player circles two groups of five. At $1.00 per game, $3.00 total is bet, $1.00 each on two groups of five, and $1.00 on one grouping of ten.

Combination Ticket

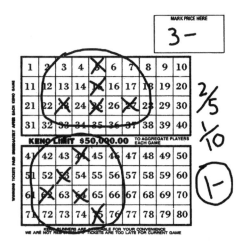

WAY TICKET

The fun of this ticket, unlike split tickets, is that you can have several winners at once on the way ticket, for groups are combined and not separated as on the split. This way you can get your favorite numbers playing in more than one combination.

Way tickets combine at least three groups of equal numbers which can be combined in several ways as straight ticket combinations. The groupings must be equal and the dollar amount bet must be the same for all groups.

For example, three group of five can be chosen. In the first group, the odd numbers 1, 3, 5, 7 and 9 are chosen; in the second group, the even numbers 28, 38, 48, 58 and 68; and in the third group, the doubles 11, 22, 33, 44 and 55.

The way ticket combines these groupings into three groups of ten-spots and this ticket would be bet on as three games. Thus, the odd numbers would combine with the evens for one ten spot, with the doubles for a second, and the even numbers and the doubles would combine for the third group.

In this example, the ticket would have 3/10 marked on the side to show that three groups of 10 are being played.

This is how the ticket would be marked:

Way Ticket

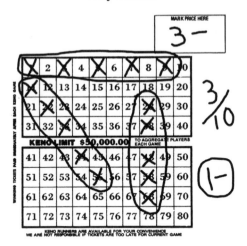

KING TICKETS

Finally, there is the **king ticket** in which one number is circled by itself, called the **king**, and used in combination with other circled groups on the ticket.

For example, along with the "king," a player circles a group of two numbers and three numbers. The game can now be played as a 3-spot (king + 2-spot), 4-spot (king + 3-spot), 5-spot (2-spot + 3-spot) and a 6-spot (king + 2-spot + 3-spot) for a total of 4 ways. If each group cost $1, than this ticket would cost $4 to play.

You can make king tickets complicated by combining the king in all sorts of variations and giving yourself a myriad of possibilities to appease your gods of chance—but in any case, when's the last time you had a chance to play with the king?

King tickets are marked similarly to the way and split tickets, showing the combinations played, the amount bet per grouping and the total bet.

Let's show the above example of a king ticket, using the number 69 as the king.

King Ticket

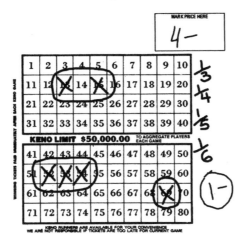

SPECIAL TICKETS

Casinos often promote their keno games in various ways, perhaps through a coupon or special incentive, and in many of these instances they'll present the player with a **special ticket**—a keno ticket that must be played a certain way and that will pay according to a different payoff structure—marked on the special payoff chart you will receive.

These tickets generally offer the player a little better deal than the regular ticket and are an incentive to get him or her to play a game, for generally speaking, it's difficult to play just one game. However, do check the payoff rate to make sure that indeed the payoff is more attractive than the regular card.

When playing a special card, make sure you indicate this on your ticket by marking **"SP"** for special on your original ticket, or otherwise following the instructions on the special ticket sheet.

WINNING STRATEGY

Keno is a game that should not be played seriously for the odds are prohibitively against the player. The house edge is typically well over 20% and can be as high as 35%—daunting odds if one wants to win in the long run.

However, keno can be a fun game—its certainly been fun enough to last 2,000 years—and the attraction of a big payoff for only a small bet keeps many players entranced.

One thing to look out for is that some casinos offer better payoffs on the big win than others so a little shopping might get you closer to a bigger payoff. For example, downtown Las Vegas casinos generally have a better payoff per dollar bet than the strip casinos.

And if you find a casino offering $50,000 on a big win as opposed to $25,000 or whatever for the same number of spots hit, by all means, play for the bigger total.

Keno is a great game to test out your lucky numbers. Picking birth dates, anniversaries, license plate numbers and the like offer a big pool of possibilities to see which ones will really pay off.

Perhaps you like the evens, odds and doubles as used in one of our examples, or a progression using every fourth number, or numbers having either a 3 or a 5 in it.

Do you play the same numbers and combinations every game or switch around when one set fails? And what if the original set then wins, or if you didn't switch and the numbers you would have played won? Oh, the heartaches!

If you know your lucky numbers, you may just give them a whirl and see if you can't walk away with a $50,000 bonanza!

Sports Betting

FIVE KEYS TO SPORTS BETTING

1. There is no such thing as a sure win, no matter who is playing who. You never know. That is why they play the game and hold the event. Bet accordingly.

2. Shop around for the best payouts.

3. Look for events or games where one side is a fan favorite. That may give you a good "wrinkle" to bet on the other side.

4. Educate yourself before you turn your money over to the bookie. It is a lot to work to find the best percentage plays.

5. Don't bet money you cannot afford to lose. Too many people have gotten caught up in sports betting and taken a hard turn down the wrong road.

INTRODUCTION

The urge to gamble on sports is a fervent passion in the United States and fuels a tremendous underground economy that runs into the billions of dollars yearly. Sports games are exciting, and for many people, putting their money where there mouths are makes the games that much more intense.

Football, baseball, basketball and boxing all have their share of aficionados, and in this section we're going to show you just what goes into the making of the sports lines, how to read them, the odds involved, and finally, how to get an edge on these lines so that you can be a winner at sports betting!

THE BETTING LINES

There are two types of lines in sports betting, the money line, which is used in baseball and boxing, and the pointspread, the line used for football and basketball.

The **money line** penalizes bettors wagering on the favorite by making them lay money, that is bet more money than they hope to win back. For example, if a bettor had to lay 6 to 5 odds, it means he would have to lay $6 to win $5.

Underdog bettors, on the other side of that coin, would receive back more than they bet as compensation for betting on the "dog." If the odds on a contest are listed as 8 to 5, a $5 bet on the dog would pay back $8 if the bet is won.

The **pointspread** tries to equalize betting money by awarding the underdog extra points and creating what is called a **spread**.

Thus, if the bookie creates a spread of 7 points in a football game and you bet the underdog, you can win the wager even if your team doesn't win the game. Either a loss by less than 7 points or an outright victory affords the underdog bettor a winning wager. An underdog defeat by more than 7 points loses the wager.

If you bet the favorite in this example, your team must win by more than seven points for the bet to be won. A three point victory by the favorite is all well and good for the team itself. A win after all, is a win. But not for those who bet the favorite. The favorite did not cover the seven point spread, and therefore, all bets on the favorite are lost.

If the favorite wins by exactly seven points, the bet is a **push**, a tie, and both favorite and underdog bettors receive their wagers back.

Thus, you see that the concept of winning at football and basketball betting, sports where the pointspread line is used, is based on winning against the spread and not necessarily on the raw outcome itself.

HOW THE LINE IS MADE

The main purpose of the betting line is to divide public opinion in such a way that money gets bet equally on both sides of an event. As such, the important consideration in setting a line is figuring how the public will perceive an upcoming contest.

This is a very important concept to understand. The bookmaker, whether run legally or illegally, is a business that makes its money by handling bets and taking a commission on the money wagered. Bookmakers really don't care which contestant wins a match—they only care that money is bet equally on both sides so that they can collect their **vigorish** or **vig**, the bookmakers built-in commission, no matter which side wins.

Thus, the betting line represents how fans perceive the game and how they will bet—not the actual match-up of the teams.

For example, a number of years back, the aging Ali, in another of his comeback tries and clearly over the hill, faced his former sparring partner, Larry Holmes who at 30 years old, was fighting in his prime. This match, clear to many prizefight experts, was really no contest. The betting public on the other hand, were still enamored with the mystique of the once great Ali, and this had driven the odds down to 8/5 in favor of Holmes.

If the betting line was made on the basis of Ali's real chances of winning, Ali would have been fighting as an overwhelming underdog, and most of the money would have come in on Holmes.

This would have created a situation called being **sided**—when most of the money gets bet on one side of a gambling proposition and comparatively little on the other.

Being sided is a tremendous risk for bookmakers for it makes them gamblers and that is not their business. Their business is to collect commissions on gambles other people take. If the bookmakers had not adjusted the line in the Ali-Holmes fight to reflect how the betting public would bet, an Ali win would have taken them to the cleaners.

As businessmen, bookmakers attempt to form a line such that they can collect profits regardless of who wins.

This same principle of the bookmakers trying to divide the betting money holds true in the betting lines for all the sports—football, hockey, basketball, baseball, boxing and other sporting events which attract gamblers.

An astute bettor who realizes this and who follows his sport carefully, can use this information to make money at sports betting.

THE FIRST PRINCIPLE OF BEATING THE BOOKIE

Now that you understand how and why the line is made, we can clearly outline the foremost principles of winning money at sports betting. First of all, we're going to look for games and sporting events where public opinions, for one reason or another, distort the line, and therefore give the sharp and ready bettor an edge in the game.

But having an edge is not enough, the edge must be sufficient enough to overcome the built-in vig that the bookie's have, and we'll discuss each sport in turn to show the exact odds you face with each betting proposition, and how best to overcome those odds.

Sports Betting Comparison Chart

Sport	Type of Line	Payoff	Winning % Needed to Break Even
Baseball	Money Line	Variable	Variable
Basketball	Pointspread	10-11	52.38%
Boxing	Money Line	Variable	Variable
Football	Pointspread	10-11	52.38%

FOOTBALL BETTING

INTRODUCTION

Every year, as constant as the seasons, sports fans gear up for the gala opening of NFL and collegiate football. Even before opening day, football fever spurs the frantic analysis and heated discussions that accompany every season, and helps fuel the mammoth underground economy of football betting. When it's that time of year, football owns the weekends and Monday nights for many Americans, a good portion of who could not conceive of life without this staple of excitement.

Betting is very much a part of football for fans, and the wagers that many bettors make add a lot of spice and enjoyment to the gridiron wars they see waged out on the field.

Let's see just what is involved in making the line, what odds you're up against, and how best to play ball.

THE FOOTBALL LINE

Football betting, whether college or pro, works according to the pointspread. The bookmakers handicap opposing teams so that they can get equal betting action on both teams, and earn their vigorish without risk. As such, football contests have a pointspread, with one team playing the favorite, and the other, the underdog.

Bettors wager according to these lines, giving points when betting favorites, and taking points when betting the underdog.

Here is how a typical line may look.

San Francisco	MIAMI	+3

You may also see that line listed as follows, but either way means the same thing.

San Francisco	–3	MIAMI

The lines, however shown, will always list the favorite first and show the home team in capital letters. In the above example, San Francisco is listed first and is the favorite and Miami, listed in capital letters, is the home team.

The number shown indicates the amount of points that the favorite, listed first, is favored over the underdog, the team listed second. So whether the number shows up as a **+** next to the underdog or a **–** next to the favorite, doesn't make a difference.

In the above examples, we see the San Francisco 49ers listed as three point favorites over the Miami Dolphins.

THE BOOKMAKERS VIGORISH

To bet on NFL or college games you have to lay 11 to 10 on all bets, whether betting the favorite or the underdog. To win $10, you have to give the bookie $11. Thus, for example, if you want to bet $50, you must give the bookie $55.

This difference between the 11 to 10 wager bettors must lay with the bookmaker and the true odds of 10-10, even-money, is the bookie's profit margin, his vig, and what allows him to conduct business.

For example, if you lay $11 to $10 on a game and win the bet, you'll get paid $21 back—the $11 bet, plus the $10 in winnings. If you bet $110, you'll get back $210 from the bookie, your original $110 bet plus $100 in winnings.

Let's see what happens when you win one game and lose one game laying 11 to 10 odds and betting $110 per game.

First Game: Win	+$100
Second Game: Loss	–$110
Net	**– $10**

You have an even win percentage, but yet have lost money. So you see, winning half your games isn't good enough to make money at football betting. If you win only half you're going to be a loser at a rate of $1 for every $22 bet, an edge to the bookmaker of 4.54%.

And this 4.54%, the bookmakers vigorish, or vig, is the figure you must overcome to show a profit on the gridiron.

Let's carry these figures over a 16 game season with a $110 bettor to see how a 50% win rate would work out. Remember, we have to lay 11 to 10 on every game.

8 Wins at $100 per win 8 Losses at $110 per loss	+$800 −$880
Net	**−$80**

Though we won 8 out of 16 games, not too bad in itself, the bookie's vig has eaten away at our stake, and we show a loss of $80!

What winning percentage is needed to overcome the bookie's vig?

52.38%. That's the magic number. As a football bettor, this is the figure that must be foremost in your betting mind. To be a winner, you must win greater than 52.38% of your bets.

LINE CHANGES

As the week progresses, the line might change up or down a little to reflect the bets coming in. For example, if the Giants are playing the Cowboys and are favored by +3 points, and more money is coming in on the Cowboys than the Giants, the bookmaker might move the line to +4, and then again if necessary, maybe +5 to encourage more money to be bet on the Giants.

However, once your bet is made, it is committed to the pointspread at which it was placed, regardless of how the line moves after. If your bet was placed when the line was +3, and the line moves to +5, your bet is committed to the +3.

TEASERS

The **teaser** bet is an inducement for bettors to wager two games or more as a group with the condition that both teams chosen must win. If just one of the teased teams lose, than the whole bet is lost. Also, a tie against the spread on either game loses the teaser as well.

The bookmaker allows 6, 6 1/2 or 7 points, depending upon the wager made, as the tease incentive for the bettor to use any way desired on the match-ups chosen.

On a two team tease, a six point bonus gets an even money bet, instead of the usual 11 to 10 lay. If 6 1/2 points is taken, than the regular 11 to 10 bet is laid, and if a 7 point tease is chosen, than the bettor must lay 6 to 5.

Let's look at a tease with the following two teams:

Chicago Bears	New England Patriots	+6
New York Giants	Green Bay Packers	+3

On a six point tease you may elect to take the underdog Patriots at 6 points more for a +12 spread and the favorite Giants who now have a 3 point spread with the 6 points added.

You could also choose those games the other way around, or play both favorites or both underdogs. Wagering any of these 6 point tease combinations allows your bet to be made at even money instead of the usual 11 to 10.

You could also play the tease taking 6 1/2 points and lay 11 to 10, or take 7 points and lay 6 to 5.

PARLAY BETS

A **parlay** bet is similar to a teaser in that the results of more than one game's results are tied together. With a parlay bet, you must pick a minimum of three teams, and all of these teams must win. A loss or tie in any of the contests spells a loss for the entire bet.

However, unlike a teaser, your teams are not given extra points—they must beat the spread straight out. The payoffs are big and that attracts a lot of bettors, but the odds are so atrocious that you would be better off throwing your money away, for more or less, that is what you'll be doing on a parlay.

A typical parlay card might pay as follows:

Typical Parlay Card

Teams	Payoff	True Odds
Three	$6 for $1	7 to 1 (8 for 1)
Four	$11 for $1	15 to 1 (16 for 1)
Five	$20 for $1	31 to 1 (32 for 1)
Six	$40 for $1	63 to 1 (64 for 1)
Seven	$80 for $1	127 to 1 (128 for 1)
Eight	$150 for $1	255 to 1 (256 for 1)
Nine	$300 for $1	511 to 1 (512 for 1)
Ten	$500 for $1	1023 to 1 (1024 for 1)

You may notice the **"for"** in the Payoff column which is a subtle gambling term telling you that you're getting less. A payoff of $6 for $1 means that you get back $6 total on a won bet, your original $1 plus $5 in winnings as opposed to the word **"to"** as in $6 to $1, meaning you win $6 for every $1 you bet, and will get back a total of $7.

As you can see by the chart, parlays are sucker bets, and we advise you to avoid them, unless you happen to be the one booking other people's parlays, in which case, you'll be making lots.

THE OVER & UNDER

There are also over and under bets in football, where you bet that the two teams combined will score more than a prescribed amount of points set by the bookmaker, **over**, or you can bet that they will score less, or **under**. The over and under betting works just like that of the pointspread betting in football. You still have to lay 11 to 10 on all your bets and will need a 52.38% winning percentage to beat the bookie.

TOUTS

One must be careful with the tout services for generally speaking, they're scam operations. These businesses are often started by gamblers who went belly-up with their own money and are now passing their worthy experience onto others at just $50 a pop or more.

You might see an advertisement, "65% win against the spread" for example or "3 out of our 4 best bets won last week," or any of a myriad of other enticing numbers. The problem is that these figures represent only a small slice of the truth. How about the week before or last year, facts which conveniently go unmentioned.

It's easy to describe a slice of the truth and make it sound appealing, which is what most of these services do. Let's say I run a two man race and my opponent beats me out at the finish line. Well, I comment, "I finished second, right behind the winner while my opponent finished next to last." Little does the listener know that only two people ran in the race.

In any case, be careful with tout services. I recommend instead, putting your money into learning more about winning and into your bets.

BASEBALL

THE BASEBALL LINE

Betting on major league baseball is done according to the money line. In baseball, whenever you bet the favorite, you must **lay odds**, bet more that the amount you hope to win, while when you bet the underdog, or dog, you will win more than you bet.

Let's see how a game may be listed and show how the money line will work.

YANKEES	Tigers	6 1/2	7 1/2

The favorite, in this example the Yankees, is listed first, and is capitalized because it is the home team.

The line in baseball is listed to reflect all payments to $5.00. The first number, 6 1/2 represents the amount a Detroit bettor, the underdog, will win for every $5.00 bet. Thus, on a won bet, the Tigers bettor will receive back $11.50—the original $5.00 wager plus $6.50 in winnings.

The second number, 7 1/2, is the amount of money a Yankee fan must lay to win $5.00. A Yankee win will return to New York bettors $12.50—the original $7.50 wager plus $5.00 in winnings for every $7.50 wagered.

This style of listing can be confusing, however, we'll show you an easy way to remember what number goes with what team and just what the line means to you as a bettor.

The favorite, which is always listed first, belongs to the larger number—what the bettor must lay to win $5.00, while the underdog, listed second, belongs to the lower number—what the bettor will win with a $5.00 bet.

Just word-associate—favorite, larger number; underdog, smaller number. And remember, all bets are to $5.00.

You might also see that same line on the Yankee-Tiger game expressed as follows:

YANKEES	-1.30	Tigers	+1.50

It is the same exact line, just written differently to reflect bets based on $1.00 as opposed to $5.00 above. Casinos will usually list the line this way.

If you bet on the Yankees, you need to lay $1.30 to win $1.00, and on the Tigers, a $1.00 bet will win $1.50. Multiply these numbers by $5.00 and you have the same numbers as the 6 1/2 and 7 1/2 figures discussed above.

This line is called a **20¢ line** for the 20¢ difference between the underdog and favorite's bet when worked out to the dollar and it represents the bookie's take on each set of bets. This 20¢ line is the standard baseball betting line, the one most bettors will face when betting on the "bigs."

The following chart shows the bookie's edge on the various lines.

20¢ or 1 Point Line

Quote	True Odds	Bookmaker's Underdog	% Edge Favorite
11-10	1-1	4.55	4.55
5-6	11-10	4.76	3.97
5 1/2-6 1/2	6-5	4.55	3.50
6-7	13-10	4.35	3.11
6 1/2- 7 1/2	7-5	4.17	2.78
7-8	3-2	4.00	2.50
7 1/2-8 1/2	8-5	3.85	2.26
8-9	17-10	3.70	2.06
8 1/2-9 1/2	9-5	3.57	1.88
9-10	19-10	3.45	1.72
9 1/2-10 1/2	2-1	3.33	1.59
10-11	21-10	3.23	1.47
10 1/2-11 1/2	11-5	3.13	1.36
11-12	23-10	3.03	1.26
11 1/2-12 1/2	12-5	2.94	1.18
12-13	5-2	2.86	1.10
12 1/2-13 1/2	13-5	2.78	1.03

Quote – The line quoted by the bookmaker.
True Odds – The actual odds between the quoted numbers for favorite and underdog which would give the bookie no edge at all.
Bookmaker's % Edge: Underdog – The bookie's edge on under-dog bets at the line quoted.
Bookmaker's % Edge: Favorite – The bookie's edge on favorite bets at the line quoted.

You'll notice that in all cases the edge is lowest when betting favorites, except in the 11-10 quote where the edge is equivalent for underdog or favorite bettors. This does not necessarily mean that favorites are the best bets. This is the bookie's edge against what he figures the true odds to be. That doesn't translate to a superior wager. We get a different view in this next chart.

The Payoff Chart

The Vegas Line	Take Odds	Profit to $1.00
+220	11-5	2.20
+200	2-1	2.00
+180	9-5	1.80
+170	8 1/2-5	1.70
+160	8-5	1.60
+150	7 1/2-5	1.50
+140	7-5	1.40
+130	6 1/2-5	1.30
+120	6-5	1.20
+110	5 1/2-5	1.10
Even	1-1	1.00
−110	5-5 1/2	.91
−120	5-6	.83
−130	5-6 1/2	.77
−140	5-7	.71
−150	5-7 1/2	.67
−160	5-8	.62
−170	5-8 1/2	.59
−180	5-9	.55
−200	1-2	.50
−220	5-11	.45
−240	5-12	.42
−260	5-13	.38
−280	5-14	.36
−300	1-3	.33

The Vegas Line – The line coming out of Vegas, though it could represent any standard line.

Take Odds – The first column equivalent in a different format.

Profit to $1.00 – The amount a won bet will return for every $1.00 bet.

On **The Payoff Chart**, we see the profit you make every time you wager $1.00 and win your bet. The + numbers on the top half of the first column indicates the payoff amount for underdogs, while the minus numbers below show the payoff on favorites.

Thus, a Vegas line of +220, means that a winning underdog bet of $1.00 pays $2.20 while a Vegas line of -220 indicates the opposite, that a winning $2.20 bet pays $1.00 to a favorite bettor.

Let's go back to our Yankee-Tiger game where the line reads +130 - 150, and see what **The Payoff Chart** shows to us as bettors.

If we bet on the Yano bearing on the Yankees, the favorite, we'd have to lay $1.50 to win $1.00. Looking at the column "Profit to $1.00", we see that we'd win only 67¢ for every dollar bet.

If instead, we bet on the Tigers, the dog, we'd get $1.30 for every dollar bet, for a net profit of $1.30.

Betting on the favorite, and laying $1.50 forces you to win 60% of the time just to break even. There's a big penalty betting favorites, and at a certain point, the winning percentage needed to show a profit on big favorites becomes too high to realistically show a profit.

The next table is very important for it shows the break even point for all bets in which odds are being laid as a favorite bettor or taken on the underdog side.

Break-Even Point Against the Line

The Line	Underdog % Needed To Win	The Line	Favorite % Needed To Win
110 Pick	52.4	110 Pick	52.4
Even	50.0	−120	54.6
+110	47.6	−130	56.5
+120	45.5	−140	58.5
+130	43.5	−150	60.2
+140	41.7	−160	61.7
+150	40.0	−170	62.9
+160	38.5	−180	64.5
+170	37.0	−200	66.7
+180	35.7	−220	69.0
+200	33.3	−240	70.4
+220	31.3	−260	72.5
+240	29.4	−280	73.5

You can see that the bigger the favorite, the greater and more intimidating a win percentage will be needed just to break even. Let's say that a series of 100 bets is made laying –1.50/1 on the favorite at $7.50 a crack, and 60 of these wagers are won.

Here's how it would look.

60 wins x $5.00 = +$300
40 losses x $7.50 = –$300
Break-Even

There's no gain and no loss. The bets have broken even exactly. To win 60% of the time is a gargantuan effort. If you could sustain that winning percentage in football betting you'd be virtually minting your own money. But against very big favorites as in the above example, you don't even make a penny!

For a big-league team to win 60% of its games in a 162 game schedule, they must win 97 games! That's usually enough to take a division title. Anything less than a 60% win ratio while laying -1.50/1 will show losses in your wagers.

The question is, how many teams that you bet on will be good enough to do that for you? And that's the real problem betting big favorites in baseball.

So you see, that even though the bookie's edge is lower when you bet on favorites, your chances of winning are not necessarily less, for you have to score a big percentage of wins just to cover the odds you lay.

Let's now look at an example where you're pursuing an even bigger favorite, at -1.70/1. As you can see on our chart, you now need to win at a 63% clip just to break even. If you win 58% of the time, it's not good enough at a -1.70/1 line, for you'll be a loser.

Let's see how this looks. Laying -1.70 equates to 81/2-5 or in dollars, betting $8.50 to win $5.00.

58 Wins x $5.00 = +$290
42 Losses x $8.50 = –$357
Overall –$67

That's a rough loss to take, especially when you've scored 58%, a pretty good win rate.

Let's now look at the previous betting situation from the other side of the coin. We'll assume a 100 $5.00 bets are made on the underdog half of the +1.30/–1.50 (6 1/2 – 7 1/2) odds. 44 of those bets win and 56 lose.

Here's how it looks:

44 wins x $6.50 = +$286
56 losses x $5.00 = –$280
Net Win +$6

Obviously, it's a whole different smoke betting on underdogs. Even with a terrible losing percentage, a profit was shown betting the underdog position at +1.30.

But then again, don't be running out to the bookie's with your hands stuffed with betting money—it's not so easy. Big underdogs are big underdogs for a reason. Favorites can be good bets just as underdogs can be good bets as well. Each situation must be looked at separately and judged on its own merits.

BETTING STRATEGIES

We feel that you should avoid betting favorites calling for a line of -150 or more. A winning percentage of 58%, which would show you good profits in football or basketball, and get your baseball team pretty close to a pennant, would leave you in the hole betting against a +150 line.

On the other hand, you may find some good spots betting as the underdog part of a 1.50/1.00 line, for, as the chart shows, you need only a 40% win rate to break even.

However, you must pick your games carefully, for when a team is listed as a big underdog, there's a reason. For example, a pitcher like Randy Johnson of the Seattle Mariners who was virtually unbeatable when he was on his game, in fact going more than 20 straight decisions without a loss, may be a matchup you wouldn't want to bet against.

What we've shown you are the cold hard numbers you face in baseball betting. Now use your baseball knowledge and handicapping skills combined with prudent money management to come out of the season as a winner at baseball betting!

BASKETBALL

Betting on the hoops is done according to a point line. If you bet on the favorite, you need to give points, and if you take the underdog, you receive them. As in football, which also works according to a pointspread, you really don't care if the team you're betting on wins or loses, only that it covers the spread.

For example, if the Los Angeles Lakers are favored by 5 points over the Boston Celtics, the Lakers must win by 6 points to cover the spread. Even if Los Angeles wins the game by 3 points, it is still a loss for Laker bettors—the team has not covered the spread.

On the other hand, Celtics bettors can lose the game by 4 points and still win the bet, for the line has given them 5 points.

If the Los Angeles Lakers win the contest by exactly five points, then the game is a push, and nobody wins or loses the bet. The bookmaker will return underdog and favorite wagers without any loss at all. No commission is made on tie bets.

Following is an example of a basketball line:

KNICKS	Bulls	+3

As in football and baseball, the favorite is listed first and the underdog second, while the home team is listed in capital letters. The points listed show how many points the underdog, Chicago in this example, is being given.

Thus, we see the Knicks, listed first, are the favorites by 3 points, and that they're playing in New York since their heading is capitalized. Or if you want to look at it the other way, Chicago is a three point underdog and is playing an away game.

THE BETTING ODDS

As in football, you have to lay 11-10 on all bets, regardless of whether you're betting the favorite or underdog. The bookie's profit comes from the difference between the 11 and the 10, which works out to a vig of 4.54%.

As a bettor trying to beat the odds, the break-even point against the bookmakers vig is 52.38% no matter who is bet on, favorite or underdog. Anything less than the 52.38%, you're in the red, anything better, you'll have profits to show.

Basketball can also be bet as an over/under bet. The bookmaker sets a number and bettors can wager whether the total points in the game will exceed the listed number or go below. The final winner is unimportant in this type of bet—it's only the total point count that matters.

Thus, if the Chicago-New York game has an over/under number of 195, and the final score is 95 to 93, bettors wagering under will win, for the total points equal only 188. Should the score be 100-95 for a total of 195 points, than the bet is a push, nobody wins.

Over/under bets are also laid at 11-10 and the break-even point for bettors, as in the regular bets against the spread, is 52.38%.

TEASER BETS

The bookmakers offer teaser bets in basketball, where two or more team are chosen and both must win for the wager to pay off. Bettors are usually given 4 points extra per game as an inducement to bet the teaser, however all games wagered in the tease must be won. If just one game is lost or tied, the wager is lost.

The extra points can be used to bet on the favorite or underdog and are added to the current pointspread at the time of the wager. Thus, if the Knicks are 5 point favorites at home against the Bulls, you can take the 4 point tease to bet the Knicks as 9 point favorites. Or maybe you feel that the Bulls with those extra points are a great bet against the Knicks and will take them as a 1 point underdog using the teaser points against the spread.

The teaser bet is laid at 11 to 10 odds like the regular wagers. The main problem with teasers is that it's tough enough to win one game at a time against the spread without having two games tied together where both contests are must wins. One win and one loss won't do here—that's a loser on the tease. Both bets must be won.

If you're a pretty tight handicapper, those extra points may make the difference and turn good bets into very good bets.

Certainly though, stay away from teasers involving more than two games. It's just too difficult to call three wins. Keep your chances of winning within the stadium.

RECORDKEEPING

The most important part of winning at basketball betting as in the other forms of sports betting, is to keep good records. All handicappers stress this point, and with good reason. To know what is going on, you need the facts at hand and also, if you're a serious bettor, there is no better way to actually see, black and white, just what is happening with the calls you are making.

BOXING

The big marquee fights create tremendous excitement and betting not only in the United States, but worldwide as well. Great bouts such as Ali-Frazier, Leonard-Duran, and Hagler-Hearns, were anticipated by millions of people, many of whom were ready to splash down some major cash if the odds were right. Fights such as Tyson-Holyfield, or ones involving some of the many recent retreads fighting in the 90's would occasionally generate some excitement. And of course, new stars are always emerging and drawing interest among the betting public.

Prize fight betting is based on the money line, as in baseball, but at a greater disadvantage to the bettor. While baseball bettors wager against a 20¢ line, in boxing, the betting fan is generally up against a **40¢ line**, a bigger hurdle to overcome.

As in baseball, the boxing quotes are based on a $5 bet. The bigger number is the amount you must wager to win $5 while the lesser number is the amount you will win if $5 is wagered.

A fight listed at 6-8 means that you must lay $8 to win $5 if you bet the favorite, odds of 8-5, and that you will win $6 on a $5 bet if you take the underdog. The $2 difference between the $6 and $8, when taken to the dollar—we divide by 5 since the above line is based on $5.00 - $2.00 divided by 5, gives us 40¢ and hence, the term "40¢ line."

Of course, you can bet any amount permitted by the bookmaker. Thus, a $100 bet on the underdog wins $120 if the underdog comes through, while the favorite bettor must lay $160 to win $100.

The money line in boxing can vary, depending upon where you place your wager and sometimes, the size of that wager as well. The following chart shows the 40¢ line.

40¢ or 2 Point Line

Quote	True Odds	Bookmaker's Underdog	Edge Favorite
"6-5 Pick"	1-1	8.33	8.33
5-7	6-5	9.09	6.49
6-8	7-5	8.33	5.21
7-9	8-5	7.69	4.27
8-10	9-5	7.14	3.57
9-11	2-1	6.67	3.03
10-12	11-5	6.25	2.60
11-13	12-5	5.88	2.26
12-14	13-5	5.56	1.98
13-15	14-5	5.26	1.75
14-18	16-5	9.52	2.65
15-20	7-2	11.11	2.78

As the chart clearly indicates, underdog betting gives better odds against the bookie and if one was to think of prizefight betting on a long term basis, betting on the dog would seem to be a superior way of wagering looking at that factor alone.

However, boxing matches should be viewed on a fight by fight basis, as each match presents an interesting call and must be judged on its own merits. Over the years, betting on prizefights has lost some of its luster as a wary public tires of the unpredictable and questionable quality of the scoring and of the ever-present undertones of tainted fights.

Too many times, a boxer has been robbed of a clear victory in the ring by judges working on questionable motives who seemed to watch a different fight than what fans saw in the ring.

And fights such as the Buster Douglas-Evander Holyfield match of 1990 that virtually saw Douglass lay down and close his eyes, don't help the picture any as well.

With all these problems, boxing is fairly tough to pick, but now and again some real doozies come along and allow the astute bettor to pick up some good action.

I would look for fights where an aging but popular champion who should by all rights be retired, is coming back for a last hurrah against a young, proven star. By popularity alone, the old champion gets a lot of money bet in his corner, but really has little chance anymore—as in the Ali-Holmes example earlier.

One may often find profitable spots near fight time when a contender shows himself to be clearly without motivation. For example, sharp bettors made some money betting against Douglass in the Holyfield fight when the one-fight champion showed up for the weigh-in looking like a beached whale and clearly out of shape.

These type of fights won't come often, but when they do, they're good opportunities to pick up a little in winnings. But remember, don't bet the ship—its poor money management to put all your eggs in one basket, and you never know what might happen.

PRINCIPLES OF WINNING AT SPORTS BETTING

1. **Find situations where emotions run high for a particular contest and drive up (or down) the odds beyond what the real odds should be.**

   Generally speaking, home town fans bet with their heart and will willingly bet against lopsided odds to support their team. Excellent bets can be found here for fans tend to ignore realities and bet blind. A good example was the Ali-Holmes matchup discussed earlier. Ali was every bit as much the people's champion as he billed himself and his fans supported him right to the end. Fine as a fan, foolish as a bettor. Smart bettors made lots of money on that fight. Look for those situations.

This lead us to the second principle.

2. Don't bet on games you're emotionally involved with.

If your game plan is to win money, and it better be if you're reading this section and betting money, than you can't be wagering as a fan. Betting emotionally clouds your judgment and allows one to make stupid and costly mistakes.

If you're a diehard fan, you could probably watch your team lose six out of seven and feel that the eighth game shows promise for the team knowing full well that your team this year just doesn't have what it takes. Lay off those games—find other ones where you can see the game for what it is.

3. Always bet within your limits.

Remember, no game or situation in life is a lock. You never know what can happen no matter what the situation appears to be. Of course, if you feel strongly about a bet, by all means, make that bet. However, and we go over this in our money management chapter, never bet above your means or way out of line from your normal betting.

It would be quite silly, to use kind language, to have one bad loss destroy a whole season of steady wins. Many foolish and greedy gamblers know that story. If greed takes over, then you're ripe as a sucker or a fool. It's a fact of life.

For those of you who believe in locks, the game that can't miss, think of the Oakland A's - Los Angeles Dodger world series of baseball in 1988 where nobody gave the Dodgers a chance and they rolled over the big, bad A's. There are many examples in baseball, basketball, football, hockey, boxing, and in fact any sport where competitors line up against one another to compete.

Or even more illustrative, in boxing, the Buster Douglas - Mike Tyson upset fight of 1990. That was a "lock" if ever there was a sports lock. Basically, you had to be crazy to bet against Tyson, who until then, was seemingly invincible. Nobody gave Douglass a chance and yet he pummeled Tyson all over the ring. Perhaps a few insiders knew something, perhaps not, but in any case, the public viewed this bout as a non-event, another walk for Tyson.

If you find betting situations you really like, by all means take advantage of them and make a bet. But always keep money management principles foremost in mind whenever money is at stake.

4. Bet only on games you think you have the edge.
Stay away from marginal games which don't fit your winning formula. Many good handicappers get brought down by making bets on teams they don't feel strongly about. Cut out the bad bets, ones you know you shouldn't make, and your good bets may keep you a winner.

5. Make your own rating system of teams.
Most professional handicappers advise you to really study your game and keep your own personal rating system of teams comparative strengths. When there's a significant difference between a way you would handicap a game and the bookie's line, then you may have a good bet.

6. Bet on consistency.
Don't let one bad week in a teams performance or one excellent week cloud a teams true ability. Every team has good and bad days just as individuals do, but one day doesn't make a team or a player.

If a proven consistent winner looks bad in one game, you may find a great betting opportunity the following week as public perception sours on that teams capabilities. Visa-versa with bad teams having good days.

7. Be flexible in your winning approach.
There is no one tried and true way of beating the bookie, and don't be conned into thinking there is one. There are many angles which can give you an edge. Look at them all before making the proper decision.

The Wheel of Fortune

FIVE KEYS TO WHEEL OF FORTUNE

1 This carnival-inspired game has poor odds, no skill, and not much else to inspire other than a quick, usually losing thrill. So don't lose too much time or money at this game.

2 Given that the odds start at a "low" 11.11% against, I would recommend the fun level be kept to minimum type bets.

3 The $5 wager is your best bet on a typical wheel.

4 The $1 wager is your second best bet on a typical wheel.

5 If you somehow manage to get ahead in this game, get out a winner and move on to something with better odds.

INTRODUCTION

The big spinning wheel, also called the **"Big Six"** or sometimes the **"Money Wheel,"** is only infrequently found in casinos outside the United States, and even within the U.S., the wheel barely gets much play. But apparently it gets some action, for the Big Six is still operating in numerous casinos.

The Money Wheel though, is fairly popular at county fairs, "Las Vegas Nights," carnivals and other such events, and generally, due to a lack of competition from other gambling games and a beer drinking and festive crowd, they get pretty good play—and I might add, very few winners.

The wheels vary in the amount of slots that could be landed upon, generally around 54. They're filled with $1, $2, $5, $10, $20 and sometimes other denominations that could be won. Some wheels might even put prizes in the slots.

Almost without exception, this quick and I think, boring game, has poor odds, and very little to cheer about. In Nevada casinos, the odds range from 11% against the player on the $5 bet to as high as 24% on others. Very steep.

PAYOFFS AND ODDS

Following are the typical odds of a Nevada-type 54 slot wheel on a $1 bet.

Wheel of Fortune • Payoffs and Odds

Wager	# of Winning Spins	# of Losing Spins	Payoff	Casino's Advantage
$1	23	31	$1	14.81%
$2	15	39	$2	16.67%
$5	8	46	$5	11.11%
$10	4	50	$10	18.52%
$20	2	52	$20	22.22%
$40*	1	53	$40	24.07%

*The $40 bet is usually indicated by a joker or "flag". In Atlantic City, the payoff on this bet is generally 45 to 1, which drops the odds on the wager to 14.81%

The overall average of all the bets combined comes out to just under 20%, not the most enticing figure for the discriminating bettor. The odds can be even worse in carnivals and fairs, depending on how the payoffs are set.

In any case, don't lose any sleep if the "Wheel of Fortune" isn't offered next time you're in a gambling situation, unless of course, Vanna White is the one operating it!

Caribbean Stud Poker

INTRODUCTION

As its name suggests, Caribbean stud poker first caught on and became popular in Caribbean casinos, but it has since spread and now can regularly be found in Las Vegas casinos and other casinos around the world. The tables, in shape and size, resemble those found in the blackjack pit and the game features a dealer and cards as well. In fact the only way to tell that this is not a blackjack game from a little distance away is the sign posted above the table that reads, "Caribbean stud poker." When you sit down, however, you see that there is a different game being played.

While Caribbean stud poker shares the same hand rankings as standard poker games—which makes it even easier for players familiar with poker to learn the game— the similarity ends there. For one, the game is played against the casino, not against other players, which is a huge difference. Also, there is no bluffing, and payoffs come as a result of having achieved a predetermined poker hand, not having outmaneuvered or outlasted other players.

Caribbean stud poker is simple to play. Five cards are dealt to each participating player and there are no draws. Your only playing decision in this game is whether to make an additional bet after you have seen your cards or to fold your hand and forfeit the original wager. Caribbean stud poker also features an additional $1 bet that is tied in to a progressive jackpot that awards bonus payouts for winning hands—even as much as hundreds of thousands of dollars if a royal flush is hit.

There is strategy involved in order to shave the house edge down to the smallest possible percentage, thus giving you the best chances to beat the casino. We'll talk about all this in this section.

Let's move on now and see what the game is all about.

THE BASICS

THE SETTING

Caribbean stud poker can be played with just one player against the dealer or with a full complement of seven players. In either case, the strategy and play of the game is the same, since you play against the house, not against fellow players. The game is played on a table that closely resembles a blackjack table, with the players seated around the curved side of the table, and the dealer standing along the flat side facing the players. In front of the dealer is a chip rack that holds the table's bankroll. From this stash of chips, the dealer will pay off winning hands, or deposit losing bets that he has collected back into it.

The minimum and maximum bets allowable are usually posted on a small placard on the corner of the table. In most casinos, $5 is the minimum bet and ante allowed. You may also choose to make the **progressive bet** by putting $1 into the drop slot.

Caribbean stud poker uses one standard 52-card pack with 13 cards of each rank, ace to king, and four suits: spades, diamonds, clubs, and hearts.

THE OBJECT OF THE GAME

Your goal in Caribbean stud poker is to draw a five card poker hand that is not only stronger than the dealer's, but which is of a high enough ranking to qualify for a bonus payout. The higher the rank of your hand, as long as your hand is stronger than the dealer's, the greater the bonus you will win according to a preset payoff schedule. However, there is one caveat: The dealer must hold a hand containing an ace and a king, or at least a pair or higher—that is, a qualifying hand—for the bonus to count.

When placing the $1 optional progressive wager in Caribbean stud poker, your goal is to draw a flush or better to receive additional bonus payouts. In particular, you would like to get a royal flush, a hand that can win hundreds of thousands of dollars.

Before we look at qualifying hands and how they affect the game, let's review the poker hands that are used to determine the payoffs in this game.

HAND RANKS

If you're a poker player, you'll notice that the hand rankings are exactly the same ones used in standard high poker games, except for the A-K hand, which is given value in Caribbean stud poker. The hands below are listed in descending order of strength, from the most powerful, the royal flush, to the least powerful hand that still pays out money to players, the A-K high.

Royal Flush

An A-K-Q-J-10, all of the same suit, is called a royal flush. It is a rare sight, one that you may never see in a lifetime of play.

Straight Flush

Five cards of the same suit in numerical sequence, such as the J-10-9-8-7 of clubs, is called a straight flush. This particular example is called a jack-high straight flush since the jack is the highest-ranking card. In a straight flush, an ace can be used as either the highest card—forming an ace-high straight flush, which is actually a royal flush—or the lowest card, as in the A-2-3-4-5 of diamonds. The Q-K-A-2-3 of clubs is not a straight flush, just an ace-high flush.

Four of a Kind

Four cards of identical rank, such as the 6-6-6-6-3, are called four of a kind. The unmatched card in the below example, the 3, is irrelevant and has no bearing on the rank of the hand.

Full House

A full house consists of three cards of identical rank and two other cards of identical rank, but different from the rank of the first three cards. Two examples of full houses are 8-8-8-J-J and K-K-K-7-7.

Flush

Any five cards of the same suit constitute a flush. The A-K-7-3-2 of spades is an ace-high flush, and the Q-10-7-5-3 of hearts is a queen-high flush.

Straight

A straight consists of five non-suited cards in sequential order, such as 10-9-8-7-6. In a straight, an ace can be used as either the highest card in the run, such as the ace-high straight A-K-Q-J-10, or the lowest card, as in the 5-high straight 5-4-3-2-A. The hand made up of the Q-K-A-2-3 is not a straight. It is merely an ace-high hand and will be beaten by any pair.

Three of a Kind

Three cards of identical value along with two unmatched cards are called a three of a kind. An example of three of a kind is 7-7-7-Q-2.

Two Pair

Two sets of equivalently valued or "paired" cards, along with an unmatched card is a two pair hand. Examples of two pair hands include 4-4-3-3-A and K-K-3-3-J.

One Pair

One set of identically valued cards along with three unmatched cards is called a pair. The hand 2-2-8-4-A is referred to as "a pair of twos." Pairs are ranked in order of value from the highest—aces—down to the lowest—deuces. Thus, a pair of aces beats out a pair of kings, and a pair of nines wins over a pair of sixes.

Ace-King

In Caribbean stud poker, a hand lacking all above combinations but led by an ace and a king, such as A-K-J-5-3, ranks below a one pair hand,. This is the weakest hand that would qualify as a dealer hand. If both the dealer and the player hold this hand, then the highest-ranked of the remaining cards decides the winner.

All Other Hands

Any hand not including any of the above combinations is a non-qualifying hand and has no value in Caribbean stud poker.

ODDS OF DRAWING HANDS

The following table shows the odds of being dealt the above hands in Caribbean stud poker. These are the same odds as in regular draw poker for the first five cards dealt.

Odds of Drawing Qualifying Hands

Royal Flush	649,739 – 1
Straight Flush	72,192 – 1
Four of a Kind	4,165 – 1
Full House	693 – 1
Flush	508 – 1
Straight	254 – 1
Three of a Kind	46 – 1
Two Pair	20 – 1
One Pair	1.37 – 1

RESOLVING TIES

Should both the dealer and player be dealt equivalently ranked hands, then the normal rules of poker rankings are used to determine the winner. This involves using the higher ranked unmatched cards to determine the better hand when there are one pair and two pair hands, or in the case of flushes and straights, using the highest cards leading those hands. Let's take a closer look at these situations.

Three of a Kind and Full House Ties

When two players hold three of a kind or full houses, the hand with the higher ranking three of a kind wins the pot. For example, K-K-K-7-7 is a higher ranking full house than Q-Q-Q-A-A, and 9-9-9-3-4 beats out 8-8-8-Q-5.

Flush Ties

When the dealer and the player both hold flushes, the flush led by the highest card wins. If those cards are tied, the next highest cards are compared, and so on down. In the unlikely event that both flushes contain identically valued cards, then the outcome is a tie or a **push.**

Straight and Straight Flush Ties

The winner of straight and straight flush ties is also determined by the lead card. An ace-high straight beats any other straight, and ties against another ace-high straight. Similarly, a king-high straight is stronger than a queen-high and so forth.

Two Pair Ties

The same holds true for two pair hands. For example, J-J-7-7-K beats out 10-10-9-9-A, and 8-8-4-4-10 loses to 8-8-5-5-9. When both pairs are evenly matched, the higher ranking fifth card, the unmatched card, determines the victor. If all cards are equally ranked, such as 5-5-3-3-2 and 5-5-3-3-2, then the hand is a tie.

One Pair and A-K Ties

If the player and the dealer hold the same pair or A-K led non-pair hand, then the hand with the highest unmatched card would win. Should the highest unmatched card in each hands be of equal rank, then the next highest ranking cards would be compared. If all cards are identical in value, then the hand is a tie. For example, if the dealer has a 9-9-K-J-5 and the player 9-9-K-Q-4, the player wins by virtue of his queen beating the dealer's jack. Similarly, A-K-Q-7-2 beats out A-K-J-10-9.

PLAYING THE GAME

In front of you will be three betting spots, one for each of the three wagers you can make. The bet and the ante wagers are adjacent to one another in a design that looks like a treasure chest. The spot closest to the dealer, and where you will place your initial wager is marked "Ante." It is rectangular in shape. The betting spot just below it, which is closer to you and enclosed in a circle, is marked, "Bet." These are the areas where you will do the majority of your betting.

The final betting area, closest to the dealer, is actually a drop slot, a "hole" in the table where you can make an optional and separate $1 wager on the progressive jackpot.

You begin by placing your bet in the area marked "Ante." You may also choose to make the progressive bet by dropping $1 into the drop slot. For now though, no money can be wagered in the area marked "Bet."

When all players have placed their bets, the dealer's first action will be to push a button that automatically collects the $1 progressive bets that were made. These bets will drop out of sight into the table, and a red light will go on in front of each player who made the bet. The ante bets remain on the table

The dealer is now ready to distribute the cards. Five cards will be dealt face down to each player. The dealer will also deal himself five cards, four face-down and one face-up to be viewed by all players. This exposed card is known as an **upcard**. There will be no further cards drawn by either player or dealer.

If you feel your five card hand can beat the dealer or qualifies for a bonus payout, you can **call**. You do so by placing an additional wager in the box marked "bet" and placing your cards face down on the table. This wager is double the ante bet. Thus, if $5 was bet as an ante, then $10 must be placed in the bet area. Similarly, if $25 was the ante, then $50 is the additional wager placed in the bet area. In the first case, you would have total ante and call bets of $15, and in the second case, adding $25 to $50, $75 would be the total.

If you do not wish to place this additional bet, you **fold** and do so by returning your cards to the dealer. Your ante bet will be forfeited and collected by the house. You will no longer participate in the hand and no additional money is at risk.

Each player in turn must decide whether to play on by placing the additional double bet in the bet box or to fold and forfeit his ante bet. Play proceeds clockwise, beginning with the player at the dealer's left and continuing on to the player positioned at the dealer's immediate right, the position at the table known as **third base**.

Calling or folding is the only playing decision you will make once the cards are dealt. When all players have played their hands, the dealer will turn over his remaining four down cards to reveal his final five card hand. These cards will be compared to your hand to see whether you have won or lost on your bets.

The dealer's first action once his cards are revealed is to determine whether he has a qualifying hand, the minimum hand required by the rules of the game for bonuses and extra payouts to occur for players holding stronger hands.

Let's see what it means to have a *qualifying* hand.

THE QUALIFYING HAND

A dealer's **qualifying hand** contains at least an ace and a king or a higher total such as a pair or better for his five cards. For example, A-K-4-3-2 (ace-king high), 3-3-7-9-Q (pair of threes), and 7-8-9-10-J (straight), are all qualifying dealer hands, while A-Q-3-4-7 is not.

Why is a qualifying hand so important? We'll take a look at that now.

When the Dealer Does Not Have a Qualifying Hand

If the dealer does *not* have a qualifying hand, then all players who have remained in the game automatically win their ante bet, regardless of whether their hand is stronger than the dealer's. For example, if the dealer holds A-J-10-8-2, a non-qualifying hand, and you hold Q-9-8-6-2 or even 7-6-4-3-2, you win. The dealer cannot win if his hand doesn't contain at least a hand of A-K strength nor can any player who has folded—that money is already collected and gone.

That's the good news. The bad news is that if the dealer does not have a qualifying hand, you win *only* the ante bet. The call bets, the ones placed in the bet area, are returned. They are not eligible for bonus payouts or even 1-1 payoffs regardless of the hand drawn.

Thus, if $5 was wagered on the ante and $10 in the bet circle, and you happen to hold three jacks when the dealer holds, for example, 2-3-7-9-K, a non-qualifying hand, then the total win would be only the $5 paid at even money on the ante bet. The non-qualifying dealer hand negates the 3 to 1 bonus that would have been paid for the three of a kind. In the above example, the $10 wager in the bet circle gets returned.

Let's see what happens when the dealer does have a qualifying hand.

When the Dealer Has a Qualifying Hand

When the dealer does have that qualifying hand, that is, at least an A-K or better, then he'll compare his hand to each of the players to see who has the stronger hand.

As opposed to the non-qualifying situation, both the ante bet and the call bet (the wager in the "bet" area) are at stake now. You will either win both bets or lose both, depending upon who has the stronger total. For example, if $5 were bet on the ante and $10 on the call bet, and the dealer held two eights to your two deuces, than you lose both bets since you have the weaker hand.

However, if you have the better hand, then both bets are won instead. Each wager, the ante bet and the call bet is paid differently. Ante bets are paid at even money, 1-1, while call bets are paid according to the bonus schedule shown below. Note that there is no bonus payout given for an A-K hand.

Bonus Payouts on the Call Bet

Royal Flush	100-1
Straight Flush	50-1
Four of a Kind	20-1
Full House	7-1
Flush	5-1
Straight	4-1
Three of a Kind	3-1
Two Pair	2-1
One Pair	1-1

We'll look at an example hand to make the bonus payouts perfectly clear.

Let's say you have a $5 ante bet and a $10 call bet and hold three nines against the dealer's pair of queens. Because the dealer has a qualifying hand, you qualify for the bonus payout on your three of a kind hand. Thus, you'll win even-money on the ante bet, $5, plus 3 to 1 on the call bet, for $30 more. The dealer would push over $50 to you, $35 in winnings plus the original $15 in bets.

In the unlucky event that the dealer doesn't hold a qualifying hand, your three of a kind would go to waste and you would only win the ante bet. You also don't qualify for bonus payouts if your hand is weaker than the dealer's. For example, if he held a pair of jacks and you held tens, your ante and call bets would be outright losers.

Note that the dealer only wins at even money, regardless of the strength of his hand. The most you could lose is what you bet, while the house could lose a lot more, according to the payout schedule.

HELPFUL HINT

To qualify for a bonus payout, three things must occur:
1. The dealer must have a qualifying hand.
2. You must have a better hand than the dealer.
3. You must have at least a one pair hand or better.

THE MAXIMUM BONUS PAYOUT

You must be aware that casinos have a limit on the maximum amount they'll pay in bonus payouts. Some limits may be as low as $5,000, while others may go as high as $50,000 or more. There is no standard so you'll need to check the limit posted on the table.

How does this maximum payout affect you? Well, not in a good way if you have bet more than you can win, because in that case, you will be denied the full amount of the payout on a big hand if your winnings exceed the table limit for bonus payouts.

Here's an example to make this perfectly clear. Let's say you wager $150 on the call bet and draw a straight flush in a casino with a $5,000 maximum limit bonus payout. Normally, you would be entitled to $7,500 —50 to 1 multiplied by the $150 bet. However, since the maximum bonus payout is only $5,000, you would lose out on an extra $2,500! That's a very big hit to take. Your loss would be even greater if that hand had been a royal flush, paying 100-1 on the bonus, meaning you would only get $5,000 of the $15,000 and lose out on the extra $10,000!

So you see, being aware of the maximum bonus payout and adjusting your bets accordingly is a key factor in your strategy considerations for this game. You don't want to get caught in a situation where you have to forego big winnings simply because you weren't properly prepared to bet the correct amount.

To protect against this happening, you must always make sure that the maximum call bet multiplied by 100 does not exceed the bonus payout. I use the number "100" because the largest bonus, on the royal flush, pays at 100 to 1. If 100 times the call bet is greater than the casino's limit, then you would not get the full payout for a royal flush.

To calculate the maximum bet that won't be penalized if a royal flush is drawn, divide the casino's maximum payout by 100. For example, if the maximum payout is $5,000, your maximum call bet should not exceed $50—$5,000 divided by 100. And if the call bet is $50, the ante, which is always half that amount, would be $25.

You can also divide the maximum payout by 200 to reach the maximum ante that will be paid off in full.

THE PROGRESSIVE JACKPOT

The optional wager, the progressive bet, is made by placing $1 in the drop slot, also known as the **progressive slot**, before the cards are dealt. The goal of this bet is to earn additional bonus payouts by drawing a flush or higher ranked hand. While a flush, full house, or other powerful hand would be great, what you ideally would like to hit is a royal flush, a hand that will pay you the full progressive amount.

On or near every Caribbean stud poker table will be a jackpot meter that goes up in value each time $1 is placed into the drop slot at any table linked to that meter. Depending upon the casino, this jackpot can be as little as $5,000 or $10,000, the general starting point after a royal flush is hit, or as high as hundreds of thousands of dollars. And obviously, in the latter case, this is where the possibilities of this wager gets to be a lot more interesting for you.

Before each hand is dealt, the dealer will push a button which causes the dollar bets to drop into the holding area below the table which holds these bets, and at the same time, causing the progressive jackpot to rise. The amount each progressive bet increases the jackpot varies from casino to casino. Some casinos put in only 49¢ of each dollar played, while others, particularly larger, more forward-thinking casinos that understand the ability of larger jackpots to draw players, may put in as much as 75¢ per dollar played to boost the jackpots faster. Obviously, the smaller the amount of money put back into the progressive, the slower the jackpot will grow.

However, the actual percentage of money that gets put back into the jackpot is not really a concern for you unless you plan on camping out and adding to the casino coffers with endless progressive bets to help build the jackpot. What really matters, is who has the highest jackpots. You want to win the thing when its got a lot of money waiting for you. How it got that high is neither here nor there. As that jackpot grows, so should your interest. Just like the lottery, you don't really care about the details of the big prize, you just want to know, "How many millions of dollars can I win if I pick the right numbers?"

What does it take to win the full amount of the progressive? Why, nothing less than the big sandwich with all the dressings—the royal flush. While drawing this hand would certainly be nice, don't hold your breath. It's a long shot—1 in 649,739, to be exact. But playing long shots is what much of gambling is about anyway. And meanwhile, you have other big hands that will give you payouts while you dream about that big salami being delivered into your hands.

The following charts contain payout schedules for progressive jackpots. The first schedule, which would more likely be found at a larger casino aggressively targeting Caribbean stud poker players, is liberal in its payout structure, and that obviously benefits you if this good pay table can be found. The second schedule is more common and pays much less on the four of a kind, full house, and flush hands. However, you'll note that in all cases, the royal flush pays the full 100% shown on the progressive meter and the straight flush, 10% of the meter.

Note that the three numbers following the name of each schedule show the payoffs given on the four of a kind, full house, and flush hands, respectively.

Payout Schedule A (Liberal)
500/250/100

Royal Flush	100% of the jackpot
Straight Flush	10% of the jackpot
Four of a Kind	$500
Full House	$250
Flush	$100

Payout Schedule B (Common)
100/75/50

Royal Flush	100% of the jackpot
Straight Flush	10% of the jackpot
Four of a Kind	$100
Full House	$75
Flush	$50

In between the 500/250/100 liberal and 100/75/50 common schedules shown above, you may find 500/150/75, 500/100/75, 500/100/50, 500/75/50, 300/100/50, 250/100/50, and 150/100/50. Charts for these payouts are presented below.

You should keep in mind that the progressive is a separate bet and is not affected by the results of the ante or regular call bet. For example, if you draw a full house and the dealer miraculously—I should say, disastrously—has a four of a kind, you would still win $250 on the $1 progressive bet—assuming Schedule A is in play—even though the call and ante bets are losers.

By the same token, you would get the full bonus payout on the $1 progressive bet even if the dealer doesn't have a qualifying hand. Therefore, when the dealer has a non-qualifying hand, you must be careful to alert the dealers to flushes and better hands before the dealer accidentally removes the cards without checking for progressive winners.

Finally, there is no maximum limit on a progressive payout as there is on the bonus payout. If you hit the royal flush, you'll get paid the full amount of the progressive meter. If that occurs, obviously, you'll be one very happy camper.

THE AGGREGATE PAYOFF ON PROGRESSIVES

On the progressive bet, one other casino rule comes into play. The bonus payout is limited to an aggregate payoff on the straight flush and the royal flush. What this means is that on a straight flush hand, say, a total of 10% will be paid out. Thus, if two players hold a straight flush on the same deal, they would split that 10%, meaning they'd get only 5% each.

For example, if the meter showed $12,000, the total pool of $1,200 for the straight flush would be divided evenly between the two winners at $600 each. This applies only to straight flush and royal flush hands on progressive wagers, not to the bonus payouts on the four of a kind, full house, and flush hands, where each player will receive the full amount listed.

The chances of two players holding a straight or royal flush on the very same hand is so unlikely—quantum degrees more than one hundred million to 1 against (the exact odds depending upon how many other players are at the table)—that this rule shouldn't be of great concern to you.

HOUSE PERCENTAGES

The house advantage in Caribbean stud poker on the regular ante and call bets, if the proper strategy is followed, is 2.56%, which is not too bad compared to other games or bets within games that can be found in the casinos. For example, American-style double zero roulette will have you bucking odds of 5.26%, which is really steep, but not as bad as proposition bets in craps, which are over 11% against you. On the other hand, the good bets in craps have you competing against a house edge of well less than 1% and in blackjack, with proper play, an actual advantage.

So, how you view the house edge in Caribbean stud poker is relative. If you like the game and have a good time playing it, you can feel much better here than at keno tables and at many slot machines, where the house edge is much more significant. When you put the house edge at Caribbean stud poker into perspective with the other games available in a casino, you see that the percentages are not all that bad. You still have to keep in mind that whenever the house has an edge, they have the expectation to win more than they will lose in the long run. In the short run, however, you can get on a roll and take their money.

The house edge on the progressive bet is relative to how much money is in the pool itself, but generally speaking, you're looking at an edge in excess of 25%. The greater the pool, the lower the house edge on the $1 bet, though keep in mind that your chances of being dealt a royal flush don't change whether the jackpot is $10,000 or $100,000. Obviously, you don't get the best odds making the progressive wager, but you do get a big payoff if you hit.

When you play the basic game in Caribbean stud poker, making the call and ante bets, your job is to keep the house edge at the minimum possible because the lower the casino's edge, the better your chances of winning their money. And that's why you always want to play your best game.

A CLOSER LOOK AT THE ODDS

On average, when you utilize proper strategy, you will make a call bet on just over half of your hands—about 52% of the time. In other words, every other hand will involve a call bet, which is double the size of the ante bet. If you think in terms of units, on one hand, you'll have a one unit bet and on the next hand, three units-one unit on the ante and two units on the call. If we simulate a progression, the first hand will be one unit, the second will be three units, the third will be one unit, and the fourth will be three units again. That's an average of two units bet per hand that you will make in Caribbean stud poker. Thus, if your ante bet is $5(one unit), you will average about $10 in bets per hand.

If you never made the call bets, which if course, would be foolish, and only made the ante bet, you would lose at a 5.25% clip, which is very steep. However, when the call bets are averaged in—and they should be—the overall house odds drop to 2.56% of the money wagered if the proper strategies are played.

You will sometimes see the house percentage for the game quoted at that same 5.25% edge, but it is misleading since it only accounts for the ante bet—before you make the advantageous call bet. It would be like quoting the house edge at blackjack without including the doubling and split opportunities, which would again, mislead the player as to the true house edge faced at the game. As stated above, playing the proper strategy on the ante and call bets, the house edge in Caribbean stud poker is 2.56%.

The call bets in Caribbean stud poker are similar to double downs in blackjack or odds bets in craps in this fashion. You only will place these bets when you either have an even game against the house, which will bring down the overall house edge on a bet, or when you actually have an edge. You never want to increase the size of a wager or risk additional money when the odds are against you. That, of course, is not a winning approach. But when the call bets give you a chance to put more money on the table when you have the edge, that's where you reduce the house edge and where you can make more money.

WINNING STRATEGY

INTRODUCTION

In this section, we'll go over the playing and betting strategies that optimize your chances of winning at Caribbean stud poker. We'll discuss the ante, call, and progressive bets, the best way to approach call or fold decisions, and an overall winning approach to putting some green in your pockets.

PLAYING STRATEGY

There is one crucial decision to make in Caribbean stud poker, whether to make the call wager at double the ante size, or to fold and forfeit the ante without risking additional money. In some cases, for example, when you have a strong hand such as three of a kind or two pair, the strategy is fairly obvious: You want the additional money out on the table. On the other hand, when your cards are weak and you don't even have an ace and a king—cards that will at least compete with a qualifying dealer total—the strategy is also clear cut: You want to fold.

The basic strategy outlined below will have you playing at a near optimal level. Playing the absolute perfect optimal strategy will help your chances of winning by only a few hundredths of a percentage point. This gain is so tiny that the extra effort needed to learn a semi-complicated playing strategy is not worth it by any stretch of the imagination. The strategy presented here is all that you need to know to play a near-perfect game with no practical loss of profit.

The correct playing strategy divides hands into two categories: those which are stronger than the dealer's qualifying total of A-K, which you'll generally keep; and hands which are weaker than the minimum A-K, which you'll throw away.

The general strategy in Caribbean stud poker is to minimize losses in bad situations. For example, holding a small pair will show long term losses, but you'll play it because you'll lose less by hoping the dealer is weaker or doesn't qualify. This is better than tossing the pair and automatically losing your ante wager. At the same time, you'll maximize winnings when your cards are strong, for example, when you have a hand of two pair or higher, a situation where you're a big favorite and get a good payout. Very simply, when you have the edge, you want to get more money on the table, and when the house has the edge, you want less money out there.

We'll look at the specific starting hands that should be played till the call bet, beginning with the strongest hands you can hold and working your way down to the weakest hands.

Two Pair, Three and Four of a Kind, Straights, Flushes, Full Houses, Straight and Royal Flushes

Two pair, three and four of a kind, straights, flushes, full houses, and straight and royal flushes are all very strong hands that not only are heavily favored to win, but which qualify for bonus payouts. The strategy for these hands is very clear even to beginning players: Get more money out there—make the call bet!

Pairs

Pairs are dealt 42% of the time in five-card poker, so this is a hand you'll see on a regular basis. The correct strategy when holding a pair—any pair—is to call, regardless of the dealer's upcard. This is a clear gain in all situations.

This doesn't mean you'll win money in the long run playing all pairs, because you won't. Do not confuse "gaining," that is, making more money doing something than not, with "profit," which means you'll expect to win money in the long term in a given situation. Your chances of winning a hand is tied in to the rank of your pairs; essentially, the higher the pair, the more hands you will win in the long run. The stronger pairs—tens, jacks, queens, kings and aces—have a positive expectation of winning against all dealer upcards. You can look at them as an excellent profit center.

However, with the smaller pairs, you may or may not have an edge against the dealer, depending on the upcard he is showing. Overall, when you are dealt twos, threes, fours, fives, sixes and sevens, your long-term expectations are negative; that is, you would expect to show a loss. However—except for the lowest of pairs, twos through fours—if your pair is greater than the dealer's upcard, you will always have a positive winning expectation. For example, let's say you hold a pair of sevens and the dealer shows a 6. You already know that the dealer's 6, if paired and not improved with another 6 or a second pair, is a loser to your sevens, so that's a big edge. You have a long term expectation of winning, not only here, but when the dealer shows any upcards of 2-6 as well in this situation.

Small pairs may be weak, but would be a huge mistake to throw them away. Keeping them is more profitable than discarding them and forfeiting your ante bet without a fight. While the dealer may have a pair 42% of the time, 58% of the time he won't and you'll win that ante bet—but not the call bet, which will be returned to you. You're putting more money out on the table by making the call bet, but of course, the times the dealer does make that bigger pair, you lose the ante bet and the call bet. But overall, it works out to your advantage. Players who throw away small pairs give up anywhere from 5-10% depending upon the pairs discarded and the situation. That's a bad loss to take.

Compare the above hand to a situation where you still hold the sevens, but the dealer holds an 8 (or higher) instead. If he pairs that 8, you're now on the losing end of the pairs. So you see, what the dealer holds as an upcard has a big effect on your winning chances. You should still put more money on the call bet in this situation, because it is still to your advantage, it is just not as much to your advantage as it would be if the dealer had a smaller upcard to your pair.

In summary, play all pairs, even small pairs, and make that call bet. Sometimes you'll have the expectation to win in the long run, sometimes you won't, but in all cases, you will come out ahead by making this play.

A-K

When you hold A-K, you have a borderline hand and your strategy will depend on the other three cards that are held and the dealer's upcard.

When Your Third-Highest Card Is a Jack or Queen, Call the Dealer

For example, the hand A-K-J-9-4 should be played against all dealer upcards including the ace. The thinking here is that if the dealer makes a qualifying hand of A-K-x-x-x (where "x" stands for any card other than those that would give the dealer a pair or another higher hand), the A-K-J or better hand is strong enough to win, thus making the call bet a profitable play.

When Your Third Highest Card Is Less Than a Jack, Call the Dealer Only if His Upcard Matches One of Your Five Cards

Examples: Call with A-K-10-5-2 vs. ace and A-K-10-5-2 vs. 2, but fold A-K-10-5-2 vs. queen and A-K-8-7-6 vs. 5.

The A-K hands are almost 50-50 in terms of long term gain. In order for calling to be the correct play, a little extra edge is needed to push the A-K hand into your favor. In the situation where one of your cards matches the dealer's upcard, the dealer is less likely to have a pair. That's one less card that can help the dealer defeat your hand, and it gives you the extra edge needed to make this a profitable play.

If your A-K hand doesn't have a jack or a queen to back it up and none of your five cards pair up with the dealer's upcard, than the correct play is to fold.

A-Q or Less

Any hand that doesn't have any of the above combinations—that is no A-K-J or better, or A-K-duplicated card—should be folded. Thus, if the best you're looking at is an unpaired hand with no straights or flushes, and an A-Q or less, you have an automatic fold. Examples: Fold A-Q-J-10-9, A-Q-8-7-6, K-Q-J-10-6, and 10-8-4-3-2.

The problem with these hands is that they're worthless. A-Q led hands are no better the jack-high or even 8-high hands. In all cases, if the dealer qualifies, these hands will lose, since by definition, a qualifying dealer hand contains an A-K or better.

The Disadvantage of Playing A-Q or Lesser Hands

There is one constant in Caribbean stud poker that will make playing A-Q or less hands disastrous: The dealer will make a qualifying hand approximately 56% of the time. At first glance, you might think that the loss is $12 for every $100 bet—56 losses less 44 wins.

That's a very convincing argument not to make this play. Giving up 12% is a foolish play. But the loss is actually much worse! When the ante bet is figured in, your disadvantage comes out to more than ten times that, about 125%! Let's take a closer look at the math behind this.

We'll use a $10 ante bet for this example. In 100 hands, the dealer will fail to qualify 44 times, and you'll win a total of only $440. Since the dealer didn't qualify, the $20 call bet is returned and only the ante bet is paid off. That's $10 for each winning hand at 1-1, even money. The other 56 times that the dealer qualifies, you'll not only lose the $10 ante bet, but the $20 call bet as well! That's $1,680 in losses against only $440 in wins for a net loss of $1,240.

Thus, for every $1,000 made in ante bets, you'll lose $1,240. That's a very heavy loss to try and overcome in this game, or for that matter, any game. An approximate 125% house edge is way too much to give up in any betting proposition.

The moral of the story: Don't play A-Q or less, no matter what kind of hunch you have going. You should never, ever think about playing these hands. To be a winner at Caribbean stud poker, you absolutely must avoid any situation that gives the house an exorbitant edge.

PROGRESSIVE BET STRATEGY

Generally speaking, unless the jackpot is in the hundreds of thousands, the progressive $1 wager is a complete sucker bet that gives the house an edge anywhere between 50-75%. Ouch!

Even when the jackpot is say $250,000, you still may be giving the casino an enormous advantage by making this bet. The exact edge the casino enjoys is a function of several factors: the bonuses paid on four of a kind, full houses, and flushes, which as we've seen, vary from casino to casino; the size of the jackpot itself; and equally important, the size of the ante bet.

This last factor, the size of the ante bet, is important because the progressive bet cannot be made as an independent wager. To play Caribbean stud poker, you must place, at a minimum, an ante bet, and only then can you make the progressive bet as well. Since each bet gives the casino roughly a 5.25% edge, the larger the average bet, the higher the jackpot must be to compensate for these wagers. Thus, if $5 were wagered on the ante, a break-even for the progressive would be far lower than if $10 were the average ante bet.

For example, if you're playing in a casino with liberal payouts, say $500 for four of a kind, $250 for a full house, and $100 for a flush, and the average ante bet is $5, then the break-even on a progressive jackpot would be around $200,000. However, if you had less liberal payouts of $100 for four of a kind, $75 for a full house, and $50 for a flush, which are found at many casinos, the break-even progressive jackpot pops up closer to $350,000 on that average $5 bet.

But make that $5 average ante $10 in a game with liberal payouts, and the break-even jackpot jumps almost $100,000 to $300,000. A $1 average ante bet would yield better overall odds on the $1 progressive, but that will rarely be found. Most casinos have a $5 minimum ante bet.

Thus, as we see, these three important factors—average ante size, jackpot size, and bonus payout schedule—influence the house edge you're up against when making a progressive bet in Caribbean stud poker.

In rare cases, you will find a monster payout that has built up, and the progressive bet may actually be advantageous. It's always nice to dream of the big hit, hence the millions and millions of people who play the lottery consistently and the many players who donate the $1 to the progressive pool in Caribbean stud poker. However, my approach to gambling is to stick to the bets that offer me the best chances of winning in the long run. And unless the progressive jackpot is in the hundreds of thousands of dollars, you would be better off avoiding the progressive bet altogether.

If a you feel the pressing need to make that $1 dream bet, you might consider the lottery. Lousy odds, but if you do hit, the payout is not a measly five figures, it's a two year cruise around the world, a dream home, instant retirement, and the most expensive cigars money can buy.

But then again, my advice is always to play rationally. Make the best bets the games can give you, and if you're winning, make sure to walk away with the casino's money in your pocket.

Betting Strategy

If you find a situation where the progressive jackpot gets into the hundreds of thousands of dollars, and you're going to play Caribbean stud poker strictly for the purpose of taking a shot at the jackpot, then you would want to keep the ante bet as small as possible in order to minimize the effect of the house edge on the ante and call bets.

Other than the advice given on the $1 progressive bet above, in Caribbean stud poker, there is no particular betting strategy on the ante and call bets that will give you an advantage as there is in blackjack. Your best betting strategy is to bet intelligently according to your bankroll and your comfort level. We'll discuss more about this later, in money management, but the most important rule of all rules when deciding on bet size and the amount to put at risk is the following: Never risk money that you cannot afford to lose. That is the cardinal guideline for any betting proposition.

OVERALL WINNING STRATEGY

The main thing to keep in mind with most games offered by the casino, including Caribbean stud poker, is that the game is a negative expectation gamble. The casino has an advantage of 2.56% on the call and ante bets when the proper strategy is followed, which is not too bad by casino standards. The progressive $1 wager, on the other hand, can give the casino as much as a 75% edge, which by any standards, is a hard nut to crack.

If you want to get the best odds possible, meaning that you give yourself the best chances of winning money, your first order of business is to avoid the progressive bet. Unless the jackpot is enormous, at least $200,000 or more under normal circumstances, this bet gives too much away to the casino. Avoiding this wager will avoid a constant $1 drain on your bankroll.

Secondly, you must study the playing strategy so that the correct moves are made and the chances of winning are optimized. As we saw earlier, there is a lot of information to remember, but successful players learn the strategies and use them all the time, not just when the mood strikes them. There is no substitute for correct play. Hunches only build the casino's profits and make players poorer. Don't be one of the crowd of losers. Prepare yourself and play a tough game.

Finally, intelligent money management decisions must be employed at the tables. When things are going poorly, which they sometimes do, you must limit your losses. Avoid taking a bad beating in any one session. And when you're on a hot streak, make sure that when the dust settles, you leave a winner.

Caribbean stud poker is like all gambling games; you will have good streaks and bad streaks. With a little luck and smart money management, you can get more from them then they get from you. Just make smart bets and remember to keep your winnings.

Let it Ride

FIVE KEYS TO LET IT RIDE

1 Play only good three card hands – pair of 10s or better, three straight flushes, three flushes with at least two 10s or better or one 10 with a one gap straight, and either a 10, J, Q or J, Q, K.

2 Similarly, do not play low pairs (less than 10s), low straights or flushes and other poor three card hands.

3 Holding four cards, Let it Ride only with 10s or better and four card flushes and open-ended straights.

4 Avoid the $1 bonus bet (lousy odds). Better to play $1 in the lottery.

5 Learn the correct strategies. Don't give the house any extra edge at all.

INTRODUCTION

Let It Ride was first introduced to the Las Vegas casinos in August 1993, and it immediately became a rousing success. The game has continued to grow in popularity and is now a mainstay of action in casinos across the country and around the world.

Let it Ride is a simple game to play. To start, you will make equal-sized bets on the three betting circles in front of your position. So, if you bet, for example, $5 on one circle, you need to bet $5 on the other two circles as well. There is also an optional $1 bonus bet that can be made. After bets have been placed, the dealer will deal three cards to each player. He will then deal two community cards face down into boxes in front of his position. These two community cards will be combined with each player's three cards to form the final five-card hand.

Winning hands are paid out based solely on their strength and the pay table that is posted at the table. You do not compete against fellow players; your only goal is to get a high enough hand to qualify for a payout. For example, you want at least a pair of tens, which pays 1 to 1, while higher ranked hands will pay even more.

The unique twist to Let it Ride, which is a very attractive feature, is that you have the option to remove one of your three bets after you've seen your three card hand. Then the dealer turns over the first of the two down cards in front of him. Now you have the opportunity to remove the second of your three bets, or if the hand is profitable, to let it ride. The third bet, however, cannot be removed. When all players have made their choices, the dealer will turn over the second community card. Your five card hand is now revealed. If you have made a pair of tens or better, you will get paid on the third bet, at the least, plus each of the other bets you let ride. And if your hand does not qualify for payout, you lose only the bets you let ride.

Let's take a closer look to see how the game of Let it Ride works.

THE BASICS

THE SETTING AND LAYOUT

Let it Ride is dealt on a blackjack-style table with a single standard pack of 52 cards. From afar, you wouldn't even know that this wasn't a 21 game unless you glanced up and saw the sign announcing, "Let it Ride."

Once you approach the table, however, you'll see a whole different game being played. On the layout in front of each player are three betting circles. From left to right, they are marked $, 2, and 1, respectively. These are the spots where your basic bets will be placed before each deal. There will be one additional bet spot in front of you, a red button where the $1 bonus bet can be made. The table also features the Shuffle Master, a device which automatically shuffles the cards after each deal.

In front of the dealer will be two card-sized rectangles, where the two community cards will be dealt. There will also be see-through plastic discard rack, where unused cards are placed after all the cards are dealt. On the layout itself, you will see the words, "Shuffle malfunction voids all plays and pays," and "$25,000 aggregate payouts per round," though casinos may choose different amounts to limit their aggregate payout. We'll talk more about this later.

The dealer stands on the flat side of the table with a chip rack in front of his position, while across the layout, along the rounded edge, are as many as seven participating players trying their hand at lady luck.

THE OBJECT OF THE GAME

In Let It Ride, the winning hands are based on standard poker rankings, with your goal being to draw one strong enough to qualify for one of the winners in the payout schedule. These payoffs range from even money on a pair of tens to 1,000 to 1 on a royal flush.

On the $1 optional bonus bet, which is a separate wager, you are also trying to get a hand of at least one pair, which will pay 1 to 1, though you would really like to see a big hand such as a straight flush, or even a royal flush, which will pay substantially more according to pay tables that vary from casino to casino.

You do not compete against other players, as in regular poker, or against the dealer, as in Caribbean stud poker. Though other players may form better hands than you, it is of no relevance to your winning chances; The strengths of other players' hands have no bearing on your chances of getting a payout nor does the strength of your hand help affect their chances either. Thus, you need only be concerned with your own cards. So, even though the game shares the same ranks as regular poker, as you see, Let it Ride is not a poker game nor does it resemble it in any way except for these hand rankings.

In Let It Ride, the goal is solely to qualify for a payout by drawing a strong enough hand. Let's take a look at those hands now.

WINNING HANDS

Following are the hands recognized in Let It Ride, in descending order of strength, from the most powerful, the royal flush, to ones that aren't any good at all, the ones that don't qualify for payouts.

Royal Flush

An A-K-Q-J-10, all of the same suit, is called a royal flush, the most powerful and rarest hand in poker.

Straight Flush

Five cards of the same suit in numerical sequence, such as the J-10-9-8-7 of clubs, is called a straight flush. In a straight flush, an ace must be used as either the highest card—forming an ace-high straight flush, which is actually a royal flush—or the lowest card, as in the A-2-3-4-5 of diamonds. The Q-K-A-2-3 of clubs is not a straight flush, just an ace-high flush.

Four of a Kind

Four cards of identical rank, such as the 6-6-6-6-3, is called a four of a kind. The unmatched card in the above example, the 3, is irrelevant and has no bearing on the rank of the hand.

Full House

A full house consists of three cards of identical rank and two other cards of identical rank, but different from the rank of the first three cards. Two examples of full houses are 8-8-8-J-J and K-K-K-7-7.

Flush

Any five cards of the same suit constitute a flush. The A-K-7-3-2 of spades is an ace-high flush and the Q-10-7-5-3 of hearts is a queen-high flush.

Straight

A straight consists of five non-suited cards in sequential order, such as 10-9-8-7-6. If a straight contains an ace, the ace must serve as either the highest card in the run, such as the ace-high straight A-K-Q-J-10, or the lowest card, as in the 5-high straight 5-4-3-2-A. The hand made up of the Q-K-A-2-3 is not a straight. It is merely an ace-high hand and will be beaten by any pair.

Three of a Kind

Three cards of identical value along with two unmatched cards is called a three of a kind. An example of a three of a kind hand is 7-7-7-Q-2.

Two Pair

Two sets of equivalently valued or "paired" cards along with an unmatched card is a two pair hand. Examples of two pair hands include 4-4-3-3-A and K-K-3-3-J.

One Pair

One set of identically valued cards along with three unmatched cards is called a pair. The hand 2-2-8-4-A is referred to as "a pair of twos." Pairs are ranked in order of value from the highest—aces—down to the lowest—deuces. Thus, a pair of aces beats out a pair of kings, and a pair of nines wins over a pair of sixes.

All Other Hands

Hands with none of the above combinations are losing hands. Since they qualify for no payouts, they have no value in Let It Ride.

ODDS OF DRAWING WINNING HANDS

Below is a table showing the odds of being dealt winning hands in Let It Ride. These are the same odds as those in regular draw poker and Caribbean stud poker for the first five cards dealt.

Odds of Drawing Winning Hands

Royal Flush	649,739 – 1
Straight Flush	72,192 – 1
Four of a Kind	4,165 – 1
Full House	693 – 1
Flush	508 – 1
Straight	254 – 1
Three of a Kind	46 – 1
Two Pair	20 – 1
One Pair	1.37 – 1

PAYOUTS

A pair of tens is the lowest ranked hand that qualifies for a payout. If your hand is smaller, say a pair of nines or threes, or an ace-high hand, then there is no payoff and whatever bets that are still active will be lost. On the other side of the coin, while all pairs of tens or better pay 1 to 1, higher combinations such as two pair and three of a kind pay even more.

The best hand, the royal flush, will pay 1,000 to 1 in most casinos that offer the game. However, you must check each time you play, as pay tables and regulations are subject to flux and can change at any time and may be different from one casino center to another. (Note that gaming commissions in some jurisdictions have mandated that casinos can't pay more than 500-1 for the royal flush, and some casinos have adopted this pay scale on their own.)

Standard Payouts

The following pay table is considered standard and is commonly found in casinos. It features a 1,000 to 1 payoff on a royal flush, higher payouts for big hands, and smaller payouts for full houses and flushes.

Standard Payout Schedule (Table A)

Royal Flush	1,000-1
Straight Flush	200-1
Four of a Kind	50-1
Full House	11-1
Flush	8-1
Straight	5-1
Three of a Kind	3-1
Two Pair	2-1
Pair of Tens or Better	1-1

Alternate Payouts

In this less commonly found pay table, there are smaller payouts on the higher-ranked but less frequent hands—flush, straight flush, royal flush, and four of a kind hands—with larger payouts on the more frequently hit hands, full houses and flushes.

The individual payouts balance each other out in the two pay tables, A and B, giving you equivalent odds overall, no matter which schedule is used.

Alternate Payoff Schedule (Table B)

Royal Flush	500-1
Straight Flush	100-1
Four of a Kind	25-1
Full House	15-1
Flush	10-1
Straight	5-1
Three of a Kind	3-1
Two Pair	2-1
Pair of tens or Better	1-1

PLAYING THE GAME

OVERVIEW

The first order of business, before any cards are dealt, is that all players must get their bets down on the felt. There are three betting circles in front of each player, marked "1," "2," and "$." The amount of the bet on one spot must be the same on all three of them. For example, if $5 were to be bet on the circle marked "1", then $5 must also be bet on the other two circles, the one marked "2" and the one marked "$." And if you choose to bet $25 per spot, then you would have $75 bet in total.

There is an additional wager that can be placed, the $1 bonus bet, which we'll cover in detail later in this chapter.

Normally, $5 is the minimum allowable bet on each circle, although smaller casinos may offer minimums as low as $3. Whatever the minimum limit, it will be clearly posted on the table, along with the maximum limit.

After all bets have been made, the dealer will distribute three downcards to each active player. The Shuffle Master machines automatically spits out three cards at a time. The dealer will gather them up, and push the cards facedown to the first active player to his left. And then he will take the next set of three cards and give it to the next player in order, until all players have received their three-card hand.

He will then take the next three card set, place two of them in the card-shaped rectangular boxes in front of him, and place the extra third card in the discard tray to his left. These two community cards will be used by all players to form their five-card hands. There are two rounds of play in Let it Ride. First you receive your three cards and choose whether to let your bet in the "1" spot ride. The second round is after the dealer has revealed the first community card and you have to decide on the bet in circle 2—keep it, or let it ride.

Beginning with the player on the dealer's left and proceeding in a clockwise direction, each player in turn must make these decisions. When the last player, the one in the third base seat (closest to the dealer's right) has acted, then the round is over and it is time to see who won and who lost.

The dealer will turn over each player's hand in turn, one by one—from the player's perspective, left to right—either collecting lost bets or paying off the winners. Thus, he will start in the third base position, and go around paying off or collecting bets from the first base position. Note that the payoff sequence is exactly opposite the order from which the cards were dealt.

A CLOSER LOOK AT THE TWO ROUNDS OF PLAY

Once your bets have been placed and it is your turn to play, you have a decision to make. Let's take a closer look at the mechanics of keeping or removing your bets.

Decision 1

After looking at your three down cards, you have the option of playing for the bet in circle 1. You must decide whether to let your bet ride or to withdraw that bet from play and return it to your bankroll.

If the decision is to let a bet ride, you place your cards under or in front of the chips in the first circle. The dealer will understand this to mean that you want to keep your bet in play, and he will move on to the next player.

If you are unhappy with the cards you're dealt and wish to remove your bet in circle 1 from play, you do so by scraping the table with the cards. This motion will prompt the dealer to remove your bet from the first circle and return it to you.

You should not physically take back your own bets; you should let the dealer perform that function.

Decision 2

After all players have made their decisions on bet circle 1, the dealer turns over one of the two community cards in front of him. You now know four of the five cards that will be used to form your final hand.

Again, just like in the first round, you must decide whether to let your bet ride or to take it down and put it back into your bankroll. The motions are the same as they are in the first round; the only difference is that now you are deciding about the bet in circle 2. If your decision is to let your bet ride, slide your cards under the bets in the second circle. And if you wish to remove your bet, scrape the table with your cards. Your bet will be removed from circle 2 and returned to you by the dealer.

Your action on circle 1 has absolutely no bearing on your decision on circle 2. The two actions are independent of each other, so don't feel pressured to make a play one way or the other based on what you did on the first round of play. For example, you may remove the bet in circle 1 and let the bet in circle 2 ride; while another player may let it ride in circle 1 but remove it in circle 2; a third may remove a bet in each of the two rounds; and a fourth may let both bets ride. All these combinations are permissible.

When all players have made their decisions on the bets in circle 2, it is time for the showdown.

The Showdown

The dealer now turns over the second and final community card and you can now see the final five card hand by combining these two community cards with your three individual cards.

Unlike the previous two rounds, the bet in the third circle, marked "$," cannot be removed. This bet is for keeps and will now be settled by the dealer along with the other bets that you have in the other betting circles, if any.

Going from his right and proceeding to his left, the dealer will turn over each player's cards and settle the wagers.

SETTLING THE BETS

Players who hold a pair of tens or any higher- ranked poker hand qualify for payouts according to the payout schedule shown earlier.

Winning hands pay out on all spots that still contain bets. For example, let's say you hold a pair of jacks, which pays 1 to 1, and have $5 bet on each of the three spots. You would win a total of $15, $5 for each of the spots. Thus $30 would be returned to you, $15 in winnings plus the original $15 wagered. If only spots 2 and $ contained $5 bets, then $20 would be returned, $10 of which would be winnings.

By the same token, players whose hands didn't qualify for the payoff will lose on all spots where they had bets. At the very least, that would be one losing spot, since bets on the $ circle cannot be removed. Players can lose a maximum of three bets each if they let all bets ride. Thus, if a player had $5 on each of the three circles and let all the bets ride, but lost in the showdown, a total of $15 would be lost. However, if the player had removed the bets from circles 1 and 2, then only $5 would be lost.

Now let's see how the $1 bonus bet works.

THE $1 BONUS BET

You have the option to make a separate $1 bet that will go toward an additional payout pool. This wager is placed into the bonus betting circle and must be made before the cards are dealt. On the table, there will be a spot marked "bonus" to accommodate this wager. The amount you can win will be determined according to the strength of your hand.

The $1 bonus side bet was introduced on October 1, 1997, after the original inception of the game, to replace the original $1 tournament wager. What sets the bonus apart from the tournament is that the bonus payouts are set according to a fixed schedule and are paid out on the spot. There are no tournament playoffs and no million-dollar bounty as there was earlier in the tournament format.

However, the bonus pay table is actually much better for the average player. Rather than building a large pool of money that gets distributed to a few, the million dollar payouts are now circulated back into the regular pay tables and get distributed among many. This concept is similar to that of progressive slot machines. The super jackpot machines pay less out to the regular players as money is saved for the big jackpot winner, while the smaller progressives keep the money flowing.

At the time of this writing, there are six different pay tables in effect for winners of the Let It Ride bonus, but more may be developed at any time, so the charts we'll present below may vary from what you'll see. Game makers are always adjusting their formulas and concepts to find the best mix of profitability for the casinos with popularity among its players. Which pay tables are used in a particular casino may be determined by the local gaming commission. Some jurisdictions allow multiple pay tables, while others allow just one. If multiple pay tables are allowed, it is up to casino management to choose which ones they'll put up for play on the floor.

Depending on the table used, payouts for the best hand, the royal flush, can range from $10,000 to $25,000, while full houses can range from $75 to $200. And while some pay tables give bonuses for tens or better, others don't start paying out unless a player holds at least a two pair hand. Still other games require a minimum strength of three of a kind.

These payout schedules directly affect your overall return on the money gambled and, of course, the house edge on the bet. With the most liberal payouts allowed, you will face a 2.14% house edge on the bonus bet. The least liberal can give the casino an edge as high as 7.28% or more, which is considerably more. Unfortunately, this schedule is the most common one offered.

Keep in mind that the amounts paid on *all* winning hands is what determines your overall chances of winning, not necessarily how easy it is to get a payout on a hand. For example, a pay table that pays out for tens or better does not necessarily have overall better odds than a pay table that pays out beginning at three of a kind.

Schedules A, B, and C, show the most common payouts.

Bonus Payout Schedule A

Royal Flush	$20,000
Straight Flush	$2,000
Four of a Kind	$200
Full House	$75
Flush	$50
Straight	$25
Three of a Kind	$5
Two Pair	$4
Tens or Better	$1

Bonus Payout Schedule B

Royal Flush	$20,000
Straight Flush	$2,000
Four of a Kind	$100
Full House	$75
Flush	$50
Straight	$25
Three of a Kind	$9
Two Pair	$6
Tens or Better	No Payout

Bonus Payout Schedule C

Royal Flush	$20,000
Straight Flush	$2,000
Four of a Kind	$400
Full House	$200
Flush	$50
Straight	$25
Three of a Kind	$5
Two Pair	No Payout
Tens or Better	No Payout

WINNING STRATEGY

INTRODUCTION

In this section, we'll go over the third and fourth card playing strategies, house percentages, and the overall strategy for winning at Let It Ride.

The main strategy considerations in Let It Ride have to do with the bets in the first two betting circles, 1 and 2. You must decide whether to let these bets ride or bring them down and play only for the mandatory bet in the third circle. These are the two decisions to make, one for each circle.

Once you've looked at your three downcards, you must make your first decision: let the bet in circle 1 ride or bring it down? The strategies you use to make this decision will be referred to as the **Third Card Betting Strategy**. After the dealer exposes a community card—your fourth known card—you must make the same decision about the bet in circle 2. We'll call this the **Fourth Card Playing Strategy**.

Let's take a closer look at both decisions.

THIRD CARD BETTING STRATEGY

Your first three cards give you a good indication of where your hand may be headed. You already know three-fifths of the cards that will comprise your final hand and can clearly determine the best way to play the bets.

Sometimes, as with three of a kind or a pair of tens or better, the strategy decision is obvious: You're already sitting with winners and should let the bet ride. A payout is already guaranteed and with a little luck, that hand may improve to a stronger rank and larger payoff. You'll also play strong hands that don't yet have a guaranteed payoff but which give you a positive expectation of winning.

On the other side of the coin, weak hands with negative expectations of winning call for a strategy of minimizing losses, and the correct play will be to take down the bet in circle 1.

Below are the six categories of Let It Ride poker hands where the optimal play is to let the circle 1 bet ride. Hands are listed from the strongest to the weakest. Remember that tens, jacks, queens, kings, and aces, are considered high cards. When they are paired, these hands pay off as a winner.

Hands That You Will Play

You'll let your bet ride with the following three-card hands:

1. Three of a Kind

This is fairly obvious. You've got an automatic winner that guarantees you at least a 3-1 payoff on all your bet spots.

2. Pair of Tens or Higher Pair

Another obvious play. You already have a 1-1 payoff and can't lose. Improving the hand will give you an even larger payout.

3. Three to a Royal Flush

You have all sorts of shots here for a payoff; a flush, a straight, a high pair—even three of a kind and two pair—and of course, the hand you would really like to get, a royal flush.

4. Three to a Straight Flush

Ditto above. There are good possibilities for improvement. You should let the bet ride.

5. Three to a Flush with Two Cards, 10 or Higher, and a Straight Possibility

It is not enough to have the flush chance alone, because you still need two additional suited cards to make the flush. In order to let the bet ride, you must also hold two high cards, which you hope to pair. There is also the possibility of the straight which brings more value as well. If all of the above conditions are met, you can let your circle 1 bet ride.

Examples of this type of hand include Q-J-9 of clubs and K-J-9 of hearts.

6. Three to a Flush with J-9-8, 10-9-7, or 10-8-7

Unlike the previous grouping, which can be played with a two gap straight possibility, these three hands have only one high card and are more marginal. In order to let your bet ride with a hand like this, you need the greater straight possibility that the one-gap hand provides, compared to the two-gap straight in the previous category.

For ease of remembering, these hands can also be thought of as a three-card flush with one high card and one gap.

Hands That You Won't Play

Unless you have one of the hands listed in the six categories above, you should remove your bet from the first circle. While there are always winning possibilities with any three starting cards, the cost of playing low percentage hands is too high to justify letting the bet ride. When you have a chance to remove a bet with inferior cards, you should always do so. That's the smart way to play.

Now let's look at some particular hands that you're not going to play. Though similar to some of the playable hands mentioned above, A-K-Q is a hand you won't play. It can only be filled one-way and is therefore a more difficult straight possibility to fill. And J-10-9 is not worth playing since it has only two high cards that can pair into a payoff. On these marginal hands, you just don't have enough juice to justify the bet in circle 1, and the best percentage play is to take the bet down.

Low pairs, that is, pairs less than tens, should not be played either. For example, with 7-7-Q, you should take down your bet. While it's possible that you'll catch the third 7 or another queen, the number of times that you don't will far outweigh the number of times you do, with a negative long-term result. That's exactly what you're trying to avoid.

FOURTH CARD BETTING STRATEGY

After the dealer exposes one of the two community downcards, you know four of the five cards that will make up your final hand. You're now faced with your final strategy decision: Should you let your circle 2 bet ride, or should you reclaim it for your bankroll?

As with the third card betting strategy, you'll play hands that give you a positive expectation of winning, and take down bets in the second circle when your expectation of winning is negative. In the obvious cases where you already have a winning combination, the clear-cut play is to let the bet ride. However, in many cases, you won't be quite as thrilled with your prospects, and you'll be more than happy to take down your bet.

Following is the correct strategy for letting bets ride or taking them down on circle 2.

Hands That You Will Play

You'll let your bet ride with the following four card hands:

1. Four of a Kind

This is an obvious winning hand paying 50-1. Let 'em ride!

2. Three of a Kind

This is also an obvious winner, paying 3-1 on all betting circles. Let 'em ride!

3. Two Pair

You already have a guaranteed 2-1 payoff with possibilities of improving to a full house for an 11-1 yield.

4. Pair of Tens or Higher Pair

You've already got a winner paying 1-1 and can improve to two pair or three of a kind with a good draw on the final card.

5. Four to a Royal Flush

One more card, and you're there with a big payoff. There are also the possibilities of making a flush or straight, and an excellent chance of catching a high-paying pair since any of your four high cards, if matched, becomes a winner.

6. Four to a Straight Flush

This is not as strong as a four to a royal flush, but it still holds excellent possibilities.

7. Four to a Flush

If you draw the flush, the payoff of is 8-1, which is greater than the odds of filling the flush. Here's why: Of the 48 unseen cards in the deck, nine of them will make the flush and 39 will not, odds of 4.33-1. Being paid 8-1 on odds of about 4.33-1 is always a great bet in my book.

8. Four to an Open-Ended Straight

If you aren't holding any high cards, this bet is a wash. Of the 48 unseen cards, eight of them will make the straight, and 40 will not—odds of 5-1. Since the payoff is exactly 5-1, you have an even chance. There is no theoretical loss or gain on the play, so you can choose whether to let your bet ride or take it down.

If you are holding at least one high card, you now gain the advantage on the four-card open-ended straight draw, since the last community card may pair with your high card for a winner.

9. Four to a High Straight

The hands 10-J-Q-A, 10-Q-K-A, 10-J-K-A, and J-Q-K-A, have two things in common: (1) The ability to match any of the four high cards into a paying winner, and (2) The possibility of filling to an inside straight. Neither factor by itself gives you enough strength to make the third bet, but taken together, you've got the percentages to let the second bet ride. This is due in part to the sensitivity of the single deck game.

Hands That You Won't Play

You don't let your bet ride on circle 2 when holding a one way or inside straight, such as J-10-9-7, as the chances of making these one way straights climb to 11-1. Since straights only pay 5-1, this is not a good percentage bet. The one exception is the four-card high straight, such as A-K-Q-J, because all four cards have pairing possibilities. Small pairs–nines and under–are not worth chasing anymore since these hands promise no payoff. Therefore, the best play in the long run is to take down the bet in circle 2 when holding one of these hands.

If your hand lacks any of the nine combinations listed above—in other words, if you're holding various degrees of junk—then you've got a negative expectation on this fourth card and the strategy is clear: Take down the bet and have it returned to your bankroll.

HOUSE PERCENTAGES

OVERVIEW

The best percentage that can be achieved at the Let It Ride table games is about 3.5% in favor of the house for the basic bets. This is assuming that you use the optimal basic strategy presented here and that the $1 bonus bet is not made.

Making poor percentage bets will raise the overall house edge higher than the 3.5% stated here and can cost you multiple percentage points. How much you give back to the house would be based on the number of mistakes or poor decisions made. For example, if you don't let your bets ride on automatic winning hands or do let them ride on terrible starting cards, this will increase the house edge precipitously. The more of an edge you give the house, in the long run, the more money you will lose.

Another factor that affects the overall house edge is the average bet size you make if you are also making the $ bonus bet. The smaller the average bet, the higher that house percentage would be. For example, a poor percentage $1 bet has a greater overall negative effect on a $5 bettor than on a $25 bettor.

Players who make bets on the optional $1 bonus spot may be giving the casino a larger edge that the 3.5% for the basic game, an edge that varies depending upon the payouts offered by the casino for the bonus.

MORE PERCENTAGES OF PLAY

In Let it Ride, as in blackjack, the general playing strategy is to minimize losses when you're dealt poor cards and maximize gains when your cards are strong. Thus, while many weak two-card totals in blackjack will be played from a perspective of losing the least amount of money, strong hands, on the other side of the coin, will be doubled down whenever possible in order to take advantage of the strong situations. The same analogy holds true in Let it Ride.

Most starting hands in Let It Ride have losing expectations for the player. In fact, in almost 85 out of 100 hands—84.5%, to be precise—the correct playing strategy dictates that both the first and second bets should be removed. It is the other 15% of the time, when your hand is in an advantageous situation, that the second or third bets should ride.

You take advantage of profitable situations by making sure money is bet on your profitable hands. In these favorable occasions, when all three bets are riding, you are able to make up the money you've lost on the other 85% of the hands. Those second and third bets allow you to make up lost ground.

Using the proper playing strategy, a total of two bets will stay in action about 8.5% of the time, and the full three bets will stay in action 7.0% of the time.

When all three situations are added up (the wagers with one bet, the wagers with two bets, and the wagers with three bets) the house edge at Let It Ride, if the proper playing strategy is followed, ends up at 3.5%.

FREQUENCY OF WINS

Using either of the two basic Let It Ride pay tables, you can expect to win a payout 23.88% of the time, or about one time in four hands. On the bonus pay tables, the frequency of winning will range up to the same 23.88% if the same number of payoffs are given, and less, of course, when there are fewer payoffs to be had.

CONCLUSION

When you play perfect basic strategy, the 3.5% house edge in the Let It Ride basic game is higher than the overall house edge of 2.56% in Caribbean stud poker, but certainly far more favorable than American roulette, with its 5.26% odds, and games such as keno, wheel of fortune and many of the slots machines spread around the casino. In Let it Ride, like many of the casino games, the house edge is totally dependent on the strategy decisions you make. If you play it well, you give up only 3.5%. If you play it poorly, you give the house much more of an edge, which is never a good idea.

One of the big draws for the original versions of Let It Ride was the hope of hitting a monster hand on the $1 tournament bet. However, the house edge on this wager was much worse than the 3.5% edge of the basic game, giving players a bigger hill to climb to emerge a winner. The newer bonus wager, with that same $1 bet, offers more favorable odds than the tournament versions, again, depending on how generous the pay table may be for the player.

A word on betting limits and understanding the amount of money you put at risk in this game: Whether betting $5 or $100 per betting spot, don't let these amounts deceive you into thinking that you are betting only $5 or $100. Because you're not. For example, at a $5 minimum table, you're not just betting $5, you're betting $15, $5 on each of the three required betting spots. And if you're laying out $100 per betting spot, you actually have $300 in wagers on the felt. This is an important consideration because you don't want to have more money at risk than you are comfortable with or can handle.

It is my recommendation to go after the best odds you can get in any game. Of course, if you really like to play a game, regardless of the odds, go for it. But do so making the best percentage plays you can and thus giving yourself the best chances of winning. In other words, play a tough game, giving the casino as little as you possibly have to. It is a mathematical truth: The greater the house edge, the less chance you have of winning. And the converse rings just as true: The lesser the house edge, the greater the chance you have of winning.

If you like the big payoffs with small bets, the overall attraction of the extra bonus bet is that it gives you a chance to win large sums of money with just a $1 wager. While the bonus bet may not have the glamour of the million-dollar jackpot offered by lottery games, it does offer odds that are worlds better than the lottery hustles.

With much better chances of winning something good for just a little money, the Let It Ride bonus bet has become popular among players. And since fun is what gambling is supposed to be about, at least you have a much better shot at winning something here than throwing a buck away on a numbers game such as bingo, keno or the lotto.

Just remember to keep losing streaks to reasonable and acceptable levels, and when winning, be sure to walk away with the casino's money. There is no better feeling in the casino than that.

Money Management

FIVE KEYS TO MONEY MANAGEMENT

1 Never bet money you cannot afford to lose, either financially or emotionally.

2 Once a big winner, always walk away a big winner. Create a slush fund of winnings that never gets dipped into.

3 Set loss limits before you sit down to play and never dip in deeper than originally planned. Never hurt yourself by one big loss.

4 Accept your losses, you can't always win. The practical application of this advice is not to chase losses with big bets that can turn a session into a disaster.

5 Gambling can be fun. Smart money management will keep it that way.

INTRODUCTION

To be a winner at gambling, a player must not only gamble intelligently, but must also make proper use of one's bankroll and keep his or her emotions under control. The tendency to ride a winning streak too hard in the hope of a big killing or to bet wildly during a losing streak attempting a quick comeback, have spelled doom to many a session which otherwise may have been a good win. Wins can turn into losses, and moderate losses can turn into a nightmare.

Winning and losing streaks are a very real part of gambling. It is how one deals with the inherent ups and downs at the tables that determines just how well a gambler will fare at the tables. In this section, we're going to present the sage advice every gambler should and must take to heart, for money management is a vital part of the winning formula.

You may be playing at an advantage or disadvantage to the house, but just because you're playing at an advantage doesn't mean you'll win in the short run, and conversely, just because you're playing at a disadvantage doesn't mean you'll lose. Anything can happen in the short run.

And that's why money management is so important. When you're winning, you have to stretch those winnings to the maximum safe level and make sure you finish a winner. And when things go the other direction, you must restrict losses to affordable amounts and protect yourself from ever really getting hurt at the tables.

If you follow the advice in this section, you'll be following the advice of professionals, and making the best use of your monetary resources. You'll always keep losses under control—and control is always a key concept in gambling—while winning sessions always end up as winning sessions.

You'll be on your way to successful gambling and when your luck falls right, you'll be a winner!

THE RISKS OF OVERBETTING

Astute gamblers have one thing in common—they know how to manage their money. Superior playing skills alone does not make one a winning player. The concept here is self control, the ability of a player to keep the game in check and never to lose sight of the winning strategies.

Let's show a simple example of how overbetting can quickly change a big winning session into a disaster. Let's say a bettor starts out with a bankroll of $250 and has been betting $5-$20 a shot and after two hours of skillful play has ridden a surge of luck to $225 in winnings. Now he has $475 in front of him.

Getting greedy and caught up in the excitement of the game, the gambler now really wants to put the squeeze on and fast, so he goes against his pre-planned strategy, if he even has one, and now goes for $50 -$100 a bet. With a little luck and a few big wins in a row, he's on easy street.

However, after three straight losses at $100 a pop, he gets frantic, and goes for one more play at $175, pushing all his money on the wager. Make or break. Another loss.

Suddenly, a careful strategy that netted $225 got metamorphosed into "if I can get lucky on this play, please" strategy, and the player is out $250!

Madness. Here was an example of perhaps a technically skillful player losing control, betting over his head, and taking what by all rights was a tremendous winning session and finishing four bets later out all his bankroll!

And what if the sequence went a little differently, and more of those big bets were won rather than lost, so that instead the player sat with $500 in winnings. We all know that type of player, and know that he wouldn't have left until the game broke him. Bets would have been raised again and then he would have been bankrupted. Or the next session would have done the job.

To win, you must want to win, and want to win bad enough that you won't give that money back to the casino.

I'm going to present a very important concept. Once you have won money from a casino, that money is yours, and not the casino's.

If you have $150 in winnings in front of you, you are not playing with the casino's money. It is your money now! If you think of your winnings as the casino's money, you won't feel bad giving it back. That's a dangerous attitude. Think of the money as yours now, and you won't be wanting to hand it back. And now maybe you'll walk away from the table with those winnings.

Let's move on the most important concept in money management.

 NEVER GAMBLE MONEY THAT YOU CANNOT AFFORD TO LOSE, EITHER FINANCIALLY OR EMOTIONALLY.

Do not gamble with needed funds no matter how "sure" the bet seems. The possibilities of taking a loss are real, and if that loss will hurt, you're playing with fire. Don't be coming into town, as they say, in a $20,000 Cadillac and leaving on a $100,000 Greyhound.

Gambling with needed funds is a foolish gamble, for gambling involves chance, and the short term possibilities of taking a loss are real, no matter how easy the game may appear, or how well the odds are stacked in your favor. Unexpected things happen in gambling, that's what makes it so interesting. But if you never play over your head, you'll never suffer.

Gambling is a form of entertainment and if you can't afford the possibility of losing—don't gamble at the stakes you were considering. Either play at lower levels or don't gamble at all. If the larger wagers of your gambling game make your adrenalin rush too hard, you're over your head and need to find a game with lower limits.

But don't overlook the emotional side as well. If the playing of the game becomes a cause of undue anxiety, for whatever the reason, than it ceases to be a form of entertainment and you need a break. Take some time away from the game, be it a coffee break or a month's rest.

Playing under anxiety not only ruins the fun of the game but also adversely affects play and can influence you to make decisions contrary to what smart strategy dictates.

Your goal in gambling is not just to win, but to get satisfaction out of the game. Keep that in mind and you can never go wrong.

THE NATURE OF THE GAMBLE

In any gambling pursuit where luck plays a role, fluctuations in ones fortunes are common. It is the ability of the player to successfully deal with the ups and downs inherent in the gamble, that separate the smart gamblers from the losers.

You can't always win—even when the odds favor you—and you won't always lose, even when the odds are against you. In the short run, anything can happen and usually does. But over the long run, luck evens itself out, and it is skill, in the bets one makes and how one plays the game, that will determine if a player is a winner or a loser.

The smart player bides his time, is patient, keeps the game under control and as a result can win when the odds are in his favor.

PROPER BANKROLLING

Overbetting (or undercapitalization) leaves a player vulnerable in two ways. First, a normal downward trend can wipe out a limited money supply (as we saw earlier). Second, and equally important, the bettor may feel pressured by the shortage of capital and play less powerfully than smart play dictates.

For example, psychology and bluffing is an important part of poker, and if one is playing with "scared money," and the other players see it, they will have a field day forcing the undercapitalized player out of pots.

If the amount staked on a bet is above your head, you're playing in the wrong game. Play in a lower limit game—at levels of betting you feel comfortable with.

KNOW WHEN TO QUIT

What often separates the winners from the losers is that the winners, when winning, leave the table a winner, and when losing, restrict their losses to affordable amounts. Smart gamblers never allow themselves to get destroyed at the table.

Minimizing losses is the key. You can't always win. If you're losing, keep the losses affordable—take a break. You only want to play with a clear head.

MINIMIZING LOSSES

The key concept in minimizing losses during a bad gambling run is to set a stop-loss limit. Before sitting at the table and making your bets, you must decide on the amount of money you'll put at stake, and should luck turn against you, restrict your losses to that amount only.

Do not go against this rule and you can never take a big beating. If things go poorly at first, take a break—simple as that.

When you're winning big, put a good chunk of these winnings in a "don't touch" pile, and play with the rest. You never want to hand all your winnings back to the casino. Should a losing streak occur, you're out of there—a winner!!!

PROTECTING YOUR WINS

Once you've accumulated a sizable win at the tables, the most important thing is to walk away a winner. There is no worse feeling than skulking away from a table after having lost all your wins back.

The general guidelines we recommend, is to put away half to two thirds of your winnings into a "**protected**" area that you won't touch under any circumstances. That money is bankable, for you won't play it. Keep playing with the rest of the winnings, putting more aside as the wins accumulate. Once the streak stops and the tides of fortune go against you, you'll leave the table a guaranteed winner for you've played it smart!

For example, let's say you're up 20 units. (A **unit** is the bet size you're using as a standard and could be $1, $5, $10, $25, $100, $500 or whatever value you want to assign.) Let's say your unit size is $5, so you're up $100. Put aside $50 (10 units) of your winnings into the protected zone and play the other $50 (10 units).

Set no limits on a winning streak. When you've got a hot hand, ride it for all its worth.

INCREASING BETS WHEN WINNING

If you want to risk more to win more, go for it—but in moderation. Increase your bets gradually when winning, never getting overzealous as in the earlier example.

For example, if your bet size is a flat $10 in a game, and winnings are rapidly accumulating, jump up to $15, and if all goes well, to $20. This way if you keep winning, the wins get larger. If however, a sudden losing streak ensues, no problem, for you have protected yourself.

If you're playing in a game where you use a bet range, such as blackjack, take a $5-$20 range up to $10-$30 gradually, and then slowly higher if you're still winning.

And all the time, as you gradually increase bets in your gambling game, continually sock away won bets into your "don't touch" pile, so that by the time the streak ends, you've already got plenty in the bank and can walk away—**a big winner**!

The Winning Word

FIVE KEYS TO WINNING

1. Prepare for the games you will be wagering on by reading the appropriate section carefully and practicing in the comfort of your home.

2. Protect your wins, limit your losses, and you're on the way to winning.

3. Make the correct strategy move on every play, all the time. Hunches and feelings are for losers. There is only one correct move or every situation and it is the winner who makes that move.

4. Never gamble with money you cannot afford to lose, either financially or emotionally.

5. Think and play like a winner.

THE WINNING WORD

Okay, this is my last chance at you in this book. I want to make you a winner. I want you to beat the casino. But to be successful at gambling, you must want to win, and like anything else, you have to work at it. Prepare for your games and play them like you want to win money. If you take your gambling money seriously, you'll find you'll leave casinos with more of it on the good days, and leave a ton less behind on the bad ones. You'll also find more good days than bad days if you follow the advice I have given you in this book.

The winning attitude goes a long way in life and it goes a long way in gambling too. Behind the will to succeed is an approach that keeps you on the proper course. What you wish for may not occur, but by thinking right and playing right, you give it every chance. And that is all I can ask you to do.

Think right, play right, and be a winner.

GLOSSARY

BACCARAT

Baccarat – The gambling card game of French origin. Also, the score of zero.

Baccarat a Tout Va – Variation of baccarat where there is no maximum limit on bets.

Baccarat Banque – Variation of chemin de fer.

Banco – The Banker position; In chemin de fer, a bet by a player covering the entire bank.

Banker – One of the two betting positions.

Banker Rules – The rules by which the banker position must draw cards or stand pat.

Burned Cards – Cards removed from play without being used.

Chemin De Fer – The European form of baccarat.

Cover – *See* FADE.

Croupier – Dealer, in French.

Dealer – Person dealing the cards; casino employee running a gambling game; croupier.

Fade – *Also* COVER. Chemin de Fer (and gambling term) describing the act of betting against the bank.

Le Grande – A total of nine points.

Le Petit – A total of eight points.

Mini Baccarat – Baccarat which is played on a blackjack-style layout, with a capacity to seat around six to seven players.

Natural – A two card count of 8 or 9.

Player – One of the two betting positions. Also called Punto. Any bettor wagering in a game.

Player Rules – The rules by which the player position must draw cards or stand pat.

Punto – The Player position.

Punto Banco – In Europe and other international locations, the name for the standard form of baccarat.

Scorecard – *See* TALLY SHEET.

Shill – Casino employee hired to sit at game and make game look busy.

Tally Sheet – *Also* **SCORECARD**. Sheet of paper used to record wins, losses and other data from a game.

BLACKJACK/SPANISH 21

Anchorman – *See* THIRD BASE.

Barring a Player – The exclusion of a player from the blackjack tables.

Basic Strategy – The optimal playing strategy for a particular set of rules and number of decks used, assuming the player has knowledge of only his own two cards and the dealer's upcard.

Blackjack – *Also* **NATURAL**. An original two card holding consisting of an ace and ten-value card. Also the name of the game.

Bonus Hand – A hand which gives the player a multiple bonus of his original bet.

Break – *See* BUST.

Burn Card – A card, usually form the top of the deck, that is removed from play. The top card is traditionally burned after a fresh shuffle and before the cards are dealt.

Bust – *Also* **BREAK**. To exceed the total of 21, a loser.

Card Counting – A method of keeping track of the cards already played so that knowledge of the remaining cards can be used to adjust strategies. A player that counts cards is called a card counter.

Composition of the Deck – A term used to describe the particular makeup of the cards remaining in the deck.

Composition Change – As cards are removed from the deck, the normal proportion of certain cards to other groups of cards change. This is called a composition change.

Dealer – The casino employee who deals the cards, makes the proper payoffs to winning hands and collects lost bets.

Doubling, Doubling Down – A player option to double the original bet after seeing his original two cards. If the player chooses this option, one additional card will be dealt.

Doubling after Splitting – Option offered in only some United States and international casinos whereby players are allowed to double down after splitting a pair (according to normal doubling rules).

Draw – *See* HIT.

Early Surrender – An option to forfeit a hand and lose half the bet before the dealer checks for a blackjack.

Exposed Card – *See* UPCARD.

Eye in the Sky – Refers to the mirrors above the gaming tables where the games are constantly supervised to protect both the player and the house from being cheated.

Face Card – *Also* PAINT. A jack, queen or king.

First Base – Seat closest to the dealer's left. The first baseman acts upon his hand first.

Five Card 21 – In Spanish 21, a player's seven-card hand which is less than or equal to 21 points.

Hard Total – A hand without an ace or if containing an ace, where the ace counts as only 1 point (10, 6, A).

Head On, Head to Head – Playing alone against the dealer.

High Roller – A player that wagers big money.

Hit – *Also* DRAW. The act of drawing (requesting) a card from the dealer.

Hole Card – The dealer's unexposed downcard.

House – A term to denote the casino.

Insurance – A side bet that can be made when the dealer shows an ace. The player wagers up to half his original bet and gets paid 2 to 1 on that bet if the dealer shows a blackjack. If the dealer does not have a blackjack, the insurance bet is lost.

Multiple Deck Game – Blackjack played with two or more decks of cards, usually referring to a 4, 6, or 8 deck game.

Natural – *See* BLACKJACK.

Nickels – $5 chips, usually red in color.

Paint – *See* FACE CARD.

Pat Card – A dealer upcard of 7 through ace, that tends to give the dealer pat hands.

Pat Hand – A hand totaling 17-21.

Pit Boss – Casino employee who supervises play at the tables.

Push – A tie between the dealer and the player.

Quarters – $25 chips, usually green in color.

Seven Card 21 – In Spanish 21, a player's seven-card hand which is less than or equal to 21 points.

Shoe – An oblong box used to hold multiple decks of cards.

Shuffle, Shuffling Up – The mixing of cards by a dealer prior to a fresh round of play.

Silver – $1 tokens or dollar chips.

Single Deck Game – Blackjack played from a single pack of cards.

Six Card 21 – In Spanish 21, a player's six-card hand which is less than or equal to 21 points.

Soft Hands, Soft Total – Hand in which the ace counts as 11 points.

Splitting Pairs – A player option to split two cards of identical value so that two separate hands are formed. A bet equal to the original wager is placed next to the second hand.

Stand, Stand Pat – A player's decision not to draw a card.

Stiff Card – A dealer upcard of 2 through 6, that leaves the dealer with a high busting potential.

Stiff Hand – A hand totaling hard 12, 13, 14, 15, or 16; can be busted if hit.

Super Bonus – In Spanish 21, an extra bonus for a hand which contains three 7s all of the same suit.

Surrender, Late Surrender – A player option to forfeit his original hand and lose half the bet after it has been determined that the dealer does not have a blackjack.

Ten Factor – Refers to the concentration of tens in the deck.

Ten-Value Card – 10, jack, queen, or king.

Third Base – *Also* ANCHORMAN. Position closest to the dealer's right. The third baseman makes the last play before the dealer's turn.

Three 7s – In Spanish 21, a bonus given for a player's hand whose three cards are all 7s.

Toke, Tip – A gratuity either given or bet for the dealer.

Unit – Bet size used as a standard of measurement.

Upcard – *Also* EXPOSED CARD. The dealer's face up card.

CARIBBEAN STUD POKER (MORE TERMS IN THE POKER GLOSSARY.)

Ante Bet – The initial bet made before the cards are dealt.

Bonus Bet – An optional $1 bet that can be made by players.

Bonus Payout – A winning combination.

Call – To make an additional wager two times the size of the ante bet, after the cards are dealt.

Drop Slot – Place where players can make the $1 bonus bet.

First Base – Seat closest to the dealer's left. The first baseman acts upon his hand first.

Fold – To give up one's cards and forfeit the ante bet.

Maximum Bonus Payout – The most the casino will pay in total to a big winning combination, even if the stated payout is higher.

Non-Qualifying Hand – A dealer's hand that does not contain at least an ace and a king, or higher combination.

Progressive Jackpot – A winning pool of money that gets progressively higher every time a progressive $1 bet is made until a royal flush is drawn is hit, whereupon the progressive jackpot will return to a stated level and begin accumulating anew.

Qualifying Hand – A dealer's hand containing at least an ace and a king, or higher combination.

Third Base – Position closest to the dealer's right. The third baseman makes the last play before the dealer's turn.

Upcard – The dealer's face up (exposed) card.

CRAPS

Any Craps – A bet that the following roll will be a 2, 3, or 12.

Any Seven – A bet that the following roll will be a 7.

Back Line – Refers to the don't pass area.

Bar the 12 – A term found in the don't pass and don't come areas which makes the roll of a 12 (in some casinos the 2) a standoff.

Big 6 & Big 8 – A bet that the 6, or the 8, whichever is bet on, will be thrown before a 7 is rolled.

Boxman – Casino executive who supervises the craps table from a seat between the two standing dealers.

Buy Bets – A player option to buy a point number and get paid at the correct odds. However, a 5% commission must be paid to buy the number.

Call Bet – A verbal bet that a wager is working. Disallowed in many casinos by the indication "No Call Bets" on the layout.

Center Bets – *See* PROPOSITION BETS.

Come Bet – A bet that the dice will win, or pass. Works just like a pass bet except that it can only be made after a point is established.

Come-Out Roll – The roll made before any point has been established.

Coming Out – A term to designate that a new come-out roll is about to happen.

Correct Odds – The mathematical likelihood that a bet will be a winner, expressed in odds.

Crap Out – The roll of a 2, 3, or 12 on a come-out roll, an automatic loser for pass line bettors.

Craps – Term used to denote a 2, 3, or 12. Also the name of the game.

Craps-Eleven – A one roll bet combining the Any Craps and 11.

Dealer – The casino employee who works directly with the player and who handles all monetary transactions and bets.

Don't Come Bet – A bet made against the dice. The bet works just like the don't pass except that it can only be made after a point is established.

Don't Pass – A bet made on the come-out roll only, that the dice will lose.

Double Odds Bet – A free-odds bet that allows the player to bet double his line wager as a right bettor, and double the line payoff as a wrong bettor.

Easy, Easy Way – The throw of a 4, 6, 8, or 10 other than as a pair, such as 1-5, 6 the easy way.

Even-Money – The payoff of one dollar for every dollar bet.

Field Bet – A one-roll bet that the next roll will be a number in the field box – 2, 3, 4, 9, 10, 11, or 12.

Free-Odds Bets – *Also* ODDS BET. A bet made in conjunction with the line, come and don't come bets, that is made after the establishment of a point. The house has no advantage on these wagers.

Front Line – *See* PASS LINE.

Hardway Bet – A sequence bet that the hardway number, the 4, 6, 8, or 10 will come up in doubles before it comes up easy, or before a 7 is thrown.

Hardway – The throw of a 4, 6, 8, or 10 as a pair, such as 3-3; 6 the hardway.

Hop Bet – A bet that the next roll will be a specific combination. Usually not found on the layout.

Horn Bet – A one roll bet that the next throw will be a 2, 3, 11, or 12.

Inside Numbers – The place numbers 5, 6, 8, 9.

Lay Bet – A wager made by wrong bettors that a 7 will show before the point number is thrown.

Line Bet – A pass or don't pass bet.

Marker Buck – Round disk used to mark either the point or to indicate that no point is yet established. Also called Puck, or Marker Puck.

Odds Bet – *See* FREE-ODDS BET.

Off – A designation that a bet is not working on a particular roll.

On – A designation that a bet is working on a particular roll.

One Roll Bet – A bet whose outcome is determined on the very next throw of the dice.

Outside Numbers – The numbers 4, 5, 9, and 10.

Pass, Pass Line – *Also* FRONT LINE. A bet made on the come-out roll only, that the dice will pass, or win.

Payoff, House Payoff – The amount of money the casino pays the player on a winning bet.

Place Bet – A wager that a particular number, the 4, 5, 6, 8, 9, or 10, will be rolled before a 7.

Point, Point Number – The throw of a 4, 5, 6, 8, 9, or 10 on the come-out roll becomes the point.

Proposition Bets – *Also* CENTER BETS. The bets located in the center of the layout.

Right Bettors – Players betting that the dice will pass. Pass and come bettors.

Sequence Bet – A bet whose outcome may take a succession of rolls to be determined.

Seven-Out – The roll of a 7 after a point has been established, a loser for pass line bettors.

Shoot – A progression of rolls ending on either an immediate decision on the come-out roll, or the sevening-out after a point had been established.

Shooter – The player throwing the dice.

Single Odds – A free-odds bet that allows the player to bet equal to his line wager as a right bettor, and equal the payoff as a wrong bettor.

Stickman – Casino employee who controls the dice with a hooked stick, calls the game and controls the proposition bet area.

Toke, Tip – A gratuity given or bet for the dealer.

Unit – Bet size used as a standard of measurement.

Working – Designation that a bet is on or in play.

Wrong Bettors – Players betting that the dice won't pass. Don't pass and don't come bettors.

Yo-Leven – Slang term for the roll of an 11.

KENO

Basic Ticket – *See* STRAIGHT TICKET.

Caller – Casino employee who calls each number as it's drawn

Catch – To match one or more numbers on ticket with those drawn. To catch three numbers.

Combination Ticket – A ticket combining groups of numbers to form two or more winning possibilities.

Draw – The random drawing of 20 numbers in a game.

Duplicate Ticket – The ticket marked in dark ink by the keno writer reflecting the numbers bet and returned to the player.

Draw Ticket – *See* PUNCH-OUTS.

Inside Ticket – *See* ORIGINAL TICKET.

Keno Balls – The 80 numbered balls, 1-80, of which 20 are randomly drawn in a keno game.

Keno Board – The lit board which indicates the 20 numbers drawn in a game.

Keno Lounge – The area set aside for keno in a casino.

Keno Runners – The casino employees who roam the casino area outside the keno lounge and take bets on keno games.

Keno Writer – *Also* WRITER. The employee who processes keno bets and issues duplicates.

King, King Number – The roaming number on a king ticket which is combined other groups or kings to make combinations in a game.

King Ticket – A combination type ticket using the king number.

Original Ticket – *Also* INSIDE TICKET. The original ticket filled out by the player and held by the casino.

Multi-Game Ticket – A ticket recorded once and played unchanged for one or more games.

Punch-Outs – *Also* DRAW TICKET. Special ticket with holes punched-out reflecting the 20 drawn numbers in a game.

Rate Card – The booklet issued by a casino showing the bets and their payoffs

Special Tickets – Tickets with different prices and payoffs from those in the rate card.

Split Ticket – A combination-type ticket with two or more groups of numbers.

Spots – The marked numbers on a ticket.

Straight Ticket – *Also* BASIC TICKET. A ticket where 1-15 spots are selected without combinations.

Way Ticket – A combination-type ticket with at least three different groups of equal numbers.

Writer – *See* KENO WRITER.

POKER

Act – To bet, raise, fold, or check.

Active Player – Player still in competition for the pot.

Ante – Mandatory bet placed into the pot by all players before the cards are dealt.

Bet – Money wagered and placed into the pot.

Big Blind – The larger of two mandatory bets made by the player two seats to the left of the dealer button position.

Blind – A mandatory bet made on the first round of betting. Also, the player making that bet.

Bluff – To bet or raise with an inferior hand for the purpose of intimidating opponents into folding their cards and making the bluffer a winner by default.

Board – *See* COMMUNITY CARDS.

Bring-In – Forced opening bet in seven-card stud, or the amount required to open betting.

Button – The player occupying the dealer position; also the disk used to indicate this position.

Buy-In – A player's investment of chips in a poker game or the actual amount of cash he uses to purchase chips for play.

Call – To match an amount equal to a previous bet on a current round of betting.

Cap – Limit to the number of raises allowed in a betting round.

Cash Game – Poker game played for real money.

Check – The act of "not betting" and passing the bet option to the next player while still remaining an active player.

Check and Raise – A player's raising of a bet after already checking in that round.

Community Cards – *Also* BOARD. The face up cards shared by all players.

Downcards, Closed Cards – *See* FACE DOWN.

Draw – The exchange of cards allowed after the first round of betting in draw poker variations.

8-or-Better – In high-low poker, a requirement that a player must have five unpaired cards of 8 or less to win the low end of the pot.

Face Card – *Also* PICTURE CARD. Any jack, queen, or king.

Face Down – *Also* DOWNCARDS, CLOSED CARDS. A card positioned such that its rank and suit faces the table and cannot be viewed by competing players.

Face Up – A card positioned such that its rank and suit faces up and is therefore visible to all players. Cards dealt this way are also known as Upcards or Open Cards.

Flop – In hold'em and Omaha, the first three cards simultaneously dealt face-up for communal use by all active players.

Flush – A hand of five cards of the same suit.

Fold – Get rid of one's cards, thereby becoming inactive in the current hand and ineligible to play for the pot.

Four-Card Flush – Four cards to a flush needing one more to fill.

Four-Card Straight – Four cards to a straight needing one more to fill.

Four of a Kind – *Also* **QUADS**. A hand containing four cards of identical value, such as K-K-K-K (four kings).

Full House – A hand consisting of three of a kind and a pair, such as 7-7-7-K-K.

Hand – The cards a player holds; the best five cards a player can present.

High-low – Poker variation in which players compete for the best high and low hands, with the winner of each getting half the pot.

High Poker – Poker variations in which the highest hand wins.

Hole Card – Card held by a player whose value is hidden from other players.

Kicker – Unmatched side card, usually referring to a pair.

Level – *See* ROUND.

Limit Poker – Betting structure in which the minimum and maximum bet sizes are set at fixed amounts, usually in a two-tiered structure such as $5/$10.

Low Poker – A form of poker in which the lowest hand wins.

No-Limit – Betting structure in which the maximum bet allowed is limited only by the amount of money the bettor has on the table.

Nuts – The best hand possible given the cards on board.

One Pair – Hand containing two cards of the same rank, such as Q-Q or 7-7.

Overcard – In hold'em and Omaha, a hole card higher in rank than any board card. For example, a jack is an overcard to a flop of 10-6-2.

Picture Card – *See* FACE CARD.

Pocket Cards – The face-down cards that are initially dealt to a player.

Position – A player's relative position to the player acting first in a poker round.

Pot – The sum total of all antes and bets placed in the center of the table by players during a poker hand and collected by the winner or winners of that hand.

Pot-Limit – Betting structure in which the largest bet can be no more than the current size of the pot.

Pot Odds – A concept which examines the cost of a bet against the money to be made by winning the pot and compares this to a player's chances of winning that pot.

Preflop – The first betting round in hold'em, when each player has only his two pocket cards.

Premium Hands – The top tier of starting cards.

Quads – *See* FOUR OF A KIND.

Qualifier – In high-low games, a requirement that a player must have five unpaired cards of 8 or less to win the low end of the pot.

Raise – A wager that increases a previous bet.

Rake – The amount of money taken out of the pot by the house as its fee for running the game.

Reraise – A bet equaling a previous bet and raise, plus an additional bet—a raise of a raise.

River – The last card dealt or its betting round.

Round – *Also* LEVEL. In a tournament, a fixed period of play that ends with increased blinds or antes or both. In any poker game, one complete turn of hands around a table, one per player.

Royal Flush – An A-K-Q-J-10 of the same suit. The highest ranking hand in high poker.

Scoop – In a high-low game, win both the high and low ends of a pot.

Set – *See* THREE OF A KIND.

Showdown – The final act of a poker game, where remaining players reveal their hands to determine the winner of the pot.

Side Pot – When one player has bet all his chips and two or more opponents remain, a segregated pot created for and that can only be won by players who still have chips to bet.

Small Blind – The smaller of two mandatory bets made by the player sitting immediately to the left of the dealer button position.

Standard Raise – In no-limit and pot-limit, a raise of three times the size of the big blind.

Straight – A sequence of five consecutive cards of mixed suits, such as 4-5-6-7-8.

Straight Flush – A sequence of five consecutive cards in the same suit, such as 8-9-10-J-Q of spades.

Table Stakes – A rule stating that a player's bet or call of a bet is limited to the amount of money he has on the table in front of him.

Tap Out – Go broke at the table.

Tell – An inadvertent mannerism or reaction that reveals information about a player's hand.

Three of a Kind – *Also* SET, TRIPS. Poker hand containing three cards of the same rank, such as 4-4-4.

Tournament – A competition among players who start with an equal number of chips and play until one player holds all the chips. Players compete for prizes, typically cash, and get eliminated when they run out of chips.

Tournament Chips – Chips used only for tournaments that have no cash value.

Trips – *See* THREE OF A KIND.

Turn – The fourth community card on board.

Two Pair – Poker hand containing two sets of two cards of the same rank, such as J-J-5-5.

Wild Cards – Cards designated as "wild" can be given any value, even as a duplicate of a card already held, by the holder of that card.

WPT – World Poker Tour.

WSOP – World Series of Poker.

ROULETTE

A Cheval – Split bet, in French.

American Roulette – Roulette as played in the Unites States, featuring wheels with both the zero and double zero.

American Wheel – 0 and 00 roulette wheel

Ball – Spherical ball spun against wheel's rotation.

Carre – Four-number bet, in French.

Colonne – Column bet, in French.

Column Bet – A bet on a "column" of 12 numbers.

Combination Bet – Any bet combining two or more individual numbers at once.

Corner Bet – *See* FOUR-NUMBER BET.

Douzaine – Dozens bet, in French.

Dozens Bet – A wager on either the first, second or third dozen numbers.

En Plein – Single number bet, in French.

En Prison – A European option on even-money bets, that allows players, when a 0 gets spun, to either give up half their bet or go for another spin and keep the original bet intact.

European Roulette – Roulette as played in Europe, featuring wheels with only the zero and offering en prison and partage.

European Wheel – Roulette wheel using the 0.

Even-Money Bets – The high-low, odd-even and red-black bets which pay off at even money.

Five-Number Bet – In American roulette, the bet covering the 1, 2, 3, 0 and 00.

Four-Number Bet – *Also* SQUARE BET, CORNER BET. A bet covering four numbers.

High-Low – An even-money bet on numbers 1-18 (low) or 19-36 (high).

Impair-Pair – Odd-even bet, in French.

Layout – The betting cloth on which players make their bets.

Odd-Even Bet – An even-money wager on either the odd or the even numbers.

Outside Bet – A wager on either the even-money, dozens or columns bets.

Partage – *Also* SURRENDER, in some U.S. casinos. Similar to en prison in that players forfeit only half their wager when an even-number bet is made and a zero (or double zero) is spun and different in that there is not option to let the entire bet ride for another spin.

Passe-Manque – High-low bet, in French.

Quatre Premiere – Bet covering the 0, 1, 2, and 3, in French.

Red-Black Bet – An even-money bet on either the red or black numbers.

Rouge ou Noir – Red or black bet, in French.

Sixaine – Six-number bet, in French.

Six-Number Bet – A bet covering six numbers.

Split Bet – A wager covering two numbers.

Square Bet – *See* FOUR-NUMBER BET.

Surrender – *See* PARTAGE.

Tourneur – The dealer, in French.

Transversale – Trio bet, in French.

Trio Bet – A bet covering three numbers.

Zero-Double Zero – The numbers on the wheel which account for the casino's edge over the player.

SLOTS

Action – The total amount of money played measured by the sum of all bets placed. Thus, betting a quarter 100 times, would be equivalent to $25 in action, or betting $1 for 700 plays adds up to $700 in action. Action does not take into account starting or ending bankroll, or wins or losses – just total $ bets.

Average Payer – A machine that is neither tight, nor loose, but in between.

Bank, Bank of Machines – This is a group of machines connected together in a structure as a design unit.

Bar – A popular symbol on the slot machines. This symbol is often found as one bar, two bars, and three bars.

Big Bertha – The gigantic slot machines of many reels, usually eight to ten, that are strategically placed by casinos near their front entrance (usually, but not always) to lure curious players into their casinos for a pull or two.

Big Coin Machine – A slot machine requiring $5, $25, or larger coin to play.

Big Coin Player – A slots player who plays $5, $25, or larger coins.

Blanks – The stops on a reel which contain no symbols, thus, blank stops, or blanks.

Buy-Your-Pay – A machine with a single payout line that will only pay on certain symbols if enough coins are played.

Cage – The cashier's cage, where players can exchange chips for cash, or change traveler's checks. The cage usually won't accept large numbers of coins. That must be done at a change booth.

Change Booth – A booth set up for the specific purpose of changing players bills into coins, or their coins into bills.

Changeperson – The casino employee who services the machines area for the purpose of changing bills into coins.

Carousels – An oval or round-shaped area containing a bank of machines at whose center, enclosed in the space, often sits a change girl.

Cashout Button – This button, when pressed, releases all the coins that were won, or at least held by the machine.

Changeperson – The casino employee responsible for changing player bills into coins. The changeperson usually roams the slots area, though he or she may be "stationed" in a carousel,

Cherry – A popular symbol on the slot machines.

Cold – A machine that is paying out less than expected, or a player on a losing streak.

Comp – Short for complimentary. The freebies given out by the casino, usually as a reward for play.

Criss-Cross Machine – *See* FIVE LINE CRISS-CROSS.

Denomination – The size of coin (or bill) used to play a particular machine. 5¢, 25¢, and $1.00 are the most popular denominations found.

Five Line Criss-Cross – *Also* CRISS-CROSS MACHINE. A multiple payline machine that has five winning directions, three horizontal and two diagonal.

Hold – The percentage or actual dollar amounts a casino wins from its players.

Hot – A machine that is paying out better than expected, or a player on a winning streak.

Jackpot – The big win on any machine – the jackpot!

Lemon – A symbol found on the slot machines.

Liberty Bell – The original slot machine invented by Charles Fey. Also, the symbol on the reels of many slot machines.

Long Run – The concept of what certain results are expected to be when occurring over many trials, thus, in the long run.

Loose, Loose Machine – A slot machine marked by frequent winners, with a high percentage payback to the players. This is opposed to a tight machine which has a low percentage payback.

Loose Payer – A loose machine.

Max Bet Button – *See* MAX COIN BUTTON.

Max Coin Button – *Also* MAX BET BUTTON. The button that plays all credits allowed, usually three or five, when pushed.

Mega-Progressive Machines – A progressive slot machine with enormous, usually million dollar jackpots.

Medium Coin Machine – A 50¢ or $1 denomination machine.

Medium Coin Player – A player who plays the 50¢ or $1 denomination machines.

Mills Machines – An early machine, manufactured by Mills, an early slot innovator and producer, that was the first to use the fruit symbols and have a jackpot.

Money Management – The strategy used by smart players to wisely manage their money while gambling.

Multiple Payline – A slot machine with more than one winning payline.

Multiple Progressives – A machine which contains more than one progressive jackpot.

Multiplier – A multiple coin slots which pays proportionately more on winning combinations for each coin played, though often the jackpot pays much more if all coins are played than if a lesser amount is deposited.

One-Armed Bandit – A colorful slang term used for slot machines.

One Credit Button – The button that plays one credit for the player when pushed. The spin reels button will need to be pushed after to spin the reels.

Payback or Payout Percentage – The expected return percentage for money wagered. A 97% payback states that the expected return on every dollar bet will be 97¢, for a loss of 3¢.

Payline – The line on the glass over the reels of the machine, behind which the symbols need to line up to be a winning combination.

Payout Meter – The display on the machine that shows the number of coins played and won on a spin.

Progressive Machines, Progressives – Progressives feature a growing jackpot which increases each time a coin is inserted into a machine which is hooked up to the progressive. When the jackpot does hit, the lucky player wins the total accumulated in the jackpot. Once a progressive is hit, the jackpot total will be reset to a predetermined total to begin climbing again.

Rating – The evaluation received by a player from the casino stating the level of action this player gives the casino.

Reels – *Also* STEPPER REELS. The spinning mechanism containing the symbols on a slots machine.

Seven – A popular symbol on the slot machines, generally showing up in the number form "7".

Short Run – A brief sequence of trials, where anything can happen, even though the odds say they may not be likely to.

Slots – Short for slot machines.

Slots Host – The person responsible for taking care of the slots players and all their needs.

Slots Palace – A casino that only contains slot machines.

Small Coin Machine – A 5¢, 10¢, or 25¢ denomination machine.

Small Coin Player – A player who plays the 5¢, 10¢, or 25¢ denomination machines.

Start – On some machines, pushing this button will spin the reels if credits are already bet.

Stepper Reels – *See* REELS.

Symbols – The various markings on a slot machine reel. The most popular are those originated by the Mills Company, which show fruits, bells, and bars. However, many casinos put in their own logos for the big payouts.

Tight Machine – A slot machine marked by infrequent winners, with a low percentage payback to the players. This is opposed to a loose machine which has a high percentage payback.

Well – The bottom metal area of the machine where winning coins fall.

Wild Play Machines – A new breed of slot machines that use wild symbols to multiply the winning payouts.

Wild Symbol – The symbol earmarked as "wild" by a slot manufacturer, could be designated as any winning symbol for the benefit of the player, or in addition, can increase the normal winning payout by a multiple.

Window – The glass area in the front of the machine where the player views the symbols and reels.

SPORTS BETTING

AL – American League

Bigs – Slang for the "Big Leagues," the major leagues. Used primarily for baseball.

Bookie, Bookmaker – The individual or business that sets the line and books the bets in sports, whether legal of illegal.

Crease – *See* DISTORTION.

Distortion – *Also* CREASE. A situation where overwhelming fan support for one of the contestants creates an unbalanced line favorable for the astute bettor.

Favorite – The team favored to win the game.

Home Team Advantage – The advantage a team inherently enjoys by playing before its fans on its own field.

Hoops – Slang for basketball.

Laying Money – Betting more money than one hopes to win back.

Laying Points – A situation where favorite bettors must give the underdog extra points in a game to equalize the contest.

Line – The points or odds set by the bookie which determine the conditions under which a bet is placed.

Money Line – The line in baseball and boxing where favorite bettors lay money, that is, bet more than they hope to win, while underdog bettors, take odds, win more than the amount they wager.

NBA – National Basketball Association

NFL – National Football League

NL – National League

Over-Under – These bets are wagers that a team will score either more, "over," or less "under," than the points listed.

Parlay – A bet combining two or more teams together in which all the teams in the parlay must win for the bet to win.

Pointspread – *Also* SPREAD. The line used for football and basketball where favorite bettors give (lay) points and underdog bettors take points.

Sided – When a lot more money gets bet on one side of a contest, the bookie is said to be sided.

Spread – *See* POINTSPREAD.

Straight-Up – Betting a game without taking or giving points.

Taking Odds – A wager on the underdog where a winning bet pays more than originally wagered.

Taking Points – A situation where underdog bettors receive extra points in a game to equalize the contest.

Teaser – A wager which ties two or more games together in a bet by giving bettors incentives in the way of extra points or better odds. All games "teased" must be won for the teaser be to win.

Vig, Vigorish – The bookmakers commission on sports bets.

VIDEO POKER

A – The ace.

Action – The total amount of money played measured by the sum of all bets placed. Thus, betting a quarter 100 times, would be equivalent to $25.00 in action, or betting $1 for 700 plays adds up to $700 in action. Action does not take into account starting or ending bankroll, or wins or losses—just total $ bets.

Bank, Bank of Machines – A group of machines connected together in a structure as a design unit.

Big Coin Machine – A video machine requiring $5 or $25 coins to play.

Big Coin Player – A player who plays $5 or $25 coins.

Bonus Quads – A jacks or better machine that offers special bonus payouts on specified four of a kind hands.

Bonus Royal – Type of video poker machine that gives a large bonus payout on a specified royal flush if hit.

Cage – The cashier's cage, where players can exchange chips for cash, or change traveler's checks. The cage usually won't accept large numbers of coins. That must be done at a change booth.

Change Booth – A booth set up for the specific purpose of changing players bills into coins, or their coins into bills.

Changeperson – The casino employee who services the machines area for the purpose of changing bills into coins.

Cashout Button – This button, when pressed, releases all the coins that were won, or at least held by the machine.

Changeperson – The casino employee responsible for changing player bills into coins. The changeperson usually roams the slots area, though he or she may be "stationed" in a carousel.

Cold – A machine that is paying out less than expected, or a player on a losing streak.

Comp – Short for complimentary. The freebies given out by the casino, usually as a reward for play. These can take the form of free or discounted drinks, rooms, shows, buffets and regular meals, and more.

Credits – The number of coins that a player has on "credit" in the machine which can be used for future play. Credits are accumulated through winnings or when money is inserted into the machine.

Deal/Draw Button – This button, when pressed, deals the cards.

Denomination – The size of coin (or bill) used to play a particular machine. The 25¢ and $1 machines are the most popular denominations found. Increasingly, larger denominations such as $5, $25, $100, and even higher are found now as well.

Deuces Wild – A video poker variation where all deuces are wild cards, that is, they can be used as any card that would most benefit the player, even though that card may already be used.

Deuces and Joker Wild – A video poker game dealt from a 53 card deck, the regular 52 card deck plus a wild joker. All deuces are wild in this game too, for five wild cards.

Discard – A card that a player chooses not to keep, instead drawing a new one.

Double Card Option – This feature, found on some video poker machines, uses a 53 card deck to deal the game. The 53rd card is actually an extra card, a double of one of the other cards in the deck, and when this card is received in a player's hand, the payout is doubled. Though seemingly attractive, this feature is disadvantageous for the player.

Double Down Stud – A video poker variation that deals four cards and gives players the option to either double their bet and receive the fifth card, or fold and give up their bet.

Draw – To take cards as a replacement for discarded ones.

Double or Nothing Button – A feature on some machines that allows winning hands to double their bet at the risk of losing it all in a one card show-down draw, high card wins, against the machine.

Five of a Kind – A hand containing five cards of the same rank, for example, 4-4-4-4-4 (one or more of these cards could be a wild card).

Five Deck Frenzy – The progressive variation of five deck poker.

Five Deck Poker – This video poker variation assigns one deck of cards to each video poker position so that in theory, a player could hold five cards of the same suit and value.

Flush – Five cards of the same suit. The hand 3-7-8-J-K of spades would be a spade flush.

Full House – A hand containing three cards of the same value (three of a kind) and two cards of another identical value (a pair). Q-Q-Q-K-K would be a full house.

Hand – The player's five cards.

High Card – In jacks or better, a J, Q, K, and A. In 10s or better, the 10 as well.

High Roller Machine – A video machine requiring $100 or $500 coins to play.

High Roller – A video poker player who plays $100 or $500 coins.

Hold, Hold Percentage – The action of keeping a card, not discarding it, or the button marked as such which is used for this purpose. Also, the percentage or actual dollar amounts a casino wins from its players.

Hold Button – The button that, when pressed, tells the machine to keep the card. When it is pressed again, it release the "hold" and tells the machine to discard the card.

Inside Straight – A four card straight that can only be filled in the middle, not on either end. For example, 5-6-8-9 is an inside straight since only a 7 will fill the straight.

J – A Jack.

Jackpot – A very big winner. Hitting the royal flush is hitting a jackpot.

Jacks or Better – The standard video poker machine that pays out for any poker hand of at least jacks or higher. Also, refers to a hand of at least the strength of jacks, that is, jacks, queens, kings, or aces, or any higher combination.

Joker Wild – A video poker machine dealt from a 53 card deck, the regular 52 card deck plus a joker which serves as a wild card.

K – A King.

Long Run – The concept of what certain results are expected to be when occurring over many trials, thus, in the long run.

Low Pair – A pair that doesn't qualify for a payout. In jacks or better, that would a hand of tens or worse.

Max Bet Button – See MAX COIN BUTTON.

Max Coin Button – Also MAX BET BUTTON. The button that plays all credits allowed, usually five when pushed.

Medium Coin Machine – A $1 machine.

Medium Coin Player – A player who plays the $1 machines.

Mega-Progressive Machines – A progressive video poker machine with an enormous, usually million dollar jackpot.

Money Management – The strategy used by smart players to wisely manage their money while gambling as to preserve their capitol, avoid big losses, and manage their wins.

Multiple Progressives – A machine which contains more than one progressive jackpot.

One Credit Button – The button that plays one credit for the player when pushed. The deal button will need to be pushed after to deal the cards.

Pair – Two cards of the same value, such as two fives or two jacks.

Payback or Payout Percentage – The expected return percentage for money wagered. A 97% payback states that the expected return on every dollar bet will be 97¢, for a loss of 3¢.

Paytable – The display on the video poker machine showing winning combinations and their payouts.

Payout Meter – The display on the machine that shows the number of coins played and won on a spin.

Pokermania – The progressive video poker game linked to the Atlantic city casinos.

Progressive Machines, Progressives – Progressives feature a growing jackpot which increases each time a coin is inserted into a machine that is hooked up to the progressive meter. When the winning combination does hit, usually a Royal Flush, the lucky player wins the total accumulated and posted in the display, and the jackpot total will be reset to a predetermined starting point.

Q – A Queen.

Quad – A specified four of a kind hand that pays a bonus amount if drawn.

Rating – The evaluation received by a player from the casino stating the level of action this player gives the casino.

Royal Flush – The A-K-Q-J-10, all of the same suit.

Second Chance – Video poker feature, sometimes found, that allows players to receive a sixth card in an additional "second draw" if the drawing of that one card would give the player a chance to make a straight or better hand.

Sequential Royal Flush – Refers to a royal flush that must be hit in an exact order by position. For example, the royal may need to be in order with the 10 being in the leftmost position, then consecutively, the jack, queen, king, and finally the ace in the rightmost position.

Short Run – A brief sequence of trials, where anything can happen, even though the odds say they may not.

Slots Club – A casino club set up to reward frequent slots and video poker players with comps and rewards.

Slots Host – The casino employee responsible for taking care of the slots and video poker players.

Small Coin Machine – A 5¢ or 25¢ machine.

Small Coin Player – A player who plays the 5¢, 10¢, or 25¢ denomination machines.

Straight – Five consecutive non-suited cards, such as an 8-9-10-J-Q. If the cards were all of the same suit, then the hand would be a straight flush (next). If an ace is contained in a straight, it must be either the highest or the lowest card of the sequence, or the hand is not a straight. Q-K-A-2-3 is not a straight.

Straight Flush – Five consecutive cards all in the same suit, for example, the 4-5-6-7-8 of clubs.

Suit – One of the following groups – heart, diamonds, spades, or clubs.

Tens or Better – A video poker variation that pays out for any poker hand of at least tens or higher.

Three of a Kind – *Also* TRIPS. Three cards of the same value, such as 9-9-9.

Triple Play – An interesting video poker variation that features the simultaneous play of three poker hands.

Trips – *See* THREE OF A KIND.

Two Pair – A five card hand that contains two sets of identically valued cards (two pairs) such as 7-7-A-A.

Two Pairs or Better – A video poker variation that requires a minimum hand of two pairs for a payout.

Well – The bottom metal area of the machine where winning coins fall.

Wild, Wild Card – Cards designated as "wild" can be given any value or suit, even as a duplicate or triplicate of a card already held.

GREAT CARDOZA POKER BOOKS
ADD THESE TO YOUR LIBRARY - ORDER NOW!

CRASH COURSE IN BEATING TEXAS HOLD'EM *by Avery Cardoza*. Perfect for beginning and somewhat experienced players who want to jump right in on the action and play cash games, local tournaments, online poker, and the big televised tournaments where millions of dollars can be made. Both limit and no-limit hold'em games are covered along with the essential strategies needed to play profitably on the pre-flop, flop, turn, and river. The good news is that you don't need to memorize hands or be burdened by math to be a winner—just play by the no-nonsense basic principles outlined in this book. There's a lot of money to be made and Cardoza shows you how to go and get it. 208 pages, $14.95

WINNER'S GUIDE TO TEXAS HOLD' EM POKER *by Ken Warren*. You'll learn how to play every hand from every position with every type of flop. Learn the 14 categories of starting hands, the 10 most common hold'em tells, how to evaluate a game for profit, the value of deception, the art of bluffing, 8 secrets to winning, starting hand categories, position, and more! Includes detailed analysis of the top 40 hands and the most complete chapter on hold'em odds in print. Over 400,000 copies sold! 224 pages, $16.95.

HOW TO PLAY WINNING POKER *by Avery Cardoza*. New and completely updated, this classic has sold more than 250,000 copies. Includes major new coverage on playing and winning tournaments, online poker, limit and no-limit hold'em, Omaha games, seven-card stud, and draw poker (including triple draw). Includes 21 essential winning concepts of poker, 15 concepts of bluffing, how to use psychology and body language to get an extra edge, plus information on playing online poker. 256 pages, $14.95.

KEN WARREN TEACHES TEXAS HOLD 'EM *by Ken Warren*. This is a step-by-step comprehensive manual for making money at hold'em poker. 42 powerful chapters teach you one lesson at a time. Great practical advice and concepts with examples from actual games and how to apply them to your own play. Lessons include: Starting Cards, Playing Position, Raising, Check-raising, Tells, Game/Seat Selection, Dominated Hands, Odds, and much more. This book is already a huge fan favorite and best-seller! 416 pages, $26.95.

OMAHA HI-LO: Play to Win with the Odds *by Bill Boston*. Selecting the right hands to play is the most important decision you'll make in Omaha. More than any other poker game, Omaha is driven by hand value. This is the *only* book that shows you the chances that every one of the 5,278 Omaha high-low hands has of winning the high end of the pot, the low end of it, and how often it is expected to scoop all the chips. You get all the vital tools needed to make critical preflop decisions based on the results of more than 500 million computerized hand simulations. You'll learn the 100 most profitable Omaha high-low starting cards, trap hands to avoid, 49 worst hands, 30 ace-less hands that can be played for profit, and the three bandit cards you must know to avoid losing hands. 248 pages, $19.95.

POKER TALK: Learn How to Talk Poker Like a Pro *by Avery Cardoza*. This fascinating and fabulous collection of colorful poker words, phrases, and poker-speak features more than 2,000 definitions. No longer is it enough to know how to walk the walk in poker, you need to know how to talk the talk! Learn what it means to go all in on a rainbow flop with pocket rockets and get it cracked by cowboys, put a bad beat on a calling station, and go over the top of a producer fishing with a gutshot to win a big dime. You'll soon have those railbirds wondering what *you* are talking about. 304 pages, $9.95.

CARO'S FUNDAMENTAL SECRETS OF WINNING POKER *by Mike Caro*. Learn the essential strategies, concepts, and plays that comprise the very foundation of winning poker play. Learn to win more from weak players, equalize stronger players, bluff a bluffer, win big pots, where to sit against weak players, and the six factors of strategic table image. Includes selected tips on hold 'em, 7 stud, draw, lowball, tournaments, more. 160 pages, 12.95.

Order now at 1-800-577-WINS or go online to: www.cardozapub.com

FROM CARDOZA'S EXCITING LIBRARY
ADD THESE TO YOUR COLLECTION - ORDER NOW!

SUPER SYSTEM *by Doyle Brunson.* This classic book is considered by the pros to be the best book ever written on poker! Jam-packed with advanced strategies, theories, tactics and money-making techniques—no serious poker player can afford to be without this hard-hitting information. Includes fifty pages of the most precise poker statistics ever published. Features chapters written by poker's biggest superstars, such as Dave Sklansky, Mike Caro, Chip Reese, Bobby Baldwin, and Doyle—two world champions and three master theorists. Essential strategies, advanced play, and no-nonsense winning advice on making money at 7-card stud (razz, high-low split, cards speak, and declare), draw poker, lowball, and hold'em (limit and no-limit).This is a must-read. 628 pages, $29.95.

SUPER SYSTEM 2 *by Doyle Brunson.* The most anticipated poker book ever, SS2 expands upon the original with more games and professional secrets from the best in the world. Superstar contributors include Daniel Negreanu, winner of multiple WSOP gold bracelets and 2004 Poker Player of the Year; Lyle Berman, 3-time WSOP gold bracelet winner, founder of the World Poker Tour, and super-high stakes cash player; Bobby Baldwin, 1978 World Champion; Johnny Chan, 2-time World Champion and 10-time WSOP bracelet winner; Mike Caro, poker's greatest researcher, theorist, and instructor; Jennifer Harman, the world's top female player and one of ten best overall; Todd Brunson, winner of more than 20 tournaments; and Crandell Addington, no-limit hold'em legend. 672 pgs, $34.95.

CARO'S BOOK OF POKER TELLS *by Mike Caro.* One of the ten greatest books written onpoker, this must-have book should be in every player's library. If you're serious about winning, you'll realize that most of the profit comes from being able to read your opponents. Caro reveals the the secrets of interpreting *tells*—physical reactions that reveal information about a player's cards—such as shrugs, sighs, shaky hands, eye contact, and many more. Learn when opponents are bluffing, when they aren't and why—based solely on their mannerisms. Over 170 photos of players in action and play-by-play examples show the actual tells. These powerful ideas will give you the decisive edge. 320 pages, $24.95.

CARO'S GUIDE TO DOYLE BRUNSON'S SUPER SYSTEM *by Mike Caro.* Working with World Champion Doyle Brunson, the legendary Mike Caro has created a fresh look to the "Bible" of all poker books, adding new and personal insights that help you understand the original work. Caro breaks 36 concepts into either "Analysis, Commentary, Concept, Mission, Play-By-Play, Psychology, Statistics, Story, or Strategy. Lots of illustrations and winning concepts give even more value to this great work. 86 pages, 8 1/2 x 11, $19.95.

MILLION DOLLAR HOLD'EM: Winning Big in Limit Cash Games *by Johnny Chan and Mark Karowe.* Learn how to win money consistently at limit hold'em, poker's most popular cash game, from one of poker's living legends. You'll get a rare opportunity to get into the mind of the man who has won ten World Series of Poker titles—tied for the most ever with Doyle Brunson—as Johnny picks out illustrative hands and shows how he thinks his way through the betting and the bluffing. No book so thoroughly details the thought process of how a hand is played, the alternative ways it could have been played, and the best way to win session after session. *Essential* reading for cash players. 352 pages, $29.95.

THE POKER TOURNAMENT FORMULA *by Arnold Snyder.* Start making money now in fast no-limit hold'em tournaments with these radical and powerful strategies! These never-before-published concepts and secrets for beating tournaments can turn any "fish" into a dangerous shark. For the first time, you'll learn why cards don't matter as much as the dynamics of a tournament—your position, the size of your chip stack, who your opponents are, and above all, the structure. Poker tournaments offer one of the richest opportunities to come along in decades. Every so often, a book comes along that changes the way players attack a game and provides them with a big advantage over opponents. Gambling legend Arnold Snyder has written such a book. 368 pages, $19.95.

BACCARAT MASTER CARD COUNTER
New Winning Strategy!

For the **first time**, Gambling Research Institute releases the **latest winning techniques** at baccarat. This **exciting** strategy, played by big money players in Monte Carlo and other exclusive locations, is based on principles that have made insiders and pros **hundreds of thousands of dollars** counting cards at blackjack - card counting!

NEW WINNING APPROACH - This brand **new** strategy now applies card counting to baccarat to give you a **new winning approach,** and is designed so that any player, with just a **little effort**, can successfully take on the casinos at their own game - and win!

SIMPLE TO USE, EASY TO MASTER - You learn how to count cards for baccarat without the mental effort needed for blackjack! No need to memorize numbers - keep the count on the scorepad. Easy-to-use, play the strategy while enjoying the game!

LEARN WHEN TO BET BANKER, WHEN TO BET PLAYER - No longer will you make bets on hunches and guesses - use the GRI Baccarat Master Card Counter to determine when to bet Player and when to bet Banker. You learn the basic counts (running and true), deck favorability, symmetrical play vs. non-symmetrical play, how and when to increase bets and much more in this **winning strategy**.

PLAY SCIENTIFICALLY TO WIN - Drawing and standing advantage, average edge, average gain, total gain, win-loss and % of occurrence are shown for every relevant hand. You won't need to know these numbers or percentages, but we've included them here so you can see exactly how the strategy works and how you can use it to your advantage.

LEARN TO WIN IN JUST ONE SITTING - That's right! After **just one sitting** you can successfully learn this powerhouse strategy and use it to your advantage in the casino. Be the best baccarat player - the one playing the odds to **win**! Baccarat can be beaten. The Master Card Counter shows you how!

To order send just $50 by check or money order to:

Cardoza Publishing, P.O. Box 1500, Cooper Station, New York, NY 10276

GRI'S PROFESSIONAL VIDEO POKER STRATEGY
Win Money at Video Poker! With the Odds!

At last, for the **first time,** and for **serious players only**, the GRI **Professional Video Poker** strategy is released so you too can play to win! **You read it right** - this strategy gives you the **mathematical advantage** over the casino and what's more, it's **easy to learn!**

PROFESSIONAL STRATEGY SHOWS YOU HOW TO WIN WITH THE ODDS - This **powerhouse strategy**, played for **big profits** by an **exclusive** circle of **professionals**, people who make their living at the machines, is now made available to you! You too can win - with the odds - and this **winning strategy** shows you how!

HOW TO PLAY FOR A PROFIT - You'll learn the **key factors** to play on a **pro level**: which machines will turn you a profit, break-even and win rates, hands per hour and average win per hour charts, time value, team play and more! You'll also learn big play strategy, alternate jackpot play, high and low jackpot play and key strategies to follow.

WINNING STRATEGIES FOR ALL MACHINES - This **comprehensive, advanced pro package** not only shows you how to win money at the 8-5 progressives, but also, the **winning strategies** for 10s or better, deuces wild, joker's wild, flat-top, progressive and special options features.

BE A WINNER IN JUST ONE DAY - In just one day, after learning our strategy, you will have the skills to **consistently win money** at video poker - with the odds. The strategies are easy to use under practical casino conditions.

FREE BONUS - PROFESSIONAL PROFIT EXPECTANCY FORMULA ($15 VALUE) - For serious players, we're including this free bonus essay which explains the professional profit expectancy principles of video poker and how to relate them to real dollars and cents in your game.

To order send just $50 by check or money order to:

Cardoza Publishing, P.O. Box 1500, Cooper Station, New York, NY 10276

THE GRI MASTER KENO STRATEGY

David Cowles Professional Winning Strategy

Finally! David Cowles, the *world's foremost expert on keno*, and the publisher of the *Keno Newsletter*, has released his **powerhouse strategy** on winning money at keno **exclusively** to Cardoza Publishing. This strategy is now available for the **first time** and is only available through us!!!

TIRED OF LOSING? LEARN HOW TO WIN! - Learn how to bet the tickets that provide the **highest payoffs** and push the percentages in your favor, how to increase winning tickets **tenfold** using way, combination and king tickets, how to set goals and plot a winning course, how to parlay small bankrolls into large fortunes by **playing smart** instead of betting haphazardly, and how to stretch your bankroll so you have **more winners** and chances for **big jackpots!**

WIN MORE PLAYING KENO! - Cowles reveals, for the first time, the magic *wager-to-win ratio* - a quick way to determine if a keno ticket is playable; also how to find the most **profitable** tickets, the *real scoop* on how to **pick winning numbers**, tips from the pros on **winning** keno tournaments and contest prizes.

THE SECRET TO THE MOST PROFITABLE BETS - Many keno tickets are blatant ripoffs. Learn to avoid the sucker bets and how to **slash the casino edge** to the bone. You can't change the odds, but you can get the best deals once you learn the *secrets* revealed here.

FREE ROOM, FOOD & DRINKS? - You bet! They're yours for the taking. You just have to know *who, how* and *when* to ask - and then *how much*.

DOUBLE BONUS! - With your order, **absolutely free**, receive two insider bonus essays: *12 Winning Tips From the Pros* - the 12 master jewels that can increase winnings drastically; and *The 10 "Don'ts" of Keno*, mistakes made by both novice and experienced players. You'll never make these mistakes again. Be a winner!

To order, send $50 by check or money order to Cardoza Publishing

5 PROFESSIONAL REPORTS TO TURN AMATEUR CARD COUNTERS TO PROS

NOT FOR BEGINNERS—FOR CARD COUNTERS ONLY

NEW AND REVISED! - These are the **groundbreaking** reports relied upon by **professional blackjack players** for more than 25 years. And now they are completely updated! This is a **very big event** for winning and pro blackjack players.

THE LEGEND REVEALS HIS SECRETS - These professional strategies are the personal work of **Blackjack Hall of Famer** Arnold Snyder, **legendary** player, author of nine books and advanced strategies, and guru to thousands of serious players.

THE PROFESSIONAL COUNTERS SECRET STRATEGIES - Start **winning** by applying the strongest betting strategy with the lowest risk. Good for all valid counting systems, some of the technical questions answered are:

- What's my advantage if the dealer deals out 4 1/2 decks instead of just 4 decks?
- Should I raise my bet at a count of +3 or +4?
- Can I beat the game if I use a betting spread of 1-to-4 units, or do I need 1-to-8?
- What's the best betting strategy if I only have $1000 and the minimum bet is $10?
- What's my win rate if I quit the table when the count goes negative?
- What's my win rate if the house uses eight decks instead of six?

You **don't need** to run computer simulations to get the answers, and you don't need a degree in probability and statistics. You simply need a set of charts where you can look up the answers —the math has already been worked out. **Accurate for all counting systems** and any size bankroll, each report is 64 pages, with 44 pages of charts. There are five separate reports for games being dealt with 1, 2, 4, 6, and 8 decks. With any betting spread, the charts show the fluctuations you can expect in an hour of play, ten hours, a hundred hours and more, so you can estimate your **best approach** to any game based on your actual bankroll. Get just the Reports that cover the games you currently play in, or get them all (and save $$$) to **be prepared** for *any* blackjack game *anywhere*.

Beat the 1-Deck Game: $25	**Beat the 6-Deck Game:** $25
Beat the 2-Deck Game: $25	**Beat the 8-Deck Game:** $25
Beat the 4-Deck Game: $25	**All five reports:** $95 (You save $30.00!)

To order, send $95 for all 5 reports (or $25 per report)—plus postage and handling to:
Cardoza Publishing, P.O. Box 1500, Cooper Station, New York, NY 10276

Win at Blackjack Without Counting Cards!!!

Multiple Deck 1,2,3 Non-Counter - Breakthrough in Blackjack!!!

BEAT MULTIPLE DECK BLACKJACK WITHOUT COUNTING CARDS!
You heard right! Now, for the **first time ever**, **win** at multiple deck blackjack **without counting cards**! Until I developed the Cardoza Multiple Deck Non-Counter (The 1,2,3 Strategy), I thought it was impossible. Don't be intimidated anymore by four, six or eight deck games - for **you have the advantage**. It doesn't matter how many decks they use, for this easy-to-use and proven strategy keeps you **winning - with the odds**!

EXCITING STRATEGY - ANYONE CAN WIN! - We're **excited** about this strategy for it allows anyone at all, against any number of decks, to have the **advantage** over any casino in the world in a multiple deck game. You don't count cards, you don't need a great memory, you don't need to be good at math - you only need to know the **winning secrets** of the 1,2,3 Multiple Deck Non-Counter and use but a **little effort** to be a **winner**.

SIMPLE BUT EFFECTIVE! - **Now the answer is here**. This strategy is so **simple**, yet so **effective**, you will be amazed. With a **minimum of effort**, this remarkable strategy, which we also call the 1,2,3 (as easy as 1,2,3), allows you to win without studiously following cards. Drink, converse with your fellow players or dealer - they'll never suspect that you can **beat the casino**!

PERSONAL GUARANTEE - And you have my personal **guarantee of satisfaction**, 100% money back! This breakthrough strategy is my personal research and is guaranteed to give you the edge! If for any reason you're not satisfied, send back the materials unused within 30 days for a full refund.

BE A LEISURELY WINNER! - If you just want to play a **leisurely game** yet have the expectation of winning, the answer is here. Not as powerful as a card counting strategy, but **powerful enough to make you a winner** - with the odds!!!

EXTRA BONUS! - Complete listing of all options and variations at blackjack and how they affect the player. ($5.00 Value!)

EXTRA, EXTRA BONUS!! - Not really a bonus since we can't sell you the strategy without protecting you against getting barred. The 1,000 word essay, *"How to Disguise the Fact That You're an Expert,"* and the 1,500 word *"How Not To Get Barred,"* are also included free. ($15.00 Value). These are bound right into the strategy.

To Order, send ~~$75~~ $50 (plus postage and handling) by check or money order to:
Cardoza Publishing, P.O. Box 1500, Cooper Station, New York, NY 10276

CARDOZA CRAPS MASTER

Exclusive Offer! - Not Available Anywhere Else
THREE BIG STRATEGIES!

Here It is! **At last**, the **secrets** of the **Grande-Gold Power Sweep**, **Molliere's Monte Carlo Turnaround** and the **Montarde-D'Girard Double Reverse** - three big strategies - are made available and presented for the **first time anywhere**! These powerful strategies are designed for the serious craps player, one wishing to bring the best odds and strategies to hot tables, cold tables and choppy tables.

1. THE GRANDE-GOLD POWER SWEEP (HOT TABLE STRATEGY)

This **dynamic strategy** takes maximum advantage of hot tables and shows you how to amass small **fortunes quickly** when numbers are being thrown fast and furious. The Grande-Gold stresses aggressive betting on wagers the house has no edge on! This previously unreleased strategy will make you a powerhouse at a hot table.

2. MOLLIERE'S MONTE CARLO TURNAROUND (COLD TABLE STRATEGY)

For the player who likes betting against the dice, Molliere's Monte Carlo Turnaround shows how to turn a cold table into hot cash. Favored by an exclusive circle of professionals who will play nothing else, the uniqueness of this strongman strategy is that the vast majority of bets **give absolutely nothing away to the casino!**

3. MONTARDE-D'GIRARD DOUBLE REVERSE (CHOPPY TABLE STRATEGY)

This **new** strategy is the **latest development** and the **most exciting strategy** to be designed in recent years. **Learn how** to play the optimum strategies against the tables when the dice run hot and cold (a choppy table) with no apparent reason. **The Montarde-d'Girard Double Reverse** shows how you can **generate big profits** while less knowledgeable players are ground out by choppy dice. And, of course, the majority of our bets give nothing away to the casino!

BONUS!!! – Order now, and you'll receive **The Craps Master-Professional Money Management Formula** ($15 value) **absolutely free**! Necessary for serious players and **used by the pros**, the **Craps Master Formula** features the unique **stop-loss ladder**.

The Above Offer is Not Available Anywhere Else. You Must Order Here.

To order send $75 $50 (plus postage and handling) by check or money order to:

Cardoza Publishing, P.O. Box 1500, Cooper Station, New York, NY 10276

CARDOZA SCHOOL OF BLACKJACK
- Home Instruction Course - $200 OFF! -

At last, after years of secrecy, the **previously unreleased** lesson plans, strategies and playing tactics formerly available only to members of the Cardoza School of Blackjack are now available to the general public - and at substantial savings. **Now**, you can **learn at home,** and at your own convenience. Like the full course given at the school, the home instruction course goes **step-by-step** over the winning concepts. We'll take you from layman to **pro**.

MASTER BLACKJACK - Learn what it takes to be a **master player**. Be a **powerhouse**, play with confidence, impunity, and **with the odds** on your side. Learn to be a **big winner** at black-jack.

MAXIMIZE WINNING SESSIONS - You'll **learn how** to take a good winning session and make a **blockbuster** out of it, but just as important, you'll learn to cut your losses. Learn exactly when to end a session. We cover everything from the psychological and emotional aspects of play to altered playing conditions (through the **eye of profitability**) to protection of big wins. The advice here could be worth **hundreds (or thousands) of dollars** in one session alone. Take our guidelines seriously.

ADVANCED STRATEGIES - You'll learn the *latest* in advanced winning strategies. Learn about the **ten-factor**, the **ace-factor**, the effects of rules variations, how to protect against dealer blackjacks, the winning strategies for single and multiple deck games and how each affects you; the **true count**, the multiple deck true count variations, and much, much more. And, of course, you'll receive the full Cardoza Base Count Strategy package.

$200 OFF - LIMITED OFFER - The Cardoza School of Blackjack home instruction course, retailed at $295 (or $895 if taken at the school) is available here for just $95.

DOUBLE BONUS! - **Rush** your order in **now**, for we're also including, **absolutely free**, the 1,000 and 1,500 word essays, "How to Disguise the Fact that You're an Expert", and "How Not to Get Barred". Among other **inside information** contained here, you'll learn about the psychology of the pit bosses, how they spot counters, how to project a losing image, role playing, and other skills to maximize your profit potential.

To order, send $95 (plus postage and handling) by check or money order to:
Cardoza Publishing, P.O. Box 1500, Cooper Station, New York, NY 10276

SAVE $200!
(regular $295 - Only $95 with coupon)

Order Now! Be a big winner! Please **rush** me the course by mail. I want to join the thousands of successful graduates **winning big money** at blackjack. I understand that the **Double Bonus** essays *and* **free** book will be included **absolutely free**.

Enclosed is a check or money order for $95 (plus postage and handling) made out to:
Cardoza Publishing
P.O. Box 1500, Cooper Station, New York, NY 10276
Call Toll-Free in U.S. & Canada, 1-800-577-WINS

Include $5.00 postage/handling for U.S. orders; $10.00 for Canada/Mexico; HI/AK, other countries, $20.00. Outside U.S., money order payable in U.S. dollars on U.S. bank only.

NAME _____

ADDRESS _____

CITY _____ STATE _____ ZIP _____

Order Now to Be a Winner! 30 Day Money Back Guarantee!   HG 2006